METTRAY

METTRAY

A HISTORY OF FRANCE'S MOST
VENERATED CARCERAL INSTITUTION

STEPHEN A. TOTH

CORNELL UNIVERSITY PRESS
Ithaca and London

First published 2019 by Cornell University Press

Printed in the United States of America

Library of Congress Cataloging-in-Publication Data

Names: Toth, Stephen A., author.
Title: Mettray : a history of France's most venerated carceral institution / by Stephen A. Toth.
Description: Ithaca [New York] : Cornell University Press, 2019. | Includes bibliographical references and index.
Identifiers: LCCN 2018060504 (print) | LCCN 2019004889 (ebook) | ISBN 9781501740190 (pdf) | ISBN 9781501740374 (ret) | ISBN 9781501740183 (cloth : alk. paper)
Subjects: LCSH: Colonie agricole et penitentiaire de Mettray—History. | Juvenile detention homes—France—History. | Reformatories—France—History. | Juvenile corrections—France—History. | Problem children—Institutional care—France—History. | Juvenile delinquents—Rehabilitation—France.
Classification: LCC HV9156.M61 (ebook) | LCC HV9156.M61 T68 2019 (print) | DDC 365/.42094454—dc23
LC record available at https://lccn.loc.gov/2018060504

To the memory of my father

CONTENTS

ILLUSTRATIONS

Figures

Tables

ACKNOWLEDGMENTS

This book would not have been possible without the generosity of many individuals, institutions, and agencies whom it gives me great pleasure to acknowledge. The late Rachel G. Fuchs was not only a mentor but also a colleague and friend whose encouragement and advice was always inspiring and incisive. I would also like to thank Marlene Tromp, whose unstinting support as director and dean was greatly appreciated. In this regard, I am pleased to acknowledge the assistance provided by a Provost Humanities Fellowship and the Scholarly Research and Creative Grants program at Arizona State University. In addition, grants from the National Endowment for the Humanities and the American Philosophical Society made much of the research and writing of this project possible. With such support I made numerous forays into the Archives départementales d'Indre-et-Loire in Tours, where Mettray's records are held. I am most grateful for the patient guidance from the staff of that institution, particularly the chief archivist of the collection, Georges-François Pottier. Additionally, I wish to thank the staffs of the Archives départementales de Hérault, the Archives départementales du Cher, and the Archives départementales de Lot-et-Garonne for their assistance in locating material related to the colonies of Val d'Yèvre, Eysses, and Aniane, respectively.

One portion of the book appeared previously. I therefore acknowledge with appreciation the permission to adapt and republish in chapter 5 of this work "The Contard Affair: Private Power, State Control and Paternal Authority in Fin-de-Siècle France," *Journal of Historical Sociology* 23, no. 2 (June 2010): 185–215.

The work has benefited greatly from the attention and comments provided by the anonymous readers of Cornell University Press. Whatever shortcomings remain reflect my own failure to address the many cogent comments they provided. I would also like to thank Emily Andrew, who took an initial interest in the project and who helped shepherd the manuscript through the review and publication process.

I must express my utmost gratitude to those closest to me who have been pillars of support for so long. My late father Andrew and my mother Betty never wavered in their faith that this work would eventually come to fruition. I cannot thank them enough. Finally, my wife Meredith and children Madeleine and Alexandra lived with this book for far too long. Without their love and patience, it would have never seen the light of day. *Merci, ma belle-famille que j'aime de tout mon cœur.*

METTRAY

Introduction

Convinced that urban poverty made children at once more vulnerable and more vicious, Frédéric Demetz, a Parisian magistrate, opened the Mettray Agricultural Colony for Boys on 22 January 1840. At Mettray, located on 700 hectares of land outside the city of Tours donated by the Vicomte Brétignières de Courteilles,[1] Demetz aimed to socialize criminal youth through agricultural work, basic elementary schooling, religious indoctrination, and strict military discipline. The institution's purpose was "to reclaim those who have never received any moral training, and who have been subjected to no other restraint than that of brute force; we propose, in short, to turn ignorant and dangerous boys into good, industrious and useful members of society. Such a problem cannot be solved by ordinary means."[2] Mettray soon became the most widely emulated institution of its day. Fifty-two facilities based on its design were opened in France during the 1840s, eventually leading to the passage of legislation in 1850 that granted private agricultural colonies a quasi-monopoly in the care and treatment of juvenile offenders. By 1853 half of all minors in corrections were held in such institutions, and by 1870 that number had risen to eight in ten.[3]

During its first three decades of existence Mettray enhanced and legitimized France's repression of criminal youth, and the establishment and diffusion of its design across the carceral landscape added a new layer to the nation's nascent prison system. Although the French state did not establish its own agricultural colonies until 1860, it did nominally regulate private institutions such as Mettray, which were required to provide annual reports to the Penitentiary Administration (which variously operated under the aegis of the Ministries of Interior and Justice). Moreover, as philanthropists and penal reformers such as Matthew Davenport Hill, Horace Mann, and Henry Barnard learned of Mettray's apparent success they visited the colony, and institutions based on the Mettray model were subsequently established in the United States, Great Britain, Australia, Belgium, Canada, and the Netherlands.[4] According to Chris Leonards such visits were not at all uncommon during the mid-nineteenth century, an "era of philanthropic tourism in which various social and moral entrepreneurs visited each other and their loci of interest."[5] Thus Mettray moved beyond the discursive boundaries of the French nation and into a growing international marketplace of ideas in which the management of juvenile delinquency was discussed and debated. Indeed, as Barbara Arneil has demonstrated, Mettray was an essential part of a much wider movement that used rural colonies to address the problem of "idleness," with institutions ranging from the "farm colonies for the mentally disabled and ill in Europe, Asia, and South/North America" to William Booth's "farm colony in Essex, . . . the CCF Metis colonies in Saskatchewan, the American Colonization Society's agrarian colony in Liberia, and the utopian colonies of the Doukhobors, Owenites, and African Americans."[6] The establishment of these colonies was driven by a basic belief that life and labor in the countryside was physically and morally redemptive.

Despite Mettray's widespread influence and its importance for understanding the history of prisons—and the fact that over 17,000 young men passed through the institution before it was closed by the Popular Front government in 1937 amid widely publicized accounts of inhumane treatment—historians have generally ignored the agricultural colony.[7] The relative paucity of historical scholarship on Mettray can be attributed to two factors. The first is practical, in that the vast collection of documents associated with Mettray's operation had long been stored in an outbuilding and was not officially transferred to the Archives départementales d'Indre-et-Loire in Tours until 2001. Prior to this, historians had to travel to the site—now a home for disabled children—to access disparate materials that were not organized in any fashion. Because the subsequent cataloging and archiving of these materials took four years to complete, it is only since 2005 that scholars have had unfettered access to Mettray's institutional records.[8] Yet, as Oliver Davis has noted, historians have generally "been content to let the dust settle on this impeccably catalogued but underused resource."[9] This book, based on an extended examination of these materials, is the first historical monograph on what was perhaps the most venerated carceral institution of its time.

The relatively modest interest in the colony's history can also be attributed to the profound shadow cast by Michel Foucault over any and all work dealing with the prison.[10] As Mary Gibson aptly notes, Foucault's *Discipline and Punish* remains "the master text" consulted by all historians of the prison because it provides the conceptual vocabulary that "pervades, sometimes imperceptibly, the entire contemporary history of crime and punishment."[11] Through his analysis of the normalizing techniques that emerged in the operations of the factory, army, and school, Foucault uncovered the various strains of a nineteenth-century discourse that cohered into a mechanism of imprisonment conceived not simply to punish but also to "reform" prisoners. The criminal body thus became the focus of a new kind of power relation in which the prisoner was made perpetually visible (i.e., the Panopticon).[12] In this setting the need for supervision slowly diminishes over time as the prisoner internalizes institutional discipline and begins to police his or her own actions to the point of self-compliance.

While the Panopticon is typically seen as the ideological and rhetorical touchstone of *Discipline and Punish*, Mettray is equally important to the overall logic of Foucault's vision: "Were I to fix the date of completion of the carceral system, I would choose the date of the official opening of Mettray. . . . Why Mettray? Because it is the disciplinary form at its most extreme, the model in which are concentrated all the coercive technologies of behavior . . . cloister, prison, school and regiment."[13] Mettray was the institutional avatar of modern disciplinary techniques that extended outward into society, anchoring what Ann Laura Stoler has termed a "carceral archipelago of empire."[14] Unlike Jeremy Bentham's largely unrealized prison house, Mettray had neither bars nor walls, yet children in the agricultural colony were nevertheless subject to what the geographer Chris Philo has called a "forest of gazes" from personnel who seemed to monitor every aspect of daily life. Even without the central watchtower of the panoptic penitentiary, children at Mettray felt the presence of a normalizing gaze that, over time, was gradually interiorized as the internal eye of conscience.[15]

Any failure on the part of the prisoner to adhere to any of Mettray's seemingly endless regulations that governed time, activity, speech, the body, and sexuality was noted and sanctioned accordingly. There were 247 separate rules that outlined behavior and comportment at Mettray.[16] The goal, according to Foucault, was to create the "obedient subject, the individual subjected to habits, rules, orders and authority that is exercised continually around him and upon him, and which he must allow to function automatically in him."[17] While this conceptualization enlightens, it also elides, as Foucault conflates rhetoric with reality. As with the Panopticon, there is an underlying presumption that Mettray functioned as the tightly governed social space envisioned by its creator, but as David Rothman has argued, "It is one thing to claim that the goal of surveillance dominated the theory of punishment, quite another to examine what actually happened when programs were translated into practice."[18] One must also be mindful, as David Garland has pointed out, that "the operation of power upon individuals [is] less of an 'automatic' process and more a matter of micro-political conflict in which the individual subject may draw upon alternative sources of power and subjectivity to resist that imposed by the institution."[19]

Given Foucault's inattention to agency, there is a presumed passivity in *Discipline and Punish* in which inmates, when they are considered at all, appear as little more than automatons who mindlessly submit to their keepers. Thus, precisely who is doing what to whom, and how power is employed or deployed, remains largely unexplored. As the sociologists Dario Melossi and Massimo Pavarini have noted, "Foucault assumes that resistance to power exists but without telling us very much about what happens when power meets with resistance."[20] While power, according to Foucault, is an all-encompassing presence in society, it is also a disembodied force, which implies that it can never be truly contested. In advancing this claim, however, the moral philosopher comes perilously close to denying the possibility of resistance even though this position does not align with his own personal politics or with his own views in later works.[21] Thus Foucault relegates the prisoner to the margins, which, as the sociologist Robert Adams notes, "squeezes out the possibility of prisoners exercising their own determining muscle."[22]

One cannot truly understand the prison without considering the imprisoned. In remarking on the "absence" of prisoners in accounts of nineteenth-century penal developments in France, Michelle Perrot asserts that "we do not hear much from them. . . . They have disappeared from their own history, so that we must follow their traces in what has been said about them."[23] The most noteworthy attempt to examine the institutional life of inmates in the context of the history of the French prison remains Patricia O'Brien's 1982 work *Promise of Punishment*, in which she argues that prisoners "must be given their place in historical studies of inarticulate groups" in an effort to "put an end to the silence of the imprisoned." By approaching the prison as a social space and adaptations to confinement as "as a form of active participation" in the punishment process, O'Brien gives a voice and a sense of historical agency to "prison populations who continue to be discussed as undifferentiated masses. . . . There is a significance to being a man, woman and child in prison."[24] Yet, the promise of O'Brien's sociohistorical approach remains largely unfulfilled—despite clear evidence in prison records of resistance—as historians have tended to focus on the broader political and social forces that have shaped carceral policy.

While Foucault maintained that the prison should not be seen as an "inert" institution—noting that periodic reform movements were one of its "conditions of functioning"[25]—he nevertheless paid little attention to prisoner resistance, noting only obliquely and without specific reference to the prison that "wherever there is power there is resistance."[26] Conversely, as the anthropologist Lila Abu-Lughod has observed, albeit in a far different context, "Where there is resistance, there is power." Abu-Lughod argues that studying the patterns and practices of resistance within systems of domination "teaches us about the complex interworking of historically changing structures of power," exposing how domination works by making it work against those who resist it.[27] Resistance, like power, is everywhere, and while it is imbricated within the power structure, it can also enable reform, which proved to be the case in the agricultural colonies.

In works after *Discipline and Punish* Foucault began to explore the power-resistance nexus more broadly, noting that that we should examine not only great radical uprisings or revolutions but also what he termed "mobile and transitory points of resistance."[28] Indeed, he posited that "it is the mundane and everyday acts of resistance that potentially produce the most profound effects."[29] While acts of collective rebellion at Mettray were rare, the "mobile and transitory" acts Foucault describes were quite common. Focusing only on the overt, public forms effectively limits analysis of resistance and reduces most prisoners to passive subordinates. As O'Brien reminds us, however, "Collective protests constituted only a minority of the responses of prisoners to their institutional setting. Most prisoners adapted and adjusted, but not without creating new subcultural forms of resistance in the process."[30]

This book is about power, how it was deployed, what its ambitions were, and how it was experienced and in some cases resisted by prisoners. Rather than romanticizing actions that were pointless or self-defeating, it highlights the ways some young men attempted to circumvent disciplinary control. Even in circumstances where it is unclear whether prisoners acted with intentionality or even in their own self-interest, their transgressions nevertheless demonstrate that in fact, many did not internalize institutional norms. While most acts of disobedience were fleeting and minor, their similarities in form and pattern suggest that prisoners experienced many of the same stresses while incarcerated.[31] Conceived as a site of moral and spiritual reform, Mettray was also a site of perpetual conflict, reprisals, and abuse, deviating markedly from its declared agenda.

On the surface, Mettray bore the quintessential earmarks of what the sociologist Erving Goffman famously termed a "total institution," virtually divorced from the outside world—an "isolated, enclosed social system whose primary purpose is to control most aspects of daily life"—and operating via a kind of hegemonic domination. Dominance in such institutions has certain characteristics, most notably in terms of material life, given its control over food, shelter, work, and clothing. There is also a symbolic or status-based aspect of domination in which the prisoner must comply with orders and manifest respect and deference to authority. These aspects of a total institution make dominance at the ideological level possible. Taken together, these different forms of domination (material, symbolic, and ideological) constitute a totalizing power that reshapes prisoner subjectivity and makes resistance inconceivable, at least theoretically.[32]

While most prisoners at Mettray served out their terms quietly, some frustrated the colony's carceral machinery by engaging in what the political theorist James C. Scott terms the "infrapolitics of the weak"—"foot dragging, dissimulation, false compliance, feigned ignorance, slander, arson, sabotage and so on"—which constitute the "hidden transcript" of resistance by which subordinate groups hinder or elude authority.[33] In his pathbreaking study of a small Malaysian village in the late 1970s Scott emphasizes the importance of analyzing not only the dramatic revolts but also the everyday, often individual and unplanned acts. While these might go unnoticed they are nonetheless important because "they make use of implicit understandings and informal networks; they represent a form of individual self-help; and they typically avoid any direct symbolic confrontation with authority."[34]

Another view is offered by the German social historian Alf Lüdtke, who in his work on spaces of labor defines acts such as pilfering, conniving, grumbling, wandering about, daydreaming, chatting, or joking as *Eigensinn*, "denoting willfulness, spontaneous self-will, or one's own meaning, a kind of self-affirmation, an act of (re)appropriating alienated social relations on and off the shop floor by a self-assertive prankishness, demarcating a space of one's own."[35] Like Goffman and Scott, Lüdtke conceptualizes the more ambiguous and elusive small acts rather than the much broader notion of resistance, the moments when the individual engages in willful behavior, briefly distancing himself from the constraints of superiors and the demands of the workplace. *Eigensinn* is an individualistic stance, an affirmation of one's own interests with the aim of making the workday or work space somewhat more agreeable. While Mettray possessed the characteristics of Goffman's total institution, there was also a liminal space between compliance and noncompliance that effectively attenuated Foucault's notion of a totalizing discipline.

Although the colony did not exist in an ideological vacuum, its modus operandi remained largely unchanged for nearly a century as it failed to acknowledge, accommodate, or adapt to changing understandings of childhood and youth amid the profound economic, demographic, political, and social upheavals of fin-de-siècle France. By the dawn of the twentieth century the lyrical image of childhood as "the sleep of reason" had come of age, so to speak, in the form of the "adolescent."[36] A new subject was born whose very existence posed a threat to society as he carried within himself (or herself) a potential dangerousness.

The inherent liminality of this age group was central to its perceived menace. It is not entirely coincidental that the "discovery" of adolescence occurred at the same time officials at Mettray first began to have serious doubts about their mission. Many were increasingly convinced that their subjects—caught between childhood and adulthood—were not just experiencing acute problems related to their own social adjustment and physical development, but that they stood at the vanguard of a new generation of lawless, amoral, and anomic youth beyond all hope of reformation. The feelings of *insécurité* this generated played a crucial role in determining Mettray's fate and, more generally, in transforming the juvenile justice system by the interwar period.

Fears of the adolescent were exacerbated by the belief that the French nation was degenerating and headed toward eventual extinction. Introduced by theorists in the social sciences, particularly the nascent field of criminology, the figure of the "degenerate" had superseded the atavistic criminal in the medico-legal imaginary by the close of the nineteenth century.[37] Degeneration theory was a capacious and malleable rubric that seemingly addressed both specific ills such as juvenile crime and more widespread fears of racial decline in the context of France's ongoing depopulation crisis. In the face of a united Germany whose population had increased by almost 20 percent from 1881 to 1901, France's population had remained nearly static, and many were convinced this *dénatalité* not only had caused France's defeat in the Franco-Prussian War but also foreshadowed national collapse.[38]

The philosopher Alfred Fouillée maintained that the harmful effects of industrialization and the advent of economic and cultural modernity imposed a severe strain on the human nervous system, leading to enervation, exhaustion, and degeneration. The insalubrious urban environment was believed to weaken the robust physical and moral constitutions of peasants drawn to the city, and this was reflected in their debilitated progeny. According to Fouillée, "The young criminal is most often a degenerate from a physical standpoint . . .

his height, weight, and muscular force diminished from his sickly constitution . . . all of which is accompanied by an obliteration of his moral sense."[39] Thus the moral qualities of the delinquent's mind were subject to the primacy of the body itself. "The fear of degeneration," according to the historian Alain Corbin, "haunted the elite and necessitated a firming up of the virility of youth,"[40] a task at which the agricultural colonies were seen as failing by the turn of the twentieth century.

To illuminate the largely unknown world of Mettray's denizens, this book delves into a store of documents—internal memoranda and correspondence, disciplinary logs, and where available, inmate files—that highlight various aspects of daily life at the institution, including living conditions, discipline, labor, sex, and violence. The young men who serve as the subjects of this work, as well as their keepers, are not presented as a faceless mass. Rather, their myriad individual stories are incorporated into the wider narrative and whenever possible, they speak for themselves. While the archival record is driven by the agendas and perspectives of the prison keepers, and although much of the documentation remains scattered or incomplete, the voices of youth are nonetheless present in the extant records at Mettray and other colonies, particularly in interviews and testimonies related to specific events and acts that occurred within the confines of the institution.[41] At times it was necessary to read between the lines of the archival record to recover these voices that speak to the depredations and deprivations of imprisonment. The recollections of former inmates, often published years after their imprisonment, are another valuable source of insight into daily life, albeit one with its own problems in terms of typicality, reliability, perspective, and historical memory.[42] Finally, annual reports, despite their somewhat formulaic character, reveal much about the day-to-day operation of the agricultural colony, both in its idealized form and in reality, as do statistics compiled from the *Compte général* that allow analysis of long-term behavioral trends and short-term anomalies.[43]

As Mary Jo Maynes has noted, historians often "have trouble conceptualizing children and youth as historical actors because so few of the sources speak directly to their experiences." According to Maynes this reflects a more "general problem of 'history from below' or subaltern history," as children do not "speak for themselves in most historical records about them."[44] Thus, it may appear counterintuitive to conceive of prisoners, particularly child or adolescent prisoners, as possessing agency. To have agency presumes the wherewithal (both cognitive and physical) to assume the specific subject position of an adult in possession of the practical and symbolic attributes associated with freedom and responsibility. Moreover, agency itself was under constant assault at Mettray as the institution undermined prisoners' capacity for autonomy by prohibiting them from making decisions related to their own existence. While captivity is intended to limit self-determination, and despite the numerous restrictions placed on prisoners and the highly regimented daily life at Mettray, many young men found ways to exercise some degree of agency. Therefore, I have endeavored to write a history of Mettray that focuses on what Michael Ignatieff has called "the living battles of the confined against their suffering."[45]

This work is not a narrow institutional history of imprisonment in which Mettray is viewed in complete isolation. At various points I contextualize Mettray's history by comparing it to three other colonies that differ in terms of size, age, location, administrative oversight, and modus operandi: the agricultural colony Val d'Yèvre, located outside the city of Bourges in the department of the Cher; the industrial colony Aniane, located outside the city of Montpellier in the department of the Hérault; and the correctional colony Eysses, located in Villeneuve-sur-Lot in the department of the Lot-et-Garonne. Each of these colonies represents a unique aspect of the larger carceral web that Mettray had woven. Established by the famed prison inspector and penal reformer Charles Lucas in 1847, Val d'Yèvre was initially a private agricultural colony that developed financial problems and subsequently fell under the control of the French state and became an institutional counterpoint to Mettray. Founded by the state in 1885 to prepare delinquent urban youths for a life of industrial labor, Aniane was one of the largest and longest-running industrial colonies in France. Finally, the relationship between Mettray and Eysses (established in 1895) was fraught because officials at the former transferred troublesome prisoners to the latter in numbers that were seen by the Penitentiary Administration as incommensurate with the size of Mettray's population.

Situated within the context of the history of juvenile crime and punishment in nineteenth- and twentieth-century France, this book aims to contribute to the scholarship on the history of childhood and adolescence and the history of masculinity. As Pieter Spierenburg has noted, until the 1970s there was a certain Whig-like quality to the historiography on imprisonment that typically characterized "the rise of the prison as the result of the benevolent endeavors of humanitarian reformers."[46] Foucault's revisionist approach was a welcome corrective to this orientation, but in much of the scholarly work that followed in the 1980s and 1990s there was a general inattention to historical detail and empirical data (as was the case with *Discipline and Punish*). Since the 1990s, however, there has been a shift away from Foucauldian abstractions and a move toward work based on deep archival research, especially as it relates to original documents and judicial records.[47] While I take issue with Foucault with regard to agency and resistance, there are multiple points of congruence between my analysis and his powerful and totalizing vision of modern disciplinary society. Nevertheless, I am in agreement with Melossi and Pavarini, who, while acknowledging the "salutary and profound impact which Foucault's perspective has had in relation to the history of the prison," also note that "it seems that the kind of detailed work required in this field is local research unconstrained by 'great visions' of an ideological nature; research which would facilitate an appreciation of local strategies and moves in the game of social control."[48] Whereas Foucault offers a view of Mettray from afar, I write from within, submerged in the disciplinary culture and secret life of the colony. I focus on the inner institutional workings of the enterprise and the various collusions, alliances, and conflicts that arose among prisoners and officials.

Historians have moved past the debate spurred by Philippe Ariès, who argued that our contemporary understanding of childhood as a distinct and sentimentalized stage in the life cycle only began to emerge in the sixteenth and seventeenth centuries. Prior to this, according to Ariès, children had been regarded as small adults; the degree of sentiment and emotional attachment we evince toward children and childhood more generally is a relatively recent historical phenomenon.[49] Ariès's arguments have elicited a great deal of criticism from a wide range of scholars, but the general contention that childhood (and, by extension, adolescence) is a social construct is not subject to debate. This work does not focus on the question of when a modern concept of childhood first appeared in France, but it does demonstrate clearly that many parents were deeply invested in the lives and the fates of their children who were housed at Mettray, and that they often endeavored to work within and occasionally outside the confines of regulations to ensure their well-being. Moreover, it explores how the evolution of one legal category (i.e., the juridical minor) impacted the operation of the agricultural colony and the structure of the juvenile justice system more generally. Self-proclaimed experts viewed minors as still needing guidance and protection. As rehabilitative practices for criminal youth were developed over the course of the late nineteenth and early twentieth centuries, new age categories were created and refined.[50]

This work builds on a wealth of scholarship focused on children in the context of legal, social, and cultural change in modern France.[51] While this literature has had a tremendous impact on the history of childhood in France as a field of inquiry, it generally relies on the ideas of child welfare advocates, politicians, and experts in the medical and social sciences in delineating changing cultural conceptions and legal protections of childhood rather than examining lived experience. The two works closest to this study in terms of focus and approach are Sarah Fishman's *The Battle for Children* (2002) and Laura Lee Downs's *Childhood in the Promised Land* (2002). The former details how the

French state defined and attempted to deal with the problem of juvenile delinquency under German occupation during the Second World War. Fishman's study is in many ways a model for this work, as she combines a "top-down" approach—focused on state policy and elite writings—with a "bottom-up" perspective that explores the impact of broad political currents on everyday lives. Through a meticulous sampling of juvenile case files, Fishman interprets the documents generated by the juvenile justice system as indicating "a two-way interaction" in which the voices of the repressed are not drowned out by "the system's distortions. The minors in court and their families . . . were not entirely powerless objects of state authority."[52] While this book follows a similar approach regarding historical agency, the focus of Fishman's work is on the juridical web in which the delinquent was caught rather than on daily life in an institution such as Mettray.

Downs examines the so-called *colonies de vacances*, or summer camps, that grew out of late nineteenth-century charity efforts—initially by religious orders, and later by socialist and communist organizations—that removed children from their urban environs and placed them in the countryside for a period of six to eight weeks. Although they were not aimed at criminal youth, the *colonies de vacances* had a mission similar to Mettray's in that they were intended to reinvigorate the minds and bodies of urban children, particularly those from the banlieues, through exposure to rural life and deep engagement with nature. The camps were also seen as providing a counterweight to the monotonous and standardized rigor of republican schools. Just as the "colonies de vacances resonated with a powerful current in French thought," designed to create "a politics of Republican virtue," so too did Mettray, which predated them by nearly half a century.[53]

As the political theorist Barbara Arneil has outlined in *Domestic Colonies*, the ideology underpinning the agrarian colonies in France was "explicitly interwoven from the outset with a Romantic focus on the countryside, a paternalistic focus on youth, and a republican focus on citizenship and virtue,"[54] principles that were deeply Rousseauian. Jean-Jacques Rousseau famously idealized the moral sensibilities and civic virtues of simple, hardworking farmers over those of the urban bourgeoisie and Parisian intellectuals, whom he believed were not dedicated to the common welfare if it came at the expense of their individual interests. He was greatly concerned about the corrosive effects of city life on the soul, and his republicanism was a central weapon in his critiques of modernity. As Annelien de Dijn has pointed out, however, Rousseau maintained that certain social practices could instill "solidarity among all citizens," rich or poor, urban or rural, and thereby address "human beings' predisposition towards moral egoism. To achieve this goal no force was more potent than patriotism."[55] Patriotism was not innate but it could be inculcated, according to Rousseau, through civic festivals that "bring people together, not so much for a public entertainment as for the gathering of a big family," where they engage in "practices, ceremonies, games and distinctive modes of dress" that instill a sense of fraternity and civic virtue.[56]

As Mona Ozouf has noted, "one of the great mythical experiences" of the eighteenth century was that of "the individual who is re-baptized as citizen in the festival . . . which was an indispensable complement to the legislative system, for although the legislator makes the laws for the people, festivals make the people for the laws."[57] Here Ozouf channels Rousseau, who believed that participation in the civic festival produced feelings of fraternity, civic identity, and perhaps most importantly from his point of view, a fervent patriotism. At the heart of the civic festival were the martial practices of the citizen-soldier, because to Rousseau, soldiering was central to becoming a citizen of the republic and to becoming a man. Military discipline and solidarity were fungible, convertible into the foundational components of civic republican life. The corporeal display of the "vigorous and warlike" citizen-soldier, who wears his uniform and participates in martial drills as part of the civic festivities of his community in the "summertime, on Sundays and on feast-days,"[58] was essential to the construction of republican citizenship. This distinctly Rousseauian vision—the intertwined conceptions of man, soldier, and citizen—was a central feature of Mettray's regime that featured an extensive array of martial activities and ceremonial practices intended to produce a totalizing civic identity that left little room for particularity or individuality.

Noting that republicanism "associated citizenship with industriousness and agrarian labor,"[59] Arneil argues that the Lockean notion of the labor theory of acquisition"(i.e., the theory of natural law that holds that property originally comes about by the exertion of labor upon natural resources), which had been used as a justification for European colonialism around the globe, was extended to domestic colonies, whose exponents advanced both economic and ethical imperatives in their "turn inward." Although these colonies, including Mettray, isolated their populations from civil society (particularly from the inherent corruption of urban areas), Arneil maintains that they were originally conceived not as repressive institutions but as benevolent ones, part and parcel of a "progressive, universalist, and Christian ideology" that sought to reform and engage the urban poor, delinquents, and the insane via "agrarian labor in a 'benevolent' way."[60] In transforming the land through their labor, the denizens of these institutions would transform themselves into industrious workers. Thus Arneil challenges the Foucauldian interpretation of the carceral as inherently coercive by focusing on the ethical components of domestic colonialism.

Mettray was initially envisioned as a colony but over time it became a carceral institution that grew increasingly punitive during its nearly century-long existence. Demetz was a benevolent paternalist, like most nineteenth-century penal reformers and philanthropists, yet corporal punishments, cellular isolation, bread-and-water rations, and the use of handcuffs and straitjackets became fundamental features of Mettray's regime. There was nothing "modern" in these sanctions, and there is no indication that the colony ever took on the omnipresent surveillance of Foucault's imagining. The moral philosopher was never particularly interested in how the colony operated or how it changed over time; instead, Foucault focused on what he saw as its disciplinary essence, which was more in the realm of rhetoric than reality. My interest is in discovering how the everyday tensions, frustrations, confrontations, and brutalities in the colony impacted its operation and ultimately led to its demise. Thus, just as Arneil offers a valuable corrective to Foucault, so too does this work, albeit from the vantage point of those who lived and worked at Mettray rather than those who shaped its original idealist mission.

Because Mettray held only male youths, one cannot truly understand its operation without addressing gender, particularly changing conceptions of masculinity in nineteenth- and early twentieth-century France. The intensely homosocial nature of the agricultural colony suggests that masculinity played a critical role in Mettray's development and history as an institution.[61] Most work on the history of gender in France has focused on the social, political, economic, and intellectual histories of women, with some analyzing changing and at times competing definitions of femininity. This book complements this corpus of work by contributing to a growing but still much less extensive literature on male identity formation.[62]

Manhood was a highly contested domain in the agricultural colony, where the regime was designed to inculcate a bourgeois heteronormative ideal that was often at odds with the model that existed among working-class and poor youth. Officials attempted to mobilize masculinity through the daily routine of labor, physical exercise, military decorum and drills, as well as through privileges offered or denied and punishments meted out. When prisoners opposed the terms of their incarceration by expressing their own alternative ideas of a resistant manhood, there was no institutional recourse in the disciplinary arsenal other than temporary exclusion via solitary confinement or transfer to a traditional prison such as Eysses. At Mettray, homosexuality was understood as a moral contagion, and the homosexual was a predatory carrier of that contagion; his presence in the colony posed a profound threat to the institution's heteronormative ethos.

The foundational work on bourgeois masculinity in modern France is Robert Nye's *Masculinity and Male Codes of Honor* (1993), which argues that masculinity was temporal, fluctuating, and construed as under threat amid the fears of cultural decadence, demographic stagnation, and racial degeneration that characterized fin-de-siècle France. Central to Nye's argument is what he defines as a male "code of honor" that reflected the "bourgeois preoccupation with moral discipline, inner values, and with the control of reproduction and sex." Over the course of the eighteenth century the bourgeoisie engaged in a protracted struggle for social recognition, adopting a code of personal self-discipline that facilitated their ascendance as a "new aristocracy of work, competence and wealth" whose ideology stressed personal initiative and independence.[63]

Not coincidentally, the concomitant democratization of military service introduced the aristocratic culture of the sword—symbol of military prowess—as honor's enforcement mechanism among the bourgeoisie. Honor was demonstrated not only by heteronormative sexual behavior but also in the contrived form of the duel, which enjoyed a renaissance as an opportunity for public display and/or defense of one's honor. According to Nye, the mutually reinforcing ideologies of honor and militarism flourished in the immediate aftermath of the Franco-Prussian War before being slowly transformed into something approximating "courage" by the outbreak of the First World War. Edward Berenson noted that the duel gave bourgeois men a way to restore a masculine "spirit of combat" by fighting "surrogate wars" with Germany in each individual duel, thereby reassuring themselves of their own personal courage as well as the nation's regeneration.[64]

It is safe to say that Demetz and his successors at Mettray were obsessed with this code of honor and related concepts such as heroism, altruism, duty, and sacrifice. The inculcation of honor at Mettray was intended to instill the paternalistic and deferential relations characteristic of French society, which at the time of the institution's opening in 1840 was still deeply hierarchical, even among the newly ascendant bourgeoisie. The social anthropologist Julian Pitt-Rivers defines honor as "the value of a person in his own eyes, but also in the eyes of society. It is his estimation of his own worth, his claim to pride, but it is also the acknowledgment of that claim, his excellence recognized by society, his right to pride"—namely, respect and deference.[65] In a wide range of ethnographic studies anthropologists have associated long-held attachments to the values of honor in Mediterranean societies with rural, pre-industrial settings. According to the anthropologist J. G. Peristiany, "Honor and shame are the constant preoccupation of individuals in small-scale, exclusive societies where face to face personal, as opposed to anonymous relations, are of paramount importance."[66]

This is not unlike the society that existed within the confines of the agricultural colony, and perceptions of honor and reputation were crucial features of manhood at Mettray. This work examines how this bourgeois code of honor—so valorized by Demetz and his successors—was transmitted and transmuted by the working-class and poor young men who inhabited Mettray in their interpersonal relations with both fellow inmates and staff and administrators. The inculcation of honor at Mettray through a variety of daily activities and rituals was intended to shape masculine identity by instilling normative ideas about appropriate manhood while also reinforcing their position in the social hierarchy. Yet, according to the novelist and playwright Jean Genet, Mettray's most notable and notorious former inmate,

> The kids that were at Mettray had already rejected traditional morality, the social morality of your society, because as soon as we arrived at Mettray we quite willingly accepted a medieval morality that insists that the vassal must obey his sovereign and which sets up a pecking order that is very apparent and based upon physical strength, on honor, and the word of honor, which was very important then. Whereas now everything depends on what is in writing, on the signed contract that is dated before the public notary, before the board of directors, etc.[67]

The archival record makes clear that honor and manhood were inextricably intertwined for inmates who struggled to make sense of their own lives and identities at Mettray. But this was not merely a matter of a youthful, masculine pride. What emerged in the colony was a particularly assertive form of manhood premised on open displays of aggression and acts (or threats) of violence, not the bourgeois self-discipline and restraint manifested within the ritualized confines of the duel. This book illuminates the ways prisoners relied on displays of physical aggression to demonstrate and defend their honor and how this propensity for violence constituted a distinct component of masculinity in the colony.

Although girls are not the focus of this work, it is important to note that most girls who were considered delinquent or in need of some form of institutional intervention were judged so because of their sexual activities (real or presumed) rather than criminal behavior (proportionally, crime rates were far lower for girls than for boys).[68] Girls who engaged in premarital sex, or were thought likely to do so by their parents or authorities, were often seen as heading toward permanent promiscuity or prostitution, and therefore posed a threat to the familial and social order. Most were sent directly to preservation schools and/or religious institutions where they were treated very differently than their male counterparts. While Mettray's primary objective was to transform male delinquents into hardworking, law-abiding citizens, institutions for girls generally aimed to instill a chaste sensibility, a task for which the nuns who staffed the penitentiary houses under the convent system—overseen by religious orders such as Bon Pasteur—were uniquely qualified.[69] Although life in girls institutions was not as well documented as in the agricultural colonies, O'Brien points out that there were published reports of riots among adolescent girls, which received "much attention from commentators because this was considered shocking behavior in girls."[70]

This work begins with an examination of the wide array of influences that shaped Demetz's vision of the agricultural colony. Mettray was a chimera, an institutional hybrid that defies easy definition or categorization. The poorhouse, the monastery, the penal colony, and the penitentiary all appear in various guises in the context of Mettray's design and regime, and the connective thread that runs through these institutions was an overriding obsession with segregation. In the case of Mettray, Demetz believed that the reform of criminal youth required their triple segregation: from their dissolute families; from the corrupting influence of adult convicts in common jails; and from the deleterious effects of the urban-industrial milieu.[71] In sum, Mettray promised to disrupt delinquency generated by criminogenic environments and pathological social associations via exposure to a rural utopia located on the margins of the modern world.

With its emphasis on discipline and the development of a masculine will through the enforcement of a strict, militaristic culture, Mettray's regimen appealed to the moral sensibilities of those who oversaw the institution. They had a deep suspicion of idleness, and labor was the fundamental precept of reform because it seemed to offer a ready-made solution for the growing disorder of the industrial age. In examining daily life in the colony this work demonstrates that beneath the administration's fondness for agricultural labor and military drill was a rather narrow idea of masculine character as fixed and dependable, rooted in the rhythmic habits of a routine designed to attenuate undisciplined natures. The *colons* of Mettray were to be molded into hardworking men (as befitting their class status), disciplined and patriotic, and homogenous in belief and outlook.

Yet, in Mettray there was a resistant culture that existed beneath the veneer of discipline and order. Indeed, the colony was a bubbling cauldron of fear, anger, frustration, and resentment that boiled over in acts of resistance by the prisoners. In examining prisoner argot, tattooing, self-mutilation, and the homosexual subculture at Mettray, this study explores the limitations of institutional power and outlines the process by which administrators came to see their young subjects' failure to interiorize a bourgeois work ethic as evidence of adolescent intractability.

This work also analyzes the pitched internecine struggles among those who worked at Mettray as administrators and guards. Despite the administrative structure designed to instill professional pride and a sense of purpose, the agricultural colony was a site of deep organizational discord that frequently impeded daily operations. While Mettray had set apparently impermeable boundaries—spatial, temporal, sexual, and cultural—those boundaries were successful only if those who policed and enforced them were perpetually vigilant. Internal records indicate that such vigilance was rarely present because the colony was chronically understaffed and underfunded.

The book concludes with an examination of three separate scandals—in 1887, 1909, and an extended period of crisis during the interwar period—that shook public confidence in Mettray and ultimately led to the decision to close the colony. These highly publicized events illuminate a protracted power struggle over the way the institution was governed, as the state endeavored to assert its dominion over the colony. Amid this turmoil there was a profound shift in ideology and practice from a period of hope to a time of disillusionment, or in Rothman's terms, from a period of "conscience" to a period of "convenience."[72] This work reveals the historically contingent nature of an institution that was nonetheless crucial to the exercise of power and authority in nineteenth- and twentieth-century France.

Chapter 1

Origins

Many penal reformers, philanthropists, and jurists were deeply troubled by a perceived increase in juvenile crime in mid-nineteenth-century France. Amid what was seen as an enormous demographic shift sweeping the poor out of the countryside and into the streets of Paris and other urban areas in search of employment and a better life, observers demonized the city, imagining it as a site of unrelenting moral depravity.[1] The inadequacy of public health measures by municipalities and state authorities exacerbated the already insalubrious environment.[2] As poverty and social dislocation became more visible, so did the perception of an ever-widening moral chasm between the *classes dangereuses* and the bourgeoisie.[3] Paris in particular was viewed as a city that had fallen dangerously ill, both literally and metaphorically, and the pathologies that afflicted it were, not coincidentally, also those that afflicted its poor. Although there was some disagreement about the extent of the illness, most agreed that its symptoms were manifest in the form of crime. Criminal statistics indicated otherwise, however; most criminal defendants were born in the departments where they had run afoul of the law, and cities began to outpace the countryside in percentage of crimes committed only after the mid-nineteenth century.[4]

The association of criminality with the poor and the concomitant though largely unstated suggestion of bourgeois victimization were pervasive among French social theorists and social critics. The perceived danger the poor posed to the ruling class and their comfortable world was exactly the measure of personal danger felt by the poor in their uncomfortable world created by the exigencies of life in a highly stratified society. According to Antoine-Honoré Frégier, the bureau head of the headquarters of the Paris police, crime was a moral pathology to which the "lower orders" of society were acutely predisposed: "The poor and the vicious classes have been, and always will be, the most productive breeding ground for evildoers of all sorts. Even when vice is not accompanied by perversity, the very fact that it allies itself with poverty in the same person makes him a proper object of fear in society: he is dangerous."[5]

Unsurprisingly, the city was blamed for the development of criminal impulses in the children of the urban poor. As the prison inspector Louis-Mathurin Moreau-Christophe bluntly proclaimed, "The child of the people of Paris from the lowest class of society . . . is essentially depraved."[6] The urban child's seeming independence from adult authority threatened long-standing notions of childhood sociability. Unlike bourgeois schoolboys and working-class apprentices whose daily lives were organized around either school or the workshop and therefore largely removed from public view, the children of the poor were highly visible in their urban environs. Whereas the child of the bourgeoisie lived in a world of the home, school, and church, the child of the urban poor inhabited only the space he could carve out on the streets. As Ariès has pointed out, in medieval and early modern cities there was little opposition to private lives lived on the street, but bourgeois reformers of the nineteenth century wanted to transform the urban space from "the familiar setting of social relations" into a natural "lieu de passage."[7] As the streets teemed with poor youths they were vulnerable to bourgeois efforts at social control.

In this context, the *gamin* (waif), most famously depicted in the character Gavroche in Victor Hugo's *Les misérables,* came to epitomize the problem of juvenile crime and delinquency in mid-nineteenth-century France. The moralist Boulangé d'Aytré maintained that while the "*gamin* is old enough to practice a trade, his family cannot make the necessary sacrifices to secure an apprenticeship. . . . [Thus] he roams the streets day and night where he encounters things he should neither see nor hear, and acquires the most vicious penchants which have dangerous consequences for society."[8] According to one anonymous prison reformer, "The *gamin* is without resources and gives in to all types of dissipations. Scarcely into the course of life, he learns the most culpable trades and eventually becomes a consummate malefactor."[9] The economist, journalist, and future prime minister of France Léon Faucher lamented: "Even before he has acquired his full strength, the *gamin* is left to his own devices. . . . This deplorable penchant manifests itself primarily as crime."[10]

Given their visibility and their presence at incidents of political violence, there was widespread concern that poor children posed a real threat to the social order. Many contemporaries believed that the *gamin* had played a role in the street violence during the Revolution of 1830 and that the child of the street was preternaturally disposed to irrational and violent impulses.[11] The jurist and politician Bérenger de la Drôme, who headed the parliamentary commission that tried the ministers of Charles X, noted bleakly: "There is not a riot that the *gamin* does not attend, and in which he does not take part. . . . For him revolution is a drama in which he can become an actor in order to satisfy his taste for adventure."[12] The anarchic sensibilities of the *gamin* were part of the rich cultural tapestry of the early nineteenth century, most clearly evoked in Eugène Delacroix's *Liberty Leading the People* (1830). Those who benefitted most from revolutionary activities (i.e., newly ascendant republicans and members of the liberal bourgeoisie) found themselves in an ideological bind regarding the *gamin*, for the same youths who had helped man the barricades during the "Three Glorious Days" could pose a threat to their own political fortunes now that they were in power.

Although the *gamin* had fallen away from an idealized notion of childhood innocence, there was a prevailing sense that he could still be "saved," but only if he was displaced from his dissolute milieu. The "rescue" and moral redemption of the street urchin was a standard leitmotiv in the vast adulatory writings on Mettray. Typical was the portrait offered by the jurist Augustin Cochin, writing of his visit to the colony. When he asked a seven-year-old boy sentenced to prison for stealing a few artichokes from a Paris street vendor why he had committed the crime, the boy reportedly replied, "My mother is in prison and I had to take care of myself. I had to eat to live." According to Cochin, "Most of the children here have similar sad stories to tell and it is why a life of family, honor and discipline, so lacking in their own homes, is so well received at Mettray."[13]

While this tale was likely apocryphal, the image was nonetheless powerful: a youth who had crossed a line into lawlessness, embodying both disorder and innocence. Indeed, a significant number of children arrested in France during the first half of the nineteenth century had committed offenses not unlike Cochin's typical denizen of Mettray. By Kathleen Nilan's estimate, roughly 40 percent of child prisoners in Paris during the 1830s and 1840s had been arrested for vagrancy, 15 percent for begging, and another 40 percent for theft (mostly petty theft).[14] Yet, the insistence on the moral origins of poverty and vice placed the burden of addressing juvenile crime not on an unjust economic system but on the prison.

During the first half of the century the focus of governmental activities with respect to the poor was not to control or regulate industry to minimize the wide-ranging social effects of the Industrial Revolution on the poor; rather, it was to morally correct and, if necessary, punish those who led irreligious, immoral, and criminal lives. If crime—and by extension, political unrest—was the product of the moral imperfection of individuals, and if vice was indeed "contagious," particularly among the poor who lived in the unhealthy urban milieu, then the most effective way to deal with the *gamin* on the city streets was by rehabilitation in prison. In this regard, however, the municipal and departmental prisons inherited from Napoléon were decidedly lacking.

"Correcting" the *gamin* necessitated his removal not only from the city but also from the communal prisons where he was housed alongside adults. While the Napoleonic Code stipulated that minors be held separately from adults and that they be provided some form of education while incarcerated, this legal provision remained a dead letter until the July Monarchy (1830–48). Prisons in early nineteenth-century France retained their premodern form, serving primarily as "depots, warehouses and way stations leading to other punishments and other places, rather than as long-term abodes and places of penitence."[15] Penal reformers such as J.-F. Ginouvrier inveighed against these common jails that were not just dirty and disorderly but "dens of iniquity" that left "indelible imprints of debauchery and crime" on boys and young men by the time of their release. "What are these children doing in prisons and jails?," Ginouvrier asked, "where they are exposed to contagion as they live beside profoundly corrupt men habituated to crime and who provide lessons in swindling and villainy."[16] The philanthropist Benjamin Appert lamented "the mixing of all convicts, especially the old with the young which results in the dangerous contagion of vice."[17] Moreau-Christophe utilized the same epidemiological trope in describing the social mores of the communal prison: "The close contact with grand criminals leads to contagion, most especially for those [such as the young] who are predisposed to mental aberrations."[18] Demetz, who as a magistrate had long been active in the prison reform movement, was similarly troubled by the state of prisons and their effects on youth: "I was struck by the number of children brought before me in the performance of my duty as a judge. Many of these stood no higher than my desk and, as there were at that time no establishments for the reformation of juveniles only, I was obliged to consign all of them to common prisons where they associated with hardened, adult criminals . . . and where they received the same treatment as adults in quarters that I knew were utterly unfit for them."[19]

The general conceptualization of vice as a contagion led Demetz and others to initially focus on conditions in the common jail, which was viewed as a uniquely criminogenic site that exacerbated rather than curtailed antisocial tendencies. While there were different theories about the causes of crime in the early to mid-nineteenth century, prison reformers were influenced by medical theories that linked moral and physical health, and therefore they endeavored to establish a regime that would attend to both.[20] Since the goal of the prison, at least in the eyes of reformers, was to enable criminals to reenter society and become productive citizens, the institution had a basic responsibility to provide prisoners with a salubrious physical environment.[21]

In this context, the reformed prison was designed to instill upright moral character through hard labor, savings, a regularized routine, and moral training to reform the criminal. Steeped in Christian notions of charity and inspired by the ideals of the French Revolution and the Declaration of the Rights of Man, penal reformers promoted the idea that punishment should be nothing more than the deprivation of liberty and that decent living conditions for all prisoners was a fundamental responsibility of the state. Consequently, the weight of sentences shifted from corporal punishment to imprisonment, and the emphasis on vengeance and deterrence was broadened to include rehabilitation. In this sense, as Foucault has noted, the prison was effectively reimagined as a utopian model of social organization.

Groups such as the Société de la morale chrétienne, founded in 1821, commenced a campaign of prison visits to study the insitutions and promote the idea that improvements were necessary not only to demonstrate to prisoners that the state whose laws they had violated was just and compassionate but also to forestall the damage occasioned by their eventual return to society. The activities of the society served as a testing ground for liberal concepts of philanthropy that emphasized the moral leadership of the educated classes and private initiative in charitable enterprises.[22] The prison was an ideal site of intervention for reformers to morally improve those they considered both inferior and dangerous.

Their efforts eventually helped inspire passage of the Prison Reform Bill of 1832, which stipulated that the penal administration provide inmates with basic necessities. Thus, the piles of straw that had been used as bedding were replaced by cots and convicts were regularly given clean clothing and bed linens. Prisoners were also given access to "elementary instruction, religious services and rudimentary libraries."[23] In addition, prisons were reorganized according to type of prisoner and length of sentence. Nine *maisons centrales* were established to house those sentenced to more than two years and the various departmental prisons (*maisons d'arrêt, maisons de justice,* and *maisons départementales*) were henceforth charged with confining only those awaiting trial or serving sentences of less than one year; long- and short-term adult offenders were no longer held in communal quarters.[24] However, while the prison reform bill rationalized and modernized the prison system in France, it was mostly silent on juvenile corrections.

Juvenile crime was blamed not only on the prison system that failed to distinguish between adults and minors but also, in the words of Demetz, on the "inferior moral standards to which children are condemned" by their dissolute parents.[25] In his study of Parisian prostitutes the hygienist A. J.-B Parent-Duchâtelet maintained that most girls and young women who turned to prostitution did so because their parents had set a poor example for them or mistreated them. A "perverse education" by parents could also produce what Parent-Duchâtelet termed "precocious" juvenile criminals.[26] As Nilan has noted, self-proclaimed authorities on juvenile crime often characterized young offenders as "precociously perverse," which implied they had reached maturity before their time; this allowed observers to preserve the romantic myth of childhood innocence while conceptualizing children who had committed criminal acts as "monstrously abnormal."[27] According to Frégier, poor and working-class parents were driven by excessive "egoism" and neglected to plan for the future. Because they wasted their wages in drink, sexual excess, and popular entertainments, they displayed a fundamental disregard for their children as well as society at large.[28] Thus Frégier characterized an entire class as living unregulated lives as their passions went unchecked by reason and morality, which were seen as the prime attributes of an enlightened and civilized people.[29]

Like most of his contemporaries, Demetz held a vaguely articulated social environmentalist view of human behavior. In castigating urban poor families, he was very much in the mainstream of mid-nineteenth-century social thought: "Raised by irreligious, disordered and vicious parents, the child cannot draw upon the moral principles on which our society is based. He is led astray by the unfortunate history of a family that kills rather than instills morality."[30] If poor and working-class families were the cradle of crime, then their children were embryonic criminals. The product of this thinking was a fully circular developmental etiology in which parental neglect was the primary cause of juvenile crime. Neglected children become unruly, and unruly children become criminals who, in turn, neglect their offspring.

In cases where a family could not assure the conformity of a recalcitrant child, the best means to instill habits of "industry, sobriety and discipline," according to Demetz, was through prolonged contact and exposure to a "new family, in which the child will learn the meaning of obedience, honor and pride and from the good example set forth by paternal authority."[31] Demetz idealized the family and sought to replicate it within the confines of his institution. The family at Mettray was designed to be a citadel against vice, its severity a rebuke and an example to those who had been raised in an environment where discipline was lacking. The director boldly proclaimed that he saw his work with juvenile delinquents as a means of "reforming the child, the family, and ultimately, all of French society."[32]

As the prison became the designated institution to deal with the social fallout of the nascent industrial age, the French government asked Demetz and the architect Guillaume Abel Blouet (who later designed Mettray) to travel to the United States and report back on developments in American corrections since the visit of Alexis de Tocqueville and Gustave de Beaumont five years earlier.[33] French prison reformers had long turned to the United States for experiential guidance as both countries tried to articulate and develop their respective national carceral systems. During the period of the revolution and empire, French reformers studied U.S. penitentiaries and adopted some of their methods of prisoner rehabilitation, most notably prison labor, which was seen as the most important means by which to ameliorate character, alter the behavior of criminals, and prepare them for their eventual return to society.[34]

Tocqueville and Beaumont spent nine months in the United States (though the original itinerary called for an eighteen-month stay), visiting over a dozen prisons and interviewing inmates and directors. Their report, published in 1833, argued the relative merits of the two principal forms of prison organization in the United States—the Pennsylvania and Auburn systems—and discussed the potential pitfalls of introducing either into France.[35] The chief advantages of the Auburn system, according to the authors, were that it was less expensive than the Pennsylvania system and did not interfere with job training or revenue-producing convict labor. Its disadvantages were twofold: there was no guarantee that prisoners would not communicate with and corrupt one another, and corporal punishment was considered an essential component of the regime. Conversely, the perceived advantages of the Pennsylvania system lay in the prophylactic and reformative qualities of absolute isolation; cells prohibited mutual corruption and encouraged personal introspection conducive to spiritual redemption. Its disadvantages were its cost and the threat that isolation posed to the mental and physical health of the prisoner.

Beaumont and Tocqueville were impressed by the willingness of the United States to experiment in corrections but they were ambivalent about whether either of the two systems were viable for France. On the one hand, while both were skeptical of the promise of rehabilitation offered by the Pennsylvania model, they nevertheless maintained that separation was the only cure for the

"dangerous contagion" of criminal association.[36] "Thrown into solitude he reflects" wrote Tocqueville of the prisoner, "and if his soul has not yet surfeited
with crime . . . it is in solitude where remorse will come to assail him."[37] On
the other hand, the authors believed that the Auburn system—with its emphasis on work in common, outside the confines of the individual cell—was
more likely to inculcate industry and obedience in the prisoner. In a letter written in 1831, Tocqueville revealed his misgivings regarding the entire enterprise: "We have the material to prove that the penitentiary system reforms and
that it does not reform; that it is costly and cheap; easy to administer and im-
practicable; in a word, that it suits or does not suit France."[38]

Given this rather tepid assessment and a continued commitment on the part
of the French government to create a national penitentiary system, Demetz
and Blouet were commissioned to embark on a similar journey and file a new
report to the French minister of the interior, Adrien de Gasparin.[39] As Oliver
Davis has noted, in addition to serving as president of Mettray's governing
board, the Société paternelle, interior minister Gasparin was responsible for
issuing circulars that established the censorship of prison mail and a ban on
tobacco, policies that impinged on the daily lives of all prisoners in France.[40]
Although Demetz and Blouet followed in the footsteps of Beaumont and Tocqueville, their report was a partisan document that strongly supported the
Pennsylvania system, which is unsurprising because Demetz had always believed that French prisons were neither punitive nor a deterrent to crime. He
wrote: "In our existing system, prison is no longer a punishment; it offers criminals asylum, livelihood, security, and the sympathy and approbation society
refuses. Far from being an object of fear it has become a way station where
criminals rest from the fatigue and tribulations of their adventurous lives, and
are given renewed force to their energy and perversity through the counsel
and encouragements of their companions in infamy."[41] Whereas Demetz was
charged by the French state with analyzing prison management, Blouet was
instructed to study prison architecture. Both were asked to determine whether
silence was perfectly maintained, whether corporal punishment was necessary,
whether U.S. penitentiaries deterred crime and reformed criminals, whether
Pennsylvania's system was unhealthy, and whether there had been any changes
in regulations since Beaumont and Tocqueville's visit.[42]

Demetz and Blouet visited seven state prisons, two of which had not been
seen by Tocqueville and Beaumont. In general, Demetz characterized conditions in local and county jails in the United States as deplorable. Corporal punishment was permitted but only if a period of solitary confinement had failed
to reform a prisoner's behavior, and only at the discretion of the head warden. Interestingly, given Demetz's total control over daily operations at Mettray,

he maintained that a warden should not possess such authority.[43] Indeed, Demetz characterized penitentiaries that adhered to the Auburn model as "either cruel or inadequate," with its severity determined by a warden who could choose to be either "humane or brutal."[44]

In theory, in the Auburn prison criminal associations were prevented through a regime of silence. This was largely impossible to achieve because even under the strictest discipline prisoners found ways to communicate, especially in workshops. Demetz and Blouet noted that at the Eastern State Penitentiary at Cherry Hill prisoners typically knew the names of their neighbors, though they did not indicate how the prisoners learned this information. Citing the Coldbath Fields Prison in London, they also remarked that the rule of silence was nearly impossible to maintain and that over 5,000 punishments had been issued for violations.[45] Demetz did acknowledge that the Auburn prison was the less expensive of the two prison systems, although he believed there was a "tendency to progressively sacrifice moral interests to those of a pecuniary nature,"[46] the same charge levelled against Mettray by many critics in the late nineteenth century.

While before his journey he had voiced some initial misgivings about the benefits of solitary confinement, Demetz later recalled that on his return to France his opinion had changed: "I left for America with a strong prejudice against the Pennsylvania system, but my ideas, in the presence of facts, have undergone a complete transformation, and I now have a need to spread my faith."[47] Demetz wrote that "justice and reason demand complete separation," and he strongly recommended penitential seclusion to the French government.[48] Under this system religious instruction could be individualized, solitude and reflection could produce reformation, and inmates could return to civil life with valuable skills without having acquired new criminal associations. Demetz also maintained that the punishment of seclusion was inherently just so long as its severity was proportionate to the culpability of the prisoner, as solitude had its greatest impact on those most corrupt and guilty.[49]

Demetz boasted that he and Blouet had formulated a system of penitential discipline and architecture that was not only superior to any in America but also "in a word, eminently French." In their final report they suggested certain modifications to the system of separate penitential discipline they had studied in the United States. Blouet produced several renderings for cellular prisons not unlike the radiating and panoptic schemes he had seen. Demetz recommended that the Pennsylvania system could be made more civilized and sociable through greater interaction between charitable institutions and the inmates, particularly as their release dates approached.[50]

To a certain degree, the debate about the Pennsylvania and Auburn systems was as much about labor practice as about punishment. Although the rhetorical contours of the debate were driven by the narrative of moral reform, the empirical divide between the two plans centered on the method of production. Given the subsequent development of an industrialized economy in France, the Auburn plan was arguably more prescient in its recognition of the factory as the organizing force of industrial life. Indeed, it was the carceral embodiment of the standard factory: long benches arrayed across a vast floor space and a silent, docile workforce supervised by guards stationed at various locations throughout the facility. Thus, the "originality" of the Auburn system, as noted by the sociologists Melossi and Pavarini, "lay essentially in the introduction of work structured in the same way as the dominant form of factory work."[51] Foucault similarly characterized the Auburn prison as an important component in the overall effort to discipline criminals and produce citizen-workers for the industrial economy, in contrast to the Pennsylvania plan, which was more antiquated, almost anachronistic, resembling the "putting-out" or cottage system that characterized the preindustrial age. The fact that Demetz endorsed the Pennsylvania model for adults (in line with the political and social tenor of the time) and yet adopted a mixed or blended system for Mettray indicated his own rather esoteric and flexible approach to prison labor and the realities of a changing economy.

The report submitted by Demetz and Blouet to the Comte de Montalivet, the new minister of the interior, was influential in solidifying the French government's position in favor of the separate system. Although Tocqueville later served on the board of the Société paternelle and generally supported Mettray as an institution, he did not particularly care for Demetz. There was a professional rivalry between the two men that derived, at least in part, from the exactitude and level of detail in the latter's report (particularly in terms of prison architecture) in comparison to Tocqueville and Beaumont's broad survey.[52] In a personal letter to Demetz, later cited in a newspaper article extolling Mettray's mission, Tocqueville nonetheless voiced his support for the colony while at the same time capturing its multifaceted character. "You seem to me," he wrote, "to have united in a happy way, the idea of the school and that of the prison, the idea of punishment and that of education, and in so doing, you have created an intermediate space between detention and freedom."[53]

Demetz also became a member of the commission of surveillance charged with monitoring the transformation of the Petite Roquette prison in Paris into an exclusively cellular establishment for juveniles.[54] When it opened in 1836 the institution was something of a carceral experiment, the first reformatory to employ a penitentiary regime of complete isolation, work, and education for juvenile offenders in France. In 1831 the Ministry of the Interior had asked Charles Lucas, the inspector general of French prisons, to outline a comprehensive plan for a model reformatory, and soon thereafter, the Conseil d'état accepted his blueprint and Petite Roquette opened its doors. The prison was initially operated on the Auburn model, with work and classes held in common during the day and youths isolated at night. Early on, Petite Roquette was deemed a great success, and supporters such as Bérenger de la Drôme attributed a fall in the recidivism rate to the beneficent influence of its disciplinary regime. In 1840, however, due to the increasing acceptance of the Pennsylvania model and a series of revolts in the reformatory itself, a system of continuous isolation was inaugurated. This new regime was criticized by many physicians, philanthropists, and penal reformers as endangering the health and mental well-being of its young prisoners. As Chris Leonards has noted, a nasty ideological battle was waged at the international penitentiary congresses in Frankfurt (1846) and Brussels (1847) between "cellomaniacs" and "agrarian colonists" led not by Demetz but by "a relative outsider," the economist and politician Louis Wolowski (a naturalized French citizen of Polish descent) who consistently referred to the solitary cell as a *chemise de pierre*.[55] Given that solitary confinement was a key component of the regime at Mettray and that Demetz had been a champion of the Pennsylvania system for adults, his silence on this issue is not surprising.

It is noteworthy that in *Democracy in America,* published the same year as Demetz and Blouet's report, Tocqueville and Beaumont included an appendix on agricultural colonies in which they recommended that France adopt such institutions for the poor:

> If such colonies were established in France, no idler could complain of not finding labor; the beggars, vagrants, paupers and all the released convicts whose numbers continue to increase and threaten the safety of individuals and even the tranquility of the state, would find a place in the colony where they could contribute to the wealth of this country by their labor. . . . By the side of these useless fields, a population . . . could be placed who are in want of soil and of the means of existence. In France, nearly two million poor are numbered and the uncultivated lands form the seventh part of the area of the kingdom.[56]

Thus, the agricultural colony was initially conceived for adult offenders, paupers, and the "idle" poor rather than for juvenile delinquents. This was not coincidental, as the French had shown great interest in the system of Dutch labor colonies (*maatschappij*) founded by Johannes van den Bosch in 1818 to assist poor urban families. On returning to Holland from Java van den Bosch claimed that the "cultivation system" he introduced overseas could serve as a model of "internal colonization" for the "idle poor" through the auspices of his benevolent society.[57] At the heart of his conceptualization of "internal colonization" was the idea that the poor should be resettled on "empty land" where their labor would increase the value of the land while also generating a "moral" or spiritual awakening in the settler. In this, as Barbara Arneil aptly notes, the "benevolent liberal Protestantism" of the Dutch state twinned the goals of reforming the poor and exploiting the economic potential of "empty land" to justify the colonies.[58]

Based on this model, several private philanthropic interests negotiated with local municipal councils to relocate pauper families primarily to the underpopulated lands in northeastern Holland where they would engage in agricultural work in return for food and shelter. Throughout the 1820s and 1830s French penal reformers, too, began to explore the possibility of resocializing released prisoners via "internal colonization."[59] According to the historian Frances Gouda, the government of King Louis-Philippe commissioned a study of the *maatschappij* system in 1832, and during that same decade several French political figures, including Jean-Paul Alban de Villeneuve-Bargemont, an archconservative member of the Chamber of Deputies, embarked on what he described as a "philanthropic pilgrimage" to Holland. In recounting his visit he offered a rhapsodic homage to life and labor in the countryside:

> The sky above displayed a softness and beautiful serenity, and everywhere we followed magnificent roads. . . . On the left and on the right, we saw new and neatly constructed farmhouses, whose simplicity did not exclude an understated elegance. Each dwelling was graced with a vegetable garden dotted with flowers. . . . Behind the houses extended the five hectares of land allotted to each household: there, the healthy and varied cultivation of potatoes, wheat, rye, cabbage, beets and vigorous and large fruit trees attested to the efforts of an active and intelligent industriousness. . . . We spent the next day traversing the colonies once again and we contemplated and admired those places that offered a spectacle so dear to humanity.[60]

On his return from America and his investigation of its penitentiary system, Demetz set out on another trip, this time on behalf of the Société de patronage des enfants libérés de la Seine (of which he was a member), in search a carceral alternative for juvenile delinquents. Accompanied by Léon Faucher, he visited several institutions that housed juvenile delinquents in Belgium and

Holland. Both men were generally dissatisfied with the agricultural colonies they saw because they were situated in the "midst of barren wastes" where, as one of the inmates reportedly remarked to Demetz, "there is not a blade of grass that has not cost us a drop of our sweat." Believing the institutions were largely failures due to the "depressing influence of an almost fruitless labor," the men returned to France without a viable model in mind.[61]

After hearing glowing reports of the Rauhes Haus (Rough house) reform school in Prussia, Demetz decided to visit this small Protestant institution located in Horn, a few miles outside Hamburg. What he discovered was not a prison but a commune that housed youths in separate cottages under the care of a "father" responsible for their moral and religious upbringing. Demetz later recalled, "I had found what I was looking for! I resolved on that very day that the Rauhe Haus would be my model. My life, and my strength would be devoted to the salvation and correction of neglected and criminal youth."[62] The founder of Rauhes Haus, Johann Wichern, sought to reform the child by imposing what Demetz characterized as a "firm, but severe discipline, tempered with paternal kindness."[63] In his design of Rauhes Haus, Wichern had been influenced by the Swiss pedagogue Johan Heinrich Pestalozzi: "It is to the charitable efforts of Pestalozzi, that we owe the establishment of agricultural colonies. His efforts have led to the establishment of new educational institutions for rich and poor, of schools of practical agriculture, as well as of agricultural reformatories, and at the same time have regenerated methods of popular education generally."[64]

Demetz believed that prison alone was insufficient to meet the needs of children and youth who required a period of moral training and tutelage above and beyond time served. "Young detainees cannot be returned prematurely to the world which led to their earlier crime," argued the former magistrate, "for they will inevitably relapse into the disordered life of vagabondage they previously knew."[65] Incarceration offered little to no hope of reformation for children if they were simply returned to the mean streets from which they came. Demetz therefore positioned Mettray as an institutional complement to the prison that would allow for the "continued recovery" of the young detainee. Placement in the colony was to be viewed as a reward for good behavior and would constitute a transitional stage between imprisonment and a free civil life.[66] Yet, throughout most of its history sentenced juveniles were sent directly to Mettray rather than after having served time in a traditional jail or prison.

Demetz set out to create an institution that would, in his words, "replicate the internal order and the strict enforcement of rules that one sees in American penitentiaries, while also following the principle of paternal government and organization based upon the family that one finds in the institution of Horn."[67] The primary mechanism of moral reformation at Mettray would be the family, which Demetz considered a bulwark against the social and moral disorder of the city. He divided Mettray into "families" of forty inmates, each of which would inhabit a separate cottage with a guard-father (*chef de famille*) responsible for supervising their activities and overseeing their moral development. In this environment, destitute and delinquent boys would experience a semblance of family life whilst learning the habits of industry and obedience to authority necessary for their new futures as "sober farmers and robust soldiers."[68]

Demetz was always careful to link the moral and economic benefits to be derived from Mettray. To this end, children were referred to not as prisoners but as *colons*, which reflected his neo-Arcadian vision.[69] The discourse surrounding agricultural labor at Mettray was distinctly moral, and its presumed virtues were considered vital to the reformation of wayward youth. In this context, Demetz remarked: "Field labor affords healthful exercise to the body, while it sufficiently occupies the mind to banish the evil thoughts which idleness is sure to induce; it affords another advantage in making rest absolutely necessary to the peasant at the very hour that his brethren who dwell in towns are entering into those amusements and dissipations which tend to enervate and demoralize the partaker."[70]

These notions were based on a deep and abiding Rousseauian faith in the restorative power of agricultural labor and a vision of rural life as simple and virtuous. The physician Isidore Sarramea proclaimed that agriculture was "the natural occupation of man as it meets all of his needs and brings to mind a constant feeling of gratitude and love for Providence."[71] As Arneil has suggested, the "countryside was an exalted physical and conceptual space lying between the corruption of the city / civilization and untamed wild / state of nature."[72] This was not merely "countryside as escapism," however, for as Ceri Crossley has pointed out, "Agricultural work—with religion in support—was understood as a process of socialization."[73] In extolling the benefits of the agricultural regime at Mettray, Cochin asked rhetorically, "What influence is more moral than that of agriculture? The healthy body fatigued from a day of agricultural labor chases away bad thoughts as the body must regain its strength through rest at night while at the same time those who live in cities engage in debauchery and vice."[74] In this sense, as Francesca Ashurst and Couze Venn have argued, Mettray may have presaged one of the principle features of the current "alternative reformatory movement," namely, "the importance given to healing and the beneficial effects of nature. . . . The emphasis on a rural setting, working with animals, making things and cultivation are today advocated by people dealing with troubled or disadvantaged children as effective forms of rehabilitation and learning."[75]

Revealing a distinctly Enlightenment sensibility, Demetz believed that hard work as a means of socialization could effectively ameliorate society's ills. Labor offered the possibility of moral transcendence, which—as Foucault notes in *Madness and Civilization*—united institutions such as the penitentiary, almshouse, and asylum in their efforts to transform subjects "who could and would work upon their release, not so much because they were again useful to society, but because they had again subscribed to the great ethical pact of human existence."[76] The implementation of a system of disciplined labor at Mettray was therefore part of a much broader "universal pedagogy" intended to "create a mass of new workers" for the state.[77] However, whereas officials understood "manhood" as the willingness to work hard, some inmates viewed labor as evidence of acquiescence or "docility" in a world where they defined themselves as men by resisting the labor regime.

Demetz firmly believed that the agricultural colony addressed the persistent and profound problem of rural depopulation. So too did Lucas, who spoke for many of his contemporaries in lamenting the "cries of distress" emanating from the countryside, supposedly stripped of its labor force by the siren call of the city. According to Lucas, while vast tracts of land "stand dormant, thousands of unoccupied men crowd the city streets without hope of ever finding any work."[78] Faucher also proclaimed, "In France, it is the interior of the country that we must colonize."[79] The agricultural colony could deliver badly needed laborers to rural areas and at the same time claim the restoration of boys' health, skills, and self-worth through hard labor in the outdoors.

The result of this seemingly irrational distribution of labor, where there were too many "unoccupied bodies" in the cities and inadequate labor in the countryside, was the improper education of children. For youngsters who were fortunate enough to have procured employment in urban industry, the modern factory—which mixed young and old, men and women, honest and dishonest in a closed environment—was seen as little different from the standard jail. The economist and physician Louis-René Villermé asserted that simple physical proximity in the factory was sufficient to endanger the morality of all workers, especially children.[80]

As an effort in social engineering akin to the deportation and exile of adult convicts overseas, the agricultural colony had the potential to reorder France by repopulating its interior with the children of the urban poor. To this end, Demetz established an affiliate patronage society intended to "exercise a benevolent tutelage over former *colons* through their placement on the farms of cultivators who will oversee their work."[81] Thus, the resocialization process at Mettray extended beyond time served to include an apprenticeship of sorts in an underdeveloped agrarian area where the former *colon* would choose to remain rather than return to an uncertain fate amid the debauched and dissipated squalor of the city.

An indefatigable master of self-promotion, Demetz extolled the virtues of his establishment at every possible turn. Visitors to the colony were provided texts heralding the institution's virtues, along with etchings, lithographs, and favorable newspaper articles. Much of this material would later be reproduced verbatim, with some personal remarks tossed in regarding the wonders of the colony and the beneficence of its founder and director, in pamphlets and brochures penned by the visitors. According to Jacques Bourquin and Éric Pierre, the visit to Mettray very quickly became a "literary genre" unto itself as these small booklets were widely disseminated throughout France and other parts of Europe.[82] As Demetz was the source of information for these publications, they frequently contained claims that Mettray's rate of recidivism was far lower than that of state-run facilities. For instance, in 1855 the director maintained that the annual recidivism rate at Mettray was less than 14 percent, compared to 75 percent for state institutions.[83] In 1872 he pegged Mettray's recidivism rate at slightly above 4 percent and claimed, rather remarkably, that the figure for state institutions was still 75 percent, sixteen years later.[84]

Mettray's early fortunes were also bolstered by the Revolution of 1848, which catalyzed fears of armies of young vagrants and delinquents terrorizing the streets. Addressing the National Assembly, the deputy A. Corne invoked the danger the urban environment posed to the political order while speaking in support of a law that would establish the agricultural colony as the institutional basis of a new juvenile carceral system in France: "Industrial work, when given to prisoners, forces them towards cities and large industrial centers. There they are exposed to all the dangers of industrial life, frequent unemployment, and the dangerous lessons given in workshops. . . . Plagued by poverty and the contagion of vice . . . they form a corrupt milieu where culpable projects are hatched and where crimes against persons and property are plotted. It is also in times of distress that resentments and anti-social forces can surface which can imperil the very foundations of public order."[85] Corne juxtaposed the steady life of agriculture against the unknown vicissitudes of industrial labor and promoted the former as a solution to both crime and the threat of revolution. "What is the profession where they will find the best chance to remain honest, peaceful and industrious workers? It is agricultural labor where they can more surely attach themselves to the soil and be imbued with a sense of order and economy, familial habits, and the love of laboriously and legitimately acquired property."[86]

Yet, as Gordon Wright has noted, it was ultimately Mettray that inspired passage of the Law of 1850, which "was intended to be a kind of basic charter covering all aspects of the juvenile delinquency problem" and would remain France's fundamental legislation on the subject for nearly a century.[87] Like the Falloux Law, which preceded it by five months, the Law of 1850 granted to private institutions a major role in the "education" of French youth.[88] Specifically, it provided public support (a modest per diem of .75 to 1.25 francs per prisoner) to private colonies in return for the "moral, religious, and professional education" of all juveniles under their supervision.[89] Mettray's predominance in the nascent agricultural colony network was apparent in the level of funding it received—three-quarters of government subsidies for such institutions from 1840 until 1870.[90] Proponents of the Law of 1850 insisted that small, private initiatives would be much more successful than large, impersonal public institutions in accomplishing the moral regeneration of the young, which is ironic because Mettray quickly grew beyond the limits of its physical capacity and regularly held well over 700 *colons* until the advent of the Third Republic.

Most of the privately operated colonies established after passage of the 1850 law were run by religious congregations. Some, such as Bon Pasteur and the Sœurs des Prisons, were specifically for girls. Indeed, in keeping with the general notion of reinforcing family ties, Corne emphasized the urgency of creating colonies and refuges for young women. "Their morality," he reasoned, "is more important to society than that of men, for the preservation of good education and good morals is principally in the hands of mothers."[91] Thus the law reflected the renewed importance of religious influence in education and reinforced traditional gender roles as well.

Three categories of minors were incarcerated at Mettray and other agricultural colonies: those acquitted because they acted "without proper judgment" (*sans discernement*) in the commission of a crime (Article 66 of the Code pénal); those convicted of crimes and given prison sentences of six months to two years (Article 67 of the Code pénal); and those subject to "paternal correction," which allowed fathers to have their children imprisoned for a period of up to one month, renewable on request, if "grievously dissatisfied" with their behavior (see chapter 5 for more on paternal correction). A fourth category of inmate was added with the passage of a law in June 1904 that allowed state authorities to send "incorrigible" minors—those housed in orphanages or hospices that received aid from Assistance publique—to correctional institutions such as Mettray. In sum, the state confined to the same institutions persons acquitted of a crime, persons judged guilty of a crime and persons who had not been charged with a crime at all, In other words, the penal liability of children was broadened to include not just lawbreakers but also those who merely demonstrated behavioral problems.

Because a magistrate could order imprisonment up to the age of twenty, minors under sixteen could receive sentences longer than adult offenders who had committed the same crime. Proponents justified this by arguing that the development of moral character in youth necessitated the formation of habits, and because habits required long periods of time to take root, extended periods of confinement were necessary. It is important to note that the legal construction of criminality and personal responsibility in minors was conflicted in nineteenth-century France. While children had long enjoyed a certain legal dispensation from full penalties for criminal acts (a tradition stretching back to the Middle Ages), the French Revolution formalized this status and the Napoleonic Code gave it an enduring expression in French law, setting sixteen as the age of criminal responsibility and introducing the concept of discretion to reconcile notions of punishment with protection for minors. As Jean-Jacques Yvorel has noted, however, *discernement* was a rather fluid legal construct that seemed to vary from a notion of general awareness that the act was unlawful (premeditation was often determinative) to broader conceptions that over the course of the nineteenth century began to take into account the development of mental faculties and the educational level of the accused as an element of judgment.[92] On the one hand, there was the general belief that children should not be held wholly responsible for their crimes. On the other hand, there was a sense that regardless of culpability, children who committed certain crimes had to be punished for their misdeeds in order to check the development of criminal impulses before they became fully formed adults.

To address this conundrum, proponents of the Law of 1850 argued that a stay in the agricultural colony should be construed not as as punitive but as offering a "correctional education." Marking the fiftieth anniversary of Mettray's opening, Berlier de Vauplane, a former magistrate and a member of the colony's Conseil d'administration, spoke to the issue:

> Children, having acted without discernment, have a need, above all else, to be educated. . . . They are not pronounced guilty for the acts they have committed. . . . Society does not inflict upon them a punishment, but it has the right to provide them with what they lack: an intellectual and moral education that will prevent them from becoming criminals and make them honest men. Therefore they are directed to a house of correction so that they may be detained and raised for a number of years as determined by a judge. . . . This is the just vision as inspired in the Penal Code.[93]

Table 1.   Juvenile Delinquents in French Penal Institutions

YEAR	PUBLIC PENITENTIARY COLONIES	ALL PUBLIC INSTITUTIONS (INCLUDING COLONIES)	PRIVATE AGRICULTURAL COLONIES	TOTAL
1840		1860	260	2120
1845		2131	1036	3167
1850		2652	2628	5280
1855		3392	6426	9818
1860	1845	2296	6242	8538
1865	1034	1196	6610	7806
1870	1028	1262	5503	6765

Source: *Statistique des prisons, 1870* (Paris, 1873), xx–xxi. See also Gaillac, *Les maisons de correction*, appendices B and C.

Thus the Law of 1850 was based on the belief that most forms of deviant behavior in youth had common origins that could be corrected through the shared "educational" regimen of the agricultural colony.

Mettray offered a new alternative to judges who, like Demetz, had previously been forced to sentence children to adult prisons or simply return them to their parents. However, because it allowed the confinement of those convicted and acquitted of crimes to the same institutions, as well as longer sentences for young offenders, ultimately the Law of 1850 increased the number of minors in corrections. Table 1 details the distribution of juveniles in all French penitentiary institutions and the increase in their numbers after 1850.

Because the state did not open its own agricultural colony until 1860—a point which was stipulated in the Law of 1850—most male juvenile delinquents were held in private agricultural colonies. Between 1850 and 1870 the proportion held in private institutions rose from 50 to 81 percent.

With initial funding provided by the July Monarchy and a donation of land from Brétignières de Courteilles—a longtime associate of Demetz who codirected Mettray until his death in 1852—the colony's first five cottages and various subsidiary buildings (kitchen, infirmary, and staff quarters) were built in 1839 to 1840.[94] The following year another five cottages were added, along with a separate chapel, the punishment quarter that initially contained twenty cells, and some additional buildings for animal husbandry. In 1844, a separate home for the director and the administration building were completed. Thus, five years after Mettray's opening its basic physical plant was complete, and it remained largely unchanged for the better part of a century.

Demetz boasted that the site was one of the most beautiful in all of France: "The climate is healthy and temperate and the soil fecund, which is an indispensable condition for a colony whose children may not yet have sufficient strength for difficult harvesting."[95] This was a critical point for Demetz, who remembered his visits to the Dutch and Belgian colonies where cultivation had been so difficult. As Dupont-Bouchat and Pierre have noted, most of the land provided by Brétignières de Courteilles—and adjacent plots leased from local landowners—was already arable without any preparatory work necessary by the *colons* other than the occasional removal of rocks from the soil.[96] Compared to Lucas's colony of Val d'Yèvre, where swamps had to be drained by the inmates, at Mettray construction and cultivation was far more efficient.

Since Mettray was envisioned as a site of moral influence rather than physical restraint, its architecture was a radical departure from traditional congregate jails or cellular-based facilities such as Petite Roquette. Because there were no bars, gates, or high walls, a young prisoner arriving at the colony's central square for the first time might have believed he was in a small village rather than a prison compound. The American educator Henry Barnard remarked: "The whole colony is not enclosed by brick walls of high palisades, but by low green hedges, over which any person could climb, and through which a boy, so disposed, could easily creep without drawing attention."[97] According to the utopian socialist François Cantagrel, who wrote many pamphlets on public works, architecture, and education, including one on Mettray, the open design of the colony was intended to inculcate restraint: "One must give to young prisoners, if not their freedom, at least the appearance of freedom. For how can they be properly prepared for social life, for their social freedom as men, if their entire education is contained within the four walls of a prison?"[98] As Davis and others have noted, Demetz effectively played on the notion of Mettray as a prison "without walls," and the phrase *sans grilles ni murailles* appeared in numerous publications, on postcards, and in iconographic works that promoted the colony's "harmonious continuity with nature."[99]

Facing new arrivals at the far end of the courtyard stood the neo-Gothic chapel, the most physically imposing structure in the colony, which had a seating capacity of 500. In her book on the horticulturist and landscape architect Jean-Pierre Barillet-Deschamps, who worked in this capacity at Mettray before eventually becoming the chief gardener of Paris under Napoléon III, Luisa Limido notes that the central position of the chapel was intended to "remind everyone, *colons* and *chefs de famille* alike," that religion was a key component of everyday life at Mettray, and one of the "principle means of moral regeneration."[100] The high bell tower, which could be seen by everyone in the colony proper, also held a guard stationed to surveille the *colons*. Mettray's disciplinary quarter was located beneath and behind the chapel. Its cells were positioned in such a way that boys being punished there for misdeeds could view Sunday Mass whilst remaining hidden from the general congregation. The words "Dieu vous voit" (God sees you) were written on the entrance gate of the cellblock to remind inmates that they were always being watched, whether by God or by guards via the panoptic features of the institution. The same inscription appeared on the walls inside each cell, along with a crucifix and the following aphorism: "God is good to those who place their faith in him. God does not seek the death of the sinner, but his submission. There is still time to do good. Prayer is the answer to all our miseries."[101] Responding to criticism from the Conseil général de la Seine, whose representatives made an unannounced and unexpected visit to Mettray in 1884, administrators insisted that this text was not an attempt at religious indoctrination; instead, it was meant to help "ward off thoughts of suicide" in inmates held in isolation.[102]

The overall layout of the colony, consisting of the central chapel flanked by two lateral wings of buildings, bore some similarities to Charles Fourier's *phalanstère*, which was designed to serve as the architectural edifice of the utopian socialist colonies he envisioned.[103] Although Demetz never referenced Fourierism in his voluminous writings—certainly the movement's positions on subjects ranging from organized religion to the family and sexuality would have been anathema to him—the architectural likeness between the two colonies was not entirely coincidental. As the geographer Colin Ripley has pointed out, Blouet's plan for Mettray owed much to the "utopian projects of the social reformers of its time, such as Fourier in France and Robert Owen in England."[104] Whereas Fourier emphasized a self-sufficient agrarian community, Owen stressed the importance of education in the moral lives of children. Mettray seemed to be a blend of the two approaches, although the education provided in the colony was of a utilitarian and practical nature.

Pamela Pilbeam has noted that the Fourierists were quite supportive of the agricultural colonies and went out of their way to show their approval as part of an effort to win "over the ruling elite" (i.e., the Orleanist establishment), many of whom, including Beaumont, Tocqueville, Lamartine, Gasparin, and even the uncompromising law-and-order prison inspector Moreau-Christophe, were founding members of the Société paternelle at Mettray.[105] The board was a veritable who's who of the French ruling class that included four interior ministers, three prime ministers, two agricultural ministers, and two justice ministers.[106] Cantagrel "reported eulogistically" on the institution, which is evident not only in his pamphlet on Mettray but also in his later writings after he succeeded Victor Considérant as editor of the Fourierist journal *La Démocratie*

Pacifique.[107] Cantagrel lauded Mettray for offering an institutional substitute for the family: "So we see an establishment that RAISES [original emphasis] these poor children by replacing their families, as much as it is possible, and providing the care and education which they have been deprived. . . . This is not only a humane institution, a work of philanthropy, it is, above all else, an effort to address the poor organization of our houses of correction. Its purpose, in the words of M. Demetz, 'fills one of the most fatal flaws in our institutions.'"[108]

Designed to convey a sense of order and community, the colony was oriented around a central square. On each side of the square were two rows of identical three-story brick cottages situated 10 meters apart. Each cottage was 12 meters long by 6.66 meters wide (39 by 21 feet).[109] Envisioned as highly circumscribed and tightly monitored spaces, the cottages had a certain panoptic quality. The lower floor of each cottage was set aside as a workshop area where *colons* did handicraft tasks in the early morning. At the start of each day, the space was divided into four separate sections by cloth partitions that rose halfway to the ceiling. Seated on a high stool above the partitions, a functionary could oversee all four areas of work at once while remaining hidden from those who labored below.[110] The second and third floors of each cottage served as refectory and dormitory spaces. For meals, the upper floors converted into a dining facility by means of two large, wooden planks that were hinged at the walls at either end of the room. When lowered, these planks created two parallel surfaces where children ate, with a space between for supervisors to pass through and monitor their subjects. Affixed to heavy wooden ceiling beams were hooks from which prisoners hung hammocks arranged so that the head of one child lay at the feet of the next to inhibit whispering or illicit sexual activity.

At the end of the room was a small alcove where the *chef de famille* slept. Covered in the front by venetian blinds, this space allowed some degree of privacy but also, more importantly, provided a vantage point from which the *chef* could see his charges without being seen. Instilling moral health necessitated an institutional order premised on the perpetual visibility of the *colon*. As in Bentham's Panopticon, the continual exposure was meant to make the observed check his own disorderly impulses while at the same time reassuring the observers.

Initially consisting of nine boys culled from the *maison centrale* at Fontrevault in Anjou, Mettray's population grew quickly during its first decade of operation, to more than 500 inmates by 1851.[111] As Pierre has noted, while the first group of youths was handpicked by Demetz as the most deserving and amenable to reform, the "conception of the colony as an intermediate

COLONIE DE METTRAY. — Un Dortoir.

FIGURE 1. Un dortoir.

stage of incarceration before a return to freedom, disappeared quickly . . . as
Mettray was no longer reserved for the best elements."[112] By 1870 its population had reached 740, well beyond the limits of Mettray's physical capacity. Yet,
Demetz remained largely unconcerned and—perhaps driven by financial
considerations—simply placed larger numbers of *colons* on outlying farms so
far removed from Mettray that they came to the colony only for Sunday
Mass.[113] With the additional *colons* came additional state funds, which, according to Dupont-Bouchat and Pierre, reduced overhead costs.[114] Mettray's population remained well above 700 until the mid-1880s when it began to slowly
decline.

Mettray was founded during a period that invited experimentation in corrections, as evidenced by the allure of carceral innovations abroad. With the
advent of the Second Empire, however, the focus of justice policy shifted to
emphasize reinforcing mechanisms of repression. Departing from the more
liberal tendencies of the July Monarchy, Louis Napoléon conceived of punishment as a retributive and intimidating force and relegated rehabilitative corrections to a secondary position. The poverty of ideas about corrections
during the Second Empire is hardly surprising. Whereas the July Monarchy
had been supported by relatively liberal social thinkers such as Blanqui, Lucas, and Guizot, the Bonapartist regime was dominated by bankers, industri-
alists, lawyers, and the military. Public policy and discourse on the prison

"question," previously the preserve of philosophers and social theorists, had become the domain of technocrats in the service of an increasingly reactionary government.[115]

Rather than improving conditions inside prisons and adapting punishments to facilitate rehabilitation, Louis Napoléon shored up the police forces and manipulated the penal codes to assure more prompt, certain, and harsh punishments. More importantly, he utilized the police not only against criminals but also against political enemies and "potential" threats to the social and political order. At the commencement of his reign, he declared: "The number of crimes committed each year proves the indispensability of improving our repressive legislation. We must assure order much more effectively than it has been previously. Above all else, I want to restore SECURITY [original emphasis] in France."[116] To this end, the prince-president centralized and bureaucratized the command structure of the police by placing municipal agents and the gendarmes under the control of the ministry of the interior and the prefects, rather than local mayors.[117] His most important "innovation," however, was the expansion and modernization of urban police forces in cities such as Paris and Lyon, which served as paradigms for the rest of the nation. Indeed, in 1854 Louis Napoléon more than tripled the size of the Parisian police force, quadrupled its budget, and started a training program for its agents.[118] The goal was to forestall political unrest and lessen the reliance on the prison as a form of social control by making the police presence ubiquitous in urban areas, leaving no street corner unseen by the gaze of authority.

Although it had been inspired by the apparent success of Rauhes Haus, Mettray was not a facsimile of the German colony but instead a complex institutional hybrid that combined elements of the U.S. Pennsylvania and Auburn systems while also adhering to the broader sociodemographic objectives of what Arneil has termed "domestic colonies." Moreover, although it was a private institution, Mettray received state funds. The public/private nature of the agricultural colony afforded it a degree of autonomy from state oversight that (at least in its early days) facilitated its rather rapid expansion. It is important to note, however, that Demetz initially envisioned Mettray as a supplement to the prison, not a prison replacement or alternative. While it did not, in fact, serve that role in the carceral network, its development remained faithful to his vision of extending the relationship of discipline not only to the youthful offender but also to the offender's family.

Anxieties over the presumed weakness and ineffectiveness of parental authority among the urban poor and working class helped pave the way for Mettray and the agricultural colony at mid-century. The laboring classes were unable to produce a disciplined workforce, and the poor sections of major cities were a dangerous and morally debased terrain. Whether through parental neglect or nefariousness, the blank slate of childhood innocence was too often inscribed with a penchant for vice and criminality. Proponents of the agricultural colony maintained that it was necessary to remove the children of the poor from the control of their parents, isolate them from the debauched culture of the streets, and reshape their physical, mental, and moral characters. By doing this, they effectively naturalized youth, reducing them to "material" to be reshaped as yeoman farmers and robust soldiers.

The theme that ran through Mettray's promotional materials was the transformation from indiscipline and disobedience to regularity and compliance. Discipline and dutifulness were the marks of successful reformation that was attributed to the institution's strict regime and the moral benefits of life and labor in the countryside. Yet, the carceral practice that made this possible also highlighted a conundrum in French law, as those acquitted of having committed a crime by having acted *sans discernment* were subject to the same sentence as those found guilty of crimes, which implied that the institutional practices of the agricultural colony were appropriate for both groups. Although Demetz maintained that Mettray's primary mission was "educational" rather than punitive, the institutional experience was also coercive and carceral, despite rhetoric that insisted that a sentence to the colony should be construed as a "reward" because it offered liberation from punishment.

The vagaries and contradictions of French law regarding juvenile offenders would not be addressed until the establishment of a juvenile justice system in 1912, and in the meantime, Mettray and the agricultural colony system flourished. Indeed, after the passage of the Law of 1850 the exercise of disciplinary authority via the agricultural colony was seemingly assured, as was Mettray's preeminent position in the colony network, even after the death of its founder in 1873. Demetz's successors had no way of knowing that the institution had, for all practical purposes, reached its zenith, and that profound changes in the French political landscape would forever alter Mettray's course.

CHAPTER 2

Regime

As Edmund White noted in his biography of Jean Genet, the Mettray family envisioned by Demetz "was of just one sex as the only women present in the colony were the nuns who ran the infirmary."[1] While the director acknowledged that Mettray's families were "fictive," he nevertheless insisted that they could provide "all the care and tenderness of a real family" and act as a "substitute for those parents who have forsaken their children."[2] That is, Mettray's "imaginary" or artificial family would be better than the "antisocial" (i.e., biological) family at instilling values in the delinquent. The organizational structure of the institution was thus based on a patriarchal conception of the family in which "fatherly" *chefs de famille* reigned supreme, as inmates were supposed to emulate those who governed the institution. Ultimately, it was Demetz and his successors as director who dominated this "familial" picture, standing in for parents who were considered at least ineffectual if not harmful to the morality of their children.

Also implicit in the structure of reform priorities at Mettray was a set of martial values and practices that Demetz believed were core components of a masculine identity. He was of the generation of bourgeois youth who had come of age in an era when the "warrior-Frenchman" as embodied by Napoléon Bonaparte represented the pinnacle of French manhood. Through an elaborate system of symbolic and material rewards, Napoléon appropriated and distributed aristocratic forms of honor among his men, establishing not only a military meritocracy but also a new model of manhood that some historians have termed "martial masculinity."[3] According to Michael J. Hughes, in promoting a masculine ideal in the French army the Napoleonic regime "transferred the military skills ascribed to the aristocracy to the entire population of France. It identified a set of warlike attributes as the defining characteristics of the French man. They included military skills, bravery, audacity, honor, a love of glory, patriotism, toughness, and an innate desire for war and combat."[4] Whereas glory, according to Hughes, might be defined as the "prestige, fame or renown that accompanied extraordinary actions or achievements," particularly, but not exclusively, on the field of battle, honor could be demonstrated through more mundane means in the civil sphere "such as honest conduct, loyal service to one's superiors and professional competence."[5]

Demetz extolled and attempted to instill many of these same qualities in his young subjects through the deployment of a variety of coercive disciplinary technologies at Mettray. According to the journalist Charles Sauvestre, Mettray's "regime of honor" was a "kind of alliance between vanity and conscience," and in making this connection, Demetz demonstrated "a remarkable knowledge of human nature, and of French nature in particular."[6] The British penal reformer Florence Davenport Hill, who visited Mettray in the 1860s along with her father, the jurist and early penologist Matthew Davenport Hill, wrote that the veneration of honor constituted Mettray's basic ethos: "An appeal to the sentiment of honor is made under many differing forms, which, excepting that of religious duty, takes precedence over all others at Mettray. . . . A strong feeling of personal honor, that is to say, freedom from personal reproach is, indeed, inculcated; but owing to the esprit de corps which is sedulously fostered, first the honor of his family, and ultimately that of the whole colony, of which he is but a minute fraction, is hardly less dear to the Mettray lad than his own."[7] In a laudatory account of his visit to Mettray, the attorney Paul Huot maintained that prisoners learned quickly that their presence in the colony should be considered a privilege and a "mark of confidence, which they are on honor not to abuse." When Huot asked a *colon* why he did not attempt to escape, the young man reportedly replied, "As there are no walls here, nothing would be easier, and I have often wished to try; but thinking of the confidence our director puts in us, it would be an act of dishonor and *lâcheté* [cowardice] to do so."[8] Demetz also referred to this notion of honor when speaking of escape: "We have told our children that they are living as though they were prisoners on parole, and that if they commit an act of cowardice by crossing the boundaries of the colony they will have abused the confidence we have placed in them. One always listens and understands that in France, no matter whom it is that we address, when we speak to them, we speak in the name of honor."[9]

Like Napoléon, Demetz militarized masculinity in elaborate ceremonies and symbolic activities to reward honorable behavior. For instance, all inmates who completed three months of incarceration without incurring any disciplinary infractions had their names inscribed on the *tableau d'honneur*, which was prominently displayed in the colony's classroom. According to Hill, the "desire to stand well in the eyes of their world," made inscription an "object of high ambition for *colons*."[10] If the *colon* later commited an infraction, his name was removed from the tableau and it would be reinscribed only after he had completed another three months of service without committing a new violation. If a *colon* manifested exemplary behavior for six months and his labor was deemed exceptional, he was given a gift, such as a billfold, and publicly saluted for his efforts at weekend assembly. After a year of "exemplary conduct" he was awarded a white stripe on the sleeve of his uniform; a second year merited a blue stripe, and at the end of a third year the prisoner was given a red stripe, constituting the tricolor, which was seen a "badge of honor."[11] This was considered an important incentive to encourage good behavior in the *colon* and a visible sign of prestige.

Just as Napoléon devoted hours to reviewing his soldiers, so did Mettray's director, who scrutinized every detail and aspect of military drill and formation. The military was the ideological touchstone for the construction of masculinity at Mettray as the *colons* were immersed in an institutional culture designed to instill loyalty, devotion, and above all else, discipline. As Foucault aptly notes (albeit not in reference to Mettray): "Discipline had its own type of ceremony. It was not the triumph but the review, the 'parade,' an ostentatious form of the examination. In it the subjects were presented as 'objects' to the observer of a power that was manifested only by its gaze."[12] After Sunday worship the entire colony assembled in the central square where each *chef du famille* delivered an overview of the week's activities, always directing their remarks to Demetz, "awarding praise or blame, rewards or punishments, as may be deserved, to each *colon* individually mentioned."[13] Huot recalled one such allocution: "I have been content with my family this week; the order, the application of work has been good and there have been few punishments; Colon D has distinguished himself by his diligence and good conduct."[14] Young men who had received demerits for laziness or committed other infractions during the week, however, were publicly shamed. At the assembly Huot witnessed, Demetz ordered a youth to stand and approach the podium. "The colon, around the age of twelve, slowly walked toward the director, giving a military salute with his hand and removing his beret. 'I am not happy with

VII. Colonie de METTRAY
Remise de la médaille de 1870

FIGURE 2.   Remise de la médaille de 1870.

you, Colon G. You made a promise to correct yourself of the bad habits which
have the effect of generating laziness in others. You have not kept your promise. Your unwillingness to work is a sickness which must be cured. Pass to my
left whereupon you will be led to your cell.'"[15]

The family whose behavior was the most exemplary during the week was
awarded a special banner to display during parade drill. Unsurprisingly, the flag
echoed the tricolor, and it bore an inscription that read: "Colony of Mettray:
Honor to the Family." Because the flag represented the honor and reputation
of the entire colony as well as its director, the family awarded this distinction marched at the head of the procession. Indeed, it was Demetz (and his
successors) who conferred the banner and to whom a family had to return it
should they fail to uphold the standard. According to Huot, the award of the
flag never failed "to produce a profound sensation. . . . The lad whom I saw
advance to the platform was pale with emotion and the joy of his brethren . . .
was conveyed by an expression of profound serenity and calm happiness."[16]
Families who distinguished themselves by their regular conduct were also publicly recognized and rewarded with inspirational prints, "representing some
trait of courage, or some religious subject; sometimes it is one of those battles
which have conferred such honor on our army; and sometimes a naval engagement, as we have several boys destined for marine service. . . . The admirable
examples in these pictures compose the ornaments of assembly rooms and
serve as a popular museum of grandeur, honor and sanctity."[17]

If individual members of the family were removed from the table of honor, the flag would be bestowed on a more deserving family. Demetz claimed that before the ceremonial awarding of the flag was established in the colony in 1850, "the proportion of children on the honor roll was 66 percent; it now, in 1855, is at 75 percent."[18] When a member of a family was transferred out of the colony because of his recalcitrant behavior, the "utmost solemnity" was observed in a ceremony where the director recounted the prisoner's misdeeds and the shame he had brought to his fellow *colons* and then the prisoner was led away, clothed in the garb of a traditional prisoner rather than a *colon*, never to return to Mettray. In some cases transfers indicated a downward spiral in the behavior of a *colon*. Indeed, many troublesome youths were repeatedly transferred from one colony to another, which shifted the responsibility for their management to other institutions, particularly the correctional colonies operated by the state such as Eysses, which took in the most difficult youths.

Although officials were always careful to describe Mettray's military regimen as only one aspect of the reform program, it was the dominant principle of the colony. At the head of Mettray's family unit stood its patriarch, the *chef de famille*, who lived with his "children" and attended to their needs "as a true father would his son."[19] A. Giraud, the colony's first accountant, penned a treatise that outlined the duties of the *colon* at Mettray. He characterized the *chef de famille* as having two distinct roles in the colony:

> First, he is a chief, a captain charged with observing the rules of discipline. Secondly, he is a tender father and a true friend; this is how the colon must consider him. Similarly, the head of the family sees the colon as a soldier who must obey without murmuring and execute quickly the order which he is given; but out of the ranks, the colon is his beloved child, over whose welfare he watches day and night; he carries in his heart a paternal tenderness which is an indefinable feeling which he must extend to each child in his care. . . . We see with happiness that the colon always greets the chef de famille with the sacred name of "father." Why would he say "yes, father" instead of "yes, sir"? The former is a truer name, more in harmony with the respective positions of chef and colon and cements the intimate union which ought to exist between the father and the son.[20]

The *chef's* primary responsibilities were policing the interior of the cottage and surveilling and supervising his so-called children. He was aided in this task by his *sous-chef* and also an "elder brother" (*frère-aîné*), who kept tabs on his fellow prisoners in return for extra provisions of food, a small stipend, and the "privilege of wearing a badge upon his arm which denotes the authority invested in him."[21] Originally the *frère-aîné* was chosen by his comrades via secret ballot, but this changed in 1845 to a process in which the *chef* recommended *colons* with records of good behavior to the director, who approved their appointment for a three-month term, renewable on request.

Placing an inmate in this position was an ingenious mechanism for maintaining discipline in the cottage because he, with the *chef* and *sous-chef*, closely observed the behavior and comportment of each inmate and noted any disciplinary infraction in a family logbook. Thus surveillance itself was a category of labor for a select group of *colons*. It was a powerful position in the colony's hierarchy as punishments were often meted out based on unfavorable notations made by a *frère-aîné*. Driven by the rewards and status afforded by the position, the *frère-aîné* participated in the surveillance of his comrades by infiltrating private domains that otherwise might have remained outside the view of the administration. Demetz once boasted: "Through them [*frères-aîné*], we know everything that occurs in play time, and indeed at all hours of the day, the Elder Brothers being on the same level with their companions; moreover, we acquire this knowledge without recourse to that system of espionage which degrades alike those who execute and those who employ it."[22] In the "elder brother" we see a demonstration of what Scott noted with regard to power relations in the prison: "Among the inmates . . . who are all subject to a common domination from the institution and its officers, there frequently develops a tyranny as brutal and exploitive as anything the guards can devise. In this domination within domination, the subordinate prisoner must measure his words and conduct perhaps more carefully before dominant prisoners than he does before prison officials."[23] In many ways, surveillance at Mettray resembled the "hierarchical observation" long considered a crucial element of all modern disciplinary institutions. Foucault alludes to the development of a position similar to the *frère-aîné* in French parish schools in the seventeenth century: "Batencour selected from among the best pupils a whole series of 'officers'—intendants, observers, monitors, tutors. . . . The roles thus defined were of two kinds: the first involved the material tasks (distribution of ink and paper, giving alms to the poor) . . . the second involved surveillance: the observers must record who left his bench, who was talking, who did not have his rosary."[24] The fact that the "elder brothers" were themselves under surveillance by the *sous-chefs*, who were under the watchful eye of the *chefs de famille*, supports, at least in theory, the panopticism of the modern prison system that Foucault described. Demetz extolled the virtues of having three levels of oversight and supervision at Mettray, which "made surveillance easier, more active and more dedicated."[25]

Yet, firsthand accounts of surveillance practices at Mettray suggest an ill-disciplined cadre of elder brothers. Although boys who served as *frère-aîné* were expressly forbidden from inflicting punishments on their comrades, over the years many abused their authority. Genet characterized the *frère-aîné* as a "bully" chosen by the authorities from among the oldest and most physically imposing members of a family.[26] According to Jean-Guy Le Dano, who was incarcerated at Mettray in the early 1920s,

> The big brothers, just like their spiritual fathers . . . had all the rights, which they used and abused. In the refectory, as elsewhere, silence was de rigueur. If your spoon made noise? The guilty must stand at attention without eating until the *frère-aîné* allowed you to sit. Sometimes, depending on how cruel he felt that day, he would not permit it; then, the soup would remain in the bowl until everyone else had left the dining hall. In the dormitory the gaffe [guard], indifferent, reading a novel, lay on his bed in a small room with a window which looked out onto the entire floor. As frequently happened, a troublemaker had to be corrected, so the gaffe would send forth the *frère-aîné*. This led to beatings. The big brother usually came out victorious, because if he held this position it was because of his size, strength, and especially his rotten mentality. If he happened to fall onto his back, his demise was immediate. He would then be succeeded in office by his conqueror, with the approval and blessing of the gaffes.[27]

The position of the elder brother also existed in other agricultural colonies (often under different monikers), and its problems were not unique to Mettray. In the industrial colony of Aniane in the Languedoc-Roussillon region of southern France, an incoming director noted in a report to the local prefect that he "realized almost immediately that oversight was largely carried out by the ranking pupils [equivalent to Mettray's *frères-aîné*], while officers and their chief supervisor seemed disinterested in what was happening right before their eyes and who seemed to possess a natural laissez-faire sensibility that was obviously not new to them. In the refectory, in the dormitories, all interventions are handled by the ranking pupils, which is entirely unacceptable."[28] The director thus ordered that "ranking pupils provide a purely moral authority, only while under the authority of surveillants, and only when it pertains to general movements throughout the colony and during military exercises."[29] Unlike at Mettray, where the position was formally abolished in 1911 due to such abuses, at Aniane it continued until the colony closed.

The dominant characteristic of colony's regime was its military order. According to an Irish visitor, among Mettray's most "remarkable features are the military principles by which it operates. . . . Military discipline, military honor and military practices are appealed to at every turn."[30] Every *colon* was required to salute all staff members, and all activities in the colony were announced by the sound of a bell. Sound also was used to mark time, structuring daily activities and coordinating and standardizing movements in the colony. When entering their cottage, *colons* had to line up and proceed in single file, without shoving or loitering. In the classroom (i.e., the refectory space in each cottage) pupils had to stand at attention and salute the instructor before they could sit. They had to sit upright and were forbidden to lean forward on the desks, to put up their legs, to turn their heads, or to stretch or yawn. At mealtimes all *colons* were to stand at attention until the *chef* entered and gave the command for one of the young men to say grace. In short, the cottage was a space of drill and indoctrination where every procedure was routinized and scrutinized.

It was expected that over the course of his sentence at Mettray the *colon* would come to see himself as a soldier who must submit to authority. Just as every soldier must obey his superior, every *colon* must "obey his *frère-aîné*; the *frère-aîné* must, in turn, obey the *sous chef de famille*; the *sous chef de famille* must, in turn, obey the *chef de famille*; the *chef de famille* must, in turn, obey the inspector; the inspector must, in turn, obey the director; and the director must, in turn, obey his conscience." Any failure on the part of the *colon* to understand the "legal duties of the *military order* [emphasis mine] of which he is now a member" was met with "severe discipline."[31] Giraud argued: "Without discipline, no army, no association of men is possible. With a well observed discipline, an army is covered in glory and honor. . . . These are the echelons of legal power in the military order; each *colon* must understand it perfectly. If we pass to the civil order, we shall find man equally subject to law and obedient to his immediate chief. The cultivator, the workman, the merchant, the bourgeois, the rentier, the proprietor, and every citizen obeys the mayor, and so on."[32] This was not the egalitarian philosophy of Rousseau or the French Revolution but a vision of a deeply hierarchical society demarcated by class.

Given its military organization, routine was a central component of life at Mettray. Each day began in the same fashion with reveille at 5:00 a.m., when all *colons* were to awaken, fold and stow their hammocks, and change into their uniforms in silence. Indeed, outside of designated times for recreation, a regimen of silence was observed, including during meals and hours of labor (as in the Auburn prison system). Following roll call (the first of eight to ten prisoner counts per day), the *colons* descended to the first floor of the cottage, where they had fifteen minutes to use the nearby toilets, which were periodically emptied by a specially designated squad of five or six boys. Genet described the scene:

The shithouse was in the yard, behind each family dormitory. At Noon and at 6:00 p.m., on the way back from the shops, we would march in line, led by the elder brother, and stop in front of four urinals. We would leave the line by fours to take a leak or pretend to. At the left were the latrines, which were four or five steps high so that the crap can was on a level with the ground. Each boy stepped from the line and went to one or the other, depending on the need he felt. He would let his belt hang from the door to show that the place was occupied.[33]

Raoul Léger, a former inmate, recalled that the walls of the shared toilets were always covered with excrement.[34] According to Genet, as late as the 1920s, there was roughly one toilet for every ten prisoners, and toilet paper was always in short supply.[35] Poorly maintained latrines and a general lack of sanitation was also a problem in other colonies. An inspection report on Val d'Yèvre from 1899 noted: "Hygiene and cleanliness leave much to be desired. . . . The latrines are badly kept. When disinfectants are used they are strewn about haphazardly, which contributes to what is already a nauseating odor. . . . The fecal waste in the latrines is so considerable that one cannot avoid contact and contamination."[36] Exacerbating the insalubriousness at Val d'Yèvre was a shortage of soap, which was rarely distributed in "sufficient quantities." According to an inspection report from 1892, "It is necessary for children to guard their meager ration of soap, or to ask for soap as a favor from other pupils, or to procure additional soap through other means."[37] As soap was a highly desired commodity, the unspoken suggestion was that it was often bartered for illicit goods or sexual favors.

The standard day at Mettray was sixteen hours, including eight hours of manual labor, ninety minutes of school, and two hours and forty-five minutes for meals and recreation. During "recreation" boys were allowed to speak and play but were strictly forbidden from swearing, arguing, or injuring each other in games or horseplay.[38] As Giraud noted, during recreation *colons* were "forbidden to speak rude words, to swear, to quarrel, to insult, to strike or to call themselves by anything other than by their own names, for nicknames always wound those who are the object; they provoke irritating responses; they engender quarrels and disputes; they excite hatred and violence; they are at last a fruitful source of punishments."[39] After dinner and evening prayer, lights out at 9:00 p.m. marked the end of a grueling day during which prisoners were under the supervision of staff who ensured that a precise, military decorum was always maintained and that not a single moment was given over to idleness, which was seen as a dangerous source of misbehavior. "It is by working," according to Giraud, "that the *colon* will avoid punishment, while doubling his moral and physical strength. When the mind, the heart and body are thus occupied, time passes quickly, without boredom, without fear, and one becomes a man without realizing it."[40] This evokes Rousseau's maxim on the dangers of idleness for youth: "Idleness, a soft and sedentary life . . . these are perilous paths for a young man, and they lead him constantly into danger."[41]

As Foucault has noted, power in modern society is, above all, power over time. This was certainly evident in the daily regimen at Mettray, which was characterized by an elaborate schedule of disciplines, regimentations, and orderings. "Power," wrote Foucault, "is articulated directly onto time; it assures its control and guarantees its use."[42]

Mettray's founding statutes specified that "the employment of time and division of the day are regulated so as to introduce the necessary variety in the exercises, to occupy the time of the inmates, and to prevent their escape from observation."[43] Yet, the rigid daily routine approximated industrial time rather than the more fluid rhythms of agrarian life, though during the busy harvest season work hours were often extended at the expense of schooling.[44] While this practice was not the subject of criticism at Mettray, an inspection general report of Val d'Yèvre in 1891 noted that "school is fully suspended at the time of haymaking and harvesting. The measure is too absolute, and it seems that at least a class could be held for younger pupils, those whose labor is almost nil in these tasks and most of whom are illiterate." The director henceforth ordered that schooling be continued "for the illiterate" at harvest time while noting that this would pose a "grave inconvenience."[45] In sum, there were five officially approved activities: working, sleeping, eating, prayer, and school. At Mettray labor was the primary focus of an inmate's life, though the work was monotonous and provided little opportunity for creativity or innovation. Because prisoners spent nearly two-thirds of their day at work, either in the fields or in the workshops, these were the sites where they were most likely to clash with officials.

Drill commands, postures, salutes, and other elements of military culture were an essential part of Mettray's social fabric. Military discipline was effectively welded onto the body of the *colon* through constant repetition and punctilious exercise. According to Foucault, "By the late eighteenth century the soldier had become something that could be made; out of formless clay, an inapt body, the machine required could be constructed; posture gradually corrected; a calculated constraint runs slowly through each part of the body, mastering, making it pliable, ready at all times, turning silently into the automatism of habit; in short, one has 'got rid of the peasant' and given him 'the air of a soldier.'"[46] Standing in formation in the central courtyard, awaiting

Table 2.   Working Days, Summer

ACTIVITIES	FROM	TO	TIME
Rise, stow hammocks	5:00 a.m.	5:15 a.m.	15 minutes
Wash and toilet	5:15 a.m.	5:30 a.m.	15 minutes
Distribution of work; handicraft labor (in cottages)	5:30 a.m.	7:30 a.m.	2 hours
Breakfast and recreation	7:30 a.m.	8:30 a.m.	1 hour
Distribution of work; field labor or atelier	8:30 a.m.	12:30 p.m.	4 hours
Lunch and recreation	12:30 p.m.	1:30 p.m.	1 hour
School	1:30 p.m.	3:00 p.m.	1 hour, 30 minutes
Distribution of work; field labor or atelier	3:00 p.m.	7:00 p.m.	4 hours
Band practice or general cleanup	7:00 p.m.	8:00 p.m.	1 hour
Dinner	8:00 p.m.	8:45 p.m.	45 minutes
Prayer and evening hymns	8:45 p.m.	9:00 p.m.	15 minutes
Bed	9:00 p.m.	5:00 a.m.	8 hours

their labor assignments during the week or before chapel on Sundays, the *colon* was expected to remain completely still "with eyes fixed only on those who command him." Talking in formation was not permitted, nor was making eye contact with another inmate, walking too fast, walking too slow, or stepping out of formation. To promote regularity and uniformity in movement, boys were always marched in straight columns led by the *chef de famille* or the *chef d'atelier*. With heads held high while maintaining a "brisk, uniform pace," the *colons* marched and behaved as instructed, as though they were members of an "elite military squadron" rather than "a herd of lost sheep. When they leave work for lunch, the return must be made in the same order as at the start, in two rows, at the same pace, and in silence."[47] In the eyes of the administrators, the proper movement of inmates through the colony's matrix demanded the fusion of individuals into a single body, an entity that had as its sole purpose controlled movement through space. Once they arrived at their place of work they remained standing at attention until they were ordered to begin, which they were required to do without "offering a single observation or uttering the slightest murmur of protest."[48] Rules demanded strict obedience and skillful and diligent performance at work; complaining was strictly prohibited. Again, here are the outlines of what Foucault refers to as the military dream of a perfect society: "Its fundamental reference was not to the state of nature, but to the meticulously subordinated cogs of a machine, not to the primal social contract, but to permanent coercion, not to fundamental rights, but to indefinitely progressive forms of training, not the general will but to automatic docility."[49]

Table 3.   Working Days, Winter

ACTIVITIES	FROM	TO	TIME
Rise, stow hammocks	6:00 a.m.	6:15 a.m.	15 minutes
Wash and toilet	6:15 a.m.	6:30 a.m.	15 minutes
Distribution of work; handicraft labor (in cottages)	6:30 a.m.	7:30 a.m.	1 hour
Breakfast and recreation	7:30 a.m.	8:30 a.m.	1 hour
Distribution of work; field labor or atelier	8:30 a.m.	12:30 p.m.	4 hours
Lunch and recreation	12:30 p.m.	1:30 p.m.	1 hour
Distribution of work	1:30 p.m.	5:30 p.m.	4 hours
School	5:30 p.m.	7:00 p.m.	1 hours, 30 minutes
Dinner	7:00 p.m.	7:45 p.m.	45 minutes
Prayer and evening hymns	7:45 p.m.	8:00 p.m.	15 minutes
Bed	8:00 p.m.	6:00 a.m.	10 hours

Weekends were set aside for "recreation," which meant physical activities rather than intellectual pursuits. Attributes associated with the idealized male form such as courage, self-discipline, bravery, and resilience were instantiated through the governance of the physical body. Thus the forging of a strong, well-disciplined body was concomitant with the development of a masculine subjectivity. R. W. Connell argues that bodily practices and experiences, as well as discourses about the body, are essential for the process of conceptualizing gender. "True masculinity," according to Connell, "is almost always thought to proceed from men's bodies—to be inherent in a male body or to express something about a male body."[50]

The emphasis on physical education and military discipline prepared *colons* "quite naturally for taking their place in the ranks of the army."[51] As Ivan Jablonka notes, proponents of the agricultural colony claimed that "after a few months at the colony, the debased boys recover the good qualities of their gender. . . . The young inmate is ready to become a soldier-laborer, capable all at once of cultivating and defending the soil of the homeland."[52] Jablonka's assessment of how virility was mobilized at Mettray supports Ann Laura Stoler's contention that the agricultural colonies were integral to the European imperial project because they provided the manpower necessary to secure, pacify, and exploit overseas colonial dominions.[53]

As specified in the general regulations that guided the colony's operation, gymnastics were considered a formal "part of the instruction, and all the pupils take part in them according to their age and strength."[54] By the

Colonie de METTRAY — Gymnastique - Travail aux agrès

FIGURE 3. Gymnastique, travail au agrès.

mid-nineteenth century the idea that gymnastics was a component of male personal hygiene had spread from Prussia to Western Europe, including France. According to George Mosse, the connection between gymnastics and the military "became an established fact from the French Revolution onward . . . as the health and fitness of recruits was a serious concern with the introduction of universal military service." Exercise—that is, calisthenics—was also a way to construct a martial yet modern form of masculinity in which the "fit body was to balance the intellect . . . as such, balance was thought to be a prerequisite for proper moral as well as physical comportment."[55]

Gymnastics aided in the development and maintenance of health by increasing strength and motor skills, but Mettray's administrators also believed that it steeled the masculine "will," and they wanted their subjects to develop a corporeal discipline. According to Demetz,

> Children possess an exuberance of animal spirits which they must have the means of eliminating, no matter how, and often this necessity has more to do with the blows they give each other than any malicious feeling. Everything which tends to fatigue them helps to keep away evil thoughts and we take care, therefore, that their games shall necessitate violent exercise so that they may be tired by their play as well as by their work; thus, at night they fall asleep the moment they lie down, and their slumber is unbroken until it is time to rise.[56]

FIGURE 4. La gymnastique.

Mettray's administrators believed that impulsive physical action could lead to homosexual activities or masturbation, whereas exercise could discipline the body and mind by dissipating one's energy. Physical fatigue was salutary because it "dispels dangerous thoughts and procures beneficent sleep."[57] Exercise would contain unproductive impulses that were a threat to the physical and moral health of boys and young men. In this regard, as Christopher Forth noted, gymnastics training was not about "vulgar displays or physical prowess" but the promotion of "moderation in the appetites and emotions."[58]

All gymnastic exercises at Mettray were performed outdoors rather than in an enclosed gymnasium. Thus, like agricultural labor, the cultivation of masculinity entailed a symbolic distancing from the deleterious milieu of the city. For youths who had suffered the enervating effects of urban life, their bodies were subject to a new type of corporeal discipline through exposure to the great outdoors. Mettray was not the only colony to emphasize corporeal health through gymnastics. At Aniane, for example, the work of moral rehabilitation was seen as necessitating "a rigorous yet rational method of physical education. While some may consider gymnastics as little more than a form of a recreation, it is integral to the intellectual and moral improvement of youth. This is so well understood that most believe that gymnastics is the most powerful means of action in the pedagogy of the abnormal."[59]

Gymnastics at Val d'Yèvre also took place outdoors. One of the unique features of the exercise regimen at this colony was scaling the so-called *mur d'assaut* (assault wall), which was painted to resemble the façade of a house, with windows and doors. The wall was built in 1884 under the supervision of a former director who had operated a gymnasium in Joinville (Haute-Marne) before entering the penitentiary service. An inspection report from 1891 made note of the *mur d'assaut* and the "unfortunate public comments it has generated," which resulted in a recommendation that it be removed. While the director argued that climbing the wall was "excellent exercise for the arms" and that in his opinion it did not "give pupils the idea of scaling a house with bad intentions," he agreed to permanently suspend its use, a move that was supported by the local prefect.[60] Given that the "father" of gymnastics, the German educator Friedrich Ludwig Jahn, advocated physical training with obstacles such as walls and slopes that could be scaled using ropes or with the assistance of others, their use in the agricultural colony is not as surprising as it might seem.

Sports such as soccer and basketball were also part of the physical educational regime in many colonies. At Aniane, team sports were valued not only for the physical demands they placed on pupils but also because "they obligate the performer to put forth his best efforts and submit his will to the achievement of a common goal which helps develop a sense of discipline, abnegation and sacrifice." On a more practical and utilitarian level, the effects of "strengthening and developing the body through exercise" were lauded for fostering "maximum job performance with minimal physical fatigue."[61]

Although team sports were not introduced at Mettray until after the First World War, pupils in the colony boxed (as at Val d'Yèvre) and were taught to swim in a nearby pond. Those who evinced an interest in naval pursuits could set sails and learn navigation aboard a former sailing vessel, complete with masts and rigging, which the Ministry of the Marine had donated to the colony.[62] Demetz often boasted of the surprising naval emphasis at landlocked Mettray in the colony's annual reports circulated to benefactors, philanthropists, and politicians:

> Why, it may be asked, do we have sailmakers in our agricultural institution? We offer one word on this point. All our colons sleep in hammocks, and we require workers among us who can provide and repair this sort of bedding. Further, it must not be forgotten that we have at Mettray many boys from the coast of Bretagne who have already made voyages and are irresistibly attracted by a seafaring life. One of our masters, who was formerly the mate of a vessel, teaches them the maneuvers of a ship, and gives them useful instruction in a sailor's vocation, which seems to be by nature theirs.[63]

Whatever the nature of the physical activity, sports formed the basis of a pedagogical triumphalism at Mettray and other juvenile colonies. The triumph was not so much over the weakness of the youthful body as over the unreason and effeminacy—the willfulness as opposed to the will—of the *colon's* soul. The physical development of the corporeal form was a visible manifestation of achievement. Over time, exercise generated displays of change in muscles, health, and growth, all of which could be interpreted as a demonstration of the institution's raison d'être—the transformation of boys into men.

On Sundays at Mettray, all *colons* engaged in parade and fire drills after morning mass. The parade was a means of instilling an esprit de corps in the inmates through "the precision of movements, the instantaneous obedience to order, the neatness of the uniform and the attention to every detail that is shown."[64] Administrators believed that military drill was more virtuous than even physical exercise—and certainly play—because it required a formal symmetry that demanded diligence and alertness, attributes much admired by adults. Demetz maintained that military drill also inspired a sense of brotherhood among participants who would otherwise be atomized in general society. Through collective activities such as marching in time, military drill effectuates, according to historian William McNeill, an "artificial, primary community" that gives "new meaning and direction to life."[65] As Christopher Forth has noted, whether or not one accepts McNeill's "trans-historical claim" about the "primal" nature of such experiences, it is nevertheless "easy to see how 'muscular bonding'" functioned as a means of masculine identity formation and socialization.[66]

Demetz recognized another essential function for military drill, particularly as it related to the small drum and bugle corps that accompanied the boys on parade. The parade was a way to legitimize and constitute Mettray's authority. Whether performing for the governing board or visitors or marching through the village of Mettray during a saint's day festival, the boys always appeared in special dress uniforms: grey cloth double-breasted jackets with brass buttons, light trousers, khaki leggings, and blue Breton berets. The *chefs de famille* wore officers' uniforms with peaked caps. The uniform conveyed the idea of soldiering and facilitated the staging of a militarized masculinity at Mettray.

Seeing the *colons* in neat uniform rows marching in time to a precise military band reminded reformers, legislators, and the public of the reformation that Mettray made possible. The boys and young men before them were no longer recalcitrant delinquents but respectful, orderly young patriots eager to rejoin society and accept their socially determined roles as disciplined soldiers and obedient workers. The spectacle of martial order evoked a certain awe in

COLONIE de METTRAY. - Revue du Dimanche

FIGURE 5.   Revue du Dimanche.

many visitors to the colony who saw in such exhibitions vivid evidence of a metaphysical miracle they described in euphoric accounts. Indeed, in an 1883 competition with other agricultural colonies Mettray was awarded first place in military maneuvers.[67]

The notion that military drill instills more than physical strength was deeply Rousseauian: "What view of hunger, thirst, fatigues, dangers and death can men have if they are crushed by the smallest need and rebuffed by the least difficulty? Where will soldiers find the courage to bear excessive work to which they are totally unaccustomed?"[68] Whereas the weak body succumbs to the appetites, the strong body that has been fortified through exercise and drill can resist such weaknesses and temptations. Just as ancient Rome instilled the moral virtues of patriotism and fraternity in its legionnaire citizen-soldiers, so did Mettray, as it constructed manhood itself through military training. Both Rousseau and Demetz saw martial practices as central to their vision of masculinity and republican citizenship, concepts that were inextricably intertwined. To be a man was to be a soldier, and to be both was to be a citizen.

The intense emphasis on physical training and the literal display of the corporeal form was tied to broader anxieties regarding masculinity in nineteenth-century France. As Mosse has noted, "Manly honor meant not only moral but general physical toughness. Physical skills and dexterity had always been prized as necessary to defend one's honor, but now the new society in the making looked at the entire male body as an example of virility, strength and courage expressed through proper posture and appearance."[69] At the Protestant agricultural colony of Saint-Foy, Director P.-F. Martin-Dupont described the young men who first arrived at his institution as "pale, disheveled and looking like ghosts."[70] But the effects of life and work in the countryside, along with physical exercise and military drill, regenerated their languid and enervated bodies. At Saint-Foy and at the colony of Saint-Hilaire boys not only boxed but also engaged in *canne de combat* to make virile both body and soul.[71]

To reproduce the social order in a new generation of youth, young men had to learn their relative positions in the social hierarchy. To this end, education was considered important—not for the child's intellectual development, but to instill the "love of order, the desire to work and the respect for laws."[72] Mettray trained its denizens to conform and obey and to regard social inequality as natural, thereby ensuring its cultural reproduction. The level of instruction at Mettray was "equivalent to that received by the working class in the cities," with a heavy emphasis on practical training and the acquisition of basic knowledge. In addition to catechism, *colons* received instruction in reading, writing, and basic arithmetic as well as weekly lessons in instrumental and choral music. Demetz believed that "singing promotes good order, prevents conversation among *colons* while moving from place to place, fixes good thoughts and good words in their memory and attaches them to the institution where they first felt these happy influences." Furthermore, a "knowledge of instrumental music ensures them good pay and the prospect of advancement in the army."[73]

Instruction in the colony was initially provided by a single *instituteur principale* (schoolmaster), but the size of Mettray's inmate population quickly made such an arrangement impossible. Only one year after opening, classes were moved from a space in the central administration building to the refectory areas of the cottages, where the *chefs de famille*—assisted by their *sous-chefs* and tutors chosen from the *colons* considered to be the best and brightest— led written drills and rote recitation exercises each day. During this period the schoolmaster made his rounds, passing from one cottage to the next, observing, monitoring, and occasionally "animating and directing" class activities. While this situation was not ideal, Demetz considered the *chefs* to be "well-educated men who make excellent teachers and their presence among the boys will prevent the infraction of rules which otherwise so large an assemblage would have the opportunity of committing." He claimed that while there were twenty-four disciplinary infractions under the "old arrangement" in the standard shared classroom, there were only two recorded in the cottages during all of 1841.

Colonie de METTRAY — La Grande Classe

FIGURE 6. La Grande Classe.

Colons also participated in a weekly class on agronomy and animal husbandry, in keeping with the colony's goal of training future farmers.[74] Sauvestre reported that "there is little to no development of the intellect at Mettray," which he found commendable: "Such an education would have the effect of pushing the *colons*, upon their exit, into professions where certain bad temptations would be sure to assail them. These boys need to engage in manual trades and labor which requires the expenditure of muscular strength so that they can better maintain a certain level of physical and moral equilibrium."[75] The Fourierist Cantagrel summarized the utilitarian basis of Mettray's pedagogy thusly: "Education is proportionate to the condition in which the children will one day find themselves. They know they are destined to earn their living by the sweat of their brow and that work is their future."[76]

Those youths who did not respond to the class-based education provided at Mettray were subject to a graduated series of punishments that were intended to force them into submission and compliance:

1. A public or private reprimand.
2. Exclusion from recreation during appointed times of day.
3. Removal from *tableau d'honneur* (if applicable).
4. Loss of rank as elder brother (if applicable).
5. Confinement to punishment quarter.
6. Having to stand for a length of time in the punishment quarter.

7. Placement in a light or dark cell.
8. Placement in punishment quarter with only dry bread and water.
9. Transfer to a house of correction in extremely grave cases, especially for acts of "immorality" (i.e., homosexuality).[77]

According to Demetz, "Of all the punishments which unhappily we are under the necessity of inflicting, we must confess that the cell alone exercises a moral influence; all the rest, such as dry bread and water, have a useful effect on children under nine years of age, but only irritate the older boys. Our officers have been struck with the change that seclusion in the cells has produced in the most obstinate dispositions."[78] Although isolation seems to be at odds with the mission and method of an "open-air" colony, Demetz believed it was a critical component of the regime. "Some people have thought very absurdly that solitary confinement should be thrown aside now that such success has been attained at Mettray, where the boys are associated together. But this is a very serious error which it is our duty to correct. Such confinement, instead of being opposed to our system, is in perfect harmony with it, and is, in our opinion, its indispensable complement."[79] For Demetz, the punishment of solitary confinement was not simply leaving the *colon* to rot in a cell; it was a tactic of surveillance, persuasion, and calibrated deprivation. Isolation was, in his view, a quintessentially modern punishment in which the prisoner, amid the silence and the dark (depending on the nature of the infraction, a child might be placed in a *cellule obscure*), would be forced to reach into the parallel darkness of his own heart, his own soul, in search of a metaphysical resolution for his suffering.[80] In contrast to a regimen where nearly every moment was filled by the activities of daily life in the colony, the cell offered nothing but time for painful circumspection. According to Demetz, solitary confinement was necessary as a means of deterrence: "The course of treatment pursued at an agricultural colony does not admit of sufficient severity to intimidate undisciplined dispositions, some of whom retain their vicious propensities, unless the fear of being sent to the cells can be made to exercise a wholesome influence over them."[81]

Conditions in the cellular quarter at Mettray were generally quite awful, so that fear was warranted. Le Dano recalled:

The cell was nothing like I had ever known. . . . Here, the rats had a priori, the right of way. There was no toilet, no latrine. At the base of each cell was a gutter which acted as a collective toilet. . . . For those located nearest the entry of the building, the stream moved at least halfway down the cell block; those at the end of the row had to live with the shit when it grew too large to be washed down the mouth of the drain. Frequently, the gutter overflowed which meant that the flooding of the cells was inevitable. The cells located at the end of the gutter were reserved for the les durs (the hard heads). For those who didn't want to die of asphyxiation, they had to take an interest in closely monitoring the gutter and, if necessary, make use of their hands to assure its continued function.[82]

A *colon* who had finished serving a stint in the correctional quarter reportedly told Huot, "While I would prefer the blows [i.e., corporal punishment], I know that it is the cell that makes me better."[83] Early chroniclers of Mettray such as Huot noted that Mettray's cellblock was relatively empty during his visits: "There were only seven detainees in the quarter; when I returned on Wednesday, there were only six; when I returned for a third visit there were twelve. Certainly, out of a population of 500 *colons*, this number is not distressing."[84] By the close of the nineteenth century, though, the cellblock at Mettray was often at capacity as officials increasingly utilized isolation as a form of punishment.

Despite the insalubrious environs of the cellblock, Sauvestre extolled the colony's system of punishments and rewards as a "work of genius."[85] For an individual act of good behavior, a *colon* was awarded a point that was recorded on a pink card bearing the name of the inmate and the date of the award. Although the possession of currency at Mettray was strictly forbidden, the cards had a monetary value of five centimes, which could be redeemed at the colony's canteen for small *rustiques douceurs* such as pieces of cheese, fruit, or sweets. By granting rewards or threatening to withhold them, officials endeavored to alter behavior and mold subjectivity.

Although it was never explicitly recognized as payment for labor in institutional documents, five centimes per day were paid into prisoners' savings accounts during their incarceration. Saving was a disciplinary tactic intended to teach the importance of foresight (*prévoyance*), or providing for the future. There was a widespread belief among penal reformers that lack of foresight was the primary failing of the poor and working class. This mentality led its victims to search for pleasure in the present, neglecting the needs of their families and leaving them prey to destitution and crime in times of economic crisis. Demetz was very much in the mainstream of social economic thought in teaching the value of savings as a remedy for this "deficiency" in the moral character of the dangerous classes.[86]

Mettray had the right to exact labor from the *colon*, and it maintained stewardship over his saved earnings until his release. Thus there was no correspondence between the rights and obligations one might associate with employer and employee. *Colons* had no legal right to receive pay for the labor they provided, and an unfavorable disciplinary report could easily result in the forfeiture of their wages and/or savings. The pitifully low wages did not reflect the value or worth of the labor performed; instead, they were a symbolic reward for good behavior both at work and in the colony generally. In the 1930s critics of Mettray claimed that an increasingly harsh disciplinary policy that collected monetary penalties drawn from the savings of *colons* for minor rule violations was designed to offset the financial mismanagement of the institution (for a full discussion, see chapter 6).

Although it was exceedingly rare, there were occasions when the administration agreed to release an inmate to his family before the end of his sentence. Generally, Demetz was in no hurry to return children to their parents. In his view, parents were powerless in comparison to the institutional setting of the agricultural colony when it came to facilitating meaningful moral change in their offspring. Mettray effectively displaced parents, albeit temporarily, until the counter-morality instilled by the natal family had been defeated. Since parents could not be relied on to instill authority, discipline, and obedience in their sons, the agricultural colony served as the last refuge of childhood.

Evidence of one such early release appears in an extended exchange of correspondence between an illiterate mason and local officials. An unnamed scribe writing on behalf of the man addressed a letter to the Ministry of the Interior in August 1851 claiming that his son "might be eligible for early release for his good conduct. The petitioner also wishes to receive news of his son, as he has received no letters from either him or the director of the Mettray colony. It is his hope that you would employ your authority to return the boy to his parents who grow more worried about their child and who believe that his future conduct will be that of a dutiful son who has recognized the wrongdoing of his young age."[87] The ministry forwarded the request to the prefect, who in turn contacted Mettray's director for information. In response, Demetz wrote:

> Since his arrival in May, the child has been placed in cellular confinement for insubordination and theft, not to mention a great number of smaller punishments that we have been forced to impose because of his excessive laziness. Despite being subject to a discipline as severe as that which exists at Mettray and being the object of continual surveillance, we have not been able to get more out of him. Thus, what can we expect when he is returned home to his parents whose condition requires that they are continually absent from the home? Paris offers so

many dangers for children. This is particularly pertinent in this case as I do not have to remind you that the young man was arrested in the cabaret of Paul Niquet, which is one of the most disreputable establishments in Paris.

p.s. While completing this letter I have learned that the young L. was just placed in the punishment quarter for a theft.[88]

Demetz was also careful to note that while the father claimed to have received no news about his son, he had, in fact, written to his family on three separate occasions. Moreover, according to the director, since the boy's arrival at Mettray some three months earlier he had received no mail from his family (given the father's illiteracy, this should not have been surprising). Despite the director's clear misgivings about the family's living situation and the *colon's* seeming unsuitability for release, Demetz relented at the request of the ministry.[89] In a later missive to the prefect he noted that the youngster had been given a complete set of clothing and that his train ticket was purchased by the colony, though Mettray had not received the full state indemnity for his care.[90] (When leaving the colony, every *colon* was given two pairs of pants, two shirts, one waistcoat, one cap, one pair of suspenders, three cotton shirts, two cravats, three pocket handkerchiefs, three pairs of stockings, and one pair of shoes, which together cost six francs in 1849.[91])

All former prisoners who had reached the age of twenty and had managed to not reoffend for a period of two years after release were eligible for admission to the Association de la colonie de Mettray, whose members included the administration and the colony's benefactors. On admission, the *colons* pledged the following: "With our free and full consent, we swear, on our honor, to devote ourselves to the cause of children, poor, abandoned or criminal, to snatch them from corruption, to instruct, and to lift them up. We swear, in short, to serve our whole life and with all our strength, God, the colony, and our parents."[92] As a symbol of his commitment to the colony and its mission, each *colon* was awarded a ring with the inscription "Dieu, Honneur, Souvenir, Alliance," which according to Hill signified a "devotion to the will of God, brotherly union among members for mutual support, the succor of the unfortunate, and the reclamation of evildoers." The outside of the band was inscribed with the phrase "Loyauté passe tout."[93] He also received a certificate which, according to Hill, might serve as "the chief ornament" of the former *colon's* "little dwelling." His name appeared on the certificate along with the name of the association, the signatures of the founders, and a biblical verse drawn from Hebrews 10: "Ayons l'œil les uns sur les autres pour nous exciter aux bons œuvres" (Let us be concerned for each other, to stir a response in love and good works).[94] This emphasized the linked concepts of citizenship and civic virtue so central to the republicanism of Rousseau: a true citizen of the republic is dedicated to the welfare of the community. While the ring and certificate were acknowledgements of a man's past relationship to Mettray, they also served as visceral reminders that he must sacrifice for the collective good, and that civility necessitates that he accepts the obligation to respect and assist those in need.

When a youth arrived at Mettray the director (or, as the colony's population grew, one of his subordinates) reviewed the dossier that accompanied him. This file was comprised of documents culled from various prefectural, public welfare, and prison records that outlined his crime and judicial sentence, the economic and "moral" standing of his family, and his general state of physical health. In other words, the dossier represented the entirety of the boy's life prior to his arrival at Mettray. After reading through these materials, the director would briefly interview the child to assess his morality. These interrogatories offered little in the way of additional insight into the character of the inmate, however, and were generally devoted to a recitation of rules and regulations.

After the interview the boy was sent to the infirmary where he was subject to a cursory medical examination, then his hair was shorn to the skull, which made him easily recognizable to the public should he attempt escape. Next he was given a uniform and assigned to a family based on his age, physical strength, and vocational aptitude. If the inmate's physical constitution was insufficient for outdoor work he was temporarily assigned to "sedentary" indoor labor such as laundering clothes and linens or serving food to his comrades. The director made this determination in consultation with the physician, taking into consideration other factors such as the profession of the boy's parents, the employment he was likely to find on release, and where he was born and raised. The last is noteworthy, as Demetz believed that "birthplace exerts a strong influence on man, and how completely he is a type of its characteristics." Relying on this rather amorphous geographic and occupational determinism, the director characterized "the Breton as obstinate, perseverant, religious and devout; he is best suited for field labor. The Norman and Alsatian are particularly adapted to the care of animals. Thus, they are employed in the stables. . . . The Parisians possess an abundance of intelligence and vivacity, accompanied, however, by a want of discipline, which yields only to the firmest rule and severest correction. . . . Once overcome, many work in one of the various workshops or assist in the classroom."[95]

While there is no indication in Mettray's extant records that *colons* were used as domestic help for staff and personnel, this was a common practice in other colonies. Indeed, the minister of the interior indicated in a letter to all prefects in departments where public colonies existed that the use of pupils as domestics had "degenerated into an abuse of privilege." Moreover, the salary paid to these "'pupilles domestiques' . . . is most of the time insufficient." In language rather provocative for a systemwide communiqué, the minister characterized the practice as "an abuse of children that cannot be allowed to continue." As a result, all colonies were instructed to immediately remove "pupils attached to service personnel employed as agents, and to reintegrate those pupils according to their aptitudes into the general service or workshops of the colony. No exceptions to this decision will be accorded."[96]

A prisoner's first hours at Mettray initiated a symbolic break with his past and, more importantly, the criminal milieu from which authorities presumed he was drawn. There were two more elements in the effort to submerge the prisoner's former identity: the uniform and the *matricule* (registration number). The uniform was intended to distance the youth from his past life and to forestall the development of any sense of individuality or distinction between or among prisoners. A similar rationale justified the use of the *matricule*, as the prisoner was referred to by number instead of by name. Use of numbers was also intended to improve administrative efficiency as it aided in the organization of documents pertaining to each *colon*. Effectively dispossessed of his former identity, the *colon* was refashioned via the standard-issue uniform and the *matricule* in a process that Goffman characterized, in the modern context, as a "mortification of the self" in which "the inmate is shaped and coded into an object to be fed into the institutional machinery."[97]

Describing the uniform, Demetz claimed that "we take every precaution which might recall the prison to their minds, to impress deeply upon them the conviction that at the colony they will begin a new life, where force is replaced by persuasion." Thus, the uniform "is extremely simple, and is made so as to allow the limbs of the child the greatest freedom of action, and thus promote his healthful development. Without being very remarkable it is sufficiently peculiar to attract attention to the boys in case they should run away, for it must never be forgotten that they enjoy a perfect liberty."[98] However, the standard-issue clothing, particularly the summer wear, was nearly identical to that given to the adult *bagnard* in the overseas penal colonies. The summer uniform was gray and made of lightweight cotton rather than wool. Each *colon* was also issued a straw hat for protection from the sun. (In winter, the uniform consisted of wool trousers, waistcoat, and lightweight boots that provided little protection from the cold).

As in French Guiana and New Caledonia, *colons* at Mettray were issued wooden sabots—worn throughout the year—that hindered movement and

FIGURE 7. Les sabotiers.

discouraged escape. The clogs were neither practical nor comfortable, and most prisoners suffered cuts and blisters on their feet that often became infected and necessitated medical treatment. While the sabots remained standard issue until Mettray closed in 1937, other institutions replaced them with boots in the late nineteenth century. For instance, acting on the repeated complaints from the director of Val d'Yèvre, the local prefect addressed a formal request to the Ministry of the Interior to do away with the clogs as "the feet of our children are frequently wounded by the sabots while galoshes would result in far less inconvenience."[99] In approving a proposal to make boots standard issue in the colony, the ministry instructed officials that the expenses should not be "significantly above those which result from the employ of the sabots" (which meant that the colony's ateliers had to produce the new shoes) and that the boots be expressly designed "so as to avoid the wounds occasioned by use of the sabots."[100]

Although Demetz believed that youths were more likely to behave if they were isolated from contradictory influences while in the agricultural colony, families could visit their children at Mettray. According to regulation, all visits were to take place in a designated parlor in the presence of an officer. While such monitoring may seem unduly restrictive, administrators believed it was necessary to prevent smuggling of scarce or prohibited goods into the colony, especially tobacco, which was in great demand.[101] At the root of this surveillance also lay the conviction that character could be reshaped at Mettray, but only if the young prisoner was receptive to change. This required separating him from his family, which in the eyes of the authorities had already failed him. Indeed, administrators saw prisoners' families as a moral and political challenge to their authority and their vision of correction at Mettray.

To ensure that Mettray's project of moral reformation was not undone by the corrupting influence of family, relatives wishing to visit inmates were required to request appointments via the local prefect, who in consultation with Mettray's director would decide whether visitation was warranted or posed a potential threat to the well-being of the prisoner. Family members whom the institution regarded as troublesome or an unhealthy influence were routinely denied visitation, and all those allowed onto the grounds of the colony were closely monitored by staff. The lives of prisoners and their families were deeply affected by this visitation policy. Visits provided inmates a welcome respite from the disciplinary monotony of daily life, and they were also a means by which children and parents could reestablish an affective connection in a way that written correspondence could not match. In explaining the "family system" employed at Mettray, Demetz was careful to say, "We do not conceal from ourselves the fact that the institution can never equal the reality, and consequently, whenever our wards come from respectable families, we lose no opportunity for enabling them to meet, in order to preserve the bonds of natural affection."[102] Yet, as with most features of daily life at Mettray, the contours of visitation were determined almost exclusively by administrative fiat, largely unconstrained by political or judicial interference. As one might expect, local officials wielded their power to severely circumscribe contact with the outside world, and this was most acutely experienced by families who did not meet a bourgeois, patriarchal standard that bore little resemblance to the realities of daily life for the working class and poor.

The most common justification for denying a visit was the marital status of the mother. If she was living in concubinage (i.e., in a common-law marriage), visitation was rarely permitted.[103] As Rachel Fuchs has noted, there was a "high frequency of consensual unions" in nineteenth-century France, "some of which proved to be short and unstable, others of which were stable and long-term equivalents to a legal marriage."[104] Despite the relative prevalence of common-law marriage, particularly among poor and working-class couples, officials condemned such arrangements. As there are no extant registers that detail visits, the surviving correspondence between parents and Mettray's gatekeepers provides the only evidence of the extent to which the latter hindered visitation.

Women living in concubinage who requested visitation became, in effect, subjects of investigation. For instance, when a mother sought permission to visit her son at Mettray in January 1899, three weeks after his transfer from a local jail in the department of the Vienne, the prefect contacted Director Philippe Cluze, who replied that visitation would be "unwise" because the woman was currently living with a man who was not her husband.[105] On receiving a second request from the mother in June, the prefect—again, in consultation with the director—contacted the constabulary in Tours where she lived to request information on her "conduct and morality."[106] In a response dated one week later the unnamed official noted: "The widow B is employed, and is by all accounts a hard worker, but we must remark that she lives in a state of concubinage. Additionally, her daughter Jeanne B., age twenty, who has an illegitimate child of three years of age, also lives in a state of concubinage." Interestingly, the unnamed official concluded that "there would appear to be no harm in allowing the widow B. to visit her son at the colony of Mettray where he is detained."[107] The prefect believed otherwise, however, and wrote in a note to Cluze that this was a matter beyond the purview of the constabulary and that he wished to prohibit both the mother and the elder daughter from visiting Mettray. In a follow-up note the director expressed his satisfaction with the way the prefect handled the matter: "I commend your sage decision to forbid all communication between the young boy and his family."[108]

In another case, a mother wrote to the prefect in March 1892 indicating that she wished to visit her son Léon F., whom she had not seen in three years. In her letter, she asked, "Why will the director not give me authorization to see my son? That is why I have again sent this request so that I may see him during the Easter holiday."[109] Two weeks later she wrote again as she had yet to receive a response: "I sent a request to see my son who is held at Mettray and I have attached an envelope with postage paid for your answer. If it is forgetfulness I understand, but your silence gives me real uncertainty which will only go away once I hear from you."[110] She did not know that behind the scenes there was an extended exchange between the prefect and the director about her request. For reasons that are not entirely clear from the available correspondence, the prefect interceded on behalf of the mother, requesting that Cluze reconsider his refusal of her request: "I understand that the mother currently lives in concubinage with a man whom is not the boy's father, and that the boy is illegitimate; apart from this irregular situation, however, all accounts indicate that she exhibits good behavior and shows real affection for her son to whom she writes often. She has now asked several times if she could see him. Perhaps we can make an exception in this case."[111] Yet this entreaty was rebuffed by Cluze, and the mother was not allowed to visit her boy at Easter.

If the mother of an inmate married her common-law spouse, this was interpreted by officials as evidence of a moral awakening that was rewarded by granting entry to the colony. In a case from March 1892 a mother requested to see her son but was denied because she was living with a man who was not her husband. When her divorce became final some three months later, she again sought permission to see her son, only to be refused due to her living arrangement. Finally, in August of the same year she moved from Paris to Lyon, where she was employed in the manufacture of umbrellas. More importantly, at least in the eyes of local officials, she was now legally married. The director concluded that "as evidenced by her wedding, the mother's morality has improved and the young G. can now be allowed communication with her, and her visit to Mettray should therefore be approved."[112]

Over time there appears to have been a slight moderation in the stance on unwed mothers and visitation. The extant correspondence suggests that Emmanuel Lorenzo, the colony's director from 1906 to 1911, was somewhat more flexible than his predecessors in this regard. In July 1906, after consulting with the prefect where she lived, he allowed a mother to visit her son Jean-Marie, who was had been in public assistance before being placed at Mettray, "so long as the conversation between mother and son occurs in the presence of a staff member who will make certain that inappropriate counsel or advice is avoided." After the visit Lorenzo wrote again to the prefect, noting that "we have encouraged this young boy to write his mother more often . . . and she should be allowed in the future to see her son."[113]

Although this stance was not atypical for Lorenzo, he proved much less tolerant in a case involving a man by the name of Gavignon who requested permission to accompany his common-law wife on a visit to see her son. Gavignon wrote that although he was not the boy's biological father, "We have lived together for over four years and during that time I have come to share all of her sorrows and all of her joys and that is why I would be grateful to you if you would kindly let me accompany her and, if at all possible, that you might extend the time of our visit because we will have come from so very far away" (the couple lived in Lyon).[114] On receiving the request, the prefect asked for a recommendation from the director, who replied:

> I have permitted this woman to see her son once, and I have no reason to oppose that she sees him again, but it is not possible to allow M. Gavignon to be present at Mettray as that would only serve to awaken immoral thoughts among our pupils. I am surprised that he would even dare make such a request. As for the duration of the visit, it will be set by the internal regulations of the colony; visits that are too long in duration lead to abuse and if an exception is made for one family, others will surely ask for similar treatment, which is why, I believe, that only

the mother be allowed to visit and see her son, and then only within the limits prescribed by the rules of the colony.[115]

What is notable is that the primary focus of administrative animus was the common-law male spouse rather than the unwed mother, who had been granted visitation in the past and would continue to be allowed entry in the future, which certainly represented a break from past practice. Given the tone of the response, however, it also appears that Lorenzo viewed Gavignon's request as improper because it violated his personal sense of propriety and Mettray's standard protocol on visitation.

In a handwritten note to the prefect, another single mother who was living in concubinage requested that she be allowed to see her boy, "Lucien B. . . . I have written many times now but it seems that there are always excuses. I don't understand why it is a problem that I wish to see my son. M. Préfet, I beg you to let me go to the Loire next Sunday. It would give me great pleasure to see my son."[116] After she had contacted the prefect a fourth time, Director Cluze informed the official: "I must remind you again that the dossier of the boy is disturbing; the father left the marital home which the mother now shares with another man; she appears to go from one farm to the other mending and peddling baskets; it was our interpretation upon his arrival, and it remains our interpretation to this very day, that the child should be prohibited from having any relationship with his mother. I believe that her visit would offer more disadvantages than benefits for our young pupil."[117] Cluze steadfastly refused to accede in the matter—a decision that appears to be based as much on the mother's relative penury as her marital situation—and she was not granted entry. Indeed, the reference to the mother's various endeavors to eke out a meager existence makes clear that at the dawn of the twentieth century, long-standing moralistic explanations of poverty were still extant, at least in the minds of administrators such as Cluze.

While the screening of visitors reflected long-held prejudices regarding gender and class, it is also important to recognize that the disruption of family ties was part and parcel of a disciplinary strategy intended to induce conformity and docility in inmates through their isolation from the outside world. It is also worth noting that there were situations in which the decision to refuse an inmate contact with his parents appears to have been well justified. In one instance, a father who repeatedly requested that he be allowed to see his son was refused because he had been arrested and sentenced to a year in prison for harboring a fugitive charged with murder, and it was during that time that his seventeen-year-old son had become a ward of the state and eventually was placed at Mettray. On his arrival at the colony, the youth was diagnosed with a venereal disease, which according to the director "date[d] to the period when he lived with a submissive girl in the home of his father, which, as you know, was a refuge for shady individuals, both men and women, of a repugnant morality."[118] While all requests of the father to see his son were denied, on one occasion in December 1920 he arrived at Mettray unannounced with a permit from the prefect in hand. The director acquiesced to the visit but later complained bitterly, "We had agreed that all relations between the young D. and his father were to be prohibited based upon the damning information as to his living situation. At that time you indicated that you would not authorize any visits."[119] Although it is possible this was simply an administrative oversight, the director forwarded a complaint to the Ministry of Justice, which in turn instructed the prefect to initiate an investigation of the father, who was living in the village of Saint-Cyr-sur-Loire (Indre-et-Loire).[120] The investigation concluded that "the conduct of Monsieur D. appears irregular; he exhibits a bad character and while he claims to be a laborer, he does not, in fact, work."[121] Because the information in the report was characterized by the ministry as "unfavorable," the prefect was instructed to henceforth prohibit all visits.

Parents sometimes complained that although they had received permission to visit Mettray on a certain date they had been asked to postpone or cancel their plans because their son had committed a disciplinary infraction. In one angry letter to the prefect, the father of Étienne T. complained that it had been more than five months since he had last seen his son "as he is continually being punished for some offense. . . . I ask, if you please, why he is being punished like this. I wish to see him as soon as possible because I have been sent permission in the past only to see it taken away before I can leave for Mettray."[122] Indeed, the father had received permission to visit on 30 March 1923 but was forced to postpone the trip because his son was discovered to have penned "an immoral note" to a comrade that led to his isolation in the correctional quarter. On 8 April the father received word that he could visit later that month, only to see the invitation withdrawn again, this time for an act of insubordination (the boy insulted his workshop foreman). Responding to the prefect's request for an explanation, the director replied, "While it may seem as though this young man is continually being punished, there is little point in having his parents make a wasted trip. I have authorized ten such visits in the past and will do so again should their son's behavior improve. The boy is not the victim that his parents believe. He is a vicious and unintelligent sort who is immune to all good sense."[123] The director also indicated in the note that one of his clerks had spoken directly with the boy, encouraging him to behave so that he would be granted the "pleasure of seeing his parents," and the youth reportedly replied, "I'm not fucking hurt if my parents come or don't come to see me . . . and it doesn't bother me at all to be punished for I'm the most content when I'm being punished for something."[124] In response to the father's complaint, the prefect indicated that Mettray's director "has the authority to resort to the disciplinary measures he deems necessary and the sanctions that have been imposed upon your son are entirely justified by the vicious nature of his continued insubordination. . . . Thus, your complaint has no basis and no further action is justified."[125] After committing yet another offense later that spring, Étienne T. was transferred to the correctional colony at Eysses.

This was not an unusual occurrence at Mettray or any of the juvenile colonies; there are many references in the disciplinary record to prisoners deliberately transgressing rules in order to be placed in isolation. These actions point to a desire for solitude, a retreat into the self that could be effected only by an instrumental, intentional strategic violation of regulations. As Sykes has noted, lack of privacy is a quintessential "pain of imprisonment,"[126] regardless of the carceral setting, and therefore a spell in solitary confinement might be seen as a temporary refuge from enforced sociability. Many *colons* constructed privacy within the public space of the agricultural colony, blurring the boundaries between the two to restore a sense of self, however briefly. Étienne's desire to be alone brings to mind one aspect of Alf Lüdtke's polymorphous notion of *Eigensinn* as applied to the shop floor: "An individual worker might try to be completely 'by himself': through a variety of means: by 'tuning out' or attempts to 'escape' from the confining presence of the others. In such situations, the main aim was to . . . generate elbowroom and distance oneself from the immediate environment. Bodily contact and physical proximity motivated workers to try again and again to gain some space and to be left alone. This form of obstinacy was not resistance."[127]

The presence of families in the colony could pose problems in terms of logistics and security. This was evident in an incident in June 1912 in which a father and his eldest son arrived unannounced at Mettray to visit a young inmate. An unnamed employee who greeted the pair noted that they had been drinking, and when he learned that they did not have permission to be in the colony he asked them to leave. When they refused, he retrieved Director Paul-Emile Brun and dispatched another employee to contact the gendarmerie in the nearby village of Mettray.[128] As the scene unfolded, a crowd of inmates gathered as the two visitors began to "verbally assault Director Brun and occasionally move toward him in a physically threatening manner." According to the employee, "As one might imagine, the pupils found all this amusing and exciting, and by the looks on their faces they eagerly anticipated that a fight would occur. Naturally, their sympathies were with these two men, who, without exception, acted like two apache warriors."[129] The young inmate suddenly appeared on the scene and after fighting his way through the crowd, grabbed his father's arms and reportedly yelled, "Please, I beg you, do not hit the director!" The gendarmes arrived soon after and arrested the two men. In a coda to the affair, Brun wrote to the prefect that while he had initially planned to press charges against the father, he was convinced otherwise by the entreaties of the *colon* "who begged me, with tears in his eyes, not to pursue a formal complaint against his father whose conduct he clearly deplored." At the end of his missive, the director reflected on his life and career: "Here I am, twenty-eight years as a director. I've had cases of apaches, of rogues. But this affair made me realize once again how many of our children are the unfortunate victims of their parents. Our pupil has an excellent attitude. . . . He did not want this visit. He is ashamed of his father. In this circumstance one can see that the offspring is better than the parent."[130] Although Brun did not pursue legal action he did ban the father from having any contact with his son at Mettray, including written correspondence.

For boys who were deemed unsuitable for placement with local patrons—usually boys with acute behavioral problems—the decision to return a youth to his family was often inflected by the same gender biases and paternalist presumptions as those that guided decisions on prisoner visitation. In one case, in the spring of 1909 eighteen-year-old Clement G. was scheduled for release after completing a two-year sentence for public indecency (he had exposed himself on two separate occasions to children in the small village where he lived). Based on his record at Mettray, Director Lorenzo characterized Clement as having a "very limited intelligence; he will have difficulty earning a living and we doubt that he will be able to stay in any kind of placement, which is why it would be well in his interest to place him in public assistance in his department of origin."[131] He had arrived at this conclusion only after asking the prefect of the Vendée about the current living situation of the boy's mother. The prefect had indicated that in his view it would be unwise to return Clement to the fifty-four-year-old widow "who is a hysteric and is largely responsible for the internment of her son. It was she who initiated him into the reprehensible acts which motivated his internment."[132] The prefect failed to mention that when officials in the Vendée arrested the boy they labeled his mother a "nymphomaniac," a fact noted in the trail of documentation that accompanied Clement's arrival at Mettray. It is clear from the perfunctory responses to questions about the offense that appear on a standard form issued by the Ministry of the Interior: "Q: What were the causes of the offense or the crime committed? A: The bad instincts and bad examples of the mother. Q: Was the child inspired to commit the crime or offense by his parents, his masters, or other persons having authority over him? A: By his mother, who is recognized as a nymphomaniac by authorities in the department."[133] Although the record does not indicate how officials—in this case, the mayor of the village of Chauché—arrived at this conclusion, it appears that the son's aberrance was interpreted as somehow the result of the mother's supposed sexual proclivities. The fact that she was by all accounts destitute, without employment, and therefore unlikely to be able to provide for her son was only a secondary concern, receiving far less attention in official documentation than her presumed sexual behavior.[134]

To reform the unruly denizens of Mettray, it was necessary to inculcate not only a masculine identity through exercise and drill but also a certain class subjectivity through labor. Labor was both the instrument and symptom of reform, as the prisoner was forced to work until he did so willingly, both in the colony and in society at large on his release. Agricultural labor had a moral significance because it addressed a perceived demographic crisis (i.e., rural depopulation) and also provided a set of skills and values appropriate for the prisoners' futures as tillers of the soil. Demetz's vision was grounded in a romantic belief that life in the countryside was emblematic of an earlier, simpler world, but it was also premised on the conviction that agricultural labor could resocialize those who had contravened society's laws.

Most boys at Mettray were engaged in the cultivation of vegetables and grain crops such as corn and wheat. They also attended to livestock and farm animals in the colony. During the winter, most were assigned to various workshops where they labored as blacksmiths, cobblers, tailors, or masons. As the number of children in the colony increased, so did the size and scope of the agricultural enterprise. From a single farm field adjacent to the central square in 1840, the area under cultivation had expanded to 176 hectares, which included 75 hectares of wheat, 37 hectares of rye and oats, 40 hectares of beans, 20 hectares for cattle grazing, and 4 hectares for various vegetable crops (17 hectares lay fallow) by 1871. By 1890, the fiftieth anniversary of the colony, well over 250 hectares of land was devoted to agriculture, and there were multiple stables and pens for the more than 150 head of livestock it owned.[135] This expansion came at a high cost as purchases of land and loan repayments "weighed heavily on the budget . . . and [the growth] generally did not contribute to improving the living conditions of the *colons*."[136]

Mettray's routine remained largely unchanged throughout its nearly century-long existence. The regime was intended to be a source of moral inspiration and an aid in the project of "character building," which necessitated overcoming the child or adolescent's predisposition to unreason. Work was the cornerstone of the colony's disciplinary edifice, its primary virtue inhered in symbolic identification with the human condition. Demetz associated work with the moral virtues of a regulated life, obedience to authority, acceptance of one's position in society, and simple industriousness. Thus he justified the labor regime at Mettray by arguing that labor prepares the criminal for life in civil society on release. Organized and productive labor was also meant to compensate for the cost of operations, at least in part. While Demetz always emphasized the moral rather than the economic value of labor in his rhetoric, republican critics claimed that unscrupulous entrepreneurs in juvenile corrections were exploiting child labor for profit, a charge Mettray would not escape.

Mettray's regime was also shaped by a focus on governing the bodies of its young subjects. In adhering to a regimen not dissimilar to that seen in the military, the goal was not only to make *colons* fit and obedient but also to strengthen group cohesion and inspire the development of courage, self-confidence, and a martial-like spirit. Not only the body but also the masculine "will" would be steeled through exposure to Mettray's rigorous regime. Physical exercise and military drills, combined with the regimentation of every aspect of daily existence, were intended to transform *colons* into a depersonalized, homogenous group. The dress uniforms, the drum and bugle corps, and the elaborate array of rituals and military-style codes of conduct were also part and parcel of Mettray's disciplinary repertoire. Yet, despite the unyielding nature of the regimen, discipline and control in the colony was far from complete. Though designed to produce what Foucault called "bodies both docile and capable,"[137] Mettray's approach was undermined by acts of resistance by prisoners in the late nineteenth and early twentieth centuries.

CHAPTER 3

Resistance

The goal of replicating the family at Mettray was complicated by an underlying concern about sexual "corruption." As Foucault notes in *The History of Sexuality*, this concern was based on a rather vexed understanding of childhood sexuality that acknowledged that "children indulge or are prone to indulge in sexual activity" but nevertheless construed it as "contrary to nature" by virtue of the "physical, moral, individual and collective dangers it posed."[1] According to Vernon Rosario, however, "Children, who Rousseau had represented as naturally innocent and good, were increasingly viewed with skepticism and distrust" during the nineteenth century as the body of the child became a site of vigilance.[2] Mettray's design generally supports Foucault's contention that although sex was never explicitly discussed in the implementation and design of institutions such as the school or reformatory, it was nevertheless "a constant preoccupation. . . . The builders considered it explicitly, the organizers took it permanently into account."[3]

Sexuality was a subject of high anxiety for Mettray's administrators, and the ways it was expressed (i.e., homosexuality and masturbation) were viewed as a repudiation of social and religious strictures. "Premature" sexual activity of any kind could jeopardize the moral and mental well-being of their young subjects, so officials worked to root it out. This concern grew over the course of the nineteenth century as the rhetoric of national decline in fin-de-siècle France cast sexuality as a dangerous force, a threat to civilization in need of taming. According to Robert Nye, psychiatrists and physicians began to pathol-ogize a host of sexual behaviors, particularly homosexuality, which was read as "a symptom of profound individual pathology, and, at worst, a sign of im-minent (i.e., national) collapse."[4]

The most notorious exponent of these ideas was the physician Auguste Am-broise Tardieu, who characterized homosexuality as "the shameful vice for which modern languages do not have a name."[5] The medico-legist argued that there was a direct connection between homosexuality and crime and that ho-mosexual acts were an expression of France's social and cultural decline. In proscribing sex acts he deemed "unnatural," Tardieu reified the "natural," thereby setting the stage for medico-legal intervention. Sexuality could be ex-pressed only within the confines of heterosexual marriage and for the pur-poses of procreation; anything else was the result of mental, moral, or physical abnormality.

As Michelle Perrot has argued, the disgust of homosexuality behind bars among prison keepers was an expression of a "castrating prison which was the ultimate intensified image of sexual repression" of society at large.[6] Inter-twined with long-standing moral proscriptions against same-sex relations was a more practical issue for administrators, who believed that such relationships impinged on the maintenance of discipline in the colony because they height-ened jealousies and fueled rivalries among prisoners. Administrators consid-ered all forms of sexual expression among youngsters to be unhealthy and a threat to internal order, but their actions with regard to homosexuality in par-ticular also reflected their desire to impart a bourgeois masculinity based on notions of self-discipline and control. The focus on the sexuality of prisoners underscores the "civilizing" role that Mettray assumed in rehabilitating and reforming its young subjects. Vocational training and education were impor-tant, but so was the cultivation of "appropriate" behavior. For recalcitrant young men to learn how to conduct themselves properly, it was first neces-sary that they learn self-control. Self-control entailed not only the curbing of inappropriate conduct but also the mastery of one's own body, which was most directly manifested in terms of sexuality.

Autobiographical accounts by former inmates indicate that there was some-thing approaching a homosexual subculture at Mettray. Generally, subcul-tures in prison emerge when social groups adopt their own identities and practices in relation to prison authority, often in response to blocked aspira-tions or ambiguous or low status. Even in a restricted environment, certain modes of behavior and social habits persist through shared needs and a shared culture. Subcultures are expressions of cultural and material experiences that are distinct from the wider culture. As O'Brien notes, inmate subcultures allow prisoners to "appropriate, distort and recast the values of disciplinary society."[7]

Prison subcultures are often understood as manifestations of collective resistance to the normalizing power of a "total institution," but it is important to note that they can divide as well as unite prisoners. While individuals such as Jean Genet appreciated the opportunity to forge intimate and affective ties with other inmates, others were extremely critical of such behavior, particularly when it involved younger boys. Le Dano remarked rather blithely, "Pederasty is the most popular sport at Mettray; half the *colons* joyously violate the other half who are their victims."[8] Bernard Caffler, a former inmate, recalled that on his arrival in the colony he was asked, "Who are you going to team up with? You have to take on a boss, '*un caïd*' [kingpin]. Without a protector you will be miserable."[9] The journalist Henri Danjou, in a series of articles that appeared in *Détective* magazine in 1931 (which was expanded and published as a book the following year), noted the prevalence of exploitative relationships throughout the entire system of the juvenile colonies, both private and public. He wrote, "Reigning over all children of the *bagnes* [penal colonies] . . . is the *caïd*, the kingpin, the master of the prison. . . . The leader who will defend a pupil against the brutalities of others, even those of his own gang. And, in exchange for this protection, the *caïd*, like a lord of the manor, enjoys the 'droit de seigneur' [the right of the lord to deflower local maidens before they marry]."[10]

Evidence of this subculture is apparent in the argot that demarcated the boundary between the *colons* and the authorities. Prison argot was a subject of great interest in France, not only for penal administrators but also for the public, who were fascinated by the *jargon du vice* that frequently appeared in the works of Victor Hugo.[11] Genet noted the "extraordinary power" of Mettray's *colons* to "create words. Not extravagant words, but to designate things, words which children repeat to each other, thus inventing an entire language. The colonists' words, invented for a practical purpose, had an exact meaning: a 'gear' was an excuse. They would say 'Not a bad gear.' 'To fox' meant to gripe. . . . A 'doe' was a person who runs away, a person who escapes. . . . By mingling with other words whose authentic nobility goes back to time immemorial, these relatively new ones isolated us from the world even more."[12] According to Le Dano, if a prisoner at Mettray had successfully escaped, or if he was transferred out of the colony for bad behavior, the other inmates would "not speak of the disappeared. 'He made the leap' ('faire le saut'), they would say, and that would be the end of it."[13]

At Mettray there also existed a specialized argot that referred to a sexual hierarchy. According to Genet, there were three basic categories in this subculture: the *marles* (the oldest and strongest members of a cottage); the *mignons* (boys "protected" and granted favors by the *marles* in exchange for sex); and the *cloches* (the lowest category, boys who were physically weak and frequently abused by the *marles*). There were physical confrontations between *marles* when they vied for control of a *mignon* or tried to maintain their positions of power in the cottage. Such skirmishes were often allowed to unfold to defuse tension, to resolve conflicts, or to serve as a form of entertainment. According to the former convict Raoul Léger, there was an unspoken practice among guards to intervene in brawls only when it became apparent that one combatant had fully defeated the other.[14] Genet noted that when "guards don't make a move while a deadly battle rages, you think they're brutes, and you're right. I like to think they are petrified by the wrathful spectacle, the grandeur of which was beyond them."[15] Once a clear victor had emerged, Mettray's true social order—based on intimidation, fear, violence, and brutality—was restored. These incidents of interprisoner violence and conflict betrayed the presence of an inmate subculture that operated according to its own social control mechanisms. That is, there was a parallel and autonomous society that existed within the agricultural colony, one with its own social mores and rituals.

Conflicts between prisoners were rarely mentioned in official reports unless they involved serious injuries. It is likely that fights were so common that they did not merit much attention. Details of one conflict, however, appear in the correspondence between Director Cluze and the préfet d'Indre-et-Loire. In December 1910 sixteen-year-old Charles P. entered his cottage and "approached seventeen-year-old Jean W. from behind and coldly stabbed him twice in the back with a knife." In a note that outlined the circumstances surrounding the assault, Cluze implied that the attack was part of an ongoing dispute that involved an unnamed younger *colon* in whom both prisoners had shown a "particular" interest. As the director considered both assailant and victim to be "bad subjects: angry, vindictive and violent with a penchant for immorality," they were both placed in solitary confinement (Jean W.'s wounds were minor) before being transferred to the correctional colony at Eysses.[16]

Another violent incident in which homosexuality played a role occurred at Aniane in 1909. One day while working in the mechanics workshop a seventeen-year-old youth, Joseph E., "suddenly, and without warning . . . grabbed a red-hot poker from the forge and plunged it into the abdomen of eighteen-year-old Jean L."[17] The victim did not survive the seemingly unprovoked attack—he suffered extensive bleeding and developed peritonitis, which eventually led to his death in a local hospital. During the initial investigation of the incident,

Aniane's director noted that the attack was "carried out spontaneously and without prior discussion; neither the supervisors nor the foremen or the children of the workshop saw anything or heard anything, which is unfortunate as they were not able to have prevented this very regrettable assault of which Joseph E. is guilty." In the judicial inquiry that followed, the assailant initially claimed that he had struck the victim "out of anger because he did not wish to accept the immoral propositions of Jean L." He later admitted, however, that Jean L. had publicly "accused him of committing immoral acts on certain younger pupils, and that while this was a false claim, for the sake of protecting his honor and his reputation, he, in a moment of anger, struck his calumniator."[18] The paucity of documentation pertaining to this event makes it difficult to assess its significance in the prison culture that existed at Aniane. Nevertheless, it does suggest that masculinity at Aniane was linked with power and that violence was the principal means of protecting one's "honor," particularly when accused of engaging in homosexual activities with a younger prisoner. This brutal enactment of an honor-shame code as a means of resolving conflict and regaining honor bears little resemblance to the bourgeois duel. According to the sociologist Peter Berger, there is a general societal expectation that "men should exhibit manliness and women shame, but the failure of either implies dishonor for the individual, the family, and in some cases, the entire community,"[19] which in this case extended to the colony. For his crime, Joseph E. was sentenced to three years in prison by the Cour d'assises de Hérault.

Inmates suspected of or caught engaging in homosexual acts were permanently removed from Mettray via transfer. According to Huot, "Of the few transfers which have occurred to date, almost all were the result of immoral acts. We cannot praise too highly the director who exercises in such cases the utmost severity."[20] While officials anticipated that prisoners might engage in homosexual activities, they considered those who did to be beyond hope of correction. Director Brun described homosexuality at Mettray as

an immorality which is the plague of all agglomerations of youth such as ours where each child brings with him his own set of bad morals. We cannot ignore the mentality of our children when considering all of what takes place here. We, the educators, are not surprised, but acts which resemble those of human beasts leave an indelible impression. We have seen the most repugnant acts of bestiality and we now have evidence that some escape for the sole purpose of satisfying their desires. Just the other day, two pupils, Robert R. and Richard G., having escaped from the colony, were discovered engaging in an act of sodomy. Sad subjects such as these must be classified in the category of "abnormal." Among them this single vice finds a suitable environment to develop. Their general moral sense is completely obliterated as a result.[21]

Acting on the director's request to transfer the two young men, the préfet d'Indre-et-Loire noted in a letter addressed to the Penitentiary Administration, "The facts as Mr. Brun has outlined merit our serious attention and must be met with serious force as repugnant acts such as these have become far too numerous."[22]

The practice of transferring young men suspected of engaging in homosexual activities was not limited to Mettray. At Aniane in February 1900 two prisoners escaped while out on work detail and were captured the next day by the gendarmerie. While awaiting transfer back to Aniane they were held together in a cell in the Montpellier jail, and there the two fifteen-year-old boys, Jules D. and Henri A., were discovered "engaging in an act of pederasty" by guards. On receiving a telegram from the gendarmerie relating what had happened, the director at Aniane initiated an investigation, led by the *surveillant-chef*, which established that "Jules had the power to drive Henri to engage in such acts" and that he had "enjoyed unhindered access to [Henri A.] to fulfill his deplorable passions."[23] The director decided that the two inmates had to be separated and that Jules D., "the most culpable of the two," should be transferred to the correctional colony at Eysses.[24]

What is noteworthy about this case is not that Jules D. was transferred but that Henri A. was returned to Aniane. The documentation is quite limited but it appears to show that officials reasoned that the relationship and sexual activity between the two was not consensual but coerced, even though they were the same age and there was no indication of physical violence or threats (like the boys in the Mettray incident, the pair had escaped together). The episode points to the director's rather simplistic understanding of sexuality that effectively categorized all sexual acts as either forced or voluntary. Because Henri A. had been labelled the "passive" partner by the gendarmerie, Aniane's director conceptualized him as a victim of Jules's machinations and therefore not a "true" homosexual whose "predatory" presence would pose a threat to the social order of the colony.[25] Policing the boundaries of the young men's sexuality was an anxious and ultimately futile project because it failed to acknowledge that, particularly among adolescent boys in a cloistered, same-sex environment such as the colony, a "situational" homosexuality was possible and it was not evidence of what authorities believed was an unnatural perversion.

Prisoners' homosexuality was seen not as merely youthful sexual experimentation but as a manifestation of unacceptable autonomy over their own bodies. Officials' decisions to exile youths who engaged in homosexual acts reflected not only the prevailing notion that any kind of sexual impulse was antithetical to long-standing notions of childhood "innocence" but also their abject horror at such behavior. In their minds, homosexuality was an embodied and identifying "habit." A habit was understood as a rigidification of one's nature, and administrators required that their subjects were individuals whose "innocence" was intact, whose childlike nature was still fluid and therefore still amenable to moral reform.

Homosexuality was considered a deliberate act of disobedience, but whether it was also an act of resistance depends on context. A sexual encounter between two young men was not resistance in the same way that failing to obey an order or attempting escape might be considered an act of protest. The latter two were public acts of defiance, whereas inmates who engaged in illicit sex usually tried to hide their activities. Homosexual encounters were a way for some prisoners to experience sensual pleasure and in some cases forge emotional bonds in a manner that was expressly forbidden.[26] Yet, as the criminologists Mary Bosworth and Eamonn Carrabine have noted in a contemporary context, the assumption that "resistance must be visible to an outside audience precludes an appreciation of more personal and intimate challenges to authority . . . such as those entailed in the practice of disallowed forms of sexuality."[27] In this sense, it is possible that prisoners' refusal to remain celibate was seen by officials as a rejection of the heteronormative and procreative model of sexual relations and therefore subversive of the goals of imprisonment at Mettray.

Masturbation, too, was seen as an "immoral" act that necessitated discipline and punishment. In the eyes of many physicians and social theorists of the mid- to late nineteenth century, the "masturbator" prefigured the "homosexual." Long-standing moral injunctions against the "solitary vice" were linked with concerns about the supposed deleterious health effects of masturbation. The extensive and obsessive cataloging of ailments associated with masturbation—particularly those related to nervous disorders—generated great anxiety from the late eighteenth century. Masturbation fears were intertwined with the emergence of a commercial economy and the birth of cultural modernity, which seemingly offered greater opportunities for sensual pleasure. According to Thomas Laqueur, "Masturbation became a problem . . . because it represented in the body some of the deepest tensions in a new culture of the marketplace; solitary sex was to civil society what concupiscence had been in the Christian order."[28] Masturbation was not only considered antisocial, it was also seen as one of the unfortunate consequences of modernity. Indeed, by the close of the nineteenth century, as Robert Nye has pointed out, "Masturbation, which had always been deplored by doctors and accorded a causal role in a variety of mental and organic illnesses, now [post-1870] became a symptom of degeneration prefiguring subsequent more serious disorders."[29]

In the prescriptive literature of the day it was commonly asserted that masturbation led to impotence and a general emasculation, which was disquieting particularly in the context of France's depopulation crisis. Indeed, what had been viewed as an act of self-indulgence came to be seen as symptomatic of a general moral and physical decline that threatened to undermine the future of the French nation. The physician Claude François Lallemand, who "discovered" the "disease" spermatorrhea (i.e., "excessive" discharge of semen resulting from high levels of sexual activity), maintained that frequent masturbation led to lassitude, impotence, and in extreme cases, death.[30] According to Lallemand, masturbation irritated the seminal tract, causing an overabundance of seminal emissions and excitement, which led to more masturbation, exacerbating the condition. Men who suffered from spermatorrhea were advised to avoid all sexual activity. Physicians also warned of the threats to normative masculinity that masturbation posed: lack of confidence, general loss of control over emotions, nervousness, poor concentration, and perhaps most importantly, an inability to work productively.[31]

According to Foucault, masturbation was seen as "incompatible with a general and intensive work imperative. . . . At a time when labor capacity was being systematically exploited, how could this capacity dissipate itself in pleasurable pursuits, except those—reduced to a minimum—that enabled it to reproduce itself?"[32] Because it purportedly left one languid and enervated, masturbation was a direct challenge to a regimen that extolled and inculcated the moral value and purpose of labor. In his *thèse de doctorat* that examined the correctional colony at Aniane, the attorney André Mailhol noted: "Some pupils, troubled during the period of puberty, grow stupid and lethargic after engaging in years of vicious practices such as masturbation. We saw a maniac at Aniane, age seventeen and a half, who was no longer capable of clearly articulating a word; the director had tried every means to correct him but it was all in vain. All those who engage in masturbation, or pederasty, are incapable of any effort; you cannot get any work from them and they are not susceptible to amendment."[33] This was in spite of a daily regimen expressly designed to induce a level of fatigue that would render inmates less likely to engage in what Demetz's immediate successor, Jean Blanchard, termed "the shameful habits that are all too frequent in institutions such as ours."[34]

The eminent criminologist Henri Joly claimed that Demetz regularly showed pictures of boys who supposedly had died in the commission of the "act," or in the "convulsions of the vice," to inmates who were discovered or suspected of engaging in masturbation. According to Joly, a witness who viewed these images testified to the "startling effect" they produced on the boys who saw them.[35] More typically, prisoners were punished by a stay in solitary confinement—a somewhat counterintuitive practice given the solitary nature of the act itself. The director of Aniane noted in an 1889 report that "young spirits, already dominated by detestable impulses, are left to themselves in cells. . . . I strongly fear that, during the long hours of seclusion that the cellular regime imposes, through a series of actions and reactions, the pupils acquire and develop bad instincts. It is elementary psychology."[36] The former prisoner Caffler recalled that solitary confinement usually was paired with another punishment known as the *piquet* in which inmates were required to walk up to twenty kilometers a day in the courtyard adjacent to the cells.[37] This is likely an exaggeration; Genet (who was not unfamiliar with hyperbole) described the *piquet* as merely "two hours of constant, fatiguing movement" each day.[38] Le Dano's description of the *piquet*—a forced march that allowed for "two minutes of rest every hour while facing the wall in a small rectangular courtyard"—was perhaps most accurate.[39]

An inspection report of the colony of Val d'Yèvre characterized the *piquet* as unduly harsh, so the Ministry of the Interior ordered that "marches should last no more than fifty minutes and should include periods of rest every five minutes." In response, the director of Val d'Yèvre complained that "a fifty-minute walk punctuated by a five-minute period of rest is much too sweet. I cannot help but think of our young soldiers who carry a load of twenty-five kilos on their back for up to seven or eight hours a day without halting their marches every five minutes to rest." The préfet du Cher shared the director's sentiment—"such exercise is not contrary to the physical health of the pupils"—and argued that the *piquet* aided in the "development and maintenance" of prisoner "morality" as well.[40] The extant record does not indicate whether the practice continued unchanged, but it does shed light on the widely held belief that libidinal impulses could be curbed by extended periods of physical exertion.

Notwithstanding Mettray's meticulous design intended to normalize the surrender of prisoners' privacy, inmates found ways to circumvent panoptic surveillance. In what Colin Ripley termed a "tactical re-appropriation of the colony's strategic discipline," prisoners situated their hammocks so as to obscure the view of the *chef* and create "tents" for illicit sexual encounters.[41] They arranged trysts in communal lavatories, in open areas between buildings, and in nearby fields and wooded areas. These were sites where *colons* had some autonomy with limited interference. While they were contingent and unstable spaces within the juvenile geography of the colony, always shifting and subject at a moment's notice to violent closure by officials, they nonetheless constituted a zone of noncompliant consent, or *Eigensinn*, in Alf Lüdtke's framing.

As Goffman noted, presentations of self are precarious in total institutions, where the clothes provided are purposely dull and institutional life fails to corroborate an inmate's prior conception of self.[42] Mettray's standard-issue uniform was intended to depersonalize the wearer, but prisoners adapted their clothing according to the precepts of a different semiotic code. The *cloches* wore their uniforms according to regulation to express their general submissiveness; the *marles* put metal wire into their berets so they could be worn at a steep angle and hemmed the cuffs of their pants so that they broke more sharply than those of other prisoners.[43] This practice indicated a desire to test the boundaries of regulations, albeit slightly, and to assert their group identity. While the changes to the uniform could be understood as a form of "willfulness" (*Eigensinn*), they should not be construed as acts of resistance against the institution. Yet, in their presentation of self—in terms of both their outward appearance and their positions within the subcultural sexual hierarchy—young men subtly subverted the exigencies of surveillance and regulation at Mettray. This "tactic of the body," or more specifically, "tactic of clothing the body," represented a moment of nonconformity that did not call into question the nature of the relationship between inmates and officials.

It was uncommon for a *cloche* to be tattooed, but many of the powerful *marles* were festooned with images. Genet references tattoos only in regard to the distinctions the images conveyed within the homosexual subculture at Mettray, but there were also many heterosexual inmates who were tattooed.[44] As O'Brien noted in her study of nineteenth-century French prisons, tattooing was a means to counter the "depersonalizing life of the institution" and was therefore typically understood by prison administrators as a form of inmate resistance.[45] Tattoos stood in contradistinction to the standard-issue uniform and the *matricule*, by which the regime endeavored to extinguish a prisoner's former identity. They were a visceral response to the obsessive, repetitive roll calls and other depersonalizing features of the regime. In some small measure, the tattoo represented a reaffirmation of self, a form of adornment and individual expression that, unlike illicit contraband, could never be confiscated by officials.

There are only a few references in the record to individuals caught and punished for the act of tattooing in the juvenile colonies. The physician Etienne

Martin noted in a study of tattooing among juvenile delinquents in 1910 that it was "forbidden" to tattoo or be tattooed in a reformatory institution. According to Martin, "Infringement of the rule results in a sentence of ten days in a cell. However, I have noted tattoos which have no doubt been completed while in correction."[46] Officials viewed the tattoo as not just a manifestation of independence but also an external sign of a deeper criminal nature. As Gemma Angel has noted in the contemporary context, the very act of deliberately "breaching, damaging or breaking the skin . . . encodes the mark as a culturally transgressive symbol."[47] Tattooing was a self-inflicted injury with a deep psychological meaning, according to Alexandre Lacassagne, a physician and early pioneer in French criminology who famously described tattoos as "speaking scars."[48]

Unlike Cesare Lombroso, for whom tattoos were akin to the atavistic stigmata associated with certain criminal "types," Lacassagne viewed them as evidence of "degeneration," which by the close of the nineteenth century had superseded atavism as the preeminent explanation for crime.[49] It is beyond the scope of this work to delineate the process by which the tattoo became a focal point in a much broader debate between the biological determinism of Lombroso and the more environmentally situated explanations of crime as exemplified by Lacassagne, but the differences in the two approaches can sometimes be overstated.[50] Throughout the 1870s and 1880s anthropologists sought to extend the frontiers of criminology by building systematic classifications of criminal anatomy. Although French criminal theorists eventually came to see the criminal as having been shaped by his or her environment (i.e., by poverty, ignorance, and imitation), biological factors were rarely absent from their writings.[51] Thus, it was not atypical for experts to disavow the Lombrosian notion of the "born criminal" while nevertheless maintaining that certain somatic signs consistent with degeneration were prevalent among criminals. As the Belgian criminologist Louis Vervaeck noted, the concepts of atavism and degeneration were "very close to identical," and the distinction, at least in terms of tattooing, was minimal, as "both theories make the tattooed individual into an abnormal being, whether this is because he has remained or has become a savage."[52] Indeed, Martin, who was openly critical of Lombroso, nevertheless maintained that "there is a general absence of pain in children and adults who are tattooed," which was generally interpreted as an innate trait of the "born criminal."[53]

Because the skin is a highly sensitive medium, its deliberate breach may explain, at least in part, why the long held belief that criminals were insensitive to pain was extended to include the tattooed. In his study of tattooing among incarcerated juvenile delinquents, Martin proclaimed that understanding the

phenomenon was critical: "We find every day in prisons criminals who aston-
ish us by their infantile appearance. . . . Some are vagabonds; others are young
thieves, and some are already murderers. Tattoos among these children appear with an extraordinary frequency. . . . One can follow, step by step, through
the iconic form of the tattoos, their careers and subsequent moral development. The older the child, the more he has affiliated with dangerous company,
the more tattoos he is likely to have, most of which will have an increasingly
villainous appearance."[54] The physician described the most common images
and motifs he had found, which included: initials, names, dates, stars, daggers
and swords, rings around the fingers, bracelets around wrists, and images of
hearts, often with someone's initials and many of which were cracked or
pierced by an arrow, presumably in reference to a past romantic relationship.
Rarer were ornate or detailed religious images, though crosses and crucifixes
were common, as was the pronouncement "Dieu voit tous" ("God sees all,"
often with an eye drawn above it), which is seen in many jails and prisons
throughout France and the Francophone world.[55] Martin noted that it was not
unusual for youths to disguise or refashion their tattoos while incarcerated,
presumably to thwart the authorities' efforts to identify them if they attempted
escape.[56]

Like the furtive maneuvers surrounding sex, the practice of tattooing had
to remain hidden in the juvenile colonies, which meant that it was generally
a nighttime activity. Inmates repurposed various items for etching the skin,
including forks, nails, sewing needles, fountain ink, and pieces of coal and/or
charcoal, which were crushed into a fine powder and mixed with water.
Where tattoos appear in the records, most of the marks, however banal, were
clear articulations of emotion: of hate ("Mort aux vaches," i.e., Death to
cows [sl., guards]); of love ("Ma Claire"); of defiance ("Incorrigible"); or of
melancholy ("Enfant du malheur," i.e., Child of misfortune). According to
the former inmate Alan Kerdavid, many *colons* had their *matricules* tattooed
onto their arms, perhaps as a symbolic means of reappropriating them for
their own purposes.[57]

The administrative documentation also contains references to more elaborate designs. One young man who was charged with complicity in a collective escape plot at Mettray was described by officials as "having a cockroach
tattooed on his forehead" (it seems likely he had this tattoo before his arrival
at Mettray, but this cannot be confirmed).[58] The journalist Henri Danjou related that during a visit to Eysses he saw under a boy's half-open shirt "his name
crudely tattooed in blue ink interwoven with chains, along with an ace of
spades," and at the colony of Belle-Île he came across another boy whose body
was completely covered in tattoos, "even his eyelids."[59]

On the one hand, the practice of tattooing in the dormitory points to the existence of an autonomous social space created by and belonging to a contingent of individuals who engaged in the activity. On the other hand, local officials attempted to catalog the tattoos of their subjects as an additional mechanism of surveillance. On arrival in the colony, each inmate underwent a medical examination that included a detailed inspection of his arms, hands, chest, head, fingers (and the spaces in between) for tattoos or any other identifying scars or marks. This information was recorded (or updated, in the case of a transfer from another carceral institution) on a standardized anthropometric/identification card that also contained other information such as hair color, skin complexion, eye color, height, and weight. The practicality of this endeavor is obvious, but the minute inspection of the prisoner's body was also driven by the need to accumulate knowledge and assert power over the subject.

Before the *colon* was situated within the deferential landscape of the agricultural colony, it was first necessary to strip away his corporeal agency. Forcibly subjected to the medical gaze, the new arrival experienced himself as a humiliated and powerless subject of institutional knowledge. This was an early use of modern "bio-data," as officials endeavored to "know" their subjects while simultaneously reinforcing their dominant position over the "docile bodies" of their charges. Thus, in addition to the advantages such information provided in terms of policing, there was also something of a psychological imperative at the heart of the procedure.

Yet one had to be careful in assuming the omniscient gaze of the physician in the juvenile colonies. The director at Eysses described the case of a young man, Mathieu M., who had recently entered the colony in 1937. On arriving, the boy first approached a guard and then the *surveillant chef*, asking that he not be classed among the general population because he feared serious violence from three other pupils who had also been transferred from the colony at Belle-Île, where they had all been housed together. In a letter to the Penitentiary Administration the director wrote: "Mathieu M. informed the *surveillant chef* that these boys had not only beaten and burned him with a red-hot iron of some kind, but they had forcibly tattooed him on three different points on his left side and chest. While two of these miscreants immobilized the boy, the third burned and tattooed him in turn. . . . Under the threat of continued beating, he had three points tattooed on his left hand, with the aid of belt buckle that had been sharpened" (presumably in a workshop).[60] Somehow, these marks had been missed in the corporeal inspection when Mathieu arrived at Eysses because there was no indication of any such tattoos on his identification card—given the extent of the or marks it seems likely that he was never actually examined. A later examination, however, uncovered, in addition to the tattoos, nineteen separate scars of recent origin on various parts of his body (chest, shoulders, back, wrists, hands, neck, and buttocks). The *surveillant chef* noted in his report to the director that whenever the three youths in question "see Mathieu M., they do not fail to threaten him. Upon leaving the cellular area yesterday, as he descended to the courtyard, they all said that 'they would take care of him.'" It is likely that Mathieu M. had been targeted because he was viewed as some kind of an informant at Belle-Île. Indeed, the director hints at this in his correspondence with the Ministry of Justice, noting that the "presence of the boy is not possible among the population. Given his reputation he must not only be protected from the three wards that have been designated, but also from the 'hard-heads.' I therefore ask your permission to keep the young man in isolation as long as his security is threatened, or until I can find a post away from the general population."[61]

Inmates etched not only their skin but also the walls of the disciplinary cells where they were held for acts of disobedience. The former convict Le Dano described the cell walls at Mettray as defaced with prisoner graffiti. "'Kalifa [guard] is a bitch'; 'Hello to the friends of woe.' Two intertwined hearts with an arrow piercing both claiming that Coco and Janot are united for life. Above them a sentence written, it seems, in paint, attracted my attention: 'Baudet is dirty rubbish, one day I will cut him open.' The letters are unequal and poorly made by trembling hands."[62] These efforts could perhaps be read as acts of resistance in the sense that many were expressions of bitterness and anger from which prisoners could draw strength in the stark austerity and isolation of the cell. Kerdavid, who was later transferred from Mettray to Aniane for a disciplinary infraction, also noted the prevalence of graffiti in the cellular quarter at Aniane: "Here is the House of Silence, the Kingdom of Suffering. I got twenty days in the cell for a bitch. Death to the *vaches* [cows; slang for guards]! Child of Cayenne and forced labor. X and Z, brothers of misfortune."[63]

The most commonly destroyed objects were schoolbooks, uniforms, and bed linens. A 1935 inspection report on the state of education at Mettray declared that while "we have workbooks for class, they are always in a deplorable state. Pupils frequently rip out pages and those that remain are covered with the most obscene writings and drawings imaginable."[64] There are also repeated references in the disciplinary records to inmates who, on first arriving in the colony, "destroy their clothes and rip up their bed linens, all of which are brand new."[65] Crafted from cheap, coarse fabrics, the clothing at Mettray was made by a detachment of prisoners not selected for agricultural labor—usually younger boys who were not as physically mature as older youths—which meant that they were often ill-fitting and poorly constructed.[66]

In a belated effort to address the destruction of new property and other behavioral issues related to prisoners' admission to the colony, the administration began work on an observation section to house new arrivals for a period of two and six weeks to ease the transition to daily life at Mettray. In the building that formerly housed the Maison Paternelle (see chapter 5), youths were to be confined and observed by two guards in "constant rapport" with the inspector general about each prisoner's behavior. On the grounds adjacent to the building, the prisoners would tend a small garden and do basic field-work as a separate labor contingent before being admitted to a family in the colony proper. The decision to create the observation section was not made until 1933, however, and due to numerous delays and cost overruns in the renovation it was not completed before Mettray's closure in 1937.[67]

The verbal culture of the agricultural colony was crude, though this aspect of daily life is somewhat obscured in official records. Documents penned by administrators, particularly directors' correspondence, were generally written in the language of respectable bureaucrats, so Mettray often appears to have been more civil than it actually was. Yet, it is nonetheless clear that although inmates were formally prohibited from cursing, their use of foul language often shocked officials. According to Director Brun, "Filthy words naturally leave their mouths . . . for they do not know any others."[68] In imposing a code of conduct pertaining to language, administrators articulated a bourgeois standard of masculinity for inmates that was, in effect, a rejection of the coarseness of poor and working-class life. As evidenced in individual disciplinary reports, however, daily interactions between prisoners and officials were sometimes profane.

While not every incident made its way into the reports, certain exchanges raised the ire of staff. The historians Tamara Myers and Joan Sangster note that "verbal retorts" are generally the most common form of prisoner resistance, and given the public nature of these confrontations, they are usually construed as a direct challenge to authority.[69] This was certainly the case at Mettray, where the charge of failure to obey an order was generally preceded by a verbal assault on a guard or official. In this sense, many inmates were recidivists—not necessarily in crime but in the art of "insolence," via the abusive language they hurled at their overseers. One such individual was sixteen-year-old Guillaume B., who had been arrested for robbing a laborer of his billfold containing sixteen francs. His numerous transgressions during his eleven-month stay at Mettray included smoking and petty theft, but his most frequent offense was insolence. In most respects Guillaume was typical—he had humble socioeconomic origins and only a limited education—but his punishment record (only a small portion of which is excerpted below) is extraordinary. Guillaume B. had a profound aversion to authority and his continued defiance indicated that that he was seemingly immune to the increasingly harsh sanctions meted out by staff.

February 24, 1923:   Disorder and refusal to obey in class; arrogant response to reprimand of instructor: "You are a damn idiot." (Two days dry bread ration);

March 7, 1923:   Refusal to leave the latrines when so ordered; told *surveillant* that he "would exact his revenge later." (Four days *piquet*);

March 22, 1923:   Arrogant response to *chef d'atelier* after observations of his work. (Three days cellular confinement and *piquet*);

April 4, 1923:   After observation of his work, responded to *chef d'atelier*: "I don't work for you." (Three days cellular confinement and three days *piquet*);

April 27, 1923:   Chatting in dormitory followed by coarse response to the *chef de famille* after being reprimanded. (Four days cellular confinement and *piquet*);

May 22, 1923:   Refusal to obey followed by coarse response to *surveillant*. (Seven days cellular confinement and *piquet*);

January 2, 1924:   Upon being reprimanded for chatting in dormitory, responded with an immoral proposition to *surveillant*. (Ten days cellular confinement and *piquet*).

After accumulating over forty entries in his disciplinary record the young man was finally transferred to the correctional colony at Eysses in July 1924. Such exchanges demonstrate that while the institution prohibited foul language, officials could not eliminate it. Power at Mettray was not seamless, and small speech acts did occasionally disrupt the status quo.[70]

"Verbal retorts" were usually spontaneous expressions of frustration and anger but they were also public acts that elicited a swift and certain punishment. In contrast, gossip—characterized by Scott as covert and diffuse—was a relatively safe means by which prisoners could attack officials without fear of sanction.[71] This was not the case for fifteen-year-old Victor R., however, who was discovered to have trafficked in a rumor that Director Brun beat his wife. In June 1919 when the young man's parents were visiting their son at Mettray he told them that Mme. Brun had not been seen in public for a number of days because she bore the marks of a recent beating. The boy's story would have never been exposed had his parents not been overheard discussing the

Hôtel de la Colonie de Mettray (I.-et-L.).

FIGURE 8.   Hôtel de la Colonie.

matter later that evening by the proprietress of the "Hôtel de la Colonie," which Demetz had established in the village of Mettray for visitors to the colony. The woman told an unnamed "agent" of the colony who informed the director. Victor's visiting privileges were abruptly revoked and he was subsequently transferred to Eysses on what appears to have been a trumped-up charge of trading in tobacco (he was discovered to have in his possession two cigarettes, which authorities maintained had been given to him during his parental visit, a charge that his father vehemently denied).[72]

The prohibition on the possession and consumption of tobacco at Mettray was taken very seriously by authorities. Indeed, smoking was seemingly condemned as much as illicit sex, and easier for officials to address. According to Sauvestre, tobacco was "the grand passion of all prisoners at Mettray . . . not only for snuff, but especially for smoking."[73] If a *colon* was caught with tobacco he was usually punished by a stay in solitary confinement. There was a general concern that prisoners who procured tobacco could wield undue power and influence among their peers and thereby potentially pose a threat to discipline and order. Although there is scattered evidence that there was active trading of other goods and services among inmates, only cigarettes were transformed from a commodity into a form of currency, because they were easy to conceal, portable, somewhat durable, and always in high demand. Thus, in addition to the formal economic system at Mettray—individual savings accounts supplemented through daily labor, a commissary that dispensed certain foods as a reward for good behavior—an informal economy premised on the trade in contraband cigarettes developed during the late nineteenth and early twentieth centuries. A secondary but very real concern of authorities was that the presence of matches in the colony could lead to accidents or deliberate acts of arson.

The prohibition against tobacco was also based on the bourgeois view of smoking as an inappropriate leisure activity. Smoking was associated with gambling, drinking, and cabarets and dancehalls, all of which were considered dangerous gathering places for young males. Social clubs, schools, Masonic lodges, and National Guard units were accessible to elite and bourgeois males, but for those who "lacked wealth or cultural capital these sites often remained unattainable, and their lower-class ersatz offered much more unstable homosocial spaces where the rites of passage between boyhood and manhood could take place."[74] In spite of tobacco's increasing popularity and pervasiveness in French popular culture—and the fact that it was permitted in other juvenile facilities in Europe and North America—officials at Mettray never considered offering it as an inducement to good behavior and restricting it as a punishment for transgressions. Like swearing, smoking was one of a repertoire of activities that working-class and poor youths considered indicators of masculinity. By smoking they undermined Mettray's efforts to instill a bourgeois subjectivity, at least in terms of leisure.

Smoking at Mettray was an act of both rebellion and pleasure. Prisoners who engaged in the illicit trade and consumption of tobacco effectively rejected the values the institution sought to impart, but there was also something else at play. As Richard Klein noted in his study of tobacco, smoking serves no purpose other than to enact a structure of desire; it is a visceral, tactile, and corporeal experience that corresponds to something other than the "necessities of life."[75] Genet described the important role that tobacco plays in prison life more generally: "The cigarette is the prisoner's gentle companion. He thinks of it more than of his absent wife. His charming friendship with it is largely due to the elegance of its shape and the gestures it requires of his fingers and body. . . . He had his case, his tinder, which was made of a burned handkerchief, his flint, and the steel swivel. For the distinguishing mark of the big shot was this small piece of steel which he struck the flint to light the cigarette butts on the sly."[76]

Certain work tasks opened avenues to procure goods and services in Mettray's vibrant and diverse underground economy. Access to resources obtained through work could be a source of commerce and even power in the agricultural colony.[77] Cleaning tasks provided access to chemicals that could be drunk or inhaled. Kitchen staff pilfered knives, forks, and other implements that could be used as weapons, as well as baked goods, bread, sugar, and meat.

Those working as clerks stole paper and ink for writing and tattooing. Together with the items that inmates could purchase at the canteen, the goods and services available from the underground economy helped to alleviate the austere conditions of daily life. Prohibited from constructing their own legitimate social worlds, *colons* built an underground community that operated outside the institution's routines.[78]

Passing illicit notes between prisoners was the most common way inmates silently and clandestinely communicated with each other outside the allotted times for recreation. Boys passed notes at work, in the cottage dormitories (particularly in the refectories), in the toilets, during mass, and even in the cellblock. Guards often intercepted these notes, so it was a risky means of communication, but it was nevertheless effective at maintaining what was likely a constant dialogue among inmates.

One of the privileges most valued by prisoners was receiving private mail, which provided an opportunity for contact with the outside world. Of course, mail was not truly private; both incoming and outgoing correspondence was read and censored. Any letter critical of Mettray, its officials, or any aspects of the regime was seized. In one such letter a seventeen-year-old boy, Jean-Pierre B., not only impugned Director Brun but also made vague allusions to the burgeoning anarchist movement in Paris. "Dear Sister, I write these words to tell you that I am at the 'college' of the Touraine, the famous colony of Mettray. My director cares about only one thing: his profit, for I am in a bagne. . . . You must know that he steals from us our labor. He should carry the money he steals from us in a sack like an ordinary thief would." The letter concluded with a salute—"Vive la liberté! Vive LIABEOEUF [*sic*]"—and contained a brief postscript: "Please deliver to the learned justices of Paris a wagon of dynamite to avenge me." Beneath the postscript was a crude drawing of a man, labeled "Flic" [slang for policeman], holding a bomb with a lit fuse.[79] In requesting Jean-Pierre's immediate transfer Brun did not directly address the content of the letter, but he alluded to its "scurrilous" nature, which in his view was a vivid testament "to the despicable mentality of this pupil." The prefect agreed with Brun's assessment and Jean-Pierre was transferred to Eysses.

In another case, inmates utilized the epistolary form in an attempt to influence the selection of a new director at Val d'Yèvre. In April 1912 the colony's bursar found an envelope in his office mailbox that was addressed to Director Briavoine, who had announced his retirement a short time earlier. The envelope contained a rather remarkable missive that was supposedly written on behalf of all the pupils at Val d'Yèvre. The letter threatened violence if Briavoine's assistant director, Amable-François Démarez, was not chosen to succeed him.

Monsieur Director,

It is with regret that we have learned of your departure because you have been so good to us, but we demand that if you do leave that M. Démarez become director because we know that he is good. Some of our comrades tell us that this is not to be the case. If this is so, we have prepared a very serious revolt. We demand M. Démarez and if it is not him, we have decided that whomever is named will not last long, because we will do what we have to in order to defend what is ours. You can be sure that we will keep our promise. From this point on, we will not utter a single word until the signal has been given. M. Director, you have nothing to fear so long as you remain here, we do not want to bother you as you have been good to us. . . . But this is what we demand and we will remain quiet until it is time to act.

The 236 comrade pupils who stand in solidarity.[80]

Briavoine immediately sent a note to the Ministry of Justice along with a copy of the letter, attributing its defiance "to the workers' doctrines of unionists and anarchists who disturb the world, and which have now settled in Val d'Yèvre. . . . The principle of authority is weakening everywhere, and it is now completely unknown. The pupils are going to choose their director just as the workers wish to choose their foremen, all with brutal pressure, under the threat of sabotage and, indeed, perhaps murder."[81] The director advised the ministry to consider taking all "necessary precautions and whatever security measures are necessary to maintain order" once his successor was named. Since Démarez was later appointed to the position, the threatened "mutiny" apparently did not take place and there was no disciplinary action taken with respect to the letter.

Because of the dispersed nature of labor at Mettray, both within the confines of the institution and on adjacent farms at a remove from the colony proper, administrators believed that any resistance was most likely to occur on worksites. Most understood that labor—whether performed outdoors in the idealized agrarian setting or in the indoor workshops—did not liberate inmates from the experience of confinement. Labor in the agricultural colony was intended generate obedient, self-correcting workers ("docile bodies"), but it was also a central site of struggle between *colons* and officials. Indeed, there were myriad ways that the former resisted the efforts of the latter, who tried to instill appreciation of the dignity of hard work and how it could restore one to useful and productive citizenship.

There are references in the archival record to sporadic work stoppages, which, while short-lived and not highly coordinated, were nonetheless troublesome for administrators. At Val d'Yèvre in January 1899, a few hours after two pupils were transferred to Eysses for deliberately breaking tools, another pair of youths, Albert J. and Marcel M., threw down their tools (hammers for breaking stone) and then sat on the ground. They were soon followed by four more pupils who refused to work. Ordered to resume their tasks or face punishment, the youths began to swear at the guards and sing the "most profane songs imaginable," which "provided a dangerous example to the other pupils who began to take notice and a few who began to join in the singing." (The punishment registers frequently mention singing, and particularly the singing of provocative, obscene songs such as those associated with this act of rebellion).[82] Eventually, nine more prisoners joined in the work stoppage, and when guards tried to take them to the punishment cells "they were threatened malevolently" by the pupils who had armed themselves with various tools, stones, and iron buckets.[83] It was only after the local gendarmerie arrived that the boys were subdued and placed in isolation. According to the report on the incident, one of the boys said to the guards who led them to the punishment cells, "Why work? We are here, we have our food just like those who work. Work means nothing to us. It is not worth bothering with as we can't do anything anyway."[84] Nearly all the young men charged in the incident were transferred to Eysses.

While this protest was brief and there is no evidence of definitive objectives or stated demands, it is noteworthy because it points to a fundamental problem with inmate labor that all the agricultural colonies shared: confinement did not afford *colons* the opportunity to choose the place and conditions of their occupation. That freedom made harsh, manual labor at least somewhat tolerable for the average worker, but within the confines of the colony such autonomy was not allowed. Inmates were forced to labor, and any collective refusal to work was viewed as little different than a riot, though it was usually referred to in administrative correspondence as a "mutiny." The inmates' routine was rigorous and rigid, and there was nothing for them to spend their modest wages on other than a few perishable food items in the canteen. Inmates rarely had the opportunity to socialize with their comrades, and they were discouraged and/or forbidden from venting frustrations or discussing problems in the workplace with those who oversaw their labor. Ironically, while labor in the colony was intended to replicate conditions in the world outside, it may have had the unintended effect of uniting inmates against their keepers and imbuing a sense of collective identity as workers—citizens—who possessed certain rights, which continued after their release.

Collective revolt was uncommon, but there were countless individual incidents of resisting the labor regime. For instance, Pierre C. was transferred from

Mettray to Eysses in 1897 for "excessive and chronic laziness." His punishment record, only a portion of which is excerpted below, is noteworthy for the number of citations related to his steadfast refusal to work at a level that the institution deemed satisfactory.

November 4, 1893: Excessive laziness (1-day cellular confinement)
November 18, 1893: Excessive laziness (1-day cellular confinement)
January 14, 1894: Excessive laziness (1-day cellular confinement)
February 18, 1894: Excessive laziness (1-day cellular confinement)
February 25, 1894: Excessive laziness (3-days cellular confinement)
March 11, 1894: Excessive laziness (1-day cellular confinement)
November 17, 1894: Extreme laziness in the tailor workshop (1-day cellular confinement)
November 25, 1894: Excessive laziness (1-day cellular confinement)
December 7, 1894: Laziness, disorder in the atelier, ridiculing his chief (3-days cellular confinement)
December 14, 1894: Excessive laziness (1-day cellular confinement)
December 21, 1894: Excessive laziness (1-day cellular confinement)
February 9, 1896: Excessive laziness (1-day cellular confinement)
February 22, 1896: Excessive laziness (1-day cellular confinement)
March 21, 1896: Excessive laziness (1-day cellular confinement)
April 21, 1896: Formal refusal to work (6-days cellular confinement)
May 28, 1896: Excessive laziness (1-day cellular confinement)
June 13, 1896: Excessive laziness (1-day cellular confinement)
June 27, 1896: Excessive laziness (1-day cellular confinement)
July 28, 1896: Excessive laziness (1-day cellular confinement)
August 22, 1896: Excessive laziness (1-day cellular confinement)
October 31, 1896: Excessive laziness (1-day cellular confinement)
November 21, 1896: Excessive laziness (1-day cellular confinement)
November 28, 1896: Excessive laziness (1-day cellular confinement)
February 13, 1897: Excessive laziness and very poor work (2-days cellular confinement)
April 6, 1897: Insolence to all observations (3-days cellular confinement)
May 4, 1897: Formal refusal to work (3-days cellular confinement)
June 17, 1897: Refusal to obey and insubordination (8-days cellular confinement)
September 23, 1897: Refusal to obey (3-days cellular confinement)
September 26, 1897: Formal refusal to work (3-days cellular confinement)[85]

What is also striking about this record is that the institution repeatedly meted out the same punishment for the same infraction over a period of nearly four years, despite its ineffectiveness at ameliorating his behavior. Indeed, Pierre C. was assigned to work in three different areas at Mettray—in the field, the tailor workshop, and the stables—even though the record demonstrates that he was resisting not specific tasks but the act of labor itself. Although changes in an inmate's work regime could be approved only by the director (as stipulated in the general regulations that governed the colony), "fecklessness and laziness cannot be the reason by which one is granted a transfer to another workshop."[86] It is unclear why an exception was made in this case.

This record of recalcitrance highlights one of the central challenges Mettray faced. How should an institution premised on the economic, disciplinary, and moral value of labor respond to inmates such as Pierre C. who would not work, aside from punishing them and/or eventually transferring them to another institution? Challenges to the primacy of labor were a source of profound tension in both practical and ideological terms. Practically, pupils such as Pierre C. undercut the economic value of labor in the agricultural colony, forcing officials at Mettray to formulate alternate accommodations. Such confrontations pointed to the impossibility that the labor regime could ever effectively meet its objective to reform young delinquents. Indeed, labor at Mettray was a conflicted and contradictory project that operated under a complex set of rationales and competing objectives that made it difficult to balance the imperatives of discipline and moral reform that underpinned the institution. There are also frequent references in the punishment records to inmates who physically harmed livestock animals, particularly horses, perhaps simply out of cruelty, or perhaps to inhibit labor and production in the colony.[87] Incidents involving the deliberate destruction of property were also common. In one such case, Jean K., who did not wish to work on landscape detail in and around the colony, "stuffed rags into the pipes" of a garden, flooding it.[88]

Some of the most violent acts committed by inmates at work at Mettray were self-inflicted. This kind of behavior could be understood as an instrumental form of resistance. Feigning illness was one of the few ways that *colons* could control their participation in the workforce. Mettray's physician was vested with considerable power because only he—by virtue of his medical training and professional acumen—could distinguish between prisoners who were truly ill and those who were merely feigning illness or deliberately incapacitating themselves to avoid the rigors of hard labor. In the encounter between doctor and *colon* the tension between medicine and labor was expressed as a disciplinary exchange. Those judged to be sufficiently ill or incapacitated were excused from hard labor, particularly field work, for the duration of their illness. Thus the *colon's* body was a site of both coercion and resistance. Feigning illness was widespread in the colony and usually was attributed to the "bad" character of the prison population generally.

Inmates were well aware of the physician's power to excuse them from labor detail or even admit them to the hospital in Tours, which was considered a haven of rest and abundant food, so many did their best to try and manipulate him. The unfortunate consequence of this practice was that young men who were truly sick or injured had to overcome the physician and staff's general skepticism before receiving any medical treatment. There was a general distrust of prisoner claims regarding their physical and mental health, and because of the poor sanitary conditions in the colony and problems in the preparation of food, many prisoners became ill and an untold number died.[89]

A common ruse was to ingest various chemicals that were readily available in the colony. For instance, many prisoners consumed the disinfectant used in the spittoons and toilets at Mettray. Consumption of even a relatively small quantity of naphthalene (*crésyl*), which was made from coal tar extract, led to nausea, vomiting, diarrhea, and in acute cases of poisoning, liver and kidney failure. Some boys deliberately cut themselves and then rubbed human or animal excrement or detritus into their wounds to infect them. Others stuck foreign objects up their noses or drove nails—or needles, pins, pieces of metal, or even tree bark—into their legs, hands, of feet. One *colon*, Jacques M., threw himself into the path of a horse-drawn wagon in May 1920 to escape a sentence in the disciplinary quarter for illicitly smoking and selling cigarettes to his comrades.[90]

Although self-mutilation was an inherently self-destructive act, it also offered a way for prisoners to reclaim their own bodies while also, in some small measure, subverting a regime that depended on those bodies for their labor. There are no comprehensive statistics on the scale and scope of the practice, but there was an internal disciplinary file labeled "Senseless Acts Committed by Various Pupils to Harm Themselves" that detailed thirty-two cases from 1919 to 1923 in which prisoners either mutilated themselves or made themselves ill.[91] If these are, in fact, the only records of self-mutilations that were kept at Mettray, that is disturbing, because it is impossible to believe that these practices were limited to this brief four-year period. It is also noteworthy that there are no records of prisoners' work injuries, as opposed to acts of self-mutilation, which indicates that if the administation had concerns about work safety they were limited to staff rather than inmates.

It was not uncommon for a prisoner to enlist the help of a comrade in an act of self-mutilation. In November 1925 Pierre B. asked a fellow inmate with whom he worked in the brush-making atelier to cut off his left index finger.

According to a directorial report, the fourteen-year-old boy waited until a time "at which there was a lot of movement in the atelier" to sever Pierre's finger with a sharp blade used in the fabrication process. When asked why he had done it, the boy said simply, "Pierre asked me to cut off his finger and I didn't wish to refuse him." In the documentation requesting the transfer of both boys to Eysses, Director Jacques Lardet lamented that "the disturbing mentality of these two unstable creatures is increasingly common among our pupils."[92]

Another boy, Leroy L., asked a comrade to place his left hand between the twin rollers of an industrial-sized wringer in the prison laundry. Reminiscent of the social-scientific theory linking insensitivity to pain and criminal predisposition, local officials noted that "witnesses saw the prisoner endure what must have been a most horrible pain without blinking, without the slightest contraction of his face. It seems as though unfortunate children such as these are anesthetized naturally, and their insensitivity to pain, if not completely absent, is much higher than what one would see in a normal child."[93] White observed in his biography of Genet that such descriptions of prisoners at Mettray were not atypical: "Steiner is truly a mental case; he's brooding and silent and doesn't want to do anything."[94] The notion that prisoners may have chosen to destroy their bodies as an expression of profound alienation and discontent seems not to have occurred to officials who viewed such acts as "madness" or evidence of a type of irrationality that was beyond all explanation and understanding. Indeed, officials failed to recognize or even acknowledge the possibility that prisoners' self-destructive behavior could be construed as a powerful indictment of not only the labor regime but also their own self-righteous belief that they were firm yet benevolent rulers.

Other inmates feigned insanity. One day sixteen-year-old Constant L., who had a long history of disobedience and "immoral" conduct, "suddenly burst into the dining area of his family cottage wielding a knife and babbling rather incoherently after apparently cutting his wrists."[95] An inquiry into the young man's psychological state concluded that Constant L. was not insane but a "very intelligent and hotheaded rebel who is simulating a state of violent agitation that only gives the appearance of madness." Although there is no indication how the physician arrived at this conclusion, there is evidence in the accompanying documentation that a fellow prisoner told the authorities that Constant L. had said he wished to be sent to an asylum "where he wouldn't have to work." Placed in solitary confinement for two weeks, the young man continually threatened to harm himself and his guards. Finally, he became so unruly that he was put into a straitjacket for several days and then transferred to Eysses.[96]

One of the enduring realities of daily life in a carceral institution is that prisoners are desperate to escape their captivity. Escape is the most obvious indication of prisoner agency and resistance because it is a clear and unambiguous act of defiance against the regime. Protecting against escape at Mettray was especially difficult given its open design. As the institution relied on field labor on farms at a remove from the colony itself—up to 2 or 3 kilometers— agricultural detail provided a dangerous invitation to escape, particularly when there was only one guard to oversee twenty-five to thirty youths at a time. Although the *Règlement général* of August 1869 stipulated a minimum of six agents per 100 detainees for public colonies, by the late nineteenth century Mettray regularly failed to maintain this minimal standard.[97]

Escapes were usually spontaneous, with little or no prior planning, and rarely involved the complicity of family and friends outside the colony. Despite the impulsive nature of the act—which often was provoked by harsh reprimands, revocation of certain privileges, or squabbles with fellow inmates— administrators considered escape a very serious offense. From the perspective of the institution, successful escapes undermined its legitimacy in the eyes of its subjects and highlighted the limitations of its power. Recaptured inmates were punished by a period in solitary confinement, or for a repeat offense, permanent transfer to another facility.

As a staunch defender of Mettray, the journalist and novelist Jules-Hippolyte Percher (pseudonym Harry Alis) maintained that "escape is not the right word, since there are no barriers [at Mettray]; it would be better to say that they desert. It is a childish adventure, always the same; the child leaves on a whim, under the sudden thrust of the instinct of vagrancy, he is soon recognized in a village, arrested and brought back to the colony."[98] While the majority of escapees were recaptured, most on the same day, one should not underestimate the resolve and determination of the many escapees who took great physical risks to try and secure their freedom. During one escape attempt, a youth who did not know how to swim drowned in a nearby river (the Choiselle) while trying to evade authorities.[99] In another case, a fourteen-year-old boy, Denis D., tried to hop aboard a moving train bound for Mans on 13 January 1920; he miscalculated the jump, his right arm was ripped from its socket, and his lifeless body was found about 1,800 meters from the train station in Tours.[100] Escapes became increasingly frequent during the interwar period and led to increased public scrutiny of the colony.

Escape from prison can be both literal and figurative. As Thomas Ugelvik has noted, the mere act of planning an escape can be regarded as a form of resistance, even if the plan is never executed, because it provides a means by which one can avoid the "boredom, monotony and impassivity of everyday prison life."[101] The literary scholar Michael Hardt wrote in his work on Genet: "Prison wastes time, destroys time, empties time. The time is empty because of the repetitiveness of the prison schedule and routine. Time has no duration, no substance, because of the precise repetition of its component parts, the homogeneity and the lack of novelty. Time moves at a snail's pace; the day is never-ending."[102] In this vein, the former *colon* Le Dano characterized existence at Mettray as "terribly monotonous. . . . One can say that it is boring because there is nothing different on the horizon but refectory, dormitory and workshop. I'm bored to death. Summer is here and with it my ideas of escape slowly awaken."[103] When a prisoner contemplates escape, no matter how fantastic or unrealistic the plan may be, the very idea diminishes the disciplinary power of the prison. The inmates' obsession with "getting out" was precisely the attitude that officials feared would undermine the process of reeducation and rehabilitation. The individual who contemplates or dreams of escape, without ever acting on that impulse, has not been subsumed; his subjectivity remains intact despite the disciplinary regime.

What are we to make of prisoner resistance at Mettray? These acts were in no way unique to the colony—they are a common feature of daily life in all carceral institutions, past and present. As in all prisons, most inmates at Mettray were seemingly compliant and passed through the colony in good order. As evidenced by the rigid emphasis on military bearing and comportment, officials at Mettray were preoccupied with rules and regulations at the expense of reformation and rehabilitation. Yet, the elaborate rules failed to deter infractions, which demonstrated the limitations of power and authority in the colony. Mettray's social order developed informally and haphazardly over time as prisoners interacted with the system and their keepers to address the problems posed by their incarceration. Power was not static, or rigidly hierarchical, but located along a continuum where the prisoners themselves evinced some degree of agency.

While their acts of resistance were perhaps inexplicable to administrators and staff, it is conceivable that they were a response to the grinding nature of Mettray's regime. Intended to transform boys into men, the rigidity and monotony of daily life dehumanized them as it deprived time of all meaning, blurring each day into the next. Whether or not their actions were intentional, whether or not they understood that they would be punished for their actions, and whether or not they intended collective action or simply sought a break from the daily routine, the young prisoners' transgressions must be read within the broader context of the relationship between domination and resistance. Thus, while Foucault claims that an ever-encroaching normative discipline was Mettray's historical dialectic, the archival record indicates otherwise, as inmate activities were frequently focused on finding ways to subvert, thwart, and evade authority and disciplinary power.

Chapter 4

Discord

People who work in prisons are the little noticed custodians of penality. They are a presumed presence, a necessary albeit underappreciated component of the carceral machinery. Prison officials and staff have always embodied the "power to punish,"[1] yet they receive little attention. Punishing is viewed as a demeaning and dishonorable task; there is "no glory in punishing," according to Foucault, and "those who carry out the penalty tend to become an autonomous sector; justice is relieved of responsibility for it by a bureaucratic concealment of the penalty itself" through the various efforts of "warders, doctors, chaplains, psychiatrists, psychologists, and educationalists."[2] While cellular imprisonment advanced the birth of modern penology in the nineteenth century, prison managers and staff were largely absent from contemporary discourse. According to Christian Carlier, "It was as if the Auburn, and especially the Pennsylvania system, had the aim of putting an end to the guard-prisoner relationship, which was perceived as ontologically unhealthy, perverse and dangerous."[3]

The disdained, stereotypical "turnkey"—the corrupt jailer who asserts his dominance through control of the canteen, assignment of work, and imposition of punishments—stands in contradistinction to the role envisioned for the "surveillant" at Mettray. During the colony's first three decades those who worked at Mettray were lauded by contemporaries who saw them as central to its mission. The famed English lawyer and penologist Matthew

Davenport Hill, who visited Mettray in 1848, remarked, "Their devotion to their employment, their perfect knowledge of all the principles on which the institution is founded and of the best means of carrying these principles into effect, their enthusiastic attachment to the generous men to whom France and the world owe this noble establishment, the kindness evinced towards their wards, and the grateful spirit in which their notice of these poor lads was received, left me no room to doubt that I was among realities, not surrounded by mere shows and forms."[4] Another visitor, this one unnamed, also lauded the dedication and moral example set by Mettray's staff: "That M. Demetz has been able to find and inspire so large a number of efficient workers with such pious and patient zeal is a fact that makes one hesitate which to admire most, him or his agents. But nothing is more contagious than goodness, especially goodness in action, and of which the effects are as obvious and undeniable as these are."[5] Whereas the guards who worked in the *maisons centrales*, according to Cochin, "have little morality and leave much to be desired . . . those of Mettray are loved for their sense of justice and esteemed for their capacity. They look upon it as an honor to devote themselves to such work; they are intelligent and educated, religious and moral, disciplined and patient."[6]

On being congratulated by a visitor for having created the "best reformatory in the world," Demetz reportedly replied, "It is because I have the best assistants in the world."[7] Mettray's founder attributed the devotion and professionalism of his staff to the work of the preparatory school (*école préparatoire*) he had established for their education: "To train young men and turn them from evil to good is a charge not to be entrusted to the first assistants who may offer themselves. This important ministry requires disciplined minds, sincere self-devotion and morals above suspicion."[8] Prior to the opening of the colony, twenty young men drawn from the surrounding area—all age fifteen or older, having completed their *certificat d'études*[9]—were admitted to the school, where "they took up a life of self-devotion, put on the farmer's dress, submitted to the discipline they were to enforce upon others, and gave themselves up to the inspirations of their chiefs. . . . At the end of six months they received the first colonists. . . . As far as is practicable no person employed in this institution, even as *contremaître*, has not passed through this school."[10] The education and social reformer Mary Carpenter, daughter of Matthew Davenport Hill, concluded that Mettray's "singular success" was "directly attributable to the attention paid to the education and training of the masters, and the youngest assistants."[11]

The school's curriculum consisted of religion, French language, history, geography, arithmetic, bookkeeping, gymnastics, swimming, music, and basic agronomy. John Ramsland noted that while 155 students matriculated over the course of nearly nine years (1839–48), only thirty-seven were employed at Mettray, where they variously served as "clerks, accountants, cashiers, teachers, and heads or deputy heads of families."[12] The rest were either preparing for a teacher's certificate or employed in one of France's other agricultural colonies. According to the American penal reformer Enoch Wines, Mettray's founder considered the school essential to the colony's mission and "was often heard to say that if it were ever closed the colony would be destroyed."[13] However, declining enrollments and budget shortfalls eventually led to the school's closure after which all lower-level hires were provisional, pending the successful completion of a three-month probationary period and the final approval of the préfet d'Indre-et-Loire.

Foucault argued that the essential element of the normal school program at Mettray "was to subject the future cadres to the same apprenticeships and to the same coercions as the inmates themselves. They were taught the art of power relations. It was the first training college in pure discipline." Such training was necessary because absent the architectural technology of the Panopticon, the colony's open design demanded "a network of permanent observation." Thus, staff "had to live near the inmates," almost never leaving their side, "observing them day and night."[14] This constant observation belied a lack of faith in the power of discipline to inculcate self-surveillance, a point that Foucault failed to acknowledge. Nevertheless, the discourse of reform at Mettray included a model of the ideal reformatory officer who, via his preparatory education, was imbued with the qualities of discretion, propriety, and firmness necessary for the performance of his duties.

The endorsements of Mettray's staff, so prevalent in the mid-nineteenth century, particularly among British admirers,[15] bear no relation to the conceptualization offered by Foucault. While contemporaries lauded the character and devotion of Mettray's personnel, from Foucault's twentieth-century vantage point they were agents of an ever-invasive, biopolitical governmentality. The various "coercive technologies" at Mettray—cloister, prison, school, and regiment—demanded that

> chiefs and their deputies had to be not exactly judges, or teachers, or foremen, or noncommissioned officers, or "parents," but something of all these things in a quite specific mode of intervention. They were, in a sense, technicians of behavior, engineers of conduct, orthopedists of individuality. Their task was to produce bodies that were both docile and capable; they supervised the nine or ten working hours of every day . . . they directed the orderly movements of groups of inmates,

physical exercises, military exercises, rising in the morning, going to bed at night, walks to the accompaniment of bugle and whistle.[16]

Because Foucault was not interested in delineating the realities of daily life at Mettray, he was not particularly attuned to how those on the ground articulated the complex interaction between penal policy and practice. That is, he never examined how, or if, agents carried out their multiple disciplinary functions.

Subordinates regularly bypassed institutional constraints to advance their own ends and perceived needs and sometimes, exceeding their authority, meted out harsh punishments to young inmates in an arbitrary and abusive manner. Official regulations expressly forbade staff from exacting punishments on their own initiative, even when *colons* had violated rules. According to these regulations, the basic duty of staff was to ensure that daily routines were carried out in an orderly manner. The director had authority over all staff and inmates, and only he had the formal power to issue punishments. Official regulations were often disregarded, however, and unauthorized acts of violence toward *colons* were a feature of daily life at Mettray.

When this practice was uncovered by officials during a surprise site inspection in 1887, it elicited a torrent of criticism in local, regional, and national newspapers that tarnished the colony's once sterling reputation. While Jean-Jacques Yvorel, Frédéric Chauvaud, and Pascale Quincy-Lefebvre have analyzed various aspects of the press campaign against Mettray and the agricultural colony system more generally,[17] what remains largely unexplored is the institutional underside where the tensions and disjunctures between official regulations and workday practices laid the groundwork for mismanagement. The Prison Administration, operating under the auspices of the Ministry of the Interior, issued directives that delineated proper administrative practices, defined acts of staff misconduct, warned against the commission of such acts, and outlined the sanctions to which violators would be subject. Issuing these reminders of official policy and the consequences of violation was one of the few ways officials in Paris could address problems of corruption and abuse, but local agents chafed at what they saw as unwelcome interference in juvenile corrections.

By the time Mettray was closed in 1937, the pronouncements of the mid-nineteenth century lauding the devotion and rectitude of its staff were little more than a distant memory. Far more common were assessments such as that offered by the journalist Louis Roubaud, who conducted a lengthy investigation of Mettray and denounced its staff as intellectually and morally unfit to be educators: "Incapable of discerning between the wild impulses and noble revolts of those whom they call 'pupils,' they instead stimulate denunciations, tolerate vice, and impose suffering. The preventative or repressive severity by which they conduct themselves distorts their character and develops in them a certain cruelty. . . . Some of them, in turn, become truly crazy persecutors."[18] A similar characterization was advanced during a 1935 budget debate in the Chamber of Deputies focused on the protection of *l'enfance malheureuse* when the socialist deputy Jean Castagnez, a member from the Cher, described Mettray's staff as "brutal overseers" whose "painful and cruel acts give birth to a hatred in children's hearts so fierce that time cannot erase it."[19] Even Jean Genet, who romanticized and eroticized so much of his experience at Mettray, recalled in *Miracle of the Rose*: "I could weep with emotion at the memory of the fifty grownups who guarded us, regarded us, never understanding us, for they played their role of torturer in all faith."[20]

Had the staff at Mettray somehow changed, grown callous and cruel with the passage of time, or had the ground shifted beneath them, casting old practices in a new light? How did the colony, once universally recognized as a progressive, humanitarian endeavor, come to be understood as a brutal and anachronistic institution after little more than a generation? Mettray's scandals were indicative of broader power struggles among its personnel but also between the colony's various directors and republican officials over the way the institution was governed. An examination of Mettray's internal documentation reveals an establishment oblivious to the winds of political change and increasingly plagued by internal discord and internecine strife.

Governmental dissatisfaction with private agricultural colonies in the Third Republic was evident in a report issued on behalf of a parliamentary commission on prisons that condemned the regime of the colonies as well as their religious orientation. According to the head of the commission, the magistrate and center-left deputy Félix Voisin, nine private colonies had already been permanently closed based on accounts of prisoner abuse and neglect: "Children were frequently whipped, sometimes in considerable numbers, and others were left in filthy, disgusting cells and quarters. Most were subjected to a true exploitation. . . . In some colonies young detainees were denied elementary instruction, provided insufficient food, and their health was compromised as the result of unsafe buildings."[21]

Because many young prisoners came from cities—about 51 to 52 percent of all those imprisoned—a program of reeducation centered on agriculture was increasingly seen as contrary to the needs of an industrializing economy. "When children originating from the countryside are placed in agricultural work, there is nothing better. . . . But it is quite a different situation for those children originating from the cities! None of their prior experiences have prepared them for agricultural work which is entirely foreign to them, and which is often beyond their physical strength which is diminished by their prolonged exposure to city life."[22] Most prisoners who came from the urban milieu chose to return to the city after their release, which Voisin believed was "entirely natural as his family and friends are there and he desires to learn a trade that can better satisfy his tastes and aptitudes. . . . Such individuals would be better served by an educational experience centered on industrial training rather than agricultural pursuits."[23] At Mettray, as Chauvaud noted, nearly 85 percent of the *colons* were engaged in jobs directly related to the cultivation of the earth.[24] Yet, of the 206 Parisian *colons* released from 1863 to 1873, only fifteen worked as cultivators or in agricultural occupations after gaining their freedom from Mettray.[25] They either returned to the capital to engage in industrial trades or other occupations, enlisted in the army, were transferred to a hospice, or had died. According to Voisin, these figures conclusively demonstrated the error of the legislation of 1850, which emphasized agricultural over industrial education.

Voisin also accused the private agricultural colonies of exploiting the labor of juveniles for pecuniary gain, because their rates of provisional liberty (i.e., early release) were lower than in public correctional colonies.[26] The figures in the report, however, are not as damning as one might expect given the inflammatory rhetoric. In 1869 the proportion of the overall population in public colonies granted early release stood at 10.72 percent, compared to 3.07 percent in private colonies; in 1874 the figures were 6.54 percent and 4.89 percent, respectively, which indicated that early releases had fallen in public colonies and increased in private institutions. An overall average for that five-year period did not appear in the report. Nevertheless, according to Voisin, "The application of provisional liberty encounters serious difficulties in private institutions reserved for young inmates. . . . The interest of such institutions is often in opposition to the interest of the children. For a young prisoner who has displayed exemplary conduct, who has become, by his diligent application, a good worker, provisional release should be the reward for his conduct and his work! Yet there is often no such reward; the director of the private prison colony understands that losing such a strong worker will be for him a serious loss."[27]

Voisin argued that it was the duty of the state, rather than private entities, to assure the education and correction of young offenders. "This fact is indisputable: the state is the tutor of young delinquents; it therefore has the duty to pursue the double goal of educating and moralizing them in its own institutions; when such an undertaking is begun, when its success must be assured, one cannot think of relegating the state to secondary status. . . . The predominant role belongs to the state."[28] Fifteen years later, Louis Herbette, director of the Penitentiary Administration, put it more bluntly: "All services having the privation of liberty as their purpose, all services which punish or correct persons, must remain in the hands of representatives of the state."[29]

While Mettray was held up as an exemplar in Voisin's report, that assessment was largely based on the committee's veneration of Demetz, who briefly served as a member before an extended illness led to his death in 1873. Foreshadowing what would become a theme in criticisms of Mettray during the late nineteenth century, Voisin noted that the parliamentarians of 1850 had assumed that administrators such as Demetz would capably helm the nascent network of agricultural colonies: "We can say that in 1850 Mettray seduced minds, it was the institution that was regarded as the true model to follow. That the legislators expected a similar state of perfection in other such institutions we can understand. . . . The legislators of 1850, with their eyes still fixed on Mettray and its founder, who always spoke with a warmth of soul and with a religious zeal, mistakenly believed that other devotees capable of ensuring the success of such a moral work could be easily found. This was in error."[30] Though Voisin intended his critique to apply to all private correctional institutions, it was a direct repudiation of Mettray's mission and Demetz's romantic vision of the moral benefits he associated with life and labor in the countryside. The implication was clear: Mettray's success was a testament to Demetz's character, administrative skill, and strength of will rather than the institution's elaborate mechanisms of discipline and control. This suggested not only that Mettray's success could not be replicated but also that its own future would be in doubt after the death of its founder.

The report's criticisms of Mettray and the agricultural colony system more generally also pointed to a reconceptualization in the contemporary discourse on children. After the humiliating defeat of the Franco-Prussian War and in light of France's declining birthrate vis-à-vis Germany, social theorists and officials of the Third Republic perceived a need for the state to better protect and socialize children rather than relying on traditional structures such as the family, the church, and private philanthropy. In 1874 the young republic passed three new laws: one that prohibited the employment of children under the age of eight in factories as well as night labor for any child under the age of thirteen; the Tallon Law, which punished parents who handed over their children to traveling performers or beggars; and the Roussel Law, which protected infants placed with wet nurses by mandating state inspections of their homes.[31] In addition, state officials spent the better part of a decade reforming and secularizing public education, with passage of the normal school law of 1879, the Ferry Laws of 1881 to 1882, and finally a law in 1889 that made the state responsible for schoolteachers' salaries and thus better able to control what was taught in the classroom.[32]

While the divide between republicans and Catholics in late nineteenth-century France is often overstated, the French state's efforts to develop a comprehensive secular school system ran into fierce resistance from those who supported the extensive system of religious schools that had arisen since the passage of the Falloux Law in 1850. Under the auspices of the law, in these schools religious instruction was provided alongside traditional academic subjects such as reading, writing, and arithmetic. Moreover, unlike teachers in laic schools, those who taught in Catholic schools were not required to possess a teaching credential (*brevet de capacité*). The law also effectively encouraged local municipalities to turn their primary schools over to Catholic congregations by requiring only a minimal level of public investment, usually around 10 percent of an annual budget.[33] The result, as Raymond Grew and Patrick J. Harrigan have noted, was a sharp increase in the number of Catholic schools in France from 1850 until republicans firmly took control of the state in 1877.[34] The implications of this church-state schism extended beyond the realm of education to include juvenile corrections and therefore played a profound role in determining Mettray's fate as an institution.

The Voisin report became the model for assessments of Mettray in the years after its release. In the early 1880s republican newspapers began to criticize the colony, characterizing Mettray as an artefact of a bygone era and an institution that was harshly punitive, exploitative, and ultimately ineffective in educating and moralizing its charges. Sigismond Lacroix (né Zygmunt Krzyżanowski), a naturalized Polish émigré active in local and national politics and a frequent contributor to the socialist daily *Le Radical*, considered Mettray's mission and method to be wholly antiquated.[35] As a member of the Conseil général de la Seine, which was engaged in discussions regarding *moralement abandonnés* (children who were neglected by their parents and/or had engaged in prostitution, begging, or vagrancy),[36] Lacroix and several of his colleagues visited Mettray and came away disappointed. "Mettray must have been a considerable advance at the time it was founded. Unfortunately, the institution has remained frozen in its original mode, so today it is backward. Nothing has changed in the system from its first hours: they continue to apply the same rules that were posed at its beginning, without bringing into everyday practice the passion for innovation that animated its founder."[37] Echoing Voisin's charges of exploitation, Lacroix decried what he saw as an overemphasis on manual labor rather than a focus on education, "which is certainly a lucrative practice for the establishment. Clearly, the great concern of administrators at Mettray is less to reeducate the *colons* than to generate a respectable figure of income. . . . The greater part of this sum is furnished by the cultivation of its considerable land, and this cultivation is almost entirely the work of the 650 children who are detained there."[38]

In a second article that appeared two days later, Lacroix noted that although the colony "obeys the letter of the Penal Code" and *colons* are not "further corrupted, the corrupt do not improve." He also asked if there was not something more that society could do to address the problem of juvenile crime. "What society owes these young culprits, whom it admits acted without discretion, is an education in preparation for modern life" rather than a bygone agrarian era. Because Mettray failed to train *colons* in an industrial trade, "they do not develop a taste for work; as for freedom, it only makes them desire it without preparing them for it." The result was that "prisons are comprised of a rather large number of *colons* from Mettray. While the records of the establishment do not give the statistics of those who go wrong, the offices of the Ministry must surely know."[39] The recidivism rates claimed in Mettray's annual reports were extraordinarily low—typically between 4 and 5 percent—and substantially below national averages. Whether Lacroix was insinuating that the numbers were in some measure falsified is unclear.

These same criticisms appeared in Henri Rochefort's strident political daily *La Lanterne*. Adopting the same rhetorical framing deployed by Lacroix, Rochefort wrote that while Mettray "must have been a considerable advance in 1839, the world has marched on and it has become old-fashioned." He also similarly alludes to the problem of recidivism, pointing to "considerable proportion of men who were once at Mettray, but are now in New Caledonia, in the bagne," an institution with which he was well acquainted as a former deportee to the South Pacific island.[40] Most noteworthy is Rochefort's direct repudiation of Jean Blanchard, Demetz's immediate successor, and Mettray's military regime more generally. According to Rochefort, "The director is not an evidently wicked man, but he seems to have far too much confidence in the virtue of the *cachot*. How can one think well of this practice in which children spend long hours in complete darkness? We believe that Mettray has an absolutely repressive character."[41] While the author did not explicitly say that he had visited Mettray, he nevertheless described a military-style processional: "There is the arrangement of children in military formation, under the command of an adjutant. The fanfare sounds a march. The children march in silence. There is something about the parade that is disturbing. Outside of the music, it is always the same silence. The trampling of the herd. Every child but a molecule. We feel that his little personality is absorbed by the whole colony." The imposition of this regime, according to Rochefort, left *colons* enervated: "They come back into life with the imprint of this discipline, which kills their initiative once home. This does not build strong character. Do we want them to be liked caged birds who do not know what to do with their new-found freedom?"[42]

Governmental scrutiny of the colony intensified after the resignation of Blanchard in 1884 due to ill health (he died later that same year following a series of strokes). He had been one of the original twenty students who attended Mettray's normal school on its opening. Named first assistant to both Demetz and Brétignières de Courteilles, Blanchard accompanied them to the prison at Fontevraud to retrieve Mettray's first *colons* in 1840.[43] Over more than four decades, he served in various capacities—*chef de famille*, clerk, inspector, *sous-directeur*, and even mayor of the village of Mettray—before being named Demetz's successor. All departmental prisons, *maisons centrales*, and agricultural youth colonies, private as well as public, were under the general direction of the Prison Administration and the authority of the Ministry of the Interior.[44] Thus, while Mettray's board of directors had recommended that Blanchard be named director, he could not be officially appointed to the post without ministerial approval.

According to contemporary newspaper accounts, Blanchard's *sous-directeur*, M. Arnould, was initially seen as his natural successor by those who worked in the colony, including the outgoing director. Like Blanchard, Arnould had passed through Mettray's normal school and according to the conservative Parisian daily *Le Petit Journal*, "presented the same great qualities for the management of the colony where he had lived and worked since his childhood."[45] For reasons that are not entirely clear (they may have had to do with charges of financial impropriety), Mettray's board of directors thought otherwise and instead nominated M. Malval, who had been dismissed from his position as *conseiller à la cour* from Poitiers following his strident opposition to Jules Ferry's March Decrees of 1880, which closed the houses of religious orders and prohibited congregations from directing or teaching in any educational establishment. Because of Malval's opposition to the Law on the Freedom of Higher Education and his refusal to adhere to its Article 7[46]—and to the "Order of Expulsions of Congregations" (29 March 1880), which called for the dissolution of the Jesuit order within three months after its promulgation[47]—the ministry rejected his nomination. More than four hundred magistrates,[48] including Malval, had resigned their offices rather than enforce the decree, which likely explains Malval's interest in the position of director at Mettray.

In this context, Roger-Marie De Cayla—who had been director of the *colonie agricole* at Casabianda, on Corsica, for over a decade—was appointed Mettray's director on 7 December 1884. As a staunch republican, it is unlikely that his candidacy was supported by a majority of the board of directors, or by those who worked in the colony. While it is not entirely clear how De Cayla's nomination and hiring came about, the Catholic newspaper *L'Univers* speculated, "The board had made the choice of a former magistrate of great value, but the government did not agree and refused their recommendation; he was probably seen as too capable of continuing the work of Christian moralization so nobly undertaken by the founders."[49] Casabianda would soon be closed as a public health measure—the colony had suffered from chronic sanitary problems and periodic bouts of malaria during its eighteen years of operation—so the postition at Mettray was a fortuitous opportunity for the *chevalier de la Légion d'honneur* to begin anew. According to Ramsland, the directors who followed in the footsteps of Demetz and Blanchard were "not nearly as impressive. They were retired civil servants or retired military officers who did not have the same dedication and idealism of the first two administrators. Some saw their position as a sinecure. Others overemphasized the military characteristics of the institution because of their background."[50]

De Cayla held his post at Mettray for only two years before being sacked. The charge that he was an incapable administrator who had been shuffled from post to post by the Penitentiary Administration was a common refrain in conservative newspapers following his departure from Mettray. *L'Univers* claimed that De Cayla "was at seventeen houses before taking his position at Mettray, where he was about to undo the eighteenth."[51] Yet, he was characterized in a parliamentary investigation of penitentiary regimes as an "energetic director" at Casabianda and was praised for recognizing the need for additional doctors to treat sick prisoners.[52] According to the Conseil général d'Indre-et-Loire, which sent a delegation to visit the colony in 1885, "The universal fame of Mettray is destined to grow under the capable direction of M. De Cayla, with the assistance of his elite staff." They also remarked that although his administration appeared "to give the colony a more military appearance than in the past," this was a welcome trend that the delegation believed should be encouraged. Indeed, they recommended that the local prefect contact the war ministry to provide rifles to better simulate military training and drills in the colony.[53] What they did not know at the time of their visit was that Mettray's new director had taken on a monumental charge to modernize the colony, principally through reforms related to budget and personnel, presumably at the behest of the ministry and with at least the tacit support of Eugène Goüin, *sénateur inamovible*, who was president of Mettray's board of directors, the Conseil d'administration de la Société paternelle, from 1881 to 1904.[54]

In a remarkable stream of correspondence addressed to Goüin, the director claimed that Mettray's past administrative culture, particularly under Blanchard, had long been marked by graft and corruption: "MM. Blanchard and Arnould [Blanchard's presumed successor], who appeared to receive only normal salaries on paper, were in fact receiving much more. . . . I do not have to look far to understand the reason why we may have wanted to ignore the real situation. It may have been to prevent jealousies between employees, or because the real figures frightened the board, but it is certain that the accounts have never expressed the true details of expenditures that have been carried on off the books."[55] In the same missive he also complained of oddly elevated salaries for other employees (e.g., 3,700 francs for a steward, 5,400 francs for an instructor) and an overabundance of nuns, ten of whom staffed the infirmary, laundry, kitchen, and commissary, where "no more than four would be sufficient."[56] De Cayla ultimately recommended the implementation of a broad plan to economize that would necessitate the elimination of numerous posts and the termination of several longtime employees whose services he believed were no longer needed.

While Mettray had enjoyed a stellar reputation throughout its first thirty years, the one area of its operation that had always drawn the most scrutiny was its cost, particularly the cost of personnel. Even supporters such as the Count A. de Tourdonnet, who saw Mettray as the standard by which to measure the "costs and benefits"[57] of expanding the network of agricultural colonies at home and abroad to include orphaned and abandoned children, noted that "it must be admitted that it would be materially impossible to establish on the whole surface of France a system of education in line with that of Mettray. . . . Mettray cannot be regarded as a typical colony that can serve as an absolute model. The character of severity and active surveillance affected by the work, the conditions in which the colony is situated, the exaggerated size of the population, and the excessive proportion of employees would not be suitable for establishments of preventive education."[58] In lauding Mettray's effectiveness while lamenting its cost, M. Gillon, a delegate of the Comité de travail de l'Assemblée nationale (of the Meuse), had reached a similar conclusion some eighteen years earlier: "There has been much criticism of Mettray, so commendable in so many other respects, but for its luxury of personnel, which would have prompted the ruin of any other less well-established institution. . . . That one could do it more cheaply we cannot deny, but that we could obtain results as complete and successful we would have a hard time believing. . . . It is a long and difficult mission to accomplish, which requires constant monitoring and a large staff."[59]

When faced with these criticisms, Demetz consistently maintained, "To this objection we content ourselves with replying: Mettray does a lot of good. The limited number of our recidivists makes it possible to be convinced of it. One must understand that our children are the object of our constant paternal solicitude; indeed, there are no other means by which we can contribute to their moralization and secure their future."[60] Defenders of the institution such as Bonneville de Marsangy echoed Demetz's mantra: "'Mettray,' say a few, 'is excellent in every respect and gives wonderful results, but it is too expensive.' What is truly expensive, indeed, is the corruption of morals, it is the disgrace of families, it is the disorder, and it is the crime! And those who make the singular criticism of Mettray being too expensive have not thought about how the colony saves the state from the expenses surrounding a crime that would require ten or twenty years of atonement in prison."[61] In his pamphlet that was sold on behalf of the Société paternelle, Huot, too, noted: "Those who repeat this objection: 'Mettray costs too much,' forget that this establishment and its analogues, created either by private individuals or by the state, amortize the debt contracted by society vis-à-vis the beings that are abandoned and which humanity orders us to collect and moralize."[62]

While De Cayla was dissatisfied with his staff—except for the *chefs de famille*, whose dedication he found "pleasing"—his most vehement criticisms were reserved for the nuns and the priest who worked at Mettray. He repeatedly accused the nuns of having "forgotten their role as auxiliaries to the commandants whose orders they are to obey."[63] In his view, Mettray was little more than a "seminary" where children could read and write at only the most rudimentary level but knew by heart every catechism. He argued that Louis Demiault, the colony's priest, "wishes to transform Mettray into a branch of the Sacre Cœur, where there are only masses, vespers, the ringing of bells, and stupid sermons of which I've had the misfortune of hearing on one too many occasions." During one sermon, according to De Cayla, Demiault addressed the colony and declared. "We find ourselves in difficult times when authority is not in the hands of whom it should be. We must pray and invoke Providence for our nation so that we can avoid further misfortune." The director complained to Goüin and to the local diocese that by speaking in such a fashion, the priest was "not teaching children to respect authority and that he should not utter such words in an institution that is supported by the state." Much to De Cayla's dismay, his complaints did not lead to any disciplinary sanctions from either the board or local religious authorities.[64]

Adopting a tone that was alternately self-pitying and self-aggrandizing, De Cayla characterized the challenge that lay ahead in reforming Mettray's local administration:

> I am the only one here who must deal with the economic situation and the long-standing employees, particularly the nuns and foremen, who abuse their positions. . . . While Mettray has the appearance of a family

it is more akin to a city during a civil war. I have been met with true obstructionists who engage in malice and slander. . . . It is these same people who always interpret and question any reform of the colony as bad. I have unveiled the colony's wounds and its difficulties. . . . I do what I must, but I cannot deny that my health deteriorates.[65]

While presumably awaiting some official sign of approval from the board of directors before proceeding with his reform plan, De Cayla wrote in October 1886: "I proposed these measures knowing full well that they would be distressing, but we must make some sacrifices that would never happen otherwise. We cannot reform inveterate habits, we cannot make people industrious who do not know how to use their time. We must remove this veritable army of so-called employees, all of whom mutually reject work and do absolutely nothing."[66] The director failed to appreciate the irony in his assertion that it was impossible to "reform inveterate habits" or "make people industrious," which was Mettray's raison d'être, at least as it pertained to its young denizens.

Why De Cayla was so candid in his communications remains an open question. Had Mettray's director been given some sort of assurance that his position would remain secure while he undertook reforms? There are references in De Cayla's missives to the Vicomte Fernand de Villiers—the nephew of Brétignières de Courteilles, who at the time was serving as both vice president and secretary general on Mettray's board of directors—which seem to indicate that the viscount may have supported the idea of reform.[67] Yet, there are no written directives or letters from de Villiers, or for that matter, from Goüin that corroborate such an understanding. Both men had been affiliated with Mettray for four decades—de Villiers was appointed *directeur-adjoint* by Demetz in 1847 and Goüin began his service as chief of Mettray's finance committee in 1846—so neither was likely to support a thorough overhaul of the colony's personnel, particularly in view of the implication that they had failed to notice longtime financial corruption among the staff. They were also not likely be in accord with De Cayla's anticlerical sensibilities and any plan to ultimately laicize the colony. Nevertheless, the director apparently felt secure enough in his position to speak openly of the need for reform, even with those who might conceivably thwart his efforts.

There is nothing in the historical record that explains exactly what led to De Cayla's termination, but the action was officially taken on 4 December 1886. In a pointed response addressed to Goüin the following day, De Cayla maintained that he had only been doing what was asked of him. He wrote: "The shock of your decision yesterday has left me absolutely crushed. . . . In seeking to put a stop to all the abuses that are present at Mettray, I have excited—despite showing the utmost moderation—the hatred of those who work here, and the hatred of the board of directors, who don't know the situation, which makes them the victim as well." Given the tone of his earlier communications, one might argue with De Cayla's claim of moderation, yet he clearly felt that he had been misled. "You told me that you would help me and that you would be on my side. . . . I was told when I first arrived that the Board would never undertake the work and the effort necessary to be rid of these hypocritical and sycophantic rodents. 'It will be easier for them to dismiss you,' they said, which is what has now occurred. . . . God, I hope that one day you will come to regret this determination."[68]

Conservative newspapers reported that De Cayla had resigned his post, rather than that he been abruptly terminated, presumably because the board wished to avoid the possibility that the salacious details of his accusations might become public. According to *L'Univers*, "The last director, M. De Cayla, having tried to 'laicize' the staff and the spirit of the colony in the manner of the radicals, was blocked by the council who refused to enact his recommendations and later accepted his resignation on 14 January."[69] But the internal records tell a different story: initially, De Cayla refused to resign. He wrote to Goüin, "You tell me that I am to leave immediately, without hesitation and without motive, while you and all your miserable sycophants attack me and throw my innocent family into the blackest misery! I have rendered great service to the colony, yet I am told that I must leave and make it appear that I did so voluntarily. Oh no, I'm not in agreement with this idea. I will not leave quietly."[70] De Cayla was subsequently replaced on an interim basis by Charles Quesnel, an instructor who had worked at the colony for more than three decades.

In De Cayla's final letter, the former director excoriated Mettray and what he saw as its pervasive culture of mismanagement and abuse. He complained that the colony's administration was in complete disorder and that he was not given "a single document" or any information on his arrival. De Cayla claimed that low-level staff, particularly former *colons* who worked in the colony's slaughterhouse, had accumulated fortunes of between 100,000 to 150,000 francs—on average annual salaries of less than 2,500 francs—after working fewer than ten years at Mettray.[71] Without providing any supporting evidence, the former director maintained that such corruption was widespread. "Everyone here is the king of their little fiefdom; the butcher, the carpenter, the shoemaker and the nuns buy, sell, and traffic in all kinds of goods. What I say aloud many have only whispered: 'Mettray is a sponge from which everyone extracts the last drops.'" Perhaps most troubling was De Cayla's claim of what he had uncovered when he took up the post in late 1884: "When I arrived, I found a budget that was in a horrible state and I saw that staff expenditures were 54,000 francs annually, which is a relatively low figure. However, I was soon surprised to learn that this figure did not include bonuses which were paid for by borrowing funds from revenues generated by the Maison Pater-nelle. Thus, we paid 149,000 francs annually in salaries. Is it true that no one among the subscribers and donors knows of this practice?"[72] De Cayla refer-enced a series of codicils in Demetz's last will and testament in which Mettray's founder had supposedly indicated, with "remarkable candor," his belief that "it is necessary, to avoid reproaches which could be made, that some personnel expenses beyond those outlined in the budget should come out of the revenue generated by the Maison Paternelle."[73]

The former director also described a culture in which the corporal punish-ment of *colons* was a common practice: "The children have long been treated like slaves, brutalized and exploited. . . . It was still the practice at Mettray upon my arrival to commence punishing a child whenever a workshop supervisor complained, and God knows there are some who complain that are simply wrong in their judgments. Are there any individuals here who provide any form of moral support? No. There is nobody here who knows how to take the children and move their heart. Without threats, acts of violence, and the various forms of humiliations they employ, they are powerless."[74] It was not only supervisors but also the colony's nuns who engaged in abuse of the *co-lons*, according to the former director. He recounted the time he heard the dec-laration of a crying child who had been repeatedly slapped by a nun, and whose face and ears "were still quite red" from the beating. He characterized one nun, Sister Adalbert, as "a sort of executioner; no woman who is as bru-tal and rude as she should exercise any sort of moral influence over the in-mates. . . . The influence of these creatures is not good for the *colons*; indeed, it is harmful in the highest degree."[75]

De Cayla blustered and argued, claiming plots and conspiracies against him while citing the impossibility of getting good help, and finally became reflec-tive, if somewhat self-serving, in admitting that he had made a mistake in for-warding to the board of directors two reports, one from July 1886, and the other from October. "I took a chance in warning the board of the situation," he wrote. "While no one can say I was hiding the truth, it would appear as though the last one relative to personnel is likely what brought about my downfall. Perhaps I was too sharp and too brittle, but I worked harder than anyone else here." He concluded, with some degree of prescience, that Mettray's fate was henceforth sealed: "This institution will die for it can no longer be defended. It was a beautiful idea that could have succeeded, but not with the spirit of a sect with its lack of tolerance. Now it can only fatally arrive at the decadence of its ruin; this is what has happened to the great colony of Mettray."[76]

De Cayla's claims about financial improprieties at Mettray are unfortunately unverifiable because extant records are limited and there is no evidence of a second set of documents.[77] According to Genet's biographer, Edmund White, the novelist was convinced that the colony had been hugely profitable and that the administration had pocketed the state stipends provided for each *colon*, spending only a "fraction of that sum" on their upkeep. Indeed, Genet claimed that "Demetz and his heirs had made enormous fortunes,"[78] and in his correspondence with various parties interested in founding their own agricultural colonies there are scattered allusions to the immense potential for profit at the heart of the enterprise. As Oliver Davis indicated, Genet's allegations about "egregious accounting irregularities [were] far from being the private delusion of his ailing, self-sedated mind" prior to his death in 1986. Accusations such as this were prominent in leftwing press coverage of Mettray during the interwar period, with one allegation provoking a defamation lawsuit on behalf of the Société paternelle against the journalist Alexis Danan and the newspaper *Paris-Soir* in 1934.[79]

The curious circumstances surrounding De Cayla's departure from Mettray and the alleged financial irregularities at the colony were first reported in two Tourangelle newspapers owned by Daniel J. Wilson, the son-in-law of Jules Grévy.[80] With information likely provided by De Cayla, many of the accusations from his correspondence were repeated almost verbatim in the press. "We have been told for some time of singular things happening in the colony of Mettray. . . . For too long the direction of the colony has been abandoned to the sisters and the chaplain, before whom everyone bows humbly. . . . In this situation, it appears that the most serious accounting disorders have occurred. In the colony's recent history, an agent, a former *colon* himself, found a way in a few years to save 200,000 francs on an annual salary of 2,000."[81] Whereas republican newspapers insinuated that financial improprieties were a long-term problem at Mettray, conservative publications attributed any issues in this regard to De Cayla's mismanagement.[82] The former director attempted to refute those accusations by writing personal letters of protest to the various newspapers that had made the claims. *Le Petit Journal* noted that "M. Du Cayla [*sic*] has forwarded us a note which asserts that he did not allow the financial situation of the establishment of Mettray to become more serious than he found it; he also added that he was the victim of a cabal. This is a matter between himself and the board of directors. We have only to acknowledge his protest."[83]

De Cayla's brief and troubled stint as director is notable for two reasons. First, while we do not have the entire correspondence between the director and administration officials what does remain as part of the historical record reveals a bureaucratic turf war between the state and those who governed Mettray that continued largely unabated until the colony was closed. Second, as the murky circumstances surrounding De Cayla's departure entered the public sphere, the scandal made visible what had previously been unseen, framing Mettray's administration and staff as negligent, brutal, and corrupt reactionaries largely out of touch with progressive ideas about the care and treatment of children and youths.

Departmental inspections were a vital component of the effort by the French state to wrest control of juvenile corrections away from religious and philanthropic organizations. Inspections were conducted by republican prefects and state prosecutors, who issued reports that harshly castigated private institutions for abusive practices and insalubrious living conditions while remaining largely silent on similar problems in public colonies.[84] On 11 March 1887 two republican members of Mettray's surveillance council, M. Maurice, president of the civil tribunal in Tours, and M. Lardin de Musset, secretary general of the prefecture d'Indre-et-Loire, travelled to the colony and demanded entry to conduct an inspection. Articles 8 and 18 of the Law of 1850 had called for the creation of such councils to ensure some mechanism of oversight of all agricultural colonies, both public and private, but this visit was unusual because it was unannounced and only two members of the council attended.[85] During their visit the two men inspected the dank, unheated cells of the punishment quarter, where they discovered two *colons*, both under the age of fourteen, whose hands had been tied behind their backs with leather restraints for what appeared to be a long time. As evidenced by the unpleasant odor in the quarter, no provisions had been made for the boys to attend to their bodily needs while restrained. An inspection report was sent to the local prefect, M. Daunassau, who forwarded it on 17 March to the Ministry of the Interior, which called for an immediate investigation.

A commission of enquiry led by Jean-Pierre Boursaus, the *inspecteur général des services administratifs*, subsequently visited the colony and not only conducted interviews with staff and *colons* but also reviewed Mettray's financial records. After a four-day investigation in late March 1887, the committee determined that of the twenty-five isolation cells in the disciplinary quarter, sixteen were in a "good state" and the other nine were "less satisfactory" because they were generally unhygienic. In the words of the report, "These are the infamous cells placed beneath the chapel, some of which are veritable black dungeons that are icy and wet in the winter; we believe these should never be used, even if only for a few hours at a time"—a recommendation to which the newly appointed director, Philippe Cluze, along with President Goüin, agreed in principle. Boursaus maintained that handcuffs were not always removed at night or during meals and that some *colons* were held up to thirty or forty days in the cells. As there were no beds or cots in the quarter, children were compelled to lie on the floor to sleep and given only a blanket. He also noted that the head of the disciplinary quarter, M. Fourneau, regularly left his post while he attended to other tasks around the colony, leaving prisoners in the cells alone for extended periods of time. In addition, he asserted that two guards, Delalay and Vigneau, often slapped and kicked their charges as did the nuns, particularly Sister Adalbert.[86]

Slaps were a rather conventional form of reprimand, a "minor" type of violence that commonly occurred, as Colin Heywood has noted, in "peasant and working-class circles . . . in which parents routinely enforced discipline by slapping and beating" their children, often with a switch.[87] In other words, the corporal punishment of children in school or church settings in nineteenth-century France was far from unusual. This is not to say that the *colons* at Mettray viewed such treatment as inconsequential or that it did not have a debilitating effect. A slap is rich with import and semantic meaning beyond the physical pain it elicits because it humiliates, effectively infantilizing and emasculating the victim who is usually powerless to respond. Because there is no information in the report about whether the violence at Mettray was routinized, calculated, or spontaneous, the particular circumstances of the acts are unknown.

There is little indication in Mettray's archival record of such behavior, beyond what took place in the context of the scandal, but it is safe to assume that corporal punishment was a common and informal method of discipline. There is a wealth of evidence that guards and staff were routinely reprimanded for such acts in other juvenile colonies well into the twentieth century. Documents that detail these incidents suggest that slaps often were a staff member's attempt to reassert power. As the "verbal retorts" of *colons* demonstrate, guards had little social status at Mettray and other colonies, so it is conceivable that acts of physical violence may have been attempts to compensate for this, to reestablish their authority and manhood.

A guard at Aniane who was cited for kicking a pupil explained: "I recognize the reason for which I am reproached. But having ordered this pupil to walk straight in front of me, and having taken him by the arm, he insulted me, saying: 'Piss off, bastard.' I then hoisted my foot up to his behind and kicked him without hurting him, then he boasted in the courtyard that he was pleased because I had been seen by the director. I could not tolerate such an act of disrespect."[88] In another case, M. Pla, a staff member overseeing the colony's refectory, berated an inmate for dropping some bowls. When the boy responded "in a cavalier tone" that he had not done so on purpose and that he was not the agent's dog, Pla lost his composure, took off his tunic and cap, slapped the young man across the face, and yelled, "If you're a man, defend yourself." He later denied that the incident had taken place, but there were multiple witnesses, both inmates and staff members, all of whom verified the boy's story. The director noted that Pla's record of service was generally satisfactory but that he had "deliberately violated formal orders" by striking the child repeatedly, and that he did not have the "excuse of an undisciplined child provoking him, since it was only an incident of awkwardness and inadvertence." Pla was placed on three months' probation for his behavior.[89] Four years earlier, again in the refectory, a monitor struck a boy for stealing a piece of bread, leaving him with a black eye. The director noted that although the monitor had "no difficulty in recognizing the fault for which he was guilty, he expressed not the slightest regret, replying: 'What do you want? It was a momentary reaction.'" The agent's record indicated that he had committed similar acts while a trainee, both times in response to pupils who had taunted him. The director concluded that his "nervousness and temperament make him unfit to serve in an establishment for minors" and recommended his termination.[90] This was not just abuse; given their public nature, these acts were attempts to save face and intimidate inmates.

The public did not know at the time that one month before the surprise inspection at Mettray, René Goblet, Minister of the Interior, had issued a stern warning to the directors of all penitentiary colonies, reminding them that they were prohibited, "in the most absolute way possible, from carrying out any forms of corporal punishment, whether assault or abuse, toward pupils." This was not a mere recitation of official policy but a stern reminder that the ministry would not tolerate any dissension on this point from local administrators who in the past, according to Goblet, had "often resisted" measures that were "ongoing requirements of their service."[91] The directive was sent to prefects, who in turn were expected to convey the communiqué to local directors. The directors were instructed to acknowledge receipt of the missive and to indicate to the prefects that they understood its import.

Goblet's directive was in large measure in response to a scandal in the summer of 1886 at the colony at Porquerolles, an island located in the Mediterranean off the coast of Toulon. The longtime republican Léon de Roussen—who was editor of *La République Française* and a former secretary to Léon Gambetta, who had founded the daily in 1871—had purchased the Île d'Hyères in 1881 and transformed it into an agricultural colony via an agreement with the nascent Service des enfants moralement abandonnés de la Seine. They began on an experimental basis to place "morally endangered" boys at Porquerolles in 1883. Christened the "Centre d'éducation et de patronage des jeunes détenus mineurs," Porquerolles was an institutional hybrid: officially it was a "school of reform" for agriculture, but as Jean-Marie Guillon noted, most young residents referred to it simply as "the penitentiary." Most of its residents were drawn from the Service des enfants, but the "*colons* were poorly defined. . . . Some were orphans, but most were not, some came from parents deemed unwilling to raise them, but others from families who did not have the means to do so. Some were petty criminals, but most were street kids. Not all were 'unruly,' but all were judged in need of socialization and education through labor."[92] Roussen was rarely present on the island, and his common-law wife, Jeanne Thérèse Lapeyre, a novelist, *feuilletoniste*, and editor of the journal *La Famille*, managed the colony's day-to-day operation.[93]

On 24 July 1886, on a road outside Toulon, gendarmes arrested five boys, all under the age of fifteen. Under questioning by authorities the boys claimed they had been subject to physical abuse, neglect, and periodic bouts of acute hunger at Porquerolles. As Sylvia Schafer has noted, "inadequate food and clothing; irregular meals; the mishandling of the boys' wages . . . [and the] despotic rule of the director" were part of a regime that was "brutally harsh, bordering on cruel."[94] Review of Porquerolles's staff revealed "drunkenness, lack of pedagogical innovation, and arbitrariness," but more troubling was their practice of holding inmates for extended periods in one of the dank, dark cells in an isolated fort (Grand Langoustier) located at the edge of the island, where many inmates were trussed with hands tied behind their backs for days on end.[95] On 25 July, the day after the escaped boys had been recaptured, a revolt broke out in the colony when as many as eighty prisoners armed with knives, axes, and stones took over the fort, raising its drawbridge to make it impenetrable, in protest against the cellular imprisonment of an eight-year-old boy, whom the young rebels released.[96] The boys eventually agreed to surrender to authorities, but only if they could voice their grievances directly to the local prefect rather than to prison officials. In the aftermath, two guards were tried for abuse in the Toulon Criminal Court on 10 to 18 February 1887. Prison sentences of between one and two months were given to the guards and Lapeyre was fined 200 francs for negligence, while Roussen was forced to pay court costs. Of the nine children charged with leading the brief mutiny, five were acquitted and the others were charged symbolic fines of one franc. Roussen complained that he had not "gained" anything financially from the arrangement and that he would have been better served by "hiring some Piedmontese workers who would have done more work" at less expense. Indeed, four days before the revolt he had indicated to officials in Paris that he planned to close the colony because it was unprofitable.[97]

Adversaries of the Third Republic saw in Porquerolles an opportunity to lament the secularization of juvenile corrections as driven by a heartless bourgeoisie bent on shamelessly exploiting and mistreating children. Conservative newspapers framed the scandal at Mettray as an "act of revenge" for what had taken place at Porquerolles, an establishment founded by a prominent republican. The *Journal d'Indre-et-Loire* alleged that the inspection at Mettray was politically motivated and part of a broader effort by the republican state to divert criticism away from Porquerolles.[98] *L'Univers*, the most fervent of the conservative newspapers in its criticism of the Mettray investigation, characterized the two inspectors, Lardin de Musset and Maurice, as Freemasons and "high lords of radicalism" who were "seeking to find in a private establishment, reputedly clerical because a Christian morality is taught there, a counterpart to the scandal of Porquerolles."[99] The newspaper also mocked the impartiality and seriousness of the inspectors' discovery at Mettray: "What art to paint such horrors: 'Look what we have found! Dungeons, infected cells, arms tied behind the back in the most painful position!' Yes, at Mettray, as in all colonies, one is sometimes forced to lock recalcitrant children in cells and handcuff those who revolt, who assault their guards, who wish to plunge a knife into their stomachs. For out of one hundred children the state sends to the colony, there are at least fifty that are incorrigible, and twenty that can be forced to obey only by force."[100]

In reviewing the budget, Boursaus questioned whether the local administration's claim of a deficit of over 67,000 francs was "real or merely apparent" because "we were not provided accounting documents that would allow us to examine" the issue in greater detail, particularly records of the revenues provided by the Maison Paternelle. In support of De Cayla's claims about financial improprieties with regard to salaries, Boursaus also noted, "We can observe that there was a decrease in the number of prisoners which should be reflected in a reduction in staff whose salaries have risen to a truly enormous figure." The report concluded by asking, "Mettray, is it a legend? The work so noble and so humanitarian of M. Demetz, which was mainly intended for the moralization of *colons* has disappeared, and in its place, has been erected an institution designed for simple agricultural and industrial exploitation."[101]

On the heels of the surprise inspection, the republican press, most notably Wilson's local and regional newspapers, seized the opportunity to condemn Mettray. *La Petite France* charged that the "men who run the colony dream of a return to the state religion and regret losing the means of persuasion that existed during the Inquisition."[102] *L'Union Libérale de Tours* declared, "No cause can be more precious to defend than that of those unfortunate children bent under the merciless rod of the bigots fanaticized by cassocks."[103] Writing under the pseudonym Jean Frollo, Charles-Ange Laisant, editor of *Le Petit Parisien*, noted: "In France, however backward religious congregations may be, the general indignation which has manifested itself when acts of this kind are brought to public notice, should force them to renounce a method which is a remnant of barbarism."[104]

Beneath the anticlerical invective were real efforts to reexamine the boundaries of sanctioned correctional practices and the purpose of the agricultural colonies more generally. Paul Strauss, a republican member of the Council générale de la Seine who would later vote in favor of a measure to remove children of the Seine from Mettray, shared his impressions with the *L'Union Libérale*: "It is the system of penitentiary education which is bad; the means of correction play a too considerable role in the current configuration. Most assuredly, it is necessary to sometimes punish children; but it should not be with the temperament of a jailer."[105] This was also the viewpoint in an article in *La Lanterne* that focused on the exploitation of the *colons* at Mettray: "The establishment has a certain Protestant allure and a puritanical aspect. The spirit is hard and backwards. It acts to punish the sickness and to subject the child to a severe and harsh discipline. Regulatory punishments are applied for the slightest fault. Former detainees have spoken of dark cells and handcuffs. . . . To prepare young people for life they must be handled with care and not be placed in a state of suffering, depression and terror."[106] The radical socialist and future prime minister of France Alexandre Millerand lamented the inherent inequity of "mixing prisoners convicted by justice with children who have been morally abandoned, under the pretext of improvement in a prison house" and called for an immediate end to the practice.[107]

Because journalists were not granted access to Mettray, at least during the ongoing scandal, many relied on letters written by anonymous sources for their information, reassuring their readers (perhaps speciously) that the sources were trustworthy and reliable, usually by reference to their occupations or unique personal experiences. *La Petite France* noted the numerous unsolicited letters it had received from individuals, all of whom attested to Mettray's brutality:

> We call your attention to one of the twenty letters we have received on this subject. We know the former colon who wrote it. We have questioned him, and he has assured us that his story is true. We must also add that he is now a republican mayor in one of the principal towns in the Indre-et-Loire, which guarantees that he is an honest man. His

testimony cannot be questioned. "There was to my knowledge a type of torture which was used on a friend of mind. When a child was accused of an infraction to which he would not admit, they would put his face under a powerful spigot [of water] until he confessed. . . . I assure you that guilty or not, this torture is something which no one should suffer. Mettray lacks nothing, even practices belonging to the Middle Ages."[108]

A reference to what might be considered a nineteenth-century form of waterboarding also appeared in *La Justice*, where Léon Millot cited a letter from an anonymous former *colon* who, though innocent of the misdeed for which he was charged, was "placed under a powerful jet of water by guards. After a few moments, he felt as though he was suffocating" and confessed. According to Millot, "This practice, renewed from the Inquisition, was an infallible success" and a tactic "for which the interim director of the colony, M. Quesnel, is responsible."[109] *La Petite France* published a letter from another former *colon*, "now married and living in Chateaurenault," which read: "The scandal is unfortunately too true and the punishments inflicted at Mettray are most severe. There were often spankings which made one's rear end red. I have also seen children closed in the *cachots* underneath the chapel. I have seen the straightjacket used by guards during the day and night, and sometimes for as long as a week without a care for its effect." The editor noted, "This letter came from a man whom, we repeat, today, leads an honest life and is esteemed by all."[110]

Though he certainly was not a defender of Mettray, the indefatigable De Cayla wrote a letter to *La Petite France* in which he maintained that during his two years in the colony he had never resorted to placing *colons* in handcuffs, "except in two exceptional cases of extreme gravity where it was necessary to preserve the lives of guards and detainees who were menaced by two maniacs."[111] While proclaiming his own innocence, De Cayla accused members of his staff, especially workshop supervisors and the colony's nuns, of regularly abusing *colons*. He did not mention, however, that under his leadership the use of cellular confinement as a punishment had increased quite dramatically, nearly doubling from 851 placements in 1884 to 1,524 in 1885 without a corresponding increase in the total population.[112]

Once news of the surprise inspection at Mettray became public, Goblet contacted the préfet d'Indre-et-Loire to reiterate the ministry's position on the methods of discipline that should be employed in the colony. Although the handcuffs were made of leather and therefore unlikely to physically harm the wearers, their use was a form of corporal punishment that appeared to be used "in all sorts of situations." He noted that Article 96 of the Penitentiary

Administration's General Regulations (10 April 1869), which were initially conceived for the *maisons pénitentiaires* but also applied to the juvenile colonies, expressly prohibited corporal punishment of any kind. "How was it possible," Goblet asked, "that in the presence of such a formal text, and with the instructions as outlined by this administration . . . in words that even the Interim Director of Mettray should be able to understand, that such deplorable events could occur?"[113] Quesnel claimed that he never received any such instructions and that the use of handcuffs, cellular isolation, and corporal punishments had always been part of Mettray's regime.

In the eyes of the ministry, handcuffs were a "MEANS OF COERCION" (original emphasis) that should be employed only as "an absolute necessity" to protect inmates from harming themselves (e.g., a suicide attempt) or if there was an "unhealthy immorality" (i.e., masturbation). Means of coercion "should never be confused with a MODE OF PUNISHMENT" (original emphasis) because the two measures "are absolutely distinct." Nonetheless, handcuffs were not always removed at night or during meals, which consisted of bread and water for indeterminate periods——and this violated Article 101 of the General Regulations of 1869, which stipulated that prisoners could be deprived of their standard meals as a punishment for only three days at a time.[114]

Goblet's frustration with what had happened at Mettray was evident in his note to the local prefect, as was his displeasure at learning—via the inspector general's report—that it was not uncommon for *colons* to spend between twenty and forty days in cellular confinement. This duration of punishment violated still another provision of the General Regulations, Article 98, which required that the préfet d'Indre-et-Loire be formally notified any time a youth was subjected to cellular confinement for more than fifteen days. He concluded his missive by noting that corporal punishment and the use of handcuffs, cellular imprisonment, and deprivation of food were not only contrary to formal regulations but also inhumane. "The honor of our country, and the concern of the French administration forbids such punishments, even those taken against the worst criminals, and certainly without a doubt, young detainees."[115]

In response, *L'Univers* defended Quesnel and characterized the ministerial instructions prohibiting corporal punishment as naïve, misguided, and unnecessary.

It is easier to write beautiful humanitarian theories than to put them into practice. We would like to see the minister before a squad of colons. If a gamin insulted or threatened him, would he stand before them with his arms crossed? If a fifteen-year-old spat in his face, would he be content to wipe his face quietly? Experienced in the profession, M. Quesnel, a pupil of M. Demetz, knows how to employ counsel, to appeal to the sentiment of duty and honor, to encourage and reward; in this way he has acquired a great command over the minds of the colons; but as a man of experience, he is not unaware that, for certain natures, it is necessary to use rigor.[116]

The allusion to Demetz was an odd rhetorical flourish by the article's author, because Mettray's founder had forbidden all forms of corporal punishment in the colony. The memory of Demetz also had been invoked two days earlier in an article in *Le Messager d'Indre-et-Loire* that lauded Quesnel as a "veteran of his trade and a former student of Demetz" who knows better than to fall prey to "humanitarian theories which are foolish" and which could ultimately lead to a "state of revolt in the colonies."[117]

Despite these sentiments from defenders of Mettray, on his first official day on the job Philippe Cluze, Mettray's new director, demanded the resignations of Quesnel and Fourneau and formally dismissed Delalay and Vigneau, the two guards implicated in the beatings of the inmates. Sister Adalbert and another nun were withdrawn from the colony by the local diocese. Cluze also promised to adhere to the general recommendations of the commission of enquiry. Thus *colons* who had previously suffered from the cold while in the disciplinary quarter would be provided some form of bedding, either a cot or hammock. Moreover, he mandated a daily diet of soup and bread for all those in cellular confinement. Finally, physical restraints such as handcuffs and strait-jackets would be used only as a last resort and only in circumstances where the *colon* posed a physical threat to himself or others, and therefore not as a form of punishment.[118]

Although the scandal of 1887 did not result in any new legislation on the agricultural colonies, its effects on Mettray were nonetheless significant. On 26 March 1887 the physician and director of Assistance publique de la Seine, M. E. Peyron, was called before the Conseil municipal de Paris to provide, in the words of Edouard Vaillant, the socialist *conseiller municipal* representing the twentieth arrondissement, "information on the events at Mettray, which are of great concern to the public who are astonished and indignant at seeing the reproduction of the monstrosities of Porquerolles." Characterizing Mettray as an "environment of torture" and its residents as "twice abandoned: once by their parents and once by Assistance publique," Vaillant moved to immediately withdraw from Mettray all *assistés* who had come from the department. Although Peyron insisted that Mettray was not under his direction and he was not responsible for what had occurred in the colony, he was willing to accede

to Vaillant's request if given "a moral delay of a fortnight" to make the necessary arrangements for transfer. In his suggestion that the children be sent to
the Paris *dépôt de la préfecture de police* as a temporary solution—which Peyron
argued was inappropriate—Paul Strauss alluded to De Cayla's dismissal:
"Knowing the state of interregnum in which the colony of Mettray is in now
because of the change in director, which, as you know, came under the pressure of the clerical party . . . I wish to make a declaration [i.e., take a vote] here
and now." Eventually, Peyron proposed to temporarily house the youths at one
of the three children's hospitals overseen by Assistance publique, which the
council approved by a vote of forty-eight to sixteen.[119] The transfer move by
the Conseil général de la Seine reduced Mettray's population from 422 to 351
and resulted in its loss of a valuable departmental subvention.[120]

Five days later Mettray was the subject of a discussion in the Chamber of
Deputies between Dieudonné Belle, *député et conseiller général d'Indre-et-Loire*,
and Goblet. By raising the issue in the legislative assembly, Belle hoped not
only to diminish the significance of what had happened at Mettray but to also
acquit himself of any negligence as a former member of Mettray's surveillance council. Although he admitted that "serious abuses" had occurred in
the colony, he nevertheless maintained that journalists exaggerated what had
been discovered. Indeed, Belle later compared Mettray's "*cachots* with the
dungeons of the colleges of Paris; they are no more terrible. The cells are airy
and healthy."[121] He also claimed that Quesnel, as acting director, had lied to
investigators when he said that "means of correction" had always been used
in the colony: "I often saw young men forced to put on the straitjacket at night,
by order of the doctor, to stop certain excesses [i.e., masturbation]. I saw young
people who constantly attempted to escape, on whom such a regime was imposed. I saw others rushing their comrades or striking their guards and it was
necessary in these circumstances to take repressive measures. But what I never
saw was handcuffs behind the back or the cell utilized as means of coercion
and repression."[122]

In response, Goblet noted that Mettray was a private establishment governed by a board of directors and that the right of supervision over Mettray
existed only because the state placed children in the colony. Therefore, the only
sanction available to the state was the "right to withdraw the children it maintains there."[123] Interestingly, however, the minister revealed that throughout
the early days of the scandal he had been in contact with Goüin, who had said
that if there were abuses in the colony "he wished to put an end to it, and he
made a commitment, on behalf of the board, to accept all the measures that
I proposed." Thus, the state, in coordination with Mettray's board, had sanctioned those involved in the scandal, albeit not juridically as in the case of

Porquerolles. Goblet's response not only illuminated how the porous border between public and private made oversight difficult but also underscored the ambiguous space that Mettray occupied within the larger carceral network.

Following the lead of the department of the Seine, Charles Caillé, a republican member of the Conseil général d'Indre-et-Loire, sponsored a similar measure to remove *colons* from Mettray's host department and to suppress its annual subvention. Goüin was called before the council to speak on Mettray's behalf and it was clear that he intended to defend the institution at all costs. He maintained that unlike other private colonies that had been established to generate profits for their founders, Mettray was an "exclusively charitable" institution whose revenues "had always been used to perfect the establishment." While acknowledging that there were "imperfections and abuses" in the regime, he noted that "corporal punishment was admitted twenty years ago, not only in correctional educational institutions, but even in colleges," and that apart from the recent incidents at Mettray, "whenever a lower officer had hit a child" in the past "that officer was either severely reprimanded or even dismissed." Moreover, it was not the colony's founders, according to Goüin, but "an Inspector General of the state" who had first recommended the use of the *férule* (a leather-wrapped baton or stick) to discipline recalcitrant *colons*. Despite the inquiry's findings on the poor condition of many cells in the disciplinary quarter, Goüin claimed that they were "as good as those of the Tours penitentiary, and that all the inspectors, as well as all the members of the General Council who had visited, never criticized them." Finally, he addressed the use of handcuffs only to say that their use was authorized by the regulations of the ministry of the interior and that it remained an open question whether they were applied "as means of coercion or as a means of punishment."[124]

The majority of Goüin's address focused on what he called the "religious and political" issue that in his view was one of the primary reasons for the "attacks" on the colony. While proponents of secularization had argued that "children spend only a few hours each day in school and that religious instruction should therefore take place in the home," Goüin said that this was a moot point for an "establishment like Mettray, which is both a school and family for children." Thus "the administration would fail in all its duties if it did not provide the *colons* religious instruction. Among the *colons* there are very vicious children who have been corrupted by their parents. To try to correct these children, to bring them back to good without telling them about God, is to attempt a task that the administrators of Mettray cannot accept." The president added that the issue of religion at Mettray was never about crafting a political identity in its subjects. "The men who run this establishment have never been occupied with the political question. It is not a question of making the *colons* into republicans, Bonapartists or royalists. It is simply about making them honest citizens, respectful of the government, their country and its ordinary laws." He closed by asking the councillors to not follow the example of the department of the Seine and to "reject the proposal of M. Caillé, in memory of M. Demetz, in the memory of the glory that this man of good acquired, a part of which reflects upon the goodwill of the General Council," which had supported Mettray for nearly half a century.[125]

The prefect of Indre-et-Loire, Daunassau, recognized that Mettray "has provided a great service and can still do so, [but] it has, in recent years, been in complete decline." Adopting the critique of De Cayla—that Mettray was dominated by a cadre of long-serving lower-level personnel—he maintained that "little by little, the individuals of the lower orders have become preponderant, so much so that the one who has the least influence in the colony is the director himself." Daunassau also observed that the "most severe punishments, which, under the terms of the 1869 regulation, can only be initiated by the director, who is obligated to inform the prefect," were instead inflicted by lower-level staff at their discretion, a "fact that the honorable M. Goüin and the colony's board of trustees was unaware of." The prefect then proceeded to read into the record a copy of the ministerial letter sent to Quesnel that explicitly prohibited corporal punishment, noting his dismay that the president of the colony's board had failed to address the issue. "To this day," he remarked, "I have never received any communication concerning the prescriptions of this letter." Daunassau concluded that it was "undeniable that abuses occurred at Mettray: they occurred without the knowledge of the Board of Directors and they are attributable to a sub-order which, little by little, has replaced the directorate." Goüin responded that the ministerial instructions had been given to Cluze and that Mettray's new director had pledged to strictly enforce them. Because Cluze had just taken up his post, the council voted fourteen to six to reject Caillé's proposal to abolish the subvention, but they included an amendment that stipulated the issue would be revisited in August, by which time they could better assess Mettray's commitment to change.[126]

While Goüin was defensive in the April meeting, he nonetheless acknowledged that abuses had taken place and that reform was necessary. The tone of the meeting the following August, however, was much more contentious. M. Oudin, an attorney from Tours, opened the meeting by reading into the record a new inspection report compiled by a special commission charged by the Conseil d'Indre-et-Loire with visiting Mettray and reporting its findings. For the most part, the document focused on finances, education, and the practice of religion in the colony. Oudin noted that although "we do not have to assess whether there is a lack of order from an economic point of view, as Mettray is a private institution, we have been slow to discover the method of accounting that has been followed; and nothing else has been furnished to us on this subject, except upon request, and then only summary explanations." The report also claimed that education had never been given the same emphasis as religious instruction and that although it had improved in recent years with the addition of some "capable teachers" (before this, education purportedly consisted of *chefs de famille* reading aloud to their family's *colons*), it was "easy to see" in the classrooms that many of the pupils were illiterate. Deeply troubled by Mettray's religious orientation, the authors of the report supported De Cayla's remarks almost entirely, noting, "The child is treated as if he has entered one of the religious orders in a monastery; there are masses, vespers, the ringing of bells, and sermons. . . . While we respect all beliefs, permit us to say that this is perhaps not the best mode of moral education for young prisoners."[127]

Georges Houssard, a member of Mettray's board of directors, took the floor to reply to M. Oudin's *réquisitoire* (indictment) and demanded to know if the commission would vote on the measure to reject the 2,000-franc grant. Oudin angrily protested against Houssard's use of the term indictment to characterize the report, noting that "the defenders of Mettray were supplicants at the April meeting, promising to give all satisfaction. Yet, is everything now in order? The commission does not think so. It has found in the leadership a spirit that is not in line with that of the majority of the General Council and the country. . . . The colony of Mettray cannot boast of being what it ought to be; because, if all is in order, it is only thanks to the efforts of the superior administration which sought to address and eliminate the abuses." Houssard replied, "It was M. Goüin's honor to defend Mettray before the General Council [in April]. But since he has been good enough to allow me to appear before you, I can say that on behalf of the colony that honor is worth more than money. The colony of Mettray would prefer not to receive a subsidy if it comes at the cost of listening to the criticisms that have just been made."[128] At this point Goüin interrupted the proceeding to say that the archbishop of Tours had informed him the previous day that M. Demiault—the priest who had uttered the impertinent statement regarding the republic—would be replaced, and that Mettray's financial situation would be addressed through the sale of lands that it had acquired over the years. Mettray would retain, according to Goüin, "only three hundred hectares to justify the continued use of the sobriquet *colonie agricole*."[129] Notwithstanding these promises, the general council voted against awarding the annual subvention, marking an ignominious end to the scandal of 1887.

In a May 1888 address to Mettray's Société paternelle, Director Cluze characterized the surprise inspection and the journalistic coverage of the previous year's scandal as a "perfidiously organized campaign . . . the very violence of which was shocking to people of good faith." Cluze took pains to point out that the affair was not only "far from the infamous scandal [of Porquerolles] depicted for a period of three months by some newspapers of the Indre-et-Loire and even the capital . . . [but also] a far cry from the facts that were reported at the establishment of Porquerolles."[130] Nevertheless, the publicity had "added to the enormous difficulties" of his position. "I cannot conceal the fact that these newspaper articles, which cannot be prevented from penetrating into such a large colony, and where the children live almost at liberty, led to a very great relaxation of discipline. It has taken all authority, firmness, and my experience of command to take control of the situation and to keep our population calm." While Cluze did not wish to give the impression that there was a possibility of "serious collective acts, let alone rebellion," he did say that formal refusals to work, individual acts of insubordination, and escapes, especially among inmates between the ages of twelve and sixteen, "had become so frequent that they can only be explained by the events which took place shortly before my arrival . . . and a softening of the disciplinary regime" more generally.[131]

Cluze's claim that the negative publicity surrounding the affair had somehow fomented unrest in the colony was questionable, but what is more striking is his suggestion that the previous regime—the one that had been so harshly criticized for its treatment of its charges—had been lax. The director insisted that "there is no authority without a firm and vigorous discipline" and that "children of this age appear to be little afraid of the punishment of the cell." Thus, while Cluze promised to put an immediate stop to the "abuses pointed out by the inspector general" and to "scrupulously [observe] the regulations of 10 April 1869 in all its parts," he also expressed his "firm resolve to repress all that might infringe upon the principle of authority" in the colony.[132] Given his description of cellular confinement as an insufficient deterrent or remedy for recalcitrance and his juxtaposition of the Penitentiary Administration regulations with his own continued commitment to the maintenance of "authority," it does not seem that Cluze was particularly troubled by what had unfolded prior to his arrival at Mettray.

This chapter began by asking how Mettray's administration and staff, so widely acclaimed during the first three decades of the colony's existence, came to be branded by critics as brutal and incompetent. Certainly the inquiries, both administrative and journalistic, that detailed the corporal punishment of prisoners and the financial irregularities were deeply troubling, as was the institution's adherence to a "clerical" regime amid the ongoing church-state conflict. These were not criminal investigations, as those at Porquerolles had been, but they did establish the basis for institutional reform, including staff dismissals. Only lower-level staff lost their positions as the result of the scandal, but the reluctance of administrators to fully embrace the progressive tenets of corrections advocated by the Penitentiary Administration effectively undermined the coherence of the state's rehabilitational rhetoric and the plausibility of its preferred narrative of reformation. Despite their promises to eliminate the abuse of prisoners, neither Goüin nor Cluze were sensitive enough to the winds of political change to recalibrate Mettray's regime accordingly. Finally, it is important to recognize the role of the sensationalist press in framing workers at Mettray as negligent managers and clerical reactionaries, as well as the interplay of reform rhetoric and the practice of politics. It is no coincidence that there were so many young republican and socialist firebrands among Mettray's harshest critics, many of whom would go on to occupy important positions of political power in the years ahead. The popular support for a crusade against an institution that had once commanded vast public approval suggests that a generational turnover was afoot and that understandings of the juvenile delinquent were in a state of flux. While the details of the scandal of 1887 faded from popular consciousness, Mettray's reputation never truly recovered. France's most acclaimed carceral institution was entering a new age in which children and adolescents had gained an unprecedented valence and political presence—a prospect that those who administered Mettray were unwilling or unable to accommodate.

CHAPTER 5

Maison Paternelle

Tired of his son Gaston's increasingly debilitating habit of imbibing ether and his morose behavior following an unrequited infatuation with an English cancan dancer, Émile Contard, the manager of a textile factory in Marseilles, sent the fifteen-year-old to the Maison Paternelle, which opened on the grounds of the Mettray agricultural colony in January 1855.[1] The purpose of the Maison Paternelle was to resocialize bourgeois youth who had not broken any laws but whose recalcitrant behavior—particularly as it pertained to their schooling—was seemingly beyond the control of their parents. Unlike the *colons* of Mettray, whose upkeep was financed partially through a state subvention, the boys held in the Maison Paternelle were supported by their parents who paid boarding and tutorial fees of between 300 and 500 francs per month to have their sons housed and educated in a facility that bore many similarities to a traditional prison. Because each youth spent most of his day inside a locked room, alone except for the periodic visits from various tutors who were to engage him in intense academic studies in preparation for university, communication between students in the Maison Paternelle was not possible.[2] Situated behind the colony's chapel and attached by a common wall, the entrance to the building was enclosed behind an iron gate, and because the structure contained no outward-facing windows, residents never saw each other.[3]

Maison Paternelle.

FIGURE 9. Maison Paternelle, vue extérieure.

On 12 January 1909, five days after his arrival, Gaston Contard fashioned a noose from two cravats and hanged himself from the beam that stretched across the narrow expanse of his room. The suicide was sensationalized in the press and resulted in a wide-ranging inquiry by public prosecutors who charged the institution's director with illegal imprisonment, a crime that could draw a sentence of up to twenty years hard labor.[4] Although the affair has drawn the attention of a few historians, most notably Frédéric Chauvaud and John Ramsland, what has gone largely unexamined is how the incident illuminated a long-standing divide between those who believed in parental discretion over judicial oversight and those who argued that the state had an obligation to protect its youngest citizens—a duty that superseded the rights of the father.[5]

The Napoleonic Code granted extraordinary authority to the father, who if "grievously dissatisfied" with the conduct of his child could commit the youth to prison for up to one or six months (if the child was under the age of sixteen or eighteen, respectively).[6] The one limitation on this power of "paternal correction" was that he must obtain a court order from a local magistrate approving his request to incarcerate. As there were no formal written documents required outlining the reason for the request, this was a legal formality and court orders were rarely denied.

During the late nineteenth century, however, the right of paternal correction increasingly came under fire from social critics and government officials who viewed the practice as a legal anachronism not unlike the *lettres de cachet* of the ancien régime.[7] The Law of 24 July 1889 represented one of the first efforts by liberal legislators to curtail the power of paternal correction as the state began to initiate investigations and assume legal custody of minors whose parents abused the practice for reasons of economic expediency or personal convenience.[8] Although parents rarely resorted to paternal correction—on average, no more than 1,000 adolescents per year were imprisoned under this provision between 1851 and 1896[9]—the new law had great symbolic significance because it granted judicial authorities discretionary power to determine the best interests of the minor, thereby serving as a check on paternal correction. As Kristin Stromberg Childers has noted, the law "marked a decisive change in the boundaries between public and private life established by Napoleonic law and signaled a new progression in the fortunes of paternity in France."[10]

The Contard affair raised a basic legal and sociological question: was the Maison Paternelle a prison or a school? If it was a prison, then the state insisted that it was the ultimate arbiter—via the court order—in determining who was admitted. If it was a school, however, then the father had the inalienable right to have his son housed and educated as he saw fit and without judicial interference. Although it had the physical characteristics of a prison—bars, locks, iron gates, heavy doors, and a regime based on the strict segregation and isolation of its residents—officials of the Maison Paternelle insisted that it was a "college," akin to a boarding school, and therefore not subject to the court order.

This dichotomy became entwined with issues of paternal power and correction in the judicial investigation and legal debate surrounding the scandal at the Maison Paternelle. A wide variety of authorities not attached to the institution—jurists, criminologists, educators, penologists, and philanthropists—inveighed on the subject via local and national newspapers, professional journals, and international prison congresses. What was at stake in the wake of Contard's suicide was a disciplinary practice that had been private, removed from the public gaze, and by extension, exempt from public authority.

Not unlike the *colons* of Mettray, students in the Maison Paternelle were not simply passive objects of social control; they had some degree of agency. But their protests were aimed not at the institution where they were housed but at the investigation into its operation by state officials who saw themselves as the defenders of abused and mistreated children. Although the director was eventually acquitted of illegal imprisonment, the Maison Paternelle closed its doors amid the unfavorable publicity surrounding the suicide and the state continued to advance its claims over France's troubled youth in the early twentieth century.

Writing five years after its opening, Demetz maintained that the Maison Paternelle was a direct response "to one of the most serious needs of our time," as it addressed "an immense lacuna which existed in our system of education. . . . Before the foundation of our Maison Paternelle, parents not wishing to lock up their [ill-behaved] children in prison found themselves fully disarmed. And for school principals whose students had tried their patience, the only means of repression available to them was expulsion; but this expedient compromised the future of the student without remedying the evil."[11] Thus Demetz problematized not only the poor and working-class youths of Mettray but also bourgeois youths whom he viewed as "increasingly undisciplined."[12] At the 1872 international penal congress in London the American penologist Enoch Wines declared that the French educational system provided no remedies for misbehavior other than expulsion, which "is welcomed by the idle youth as a relief from what is felt by him to be an intolerable burden."[13] H. Latham, a university official from Cambridge who visited the Maison Paternelle in 1870, similarly remarked, "Expulsion has little terror for a young boy. He is glad to quit the lyceum. . . . The sting of expulsion lies in parental displeasure; but in most of these cases 'the incensed father' has been brought into action so often that the prospect has lost its terror."[14] As he had done with the Mettray colony, Demetz opened the Maison Paternelle to a wide variety of visitors from both France and abroad who were studying how to better tame and train troublesome youths. Although such visits grew increasingly rare over time, particularly after Demetz's death in 1873, they were part of a sustained public relations and marketing campaign intended to generate positive publicity for the fledgling institution.

The Maison Paternelle consisted of thirty separate rooms/cells of approximately ten feet by eight feet arrayed along two hallways or wings that radiated out from a central atrium. In the door of each cell was a peephole—similar to those used by the *chefs de famille* in the colony proper—that allowed functionaries to keep watch over the pupils, encouraging work and preempting any manifestation of misbehavior, particularly masturbation.

Whereas students at Mettray were taught, at least initially, in a traditional classroom setting, learning in the Maison Paternelle was structured around solitary contemplation away from all outside distractions. Each day began at 5:00 a.m. when the young men were awakened by staff and ordered to make their beds, clean their rooms, and make themselves presentable (there were no uniforms; students wore their own clothes).[15] Following a prayer and breakfast, each student was visited by various professors who conducted individu-

II. Colonie de METTRAY — Vue Intérieure de la Maison Paternelle

FIGURE 10.   Maison Paternelle, vue intérieure.

alized lessons in subjects such as Latin, history, French, German, and mathematics. Because these lessons were intended to prepare the young men to sit for the *baccalauréat*, the curriculum was starkly different from the education provided to the working-class and poor youths in Mettray, which emphasized manual labor and rote learning.

By most accounts this pedagogy was relatively successful; of the twenty-six pupils who took the *baccalauréat* from 1892 to 1894, eighteen passed. These results were not atypical, and observers such as the jurist Georges Delegorgue believed that they were "all the more remarkable when one considers that these young people were distinguished only by their laziness, their dissipation, and their indiscipline."[16] In its emphasis on the *baccalauréat* the Maison Paternelle catered to a clientele desperate for their sons to pass the examination to gain access to the liberal professions and thereby advance socially in the new, meritocratic republic.

The Maison Paternelle was promoted as providing an opportunity for lazy or underperforming youngsters to mend their ways and perhaps even gain a competitive advantage over their cohorts, particularly during the summer when their rivals were enjoying their vacations and not actively engaged in their studies or in preparing for the *baccalauréat*. Demetz effectively played on the anxieties of bourgeois parents, proclaiming, "It is especially during school vacation that the regime of the Maison Paternelle is of a salutary application. . . . While other students are relaxing, students in our institution are hard at work."[17] The magistrate Arnould Bonneville de Marsangy similarly maintained, "It is with the approach of summer vacation when requests for admission typically grow. . . . Every intelligent father is repulsed by the thought of his son, who has done nothing for an entire school year and has been the recipient of continual reproaches, being rewarded with a vacation at a time of year when the weather is beautiful and there are festivals and distractions of every kind which should be enjoyed only by those children who are meritorious and laborious."[18]

Although the Maison Paternelle had a stated mission of education, it also had a punitive purpose that "puts into the hands of the father a powerful weapon in the battle over authority" in the household.[19] The mere prospect of a stay in the Maison Paternelle was intended to deter bad behavior. Latham maintained that it "is held up 'in terrorem' by parents and school masters to overawe the rebellious spirit. . . . Teachers and others all declare that some such punishment is necessary as a terror, something which should take hold of the imagination of young men; and thus the mystery attaching to the place seems to do."[20] Wines also noted that the Maison Paternelle "has long been well known to young collegians of France and has been a terror to the lazy and vicious—a still greater number have felt the silent influence of its deterrent power."[21]

Demetz believed that discipline in the bourgeois household had largely collapsed over the course of the nineteenth century. While moral corruption began in the urban streets for the young men incarcerated in Mettray, for those housed in the Maison Paternelle indiscipline was the result of the inherent weakness of domestic authority. Demetz proclaimed that "it is the feebleness of parents which is the cause of this sickness which we must try to fight from the moment when the child first becomes convinced that he can act with impunity."[22] J. M. Guardia, one of Mettray's many unofficial publicists, argued that "few maladies are as grave as the insubordination of children, which is the result of the weakness or absence of parental authority. Respect for parents is necessary, for without it there is no point to education because the child is naturally spoiled, inclined to laziness, and becomes particularly undisciplined when the parent is weak or negligent."[23]

To some observers such as Henri Joly, a member of the law faculty at Paris, this lack of respect was due to a reticence on the part of bourgeois parents to physically punish their children, which he contrasted to village life, where "periodic whipping holds children in check yet does not awaken any long-term feelings of resentment or revenge."[24] According to the magistrate Louis Proal, "We admire our children as marvels. . . . We raise them as hothouse flowers, enfold them in cotton, stuff them full of delicacies and overwhelm them with

praise and caresses," and this resulted in a reluctance to corporally punish.[25]
Maurice Bruyère, a jurist from Paris, lamented that "today corporal punishment is considered to be out of fashion among those whose affection for the
sensibilities of the child is perhaps a bit exaggerated."[26] Delegorgue maintained
that "it was only a few years ago that corporal punishment was seen as having a real effectiveness . . . in compelling the child to work and keeping him
away from bad company because of the fear such punishment inspired."[27]

There was never an explicit prohibition against corporal punishment in
French law, and a high court ruling in 1889 upheld the "right to light correction" by both parents and teachers. Nonetheless, Delegorgue lamented the dis-
appearance of "the whip in our schools and in the colleges and universities,
which during the last century . . . was used to hold temperaments in check . . .
yet never awakened any long-term feelings of resentment or revenge on the
part of the child."[28] Bruyère fondly recalled the "one time in class where, before all my colleagues, I received a severe beating with a whip from my
teacher. . . . This did not leave me with any bitterness toward this brave and
honest man, whom I never ceased to love and respect until his death."[29] Joly
remembered that in his "youth many colleges employed a functionary who
was especially charged with the task of whipping and was paid quite hand-
somely for performing this very valuable service." Indeed, he suggested
that the practice be formalized by having "a constable or officer of the court"
mete out the punishment with the permission of the parents and/or school
officials.[30]

The sociologist Gabriel Tarde attributed "overindulgence" to the fact that
bourgeois families "are having fewer and fewer children in order to advance
economically and socially, . . . [which] carries the parents away, and leads to a
relaxation of moral discipline and domestic example."[31] Amid the widespread
concern over depopulation in fin-de-siècle France, Tarde maintained that while
the father of "seven or eight must be more austere in the surveillance and treatment of his children, the father of only one or two treats his child with excessive softness," thereby rendering his offspring more vulnerable to the "egoism"
inherent in modern society. By selfishly limiting family size "the paternal home
has become the poison well for religious and moral skepticism, ambitious vanity, precocious cupidity, vice, alcoholism and the disrespect of authority."[32]

The result of this "softness," according to Proal, was that bourgeois children
receive "an effeminate education . . . which depletes them of all moral and
physical energy and makes them as timid as rabbits." Whereas "spankings land
on the robust body of the son or daughter of the peasant," such punishment
is likely to "only exasperate the delicate child of the city."[33] Delegorgue reminded parents that the "right to corporal punishment still exists. . . . By virtue

of the duty to educate, parents are allowed to inflict domestic punishments for the purpose of moral amendment. . . . It is perfectly legitimate by law so long as it is not oppressive or violent . . . More important, this right is inscribed in nature."[34] Thus, the failure of bourgeois parents to corporally punish their sons was deemed not only unnatural but also indicative of the perceived destabilizing effect of socioeconomic modernity on traditional values and mores as they related to the socialization of youth.

In the context of enforcing discipline in the family, mothers were construed as singularly lacking. As Judith Surkis has noted, there was an ever-present fear among fin-de-siècle pedagogues "of feminine excesses of love" in the domestic sphere, which necessitated "an eventual intervention on the part of the teacher—and hence the state" in the form of education. Because the mother possessed an overabundance of sentiment—which was her "natural" inclination, particularly toward her sons (daughters were notably absent from these discussions)—a male presence was necessary to counteract her "implicitly sexualized and potentially unruly" instruction. It was therefore the responsibility of the father and the male *instituteur* to inculcate and reinforce "reason," which was vital for the development of a "proper" citizen of the republic. Such notions reflected deep cultural anxieties related to masculinity, and many social theorists—both republicans and conservatives—were convinced that there was an ongoing feminization of bourgeois male youth that threatened the future vitality of the nation.[35]

There was also concern about widowed mothers, whom many believed had little authority over their sons. As Theodore Zeldin noted, this was not an uncommon home situation—in 1900 more than one-third of French households were headed by single parents, mostly women. In that same year, 45 percent of adolescents had already lost at least one parent.[36] In a hagiographic treatise on the Maison Paternelle, Alphonse Dumas, a member of l'Académie du gard, maintained that boys who "refuse to obey their widowed mothers adhere to the principle that it is not dignified for a man to obey the will of a woman."[37] According to Guardia, "It is especially for the children of widowed mothers that intervention in the form of the Maison Paternelle is useful; because, in our day, if paternal authority isn't respected, it is necessary to recognize that maternal authority is even less so."[38] Matilda Betham-Edwards, an Englishwoman who visited the Maison Paternelle and wrote of her experience, maintained that French widows were too lenient toward their sons: "As might naturally be expected, the majority of youthful ne'er-do-wells, the incorrigibly lazy and the loafers are the sons of widows. Children as a rule are mercilessly—the word is fit—spoiled in France, and especially to be pitied is the fatherless lad, the 'lord of himself, that heritage of woe.'"[39] Bonneville de

Marsangy pointedly asked, "What happens when paternal power falls into the weak hands of a widow, whose son, until he reaches the age of majority, is under her control? Does she have the intelligence, the will, the firmness necessary in order to make him respect her maternal authority? Blinded by her tenderness she cannot perceive that in her foolish extravagance she has already lost her son to his evil dissipations!" Should a widowed mother choose to remarry, the magistrate believed that the domestic situation with regard to child-rearing would remain rather hopeless because "the stepfather will hesitate to utilize all necessary rigor toward the child or children of his wife, fearful that she might attribute his severity for a lack of affection."[40]

While mothers and widows were conceptualized as ill-equipped to deal with rebellious sons, the problem facing bourgeois fathers was the "lack of respect" afforded to them in French society. Dumas opined that "the younger generation no longer shows deference and respect for religion, the laws of the country, the sovereign, the old, and the father of the family. . . . The ancient prestige attached to these institutions and personages has never been weaker, a trend which shows no signs of abating. It is a fact all too clear to be misunderstood." Dumas's location of the proximate cause for the situation as it pertained to fathers is particularly noteworthy:

> It is difficult to not be adversely effected by the overexcited egoism, ambition, audacity and incredible temerity of society. . . . We live in a time when the father, absorbed by his own personality, disdains his role as sage and benevolent counselor of his sons, only following them from afar and rather absent-mindedly as he is preoccupied by his vain dissipations and foolish pursuit of wealth; and should he try to reassert his position of authority he finds that he can no longer command his sons' respect which he has lost. . . . Does this ardent pursuit of wealth not bring with it a chance of ruin, and if great wealth is achieved through legitimate means does it necessarily guarantee a useful or honorable life for one's progeny? Children are placed between the two pitfalls of prodigality provoked by the seduction of the world and avarice solicited by greed and the sterile desire to be the richest among the rich.[41]

Charles Sauvestre similarly noted:

> In our time there has been a significant loosening of family ties. Without anyone noticing or doing anything to counterbalance this trend, paternal authority fades and filial love cools . . . as we devote so few minutes to reflection: we have so much to do; the days are short; Paris

is so grand. And then, life brings with it so many other worries. The father is happy in his profession, his interests. The mother tends to her relations: the world is demanding, it imposes its duties. The days pass by as if they are a dream and also a good part of the nights; there are barely enough hours to rest despite much fatigue. Children! . . . My God! We would be very happy to deal with them if only we had the time. This would be so sweet . . . but business comes first.[42]

With the expansion of the French economy and the concomitant stock market boom of the 1850s—spurred in part by Louis Napoléon's program of easy credit and his various public works initiatives—the acquisition of wealth, or more precisely the acquisition of capital, allowed a nascent bourgeois class to transcend their social origins through marriage. Thus, while there is an implicit criticism of such social climbing in Sauvestre's view, one can also detect a concern regarding the conflict between economic self-interest and moral order as we see the faint hints of a discourse that would gain considerable momentum by the close of the century when social critics lamented the individualist ethos at the heart of a new industrial economy and its effects on the family.

In this context, Latham argued that while "the State represents the schoolmaster, and, to some extent, the parent as well, the Maison Paternelle is its rod."[43] On arriving at the institution each young man was told, "You must repent here before God. Respect yourself and your family. Show yourself to be docile and you will have in us a friend to love; resist and you will be vanquished."[44] Despite such rhetoric, however, supporters such as Bonneville de Marsangy declared that the Maison Paternelle was "far from being a prison; it is a college of repression, that is to say, a college organized on a new plan, having its particular rules and a specific purpose."[45] Whether the Maison Paternelle was a prison or college, its residents were subject to its rules and its punishments.

Isolation was the governing principle of the institution. Students had no contact with one another and visits from family members were generally discouraged; instead, the director forwarded a twice-monthly progress report to the father, mother, or legal guardian. Because all his meals were taken in the cell, the student's only interpersonal contacts were with the various professors who knew him only by his matriculation number—in order to protect the family name—and visited him each day to conduct lessons. The young men were taken on daily walks with their tutors and guards around the grounds of the colony, always out of view of the *colons*; this, along with a weekly individualized course in gymnastics, "provided a basic pattern of daily exercise" intended to effectuate physical development and counteract the sedentary and "effeminizing" nature of the cloistered regime.

Just as in the colony, in the Maison Paternelle the purpose of isolation was not just to prevent the spread of moral contamination. Amid the silence and solitude, the individual was meant to brood over his misdeeds. The goal was metaphysical in the sense that the young man—through his own introspection—would be spiritually reborn via his isolation. Bonneville de Marsangy maintained that "in the calm silence of actual solitude, the boy will think of his past life and this important memory will soon bring tears to his eyes. He will be saved once he repents."[46] Betham-Edwards characterized the regime as "an unremitting appeal to the reasoning faculty. . . . It was M. Demetz' opinion that a habit of reasoning is induced by solitude . . . hence his insistence on this point."[47] Wines assessed the regime similarly: "He sees none of his fellows and feels no influence from their presence. Left wholly to his own reflections, he retires within himself, and generally in one or two months is found a sufficient time to subdue his spirit, to change his habits, and to restore in him joy and pride, instead of being, as before, the grief and shame of his family."[48]

The regime was also meant to compel the young man to fully embrace the moral value of labor. Labor, or in this case intense study, would serve as a release from the unrelenting loneliness of the room. According to Demetz, "Nothing is more helpful than the regime of the Maison Paternelle in order to vanquish apathetic natures. Work, which is the object of aversion, becomes a need and a consolation, as without it, the student is left only to his own thoughts."[49] Wines also claimed that labor "becomes a necessity and a consolation to such a degree that books are taken from the students as a punishment for negligence and the want of occupation so weighs upon them that they soon beg to have them restored."[50] Thus, labor was both the instrument and the symptom of reform. In essence, the youth was forced to work until he did so willingly, and eventually he would associate labor with his own self-interest beyond an immediate desire to avoid the pain of isolation. Compulsory school work in the Maison Paternelle was intended to prepare young men for life in the outside world and to prevent them from being a drain on society after their release.

What is particularly striking about the contemporary rhetoric is how clearly it echoes Tocqueville and Beaumont's support for the Pennsylvania system of isolation. After their visit to the Eastern State Penitentiary in Philadelphia in 1831 they characterized the regime as follows: "Thrown into solitude . . . [the prisoner] reflects. Placed alone, in view of his crime, he learns to hate it; and if his soul be not yet surfeited with crime, and thus have lost all taste for anything better, it is in solitude, where remorse will come to assail him. . . . Can there be a combination more powerful for reformation than that of a prison which hands over the prisoner to all the trials of solitude, leads him through reflection to remorse, through religion to hope; makes him industrious by the burden of idleness?"[51] Demetz was a staunch supporter of the Pennsylvania regime of isolation for adults, and the existence of solitary confinement cells in the colony demonstrates that his support for the principle extended to children, at least those of the working class and poor. For children of the bourgeoisie and haute bourgeoisie, isolation was lauded as a highly individualized means of spiritual redemption. According to Bonneville de Marsangy, "The regime of separation allows for a distinct treatment, perfectly appropriate to the character and individual nature of each child. Thus, the house can act with great indulgence or with a just severity, according to individual needs and particular circumstances."[52]

The efficacy of the regime was supported by student testimonials that officials of the Maison Paternelle were only too happy to share with the public. Indeed, they were part of a larger public relations and marketing campaign designed to generate publicity for the institution. Through the systematic distribution of annual reports to jurists, legislators, educators, political officials, and journalists, Demetz and his successors described each component of the regime in detail and included case histories to buttress and dramatize individual stories of transformation in the Maison Paternelle. In a story that appeared in *Le Temps*, two letters written by the same child were reprinted from an annual report to demonstrate the effectiveness of the regime. In the first letter, addressed to "My Barbarous Parents," the anonymous boy, newly arrived at the institution, swore "before God" that he would "never touch a quill pen as a student. I will never open a single book during my captivity and no matter the walls or whatever torture they might inflict upon me will make me change." Six months later the same child wrote another letter to the director of the Maison Paternelle after being reunited with his family. "I have learned something which unfortunately I did not know before. I have learned that there is a serious side to life and work. Despite the extreme rigor of my punishment I can tell you that I am happy that it was inflicted upon me. Because my future was in great peril before you and my parents offered me one last chance for salvation." The newspaper also included a letter from an unnamed student who wrote to the director that while his father "believes what I have achieved here to be a sham, I will disabuse him of this notion. I spent my time of internment well and my sickness has been cured. . . . The results that you have obtained to vanquish my laziness and faults speak to the honor and methods that you employ."[53]

Demetz insisted that isolation in the Maison Paternelle was "indispensable for it removes all harmful influences" and that it provided an unparalleled opportunity to "study individual character" in order to develop and apply an "individualized" education that would meet the specific needs of each student.[54] This approach was in response to an educational system that some believed lacked flexibility and sensitivity in dealing with the individual child. Latham recounted that he had been told by an educator that

> the system of education in France is an elaborate instrument, most complete to behold, perfectly made out in all its parts; it enables the minister to say in the Chamber, "I can tell what lesson every boy in France is saying at the moment." But it is a machine and deals with all alike. The mass of boys is shoveled in at one end, the handle is turned, and the average youth comes out molded into something like the same shape, with the regulation stamp, but an abnormal subject gets thrown out or crushed. . . . "The class must be treated as one" is the axiom. . . . The mechanism must not be put out for an individual. Such rigid systems work ill in the case of strong idiosyncrasy or eccentricity.[55]

Although the Maison Paternelle was positioned as an alternative to an increasingly secularized and modernized system of education in late nineteenth-century France, some perceived it quite differently, and their discursive frame of reference was clearly carceral. In the view of Betham-Edwards, the Maison Paternelle was a jail: "Their parents' claim to their affections will seem invalidated by their invocation of this institution. . . . They will come out, as I heard that many lads do come out, with a rooted hatred of all things. . . . A gaol seems a cruel and degrading remedy for childish faults."[56] Indeed, even supporters of the Maison Paternelle referred to it as an "educational Bastille" where students were submitted to "strict isolation."[57]

In many ways, however, the Maison Paternelle resembled the typical French boarding school, which as Surkis has pointed out, was increasingly criticized by observers across the political spectrum as a "perverse" mode of education. Conservatives such as Hippolyte Taine and Maurice Barrès were particularly critical of the same-sex segregation of the boarding school, which they believed undermined traditional gender roles and had the general effect of feminizing French youth, sometimes even leading to sexual "inversion" (i.e., homosexuality).[58] With its emphasis on complete isolation, the Maison Paternelle forestalled concerns about the emasculating effects of the same-sex boarding school. Demetz justified isolation as a means of moral reformation precisely because it precluded the possibility of the student being exposed to "undesirable" outside influences, particularly other students. That is, there was no possibility for same-sex relations because interpersonal contact was impossible.

While castigating bourgeois parents for overindulgence, the Maison Paternelle promised to transform their sons' "natural" predispositions from indiscipline and disobedience to regularity and compliance with authority. Adolescence was seen as a perilous time in life when pathological penchants could become a permanent facet of one's adult character if they were not effectively addressed at an early age. There was also a sense that the traditional institutions of socialization (i.e., the school, the church, the family, and even the prison) were failing, and that this would have profound implications for future social stability. According to Guardia, "It is only severe, rigorous, and inflexible discipline which is capable of taming rebellious natures and it is on this point that families and establishments of public instruction must act. When paternal authority is unrecognized or powerless, the basic rules in the schools where the young are raised and taught in common are generally insufficient to hold back insubordination."[59] Just as he pathologized the private sphere of the working class and poor, Demetz also maintained that bourgeois families were "neglectful in combating this sickness; their feebleness is responsible for preparing their children for a sad future. Society has a right to demand an accounting from those whose negligence leads to disturbance from those in their care. . . . If the family abdicates or fails in its role, society must not. Society must defend itself by other means."[60]

In the investigation into the suicide of Gaston Contard it soon became apparent that he had been placed in the Maison Paternelle against his will. The elder Contard informed police that during their eight-kilometer drive from Tours to Mettray, his son had tried to shoot himself with a starter's pistol that he had hidden in his coat (he was disarmed by his father after a brief struggle). When they arrived at Mettray that evening the boy pleaded with his father not to leave him and then beseeched M. Delucé, the prefect of studies, to send a telegram to his mother in Marseilles demanding his immediate release. Article 382 of the Criminal Code stipulated that a child who had been incarcerated by paternal correction had the right to protest his imprisonment to the Cour d'appel, which "after having gathered all information, can revoke or modify the order delivered by the municipal judge."[61] This right was largely illusory because few minors had the wherewithal to request or formulate such a request.

During his five days of incarceration, Contard was visited in his cell by professors and staff who were unable to convince the young man to engage in his studies or to eat. Given Contard's general mental state and his continued demands to be released, Emmanuel Hilaire Lorenzo, director of both Mettray and the Maison Paternelle, requested that the elder Contard obtain a court order authorizing his son's incarceration. The document eventually arrived from Marseilles, one day after the suicide. Although the Maison Paternelle had procured the document only belatedly, officials maintained that court orders were generally unnecessary because most students were there of their own free will. Of the other eleven youths at the Maison Paternelle at the time of the suicide, ten were there without court orders.[62]

On the heels of the police investigation into the suicide, an inquiry into the Maison Paternelle and its operation was launched by the public prosecutor's office in Tours. In a letter to the families of students still in the Maison Paternelle, Lorenzo outlined the legal position of the institution: "We maintain that a student can be admitted, without a court order, by the head of the family who is acting within his full rights of paternal authority."[63] The director closed the letter by informing the parents that court officials had seized dossiers and student registers (which did not include students' surnames, only their matriculation numbers) and that while "I have taken every care to maintain your sons' anonymity in the most formal manner, the Maison Paternelle declines all legal responsibility should there be a possible violation of your secret."[64]

Two days later a local magistrate and René Besnard, the chief prosecutor, travelled to Mettray to question its residents. Their conversations were transcribed by an unnamed civil functionary. The first round of questions focused on learning the family situations of the students to determine why they had been placed in the Maison Paternelle. Although there is no way to ascertain whether the young men were coerced or pressured by administrators or staff not to cooperate with the investigation, it is important to note that there was always a representative of the institution present during questioning. Thus, while the terse answers and general demeanor of the students certainly indicate a high degree of resentment and hostility toward the investigators, it is likely that they did not feel entirely free to incriminate the institution where they were incarcerated.

After initially refusing to speak, student number 613 eventually told authorities that he was "not the type who talks." Asked by the judge whether he was "the type who thinks for himself," the young man responded angrily, "I am, but I am not going to say what I think of you. And do not bother asking me my name again because I will not tell you. It would take five hundred thousand men and one thousand horses to drag it out of me!"[65] Student number 628 similarly complained that he found the questions regarding his family to be "absolutely indiscreet."[66] When Besnard asked student number 625 what his father thought of the inquiry, the young man angrily snapped, "Although it is none of your business, I'm sure he thinks as I do, that your investigation is idiotic."[67]

When asked why he had been returned to the Maison Paternelle for a third time, student number 592 responded, simply, "Stupidity." When the judge said, "It is your father whom you should blame as he is the real reason why you find yourself here," the boy replied, "I have never disagreed with the will of my father. I am here to prepare for college. Now gentlemen, I have a long mathematical problem that is due tomorrow. I would like to be excused."[68] Asked if he would leave the Maison Paternelle if he could, student number 614 responded, "Others in this house may wish to leave but I am here of my own free will. I wish to work amid the great calm and in the most efficient manner possible." He then added, "Gentlemen, my presence here should be of no concern to you and I protest against this inquiry."[69] Another exchange was typical in that, again, the young man indicated that he was at the institution of his own free will, which implied that the Maison Paternelle was not, in fact, a prison:

> JUDGE: If you are here of your own free will, you will have dinner with us this evening in Tours.
>
> STUDENT: That would require the permission of the director.
>
> JUDGE: Then you are not truly free.
>
> STUDENT: Perhaps not, although a worker who enters his workshop freely every morning is obliged to ask permission from his superior if he can leave by regulation. My case is similar.
>
> JUDGE: I would like to remind you that you are obliged to tell us everything.
>
> STUDENT: Ah, but where is the freedom in that? In fact, you don't give a damn about us here.
>
> JUDGE: What did you think of your father's decision to place you here?
>
> STUDENT: I did not disagree.
>
> JUDGE: When you first came here and heard the door creaking as it closed behind you, and saw the bars on the windows, and the guards before your door, and that there were no means of communicating with the exterior, did you find this amusing?
>
> STUDENT: No, not at all, but I was put to work and since that time it has been a pleasure to be here.[70]

According to the unnamed representative of the Maison Paternelle who was present during the interrogations, the judge remarked to a colleague on leaving, "They could leave the doors wide open and no one would try to escape."[71]

The focus of the investigation changed in the days that followed when the public prosecutor received a letter from a former student complaining of abuse at the Maison Paternelle. A young man named Abadie described having been placed in shackles and held for days in *cachots* (the small, subterranean cells located beneath the chapel, which also figured in the 1887 scandal) as punishment for trying to communicate with another student through a hole in the wall between their two rooms. In a second letter, another youth claimed that his father had left him in the Maison Paternelle for a period of three years (1897–1900) as punishment for being ranked last in his class. Both letters soon appeared in the local and national press, presumably leaked by officials in the prosecutor's office.[72]

In addition, two former employees of the Maison Paternelle came forward to say they had witnessed abuse and mistreatment of young men. One, a master mason named Maignan, was responsible for repairs to the building and therefore had occasion to enter the *cachots*. He claimed that students were placed in iron chains and collars while in the *cachots* as a punishment (as in the 1887 scandal) and that he was asked to take these youths—sometimes even carrying them—to the infirmary after their release due to their weakened physical condition. He also recounted an incident he had witnessed where a guard, angered when a young man in the *cachots* asked for a drink of water, plunged the boy's head into a pail of excrement and screamed, "Cheers! Drink, pig!"[73] The other report came from Boire, a former domestic at the Maison Paternelle, who told authorities that he had been ordered to imprison students in the *cachots*, "sometimes three in the same day," and that when he left the employ of the institution they were still in use. He maintained that many young men were placed in the dungeons for five days or more in quite squalid conditions and that he eventually left his job out of "revulsion" over the mistreatment of the students.[74]

Not surprisingly, officials of the Maison Paternelle denied the claims and insisted that the institution was not a prison that arbitrarily restrained children's liberty or abused its residents in any fashion. Although by law, children's sentences were limited to one to six months in the institution, depending on the specific terms of the ordinance, officials admitted that some children stayed much longer. They insisted, however, that it "is the boarders themselves who often feel the need to stay longer; they understand that its only in this way that they can succeed against the weakness of their character. . . . Sometimes after having been released they spontaneously find the director and explain to him that for them to continue to achieve they must remain."[75]

After these new revelations surfaced, the investigatory team—which now included the judge, a substitute judge, two gendarmes, the same unnamed recorder, and Besnard—returned to the Maison Paternelle on the morning of 23 January to resume their questioning. This round of interviews focused less on family identity and the circumstances that led to students' placements in the Maison Paternelle and more on the disciplinary aspects of the regime, surely in response to the accusations leveled by the former students and employees. The officials subtly changed their tactics to try and gain the confidence and trust of the formerly reticent young men. Thus, at the beginning of each interview the judge prefaced the conversation by reminding the interviewee, "You must understand that we are the protectors of oppressed children and you have nothing to hide from us. We have come here to see if you have been subject to harsh treatment."[76] The efforts to elicit more information were largely futile, however. When asked if he had ever been placed in the *cachots*, student number 628 responded, "Is there such a place? Besides, I have never been lazy and there are no complaints against me."[77] Similarly, student number 651 told authorities that he "had never been struck for not having done my work" and that the only punishment he had suffered was "the suppression of the walk."[78]

After concluding this round of interviews, the team was led to the *cachots* by Abadie and Boire, the former student and domestic who had shared their experiences independently with prosecutors. When they descended into the basement the magistrates were reportedly "met with a very disagreeable odor." (This, too, bears a striking similarity to what occurred in the scandal in 1887). What they discovered was a series of small rooms with little ventilation and no outside light, one of which contained a musty mattress and a tattered blanket. In two of the other rooms they found chains. M. Juigner, a professor of mathematics who accompanied the men as a representative of the Maison Paternelle, said that to his knowledge the basement had been used to store coal and that no one had spent any time there in years.

Prosecutors made a third, final trip to Mettray, this time to question the staff of the Maison Paternelle, particularly the instructors who saw the students daily. Each professor was asked to outline what punishments were utilized in the institution. The answers were not revealing; even when confronted with registers that noted paddlings, dry bread rations, and placing children in the *cachots*, both professors and guards maintained that such things were "in the distant past" and "part of an old formulation."[79] Chanloup, a professor of English, insisted that such abuses no longer occurred.

CHANLOUP: This was more than thirty years ago when the regulations of the prisons were applied here. I know of the administration of M.

Blanchard [director 1873–84], and the regime at that time was very
harsh. . . . Since that time, we have evolved.

Judge: How so?

Chanloup: I left for a time when Mettray was under the direction of M.
Blanchard and returned in 1896 when it was under the direction of
M. Cluze. I expected when I returned that it would be the same as
when I left; but it did not take long for me to see that I was wrong.
In the earlier period, one would use the wood paddle on the boys.
They were punished sometimes twice a week in this manner. Upon
my return this punishment was no longer in place as the severe regime that I had known previously had disappeared. Corporal punishment was repugnant to M. Cluze. Thereafter, he would examine
the faults of the children and determine their sanctions. This regime
was continued under the direction of M. Lorenzo who has a horror
of such punishments in general.[80]

This statement is noteworthy in regard to the scandal of 1887 because
Blanchard had escaped condemnation for acts of corporal punishment under
his directorship, whereas his successor, De Cayla, was the frequent target of
accusations. According to M. Devos, a professor of mathematics, "Today, those
students who misbehave or refuse to work might be deprived of dessert, have
their daily walk suppressed, or perhaps receive a reprimand from the director
or the prefect of studies."[81] When asked to explain how "these young people
who have caused such problems for their families are now so easily and effectively punished," Juigner replied, "The regime is severe enough as it is. Reprimands produce a salutary effect."[82]

To determine whether Contard's reaction on arriving at the Maison Paternelle was typical, employees were asked for their impressions of the students'
emotional states on arrival. Touchent, a professor of history, made a distinction based on the age of the child, noting that for the younger boys aged thirteen to fifteen the first two days are difficult, but in most cases "this dissipates
once the student meets with his professors and realizes that he is in a college
or lycée."[83] Similarly, Guepin, a professor of German, maintained that "at the
beginning, some of them are unhappy and shocked by the regime, others are
a little angry, but this anger does not last long."[84] When asked if students "cry
or revolt by destroying things," Juigner replied that "it depends on the age and
character" of the child, but "most are surprised by the interest we take in them
and become excellent students. I do not ever remember having seen any of
them cry."[85]

These claims ran counter to those of outside observers such as Latham, who had been told by officials of the Maison Paternelle, albeit some forty years earlier, that on first arriving "the young men are frequently furious for two or three days. . . . They often tear their bedding to pieces, smash their table and chair, and do not listen to any instruction."[86] Juigner made a distinction, however, between those who were in the Maison Paternelle by virtue of a court order and those students who were there "voluntarily." Whereas the latter "accepts with satisfaction the type of special life that is provided them," the former "waits with impatience for the day when they are free to leave." Although all of the instructors insisted that they had never heard of anyone asking or demanding to leave the facility, Juigner maintained that "if a student were to come here without a court order and absolutely wished to leave . . . the director would without hesitation inform the family, and if it were necessary for us to guard him, we would accompany the child back to his home."[87]

Following the interviews and official depositions, Besnard told the press that he believed the institution was

> a cellular prison where absolute isolation is practiced. . . . The child passes his days and nights in a cell, whose door is closed by an exterior bolt with windows that are covered with iron bars; they take every meal in their room, receive their professors there, and only leave for one hour a day to walk under the surveillance of a guard. I consider this establishment, where children are detained without having committed either a crime or a misdemeanor, to be characteristic of a prison. . . . There is a guarantee against arbitrary internment in the form of a court order. It is this indispensable rule which has not been observed at the "Paternelle."[88]

Lorenzo was charged and tried for illegal imprisonment in July 1909. The case was initially dismissed on the basis that the director had acted in good faith, but that decision was rescinded by the criminal court and Lorenzo was charged and tried again, this time by the Cour d'assises du Vienne at Poitiers in February 1910.

Prior to Lorenzo's trial the defense consulted with numerous legal experts to have the Maison Paternelle defined as an institution rather than a prison. This was a crucial point because the Napoleonic Code stipulated that a court order from a judge authorizing the placement of a minor in a "penitentiary establishment" was necessary. Two professors of law from the University of Paris, A. Poittevin and E. Garçon, obliged, maintaining that the Maison Paternelle was "neither a prison, nor a house of detention, nor a private penitentiary," and that its purpose was "not to punish but to help 'raise' the child."

Although the lawyers conceded that the Maison Paternelle did not have "the exclusive character of a scholarly establishment," they insisted that its predominant features were academic. Therefore, from the point of view of civil and penal law, it was not unlike a boarding school where "students receive the best instruction from a large number of teachers and communicate with a varied group of personnel. . . . It is a severe life but it conforms to the basic needs of movement and sociability. . . . It is thus a juridical fact that the Maison Paternelle is 'a system of education.'"[89] M. L'Hôpital, a retired jurist who had placed his own son in the Maison Paternelle years earlier, testified in support of this notion: "It is not a prison that I found but a veritable college where my son worked and learned much."[90] A third lawyer, H. Du Buit, maintained that the "regime has nothing in common with imprisonment as the children are not living in strict isolation and enjoy daily walks accompanied by various personnel," and that the youths "are not detained but strictly interned."[91] The defense repeatedly insisted that "absolute isolation" was a deliberate misnomer cynically utilized by the prosecution as a pejorative "as there is no resemblance between the cell of a prison and the room where a boarder lives and works."[92] A local newspaper also accused the prosecutor of misrepresenting the institution in both the courtroom and in the press, as the "so-called 'cells' of the Maison Paternelle are airy rooms which would be the great envy of many."[93]

For some, the most salient critique was to simply point to the obvious contrast between a typical boarding school where "children live in common with other children, communicate with each other, and play with each other" and "'La Paternelle,' where one is imprisoned in a cell and there is no rapport between the child and other detainees."[94] The satirical journal *L'Assiette au Beurre* was far more explicit, characterizing the institution as "nothing more than a cellular prison . . . where wealthy children are incarcerated."[95] "With its cells and discipline of iron," the Maison Paternelle was, in the view of the journalist Lucien Descaves, "a thinly disguised *maison de correction*. . . . The Mettray agricultural colony has been in existence for seventy years and serves as a model for all others! Yet isn't it curious to find today both the cellular and the communal life of the agricultural colony present at Mettray? The latter is certainly preferable to the former, which the young detainees regard as a *bagne*."[96] Anonymous letters sent to Lorenzo also alluded to the *bagne* while criticizing the Maison Paternelle: "Your institution is nothing more than a den of bandits who murder and inflict cruelties on those unfortunate enough to be without defense. You destroy all the joys of childhood and your institution is a place of suffering, torture and atrocity where you are permitted to commit your crimes behind the closed doors of your *bagne*."[97] This linking of the Maison Paternelle with the overseas penal colonies of Guiana and New

Caledonia was a powerful rhetorical strategy that would reappear later in the press campaign against the agricultural colony of Mettray during the interwar period.

The president of the Société paternelle, H. Berthélemy, who was also a member of the law faculty in Paris, argued that the charge of illegal imprisonment was impossible to substantiate in light of the doctrine of in loco parentis, in which the "normal right of surveillance and control of a child exists with either the father of the family or the tutor."[98] Indeed, the very act of sending a child to a school of any kind presupposed certain restrictions on his or her liberty, a right to which the child had no legal claim, according to Poittevin and Garçon: "The fundamental character of detention is the illegitimate privation of liberty, that is, the victim is held in some area against his will where he is enclosed. All detention that is of this type and committed against a legal subject must be considered a punishable act. But the child is not a legal subject; he has no right to his liberty or any right to oppose the duties of education, protection, and surveillance which fall upon the father in the civil code."[99] As it was the moral and civic duty of the elder Contard to provide an education for his son, the attorneys insisted that he possessed the inalienable right to place the young man in whatever "house of education" he believed would be most useful in addressing "his particular character and aptitude." In the case of Gaston, "who was already subject to bad influences, why shouldn't his father be able to provide an education isolated from all camaraderie?"[100] Berthélemy maintained that "the child has no right to contact with the exterior or with his comrades which can be harmful. The Civil Code permits the father to prohibit his son from having contact with whomever he wishes."[101]

Du Buit argued that, having no legal right to individual liberty, at least as it pertained to paternal authority, "the child can only ask his father if he can come and go; he can only ask his father whom he can see and receive; he can only ask his father what he can and cannot do; he can only ask his father what he can and cannot read."[102] Another attorney, H. Devin, similarly inveighed, "From the moment the child is submitted to paternal power, he is arbitrarily limited by the control and wishes of the parent, who may choose whatever means of education he judges most suitable."[103] The local press, always a strong advocate of the Maison Paternelle, shared this understanding. "Critics charge that these children are under lock and key! This is true. But M. Besnard would have you believe that the father of a family does not have the same right to hold an undisciplined child under lock and key. . . . Just as fathers have the right to choose the means of instruction given to their children, they also have the right to determine the best means by which to protect their children against the dangerous enticements of youth."[104]

The fate of the Maison Paternelle was therefore inextricably intertwined with the issue of paternal correction. In this vein, the journalist Léon Bailby complained that "fathers of families still have the power of life and death over their children by condemning them to prison, which they find more convenient than correcting by persuasion or example. . . . The law must protect children. Otherwise, it is too easy for fathers to be rid of their progeny without any controls. As we have discovered, the director of Mettray has operated without such controls."[105] Even Delegorgue conceded that the power of paternal correction was "fine for those who can afford to send their child to a private enterprise such as the Maison Paternelle, where they receive a very expensive education, [but] such enterprises are well beyond the reach of most families. . . . Thus, the legislation pertaining to paternal correction is above all an aristocratic law, prepared for the children of wealthy families."[106]

Others such as Devin argued that diminished paternal power would "greatly undermine authority within the family which now, more than ever, must be strong and respected." La Touraine declared that any weakening of paternal power would be a "public danger as families will no longer be able to address rebellious natures, the very purpose for which 'La Paternelle' was intended." The newspaper also insisted that the concern over the "rights of children" was nothing more than a "pretext" by which the state "wishes to further secure its ever-growing power" by encroaching on what had been the private domain of the father. "Today the state wants all regulation, all control, at the expense of paternal authority. The state-monopoly is the ideal. It is not ours, and we have the firm conviction that it isn't for most people. M. Besnard is the first in line to claim for the state the right to stand with the child against the parent. He has discussed at length the rights of children, which he wishes to secure under the ever-growing power of the legislator. We should not weaken paternal authority on the pretext of protecting children."[107]

The minor did have the right, however, to be protected from abuse by a parent or those acting on behalf of the parent. It was therefore necessary for the prosecution to prove that the conditions of a stay in the institution were incompatible with respect to the youth's "humanity"—that is, that the privation of liberty was accompanied by abusive acts, or the detention occurred in an unhealthy place, or the absolute isolation was "prolonged." Despite the claims of abuse by former employees and students, the prosecutor Besnard failed to effectively demonstrate that the Maison Paternelle engaged in such practices.

Although the defense could not deny that students were held in isolation, at trial they called on a parade of former employees and students, all of whom testified that the regime was healthy and humane. More specifically, they effectively challenged the credibility of Boire (who had left the employ of the institution in 1874) and Abadie by demonstrating that practices such as placing students in the *cachots* had long been abandoned. The testimony of M. Chaveau, a former guard at the Maison Paternelle, was typical:

> There are no boarders of "La Paternelle" that were ever punished in the cachot. In the seventeen years that I spent there, these rooms were only used for the storage of coal. In the past they were used to occasionally hold escapees from the penitentiary colony, but never boarders from "La Paternelle." If they were punished, they were deprived of daily walks or perhaps put on a diet of bread and water; the directors were very benevolent. I left the Maison Paternelle seven years ago and I do not know M. Lorenzo, the current director, but former colleagues have told me that he is inclined to overindulge and that the guards have complained about his lack of severity.[108]

A more troublesome issue for the defense was the failure of officials to secure a court order authorizing the placement in the Maison Paternelle of Contard and, for that matter, most of the other students present at the time of the suicide. Although they had endeavored to define the institution as an educational establishment during the trial, the defense could not escape the fact that court orders had been secured for other students in the past. Officials maintained that they interpreted the civil code as requiring a court order only when the placement was against the expressed will of the minor. This interpretation raised a basic conundrum: "There exists at 'La Paternelle' a court order for recalcitrant children. A need for such an order does not exist, however, when one allows himself to be interned of his own free will. But if a court order is necessary for those who protest against their incarceration, is it not therefore a prison?"[109]

Some defenders of the Maison Paternelle argued that even if it was considered a prison, it was not legally obligated to obtain judicial ordinances because it was a private enterprise and therefore not subject to the civil code that pertained to state institutions. *La Dépêche* decried this view: "Certainly, they cannot be serious when they pretend with all sincerity that although an ordinance is necessary to open the doors of a public prison to rebellious children that this ceases to be the case when one is placed in an establishment that is essentially private." Moreover, whereas "a public prison offers guarantees of effective control, the private establishment offers no such guarantees. It depends on only the goodwill of the man to whom the father has delegated his power and authority. Because the goodwill is not sufficiently guaranteed, this leads to deaths such as the one that occurred here."[110] *Le Matin* proclaimed that if Lorenzo were acquitted it would be akin to "saying that 'La Paternelle' should be allowed to continue to function in these mysterious, disturbing and illegal conditions. . . . This illegality would be consecrated into law and this would be stupidly immoral. The jury must not hesitate. . . . Close 'La Paternelle' and all similar houses that function outside the law."[111]

The Contard affair brought into focus certain continuities—aims, practices, and approaches—between the Maison Paternelle and the prison. Like the Mettray colony itself, the Maison Paternelle existed at an uncomfortable juncture of conflicting ideologies and impulses. The institutional ambiguity worked to the advantage of the state, at least at first, because it was not responsible for providing any oversight of the regime, the living conditions, or the general treatment of those housed at the Maison Paternelle. In this sense it was not unlike private boarding schools that had long served to socialize unruly bourgeois youth in France. The Maison Paternelle enjoyed a sterling reputation during its early years, due primarily to its association with the Mettray colony and the indefatigable public relations efforts of Demetz. It was commonly viewed as an innovative example of private education for young men at risk of falling behind academically in an increasingly competitive, meritocratic republic.

Moreover, while both students and staff maintained during the investigation and trial that corporal punishment was no longer a part of daily life, it is clear from the many references to punishment registers (no longer extant in the historical record) that students were routinely paddled by officials in years past. Considering the concern voiced by social critics about the development (or lack thereof) of masculinity in French youth, corporal punishment might have been employed to acculturate young males and offset the general state of "indiscipline" in the "feminine" domestic sphere. And although it may have become a remnant of a bygone era, the placement of youths in the insalubrious *cachots* had at one time also been a common practice that had a debilitating effect on both the mind and the body. Whether the Maison Paternelle was a prison, a school, or some combination thereof, its regime was quite harsh.

By the turn of the twentieth century, the institutional ambiguity of the Maison Paternelle had become more problematic. In the context of a new system of public education and the "discovery" of adolescence there was a concomitant shift from "punishment" to "treatment" of the pathological predispositions and propensities associated with this stage of the life cycle. Nascent theories of psychosocial development stressed the need for frequent and sustained interaction with one's peers, and in this light, the complete lack of sociability in the Maison Paternelle was seen as counterproductive and needlessly cruel. An entirely separate juvenile court system with wide discretionary powers in sentencing, probationary oversight, and mandating medical and psychiatric treatment for wayward or delinquent youths was established in July 1912, only three years after the Contard affair. Legislation required that prior to any court proceeding the accused and his family be subject to social and psychological examination.

While the prosecutors in the Contard case represented those who favored limitations on paternal authority, there were others who reacted against what they perceived as a threat to "traditional" values and practices pertaining to the family. As evidenced in the vigorous parliamentary debates about paternal correction, the Third Republic was not monolithic, and there were many bourgeois parents who did not willingly facilitate the intervention of the state and/or the "helping professions" in the private domestic sphere, at least when it pertained to their own children.[112] Indeed, it was not until the 1930s that the practice of paternal correction fell into what Schafer termed a state of "obsolescence."[113]

During the two-day trial, Gaston's father testified for the defense on the issue of the court order and his son's request to leave: "Upon my return to Marseilles, I was made aware of the condition of my son by M. Lorenzo. Six times, by letter or dispatch, he asked me to secure a court order for internment. I responded to him that I had taken the necessary steps to obtain this paper, but that in any case, it was acceptable that my son remain there." Contard did not blame Lorenzo or the conditions in the Maison Paternelle for his son's suicide; he blamed himself: "If there is anyone who is guilty in this whole affair it is me. It is me who should be in the place occupied by M. Lorenzo."[114] His testimony had a profound effect on the jury, and newspapers reported that the gallery stood and applauded the verdict of not guilty as the director wept. It was not a total victory, however, because the negative publicity surrounding the affair brought about an immediate and dramatic drop in admissions to the Maison Paternelle, leading to its closure in October 1910. The trial also ended Lorenzo's career, as the Société paternelle pressured him to resign from his post as director of the agricultural colony, which he did in April 1911.

As for Gaston, the trial revealed a deeply troubled and depressed young man whose internment and isolation in the Maison Paternelle may well have precipitated his suicide but was not the proximate cause. In a letter to his sister written while he was still living in Marseilles—entered into the court record as evidence of his state of mind—the young Contard spoke openly of his plans to kill himself, long before he was institutionalized: "I wish to have father take my still warm ashes in an urn, on a fine summer's evening, and let them go where the wind will carry them."[115] Although he was the only suicide among the 2,251 young men who passed through the Maison Paternelle during its nearly sixty years of existence, Gaston's death resulted in a far-reaching reassessment of private power, state control, and paternal authority, and it served as a powerful portent of things to come for the Mettray agricultural colony.

CHAPTER 6

Denouement

In July 1903, following a series of collective work stoppages at Mettray, the préfet d'Indre-et-Loire initiated an inquiry into "the general condition of the colony and the causes which have led to the recent outbreaks of insubordination." In a report forwarded to the ministry of the interior he concluded that despite the "sometimes excessive rigor and the clerical spirit which regrettably presides in the administration of the colony, we must conclude that the condition of Mettray seems excellent. The moral state of the *colons*, however, has been less satisfactory." While work stoppages were "entirely without precedent until the last few years," according to the prefect, he could not establish that the acts of insubordination were premeditated, and ultimately he concluded that they were "without serious or profound cause."[1]

In sharp contrast, Director Cluze believed that the refusals to work were "assuming the character of a veritable plot" whose proximate cause could be traced to a punishment he had inflicted on an entire Mettray family. "The *colons* found this punishment unjust," the director maintained, "and that is why they refused to go to work, and then appealed to other families in support of their refusal." Cluze attributed the work stoppages to the "inherent immorality of the 'grands' [older youths]," who in his view dominated Mettray's inmate culture, "which explains the participation in the mutiny of so many who were older and not directly involved in the punishment." The director also bemoaned the deleterious effect on morale caused by the arrival of inmates from other colonies (in this case, the colony of Bologne), "whose moral state is worse because incidents of this same kind have already occurred. Children are told what is going on in these other settlements, and hearing about the acts of insubordination from those who witnessed or participated in similar events is enough to stimulate the imagination: the *colons* of Mettray wanted to have their own little rebellion as well."[2]

This event exemplifies what would become a leitmotif in official explanations of recalcitrant behavior at Mettray in the twentieth century—namely, that the source of the problem lay not in the institution but in the changing nature of its denizens. Whereas Demetz's annual reports were full of glowing optimism about the potential for wayward youths to work toward self-renewal through their agricultural labor, his much more pessimistic successors believed an increasing number of their subjects were inherently depraved as a result of their heredity, their environment, and their adolescent anomie. In his annual address to the Société paternelle in 1901, Cluze complained, "I note with difficulty that, if the number of pupils sent for correction to Mettray has diminished, their moral and intellectual value has diminished in larger proportion. We receive a much larger number of deeply vicious children, for whom there is little hope of amendment."[3] Fifteen years later, Director Brun, comparing his task of "moralizing the miscreants of Mettray" to the labors of Sisyphus, remarked, "I am deeply disturbed by the presence of vicious youths whose moral sense has been entirely obliterated by every kind of vice imaginable."[4] Brun's successor, Jacques Lardet, noted in 1922 that the "Penitentiary Administration continues to send us older pupils, ages sixteen to eighteen, who arrive here with habits of independence, laziness, and a false morality, from which it follows that discipline, at the present moment, is quite difficult. The administration of Public Assistance only sends us those children whom they cannot place in homes or who are unstable or vicious. Since the war, the current state of mind, in the prisons, as well as in the colonies, is that if they are older they are not worth it."[5] Indeed, throughout the entirety of his decade at Mettray, Lardet's assessments of the inmates were consistently bleak, containing a standard refrain: "I cannot report any improvement in the mentality of the pupils as we receive the worst subjects; the vicious, the liars, the lazy, the thieves, the vagabonds, etc."[6]

What led to this this profound loss of optimism among Mettray's directors? The belief that the colony's youths were increasingly troubled was not new. As early as 1883, Director Blanchard lamented that those "coming to us now are more vicious. Many are repeat offenders and so deeply perverted there is little hope of reformation. It is easy to foresee that the Penitentiary Administration will one day be obliged to establish separate and more repressive institutions to rid the agricultural colonies of those elements which compromise their operation."[7] This complaint took on new meaning when Mettray's traditional mission was redefined by the republican state, as administrators were convinced that the colony had become an institutional backwater, a dumping ground for France's most troubled youth. The *colons* who comprised Mettray's population during the colony's halcyon days had been replaced by a new breed of offender that was cynical, jaded, and irredeemably corrupt. Immune to the colony's regimented routine, this new cohort not only undermined authority and discipline but also threatened Mettray's very existence. The colony's slow decline illustrates the collision of nineteenth-century reform ideals with the social, political, and economic realities of the twentieth century. Mettray's subjects, viewed as intractable, were subjected to a regime that became increasingly punitive as they were sanctioned for a wide variety of offenses, mostly minor. Seemingly plagued by acts of indiscipline and beset by low staff morale, Mettray was forced to close in 1937.

Since the founding of the Third Republic, Mettray had been engaged in a protracted struggle with state officials over the clerical direction of the colony. During this period the Penitentiary Administration, in tandem with reform-minded justices, began to reduce the flow of inmates to private colonies. It was only the financial strain of expanding public facilities that prevented the French state from completely secularizing juvenile corrections by the end of the nineteenth century. Nonetheless, by freezing annual subsidies for private colonies and directing more youths to public institutions, the state began to wrest control over juvenile delinquents away from religious and philanthropic organizations. According to Henri Gaillac, whereas 84 percent of all juveniles held in correctional institutions in 1870 were in private establishments, the proportion fell to 47 percent by 1900 and continued to fall through the First World War.[8] While the number of public colonies for boys grew from four in 1880 to thirteen in 1912, the number of private establishments declined markedly from fifty-six to ten over the same period.[9]

Cluze bitterly complained, "For many years now, a certain number of people belonging to the political world have cast aspersions on private agricultural colonies such as ours, which is one of the most beautiful creations in our penitentiary system. . . . It is not entirely coincidental that there has been a rapid decline in the number of youths placed in private correction. What seems to have arisen is a rivalry between public and private colonies. One must ask if this is for the greater good."[10] The jurist Robert Picot, a member of the Société paternelle and the director of the Railroad of the South, lamented the "ever-increasing atmosphere of distrust that has been created around the agricultural colonies . . . which the press echoes, the courts dare not openly combat, and the Penitentiary Administration actively encourages by reducing remittances . . . which is a demonstration of its hostility."[11] As Picot noted, the number of youths entrusted to Mettray declined by 52 percent over eleven years: from 548 in 1892 to 505 in 1895, 396 in 1898, and 262 in 1903.[12]

Yet, as Mettray's population shrank, the number of overall infractions committed by inmates increased. Whereas 4,163 prisoners committed 9,147 infractions from 1893 to 1903, only 2,383 prisoners committed 11,160 infractions from 1903 to 1913; that is, 1,780 fewer prisoners committed more than 2,000 more infractions than during the previous decade. This trend accelerated again from 1913 to 1923, as 1,449 prisoners committed a total of 20,928 infractions, an 87.5 percent increase over the preceding decade. As a result, the number of infractions per prisoner rose from a level of 2.20:1 (1893–1903) to 4.68:1 (1903–1913) and again to 14.44:1 (1913–1923).

In their efforts to account for this troubling trend, officials insisted that the problem was the prisoners themselves. In the minds of early twentieth-century administrators, Hugo's Gavroche had been replaced by the "Apaches," violent youth gangs whose frightful customs, sobriquets, and warring factions were said to be reminiscent of the Native American tribes of the American West.[13] While the Apache was largely a cultural creation, the stuff of urban myth and legend, officials such as Brun believed that Mettray had been overrun by this cohort who, in his words, "ignore what is just, what is true, what is good. Conscience is a dead letter to them and personal dignity is non-existent. . . . Their character presents an obstacle that proves nearly invincible to our efforts to bring about their moral reformation. . . . These subjects seem to follow a special path whose motto could be termed, 'Resistance is Good.'"[14] Aside from a temporary spike in the mid-1880s, however, the infraction rate at Mettray was consistently low—ranging from 2 to 3 percent—throughout most of the nineteenth century. It was not until 1911 that the rate rose to over 15 percent before peaking at the unprecedented level of 25 percent in 1917. Thus, in the seven-year period from 1910 to 1917, the infraction rate more than quintupled.

While the infraction rate dropped in the immediate postwar period, annual levels remained at or above 10 percent, which was well above the rates of the late nineteenth and early twentieth centuries. Despite the increase in the number of infractions, the proportion of misdeeds that authoriites considered the most serious—theft, immorality, assault, laziness, and acts of insubordination—declined during the same period. The only category of infraction with marked growth was "Other," which included a vast array of minor rule violations. Whereas 52.58 percent of all infractions from 1893 to 1903 were "Other," the figure grew to 71.59 percent from 1903 to 1913 and to 78.11 percent from

Table 4.   Most Frequent Disciplinary Infractions by Decade, 1893–1923

YEARS	THEFT	IMMORALITY	ASSAULT	LAZINESS	INSUBORDINATION	OTHER
1893–1903	14.93%	5.13%	2.05%	16.26%	12.25%	49.38%
1903–1913	4.10%	2.03%	2.43%	10.79%	9.06%	71.59%
1913–1923	3.34%	0.90%	1.85%	10.49%	5.31%	78.11%

1913 to 1923 (see Table 4). There is no way to determine what was included in this category but it is likely that many of the acts were the "everyday" forms of resistance that James C. Scott has examined in his work.

As John Ramsland has noted, however, there is scattered evidence that "organized rebellions on the part of *colons* became more frequent"[15] from the turn of the century, as there were several attempts at "mutinies," which might explain, at least in part, the growing pessimism of local administrators. The most notorious took place at Mettray in the late fall of 1911. On 29 October an anonymous note to Director Brun complaining about the colony's rations was found underneath the carpet of the colony's conference room. It read:

> M. Director,
>
> Please excuse us for taking the liberty of addressing this request to you. Its purpose is to inform you that the daily diet leaves much to be desired. We prefer the prior regime, because we think there are not enough apples for us to do well and that what is provided is insufficient nourishment for the stomach of an eighteen-year-old. We hope that you will consider our request, which seems just to us, for we have continued to provide the same work for less food. We are united in this request.
>
> Signed,
> Your devoted pupils of families A, B, C, D, and H.[16]

The following day a second note, addressed to all inmates at Mettray, was discovered by a workshop supervisor in the woodworking atelier:

> To the Comrades of Mettray,
>
> We have come to announce an end to all our miseries, to all our pain. Once the bell tower rings, the time for revenge will be upon us, and we hope that all of you, our comrades and friends, will join in this great work to secure our freedom, which is the desire of all, to which all of us have been refused, and to avenge all the outrages that have

been forced upon us by our fellow man. So, on Sunday [5 November] at 7:15 a.m., when the bell in the clock tower rings, revenge will be ours.[17]

Later that same day, the foreman of the brush-making shop informed Brun that three pupils had told him privately of a plan to incite a general uprising, which they did not wish to join. The most important source of information, however, was the pupil Georges M., who expressed his misgivings about the mutiny to his supervisor in the laundry detail. Brun asked the young man for a report on what was planned for that Sunday morning. He wrote:

> For two or three days we have been talking about how the revolt will begin. In family C, Emile T. will stand on a table and announce that he is rebelling because of the poor food and because you have suppressed the issuance of socks. . . . In the laundry, Laurent L. has secured a hatchet. I've heard that Jean D., in the iron workshop, has made weapons for us to defend ourselves. The shoemakers have taken knives from the workshop to storm the disciplinary quarter to release all whom you've sent there. They will kill M. Guépin and M. Rouloin [both cell-block guards at the time] and then you, M. Director, and after this terrible carnage, they plan on taking the clothes and effects from the guards' cabinets. At the butchery, knives have been hidden. In family C they have sharpened the handles of broomsticks and have hidden an axe on the grounds. There is nothing more I can tell you, M. Director, but everything I have said is the truth.
>
> p.s. Someone will sound the charge with a bugle. That is now the signal.[18]

With this information in hand, and in coordination with the local prefect, seventeen gendarmes from Tours and the village of Mettray came in under cover of darkness and hid throughout the colony on Saturday night in preparation for the next morning. At the appointed time on Sunday, according to Brun, an inmate named Benoît B. attempted to snatch a bugle from the child normally in charge of the service, "but I could see this take place, and with the assistance of a *chef de famille*, I took the bugle from the boy and he was placed in a cell. Multiple rounds were then made to make certain that all rules were observed, and that no offense took place." The leaders of the failed uprising were later identified, and a total of twenty-nine pupils were placed in cellular confinement while awaiting transfer to Eysses.[19] In a note summarizing how the plot had been thwarted, Brun exclaimed, "We can congratulate ourselves for taking the necessary measures that have prevented the execution of this project."[20]

Rebellions such as this have been as much a part of the history of the prison as systems of discipline, and "mutinies" were endemic throughout the network of French juvenile colonies by the interwar period. What is noteworthy about this case is not that officials foiled the rebellion but that they used the term *mutiny* to describe it. As Alyson Brown has noted, *mutiny* suggests a "level of organization . . . that serves to withdraw justification to resistance against the state and locates the prison and prison authorities as defenders of public security." Moreover, the term has a military connotation that was particularly resonant at Mettray, with its celebrated martial regime. As Brown points out, "a mutiny is antithetical to an ethos whose fundamental tenets are duty, loyalty, honor and patriotism . . . and the use of the word reiterates that convicts have none of these attributes and that their actions are particularly illegitimate."[21]

The relative infrequency of such events typically carries the implication that someone must be at fault, usually the director, but there is no indication that Brun was sanctioned or disciplined by Mettray's board of directors. Indeed, he successfully framed the event as a personal triumph, having thwarted the mutineers through his act of bravery and administrative acumen. In an inquiry into the attempted mutiny the prefect interviewed the movement's leaders, who indicated that they had long complained of the daily diet to Brun, to no avail. Later, in an angry missive Brun expressed his dismay that the inmates had told the prefect they were dissatisfied with the rations and that the uprising was a direct result of their requests for change going unanswered:

> You have told me that they were complaining about the food. . . . I have, despite the disapproval of the board of directors, introduced the same diet at Mettray that is applied in all the state colonies. The pupils now have more food, per day, with their ration of beans, rather than the half pittance of vegetables they used to receive. If they want to return to the old regime of dry vegetables, I would be happy to oblige, as it would result in a savings of more than 2,000 francs per year. They have complained of my severity; I blame myself for being too good and allowing my humanitarian ideas of pity and commiseration to influence me too much. Besides, I have proven myself and it is repugnant to me that I should have to justify myself.[22]

There is no evidence that the diet was changed because of the mutiny and the subsequent inquiry, but insufficient rations remained a problem until Mettray's close, which points to the inadequacy of the state-mandated rations.[23]

On 25 August 1910 the colony of Val d'Yèvre experienced a similar rebellion that began when a boy rang a bell that usually served as a fire alarm. Once the signal was given, a few of the older pupils attacked and temporarily subdued the one guard present on the outlying farm where the event took place, while the rest of the crew fled to a nearby thicket and then deeper into a wooded area. When the forty-nine pupils who participated in the mass escape were located the following evening by the local gendarmerie, they agreed to surrender on the condition their leaders be permitted to speak to the prefect in Bourges to air their grievances about their diet. Following their surrender, the prefect heard their complaints, which the director dismissed out of hand, saying that in his sixteen years as head of the colony he had already changed the soup and its method of preparation six times to suit their tastes. He blamed the rebellion on the "Apaches, pimps, burglars and representatives of the Paris underworld that have been directed here since the application of the law of 12 April 1906. They wanted to free themselves and reconquer their freedom of vice: this is the truth regarding this latest incident. The bad food and the ill-treatment invoked by the escapees are only the pretexts by which they want to cover their gesture."[24] The leaders of the mutiny were sent to Eysses and the rest of the pupils were returned to Val d'Yèvre.

Mettray's population was increasingly comprised of older youths after the Law of 1906 raised the age of penal majority from sixteen to eighteen. It was also affected by another law, passed in July 1912, which formally established penal minority for children under the age of thirteen and created an entirely separate juvenile court (Tribunal pour enfants et adolescents) with wide discretionary powers in terms of sentencing and probationary oversight. These measures were the culmination of a long series of legislative interventions aimed at protection of the child and, by extension, the delinquent child, who was increasingly viewed as a victim of social and economic forces whose effects were most acutely felt by the working class and poor. During the first thirty years of the Third Republic a new spirit of reform arose among a wide range of social theorists and legislators, much as the prison reform movement had catalyzed philanthropists such as Demetz in the early to mid-nineteenth century. As Yvorel noted, "The street urchin, the boy from Paris, was more and more considered a victim"—particularly of his parents—rather than a social menace in fin-de-siècle France.[25] The theories of deviance advanced during this period emphasized the effects of the breakdown of traditional structures of socialization such as the family and suggested new alternatives beyond the "correctional education" offered in juvenile colonies.

Georges Bonjean, a magistrate active in the movement to establish special tribunals for young offenders, attributed juvenile crime to irresponsible parents: "I confirm as a fact that the child sent for correctional treatment is generally not responsible for his acts. I confirm as a fact that, by a strange determinism, it is the fault of their parents that children are punished."[26] Alfred Fouillée similarly noted that "crime in France, especially among young people," could be attributed to a "lack of education in the family. . . . Juvenile crime is above all else a profound reflection of paternal and maternal demoralization. If the number of young criminals is increasing in France, it is due to the physical and moral degeneration of parents of a certain class, which itself is increasing in size, with their descendants. Where there is vice, debauchery and alcoholism among parents, there are children in the home who become criminals."[27] Concerned reformers collected statistics on juvenile delinquents to determine how many had been physically and/or "morally" abandoned. Auguste Motet, a physician at the Petite Roquette prison in Paris, claimed that about 10 percent of young offenders were illegitimate and almost 50 percent were orphans of one or both parents. He also reasoned that because more than two-thirds of inmates at Petite Roquette were never visited by their parents while in custody, at least that many could be considered "morally" abandoned.[28]

To combat this problem reformers proposed preventative and quasi-penal measures. For example, the jurist Ernest Passez demanded that the penal code be adjusted to allow for the prosecution of exploitative parents and libertines, who were seen as the true source of juvenile crime. "The repression of vagabonds less than sixteen years of age," he wrote, "cannot be just or efficacious unless it attains, at the same time as the vagabonds, their parents, who are often the true culprits and who are responsible for the offense due to their negligence, their faulty surveillance and the abandonment of their children."[29] In 1889 and 1898 the legislature passed two laws that defined the circumstances in which paternal authority could be rescinded by the courts.[30] Introduced by Théophile Roussel and René Bérenger, both of whom were members of Mettray's Société paternelle, the Law of 1889 stipulated that the children of "mothers and fathers who by their habitual drunkenness, their infamous and scandalous conduct, or their child abuse, compromise either the security or the health and morality of their children," could be declared wards of the state. This law proved difficult to interpret and apply, however, spurring introduction of the supplementary law of 1898. The second formulation prescribed the devolution of paternal authority in cases of crimes committed by children or against children.[31]

In the Old Regime parental authority was delegated by the king, and after the Revolution it became a fundamental individual right inscribed in the Civil Code. By providing an alternative source of discipline, the exercise of paternal authority limited state power during the first half of the nineteenth century. In the Third Republic conservative Catholics—who, not coincidentally, were among Mettray's staunchest supporters—attempted to preserve this decentralized and largely privatized system of discipline by opposing laws limiting paternal authority, characterizing them as attempts to "replace the father by the state."[32] This was a critical component in the Contard affair that led to the closure of Mettray's Maison Paternelle.

Because the Law of 1898 prescribed punishment for child neglect and even for crimes committed by one's children, it effectively treated the delinquent as a victim of his circumstances by blaming those who supposedly had driven him to commit a criminal act. In this sense, the laws of 1889 and 1898 both illustrate the way an increasingly environmental construction of criminogenesis was used to justify the intervention of the French state over large segments of the noncriminal population. More pertinent for this discussion was the way the laws allowed the state to assume functions previously exercised by private institutions such as Mettray. As Kari Evanson has astutely noted, "The laws of 1889 and 1898 not only exhibited a mistrust of working-class and poor families, which was not new, but also a growing mistrust of the agricultural colony. By modifying Article 66 of the Penal Code, the Law of 1898 gave judges a third alternative when acquitting minors for acting sans discernement."[33] As Sylvia Schafer has pointed out, the Law of 1898 "made juvenile criminality both evidence of parental mistreatment, and, at least in some cases, a problem solved through the institutions of public assistance rather than those of the penal administration."[34] Judges now had more options at their disposal: they could remand a child to a private patronage, legal guardian, or Assistance publique rather than returning him to his family or sending him to a juvenile colony.

At Mettray there was a marked decline in numbers in the three youngest age groups prior to the extension in the age of penal majority. This was likely the result of an 1879 ministerial decree that advised procureures généraux (attorney generals) to avoid the prosecution of minors under the age of sixteen, except under "grave circumstances."[35] In the 1870s 11.32 percent of Mettray's population was between the ages of eight to twelve, and that figure had fallen to less than 1 percent by the beginning of the twentieth century. Similarly, boys between the ages of twelve to fourteen, a group that constituted nearly 20 percent of the overall population in the 1870s, comprised less than 2 percent of the whole by 1900. Inmates between the ages of fourteen to sixteen had been the second largest age group at Mettray (except in the 1870s when it was the largest), but there was a sharp decrease in the first decade of the twentieth century as the proportion fell from over one-quarter of the overall population in the 1890s to 16 percent by 1910. The most explosive change, however, was in the overall percentage of youths between the ages of sixteen and twenty. While this cohort was quite sizeable, constituting more than half of all prisoners, the most dynamic area of growth was in inmates between the ages of

Table 5.   Inmate Age at Mettray, 1861–1911

DECADE	UNDER 8	8–10	10–12	12–14	14–16	16–18	18–20	ABOVE 20
1861–70	0.36%	2.69%	11.34%	21.67%	31.34%	24.49%	8.11%	0.00%
1871–80	0.24%	2.20%	8.88%	19.35%	29.61%	28.93%	10.80%	0.00%
1881–90	0.00%	1.08%	4.22%	11.10%	27.27%	33.75%	22.58%	0.00%
1891–1900	0.00%	0.25%	0.75%	9.42%	26.64%	39.44%	23.49%	0.00%
1901–1911	0.00%	0.00%	0.00%	1.88%	16.02%	50.59%	30.86%	0.66%

eighteen and twenty. Whereas prisoners in this age group were a minority of the population in the 1870s, in the first decade of the twentieth century almost one-third of all inmates at Mettray were between the ages of eighteen and twenty. As a result, the mean age at Mettray rose from 14.24 to 17.55 years in the half-century surveyed (see Table 5).

There was a general assumption among local administrators that older inmates exerted a baleful influence on their younger comrades, and they were blamed for undermining discipline and authority in the colony. It does seem logical that older youths would be more difficult to manage than younger boys. Given their greater physical and intellectual maturity it is likely that they could better resist guards and were probably more skillful at evading rules while feigning compliance. If this older cohort could be removed from the colony, officials argued, Mettray could resume its role as a model institution; otherwise, Mettray could not be expected to achieve the noble aims of its founder.

During the early twentieth century Mettray's officials increasingly made reference to certain emotional and developmental challenges associated with adolescence to justify the failure of their institution to socialize and discipline its denizens. Such characterizations, though crude and simplistic, enjoyed a currency among Mettray's directors, who seemed unable to understand their young subjects. The broadly conceived transitional stage of life known simply as "youth" had been narrowed and redefined during the last quarter of the nineteenth century. Although they did not adhere to the physiological determinism of the American psychologist G. Stanley Hall, French physicians and psychiatrists nevertheless conceived of adolescence as beginning with the onset of puberty—roughly around the age of thirteen for boys (girls were understood to mature earlier)—and not ending until physical development finished, sometime around age eighteen for both sexes. It was during this period that adolescents exhibited acute emotional uncertainty and instability, a general tendency toward rebellion, and an awkward awakening of sexual desire.[36]

By the eve of the First World War it was generally assumed that any professional concerned with young people had to have at least a basic understanding of the importance of adolescence to one's future adult life. The jurist Louis Proal characterized adolescents as "jealous, angry, vindictive, cruel, and prone to lie. . . . In these souls one uncovers most of the same passions which agitate and disturb the hearts of men yet they are much quicker to explode in anger at the slightest provocation and are subject to impulses and acts of violence that result from feelings of exasperation or profound depression."[37] The physician Paul Garnier, who worked in the infirmary of the Paris prefecture of police, encountered "many juvenile delinquents who generally possessed a good lively spirit as children . . . but who, after a few years, reach puberty, with its continual progression of disturbances and diverse transformations. . . . [Thus] their tastes and habits change; they refuse to work and they do not respond to order or counsel. . . . They develop a quick temper and are more instinctual in character which manifests itself in bad tendencies and harmful dispositions."[38] The eminent psychologist Alfred Binet identified a "huge and ridiculous vanity" as the predominant trait of adolescence "which drives their selfishness and egoism. . . . Note what their relationships are with their accomplices and those who are part of the same gangs; the way in which they boast of their skill and courage with one another; the manner their comrades can sometimes push one to commit a crime by saying to them, if they hesitate, 'are you afraid? Are you not a man?'"[39]

As adolescence came to be accepted as a distinct stage in the life cycle, those who operated juvenile colonies grew increasingly concerned about their inability to contain and control the spread of mimetic corruption (i.e., "social contagion") from older to younger inmates. The first director of the penitentiary colony at Eysses, M. Grosmolard, noted: "It is a point of honor for them to demonstrate their aversion and even insolence toward authority. There is only one authority before which the judgement and the will of the young detainee will bend; it is the opinion of his older comrades and especially that of his group leader."[40] As part of an anthropometric study of the boys housed at Aniane, which generally refuted Lombrosian assumptions about the atavistic stigmata of the "born criminal," the colony's physician, Dr. Rouveyrolis, noted that there were

> more and more adolescents who are very mature. . . . It is important to speak about them usefully, to discuss their special psychology. The indulgence of the judge who, despite their precocious maturity, regards them as having acted "sans discernment," is seen by the adolescent as a humiliation which they do not accept. They accept common sanctions,

those applied to adults for the same misdeeds; but they rebel against any solution to which they have been made a special object. . . . How, among the youngest [emphasis in original], do some (those who are the softest), become the slaves of the older in all their requirements—one understands me when I say this, I think [here Rouveyrolis is alluding to homosexuality]—while others (those who are the most impulsive) reveal an astonishing boldness, despite their age, and are inspired to demonstrate that for them, "age is meaningless."[41]

According to the prison physician J. Maxwell, "To determine the means most appropriate to discipline their character one need not look any further than that which operates in their gangs; it is fear. Their leaders are obeyed by force. The general and profound perversity of the chiefs serves to only make their subjects listen more intently and slavishly follow their every whim."[42] Rouveyrolis concluded that there was little possibility of reforming adolescents: "Can we at least reeducate them? I think I can say, with certainty, that this is an incredibly difficult and often thankless task. With some luck, we can only hope to have serious results on those children who are very young, that is to say, those whose age makes reform possible."[43]

The First World War likely contributed to feelings of restlessness and discontent among the older prisoners. While Director Brun was pessimistic about the potential for reform of his subjects, Mettray's board of directors at least acknowledged that "although their moral state does not seem to improve, the great events of the war have made an impression on them. Their hearts died with the loss of their homes. The instinct of theft, the rapier, has taken on an incited development in many of the *colons*, which can be traced to the looting and robberies conducted by the *Boches* [Germans] once they invaded this country."[44] To the colony's aging staff—low salaries had long hindered the recruitment and retention of new personnel—the *colons* were seen as "little more than the enemy."[45]

The generational divide was exacerbated by the Great War, which decimated the colony's staff. Thirty of the colony's eighty-five employees were called into service in 1914, leaving behind only those who were too old to fight. Director Brun lamented that it was nearly impossible to find "men capable of replacing their delicate functions," and many of those who were hired soon left their positions with the "excuse that the work was too difficult with youths who were vicious, indocile and lacked all discipline." According to Brun, as the "pupils have witnessed the departure of so many of our personnel they have quickly learned to abuse their replacements, even by intimidation and threats." In 1915 twenty-four provisional agents either resigned or were re-

moved for reasons of their "moral incapacity, drunkenness, or other mo-
tives." Brun partly attributed the sharp rise in escapes during the conflict to a
"lack of serious monitoring" by "a staff that is comprised of agents who are
tired and dispirited," all of whom he hoped to "replace after we have achieved
a victorious peace."[46] Due to the lack of adequate manpower he was forced
to temporarily close most of the colony's industrial workshops—masonry,
brush-making, shoemaking, and painting—as "suitable foremen" could not be
located "without paying them a very high salary."[47]

Staffing was a problem not limited to wartime, however, as Mettray struggled to find qualified personnel throughout the interwar period. In 1923 Director Lardet noted that "the recruitment of agents has become more and
more difficult as work in the fields and life in the countryside does not attract
enough candidates for employment."[48] Two years later, he similarly remarked,
"When vacancies arise, we still have great difficulty in recruiting agents for
the reasons I have already outlined: insufficient benefits; not enough free time
each month; and the demands of a trip to the countryside each day. The city
attracts everyone. I have found three former retired adjutants to replace the
three surveillants who resigned this year. I will look to this again in the future
should the need arise."[49] But as Éric Pierre has noted, the quality of the personnel employed at Mettray declined in the postwar period as demobilized soldiers tended to leave their posts as soon as they found employment in
occupations that offered better remuneration. As a result, many of the posts
were filled by former prison guards of the Penitentiary Administration, most
of whom had grown old and tired from their service in adult institutions. In
addition, many *chefs de famille* failed to complete a full year of service, lasting
only three or four months in a very demanding position.[50] Administrators
made a belated effort to remedy the situation by increasing the salaries and
benefits for staff in the early 1930s, but by then Mettray's fate was largely
sealed.

It was not only the circumstances of the war and its aftermath that Brun
found troubling; he was also truly disturbed by his young subjects. In a letter
to the local prefect that was remarkable both for its candor and for the sense
of futility it conveys, the director offered a bleak assessment of Mettray's population. Brun maintained that the general character of his charges was
marked by a "viciousness" and a distinct "lack of sentiment."

They have a horror of uniformity, of order and propriety; their spirit of
destruction, however, is very well developed, and they revel in disorder
and filthiness. As for their mores, we cannot reach them, even when
employing the language of Virgil. They know all, they are ignorant of

nothing; a grand moral disorder has touched even the most remote and delicate fibers of their cerebral organization. . . . Everything they see, everything around them, does not interest them. They do not wish to understand, they do not want to know the causes, unless those things touch upon immorality. . . . They accuse society, in the personnel of the administration, of being the source of their misery and making them bad subjects. Thus, they will always fight against the laws of society and against honor. For them, our work of preservation takes on the character of torture, of agony, and an abuse of power. "We want to be bad," they say, "and no one has right to impose anything on us."[51]

According to the director, Mettray's subjects were doomed—"so habituated to insubordination and revolt vis-à-vis their chiefs, they will soon be joining soldiers at the front, where this penchant will likely prove fatal."[52]

Unsurprisingly, Brun attributed the uptick in escapes to the category of minors "that have been admitted since the application of the law of 12 April 1906." According to the director, "When one fully understands the moral organization of our pupils, especially of the oldest boys, one is obliged to recognize that escapes and attempted escapes in an open colony such as ours are to be expected, as the only hindrance are individual surveillants responsible for teams of twenty-five to thirty pupils."[53] In the thirteen years following passage of the Law of 1906, the colony received 842 minors aged eighteen to twenty. Of that number, almost one-quarter (209) were transferred to other correctional colonies for various rules violations, mostly escapes, and of these 137 were sent to Eysses. Brun could "not refrain" from noting that recidivism among this particular cohort was "particularly high. These youths do not take advice of any kind, for in these individuals the preoccupations of the honest man who leads an honest life do not exist."[54]

Both young and old *colons* attempted escape, but more problematic for local administrators—and posing a real threat to public safety—were older fugitives who committed burglaries and thefts and engaged in property destruction while on the run. Angry letters from nearby mayors demanding stricter surveillance of inmates made their way to the préfet d'Indre-et-Loire with increasing frequency during the interwar period. A declaration authored by the mayor of Boulay calling for "a more rigorous surveillance" was jointly signed by mayors of the surrounding communities of Crotelles, Château-Renault, Morand, Saint-Nicolas, Autrèche, Villedômer, Saint-Laurent-en-Gâtines, Nouzilly, Monthodon, and Saunay.[55] In addition, the Council of Indre-et-Loire issued an official statement in 1931 that condemned "the crimes and offenses committed by the residents of Mettray are a real terror for the surrounding population whose security is threatened by an ever-increasing number of escapes. Considering the insufficient surveillance of *colons* who work in large groups under the supervision of a single guardian . . . and the more perverse character of many *colons* sent to Mettray, the council demands that surveillance be strengthened and that a more rigorous selection of those who are admitted to Mettray be made."[56]

There were two felonies committed by escapees that galvanized local public opinion against the colony. On the evening of 30 August 1927 two *colons* set fire to a field of wheat near the town of Saint-Symphorien with a lantern they had stolen from a railway line under repair. The municipal council noted in an official letter to the préfet d'Indre-et-Loire that the fire had caused damage estimated at 20,000 francs for the farmer, but even more dangerous was the theft of the lantern, which "could have easily led to a railway disaster" because there was nothing in place to alert engineers to slow down on approach to that portion of the line. The council concluded that although "Mettray has the duty to subject its pupils to a serious surveillance it appears as though it is insufficient."[57]

Almost three years later, an eighteen-year-old escapee, Roger R., found a rifle in a nearby chateau and shot and seriously wounded the resident caretaker before attempting to set the house on fire. The municipal council of the commune of Chanceaux-sur-Choisille issued a strongly worded declaration demanding that "energetic measures be taken by the Ministry of Justice and the Société paternelle to put an immediate end to the misdeeds" of escaped *colons* who "pose a real danger to the population."[58] In a letter to the prefect about the incident, Director Lardet characterized the young man as highly disturbed and mentally challenged, but offered no explanation how he had easily escaped the colony. "In a boy who would have his full faculties such a crime could not be explained, but this is a mentally retarded man [note the distinction between boy and man] who had also been made to stay at the asylum of Saint-Dizier for his debility of onanism" before being confined at Mettray in 1927. According to the director, "the unspeakable act was the result of his mental aberration."[59]

Aside from allusions to mental illness, Lardet offered little in the way of explanation or justification for why escapes from Mettray seemed to be on the rise. He dismissed a demand from the municipal council of Notre-Dame-d'Oé that Mettray hire additional guards by noting that the "inspector general has made, on several occasions, the observation that the staff of the colony was too numerous, more numerous than colonies of the state."[60] In a report from 1930 he defended Mettray's efforts to maintain security while pointing out, somewhat counterintuitively, that escapes were common and frequent "in all

OPEN COLONIES [original emphasis] and the latter cannot, any more than at Mettray, prevent such acts in a certain class of unstable pupils."[61]

Not only the surrounding communities but also the local gendarmerie were dismayed by the evident lack of security at Mettray. In a letter to the local prefect the commandant of the gendarmerie of the Indre-et-Loire wrote: "The continual progression of escapes from Mettray has resulted in grave inconveniences as it impinges upon our time and has had an adverse effect on the accomplishment of our service. The apprehension of *colons* necessitates long and difficult searches, often at night while in the woods or in the fields. . . . I must ask that something be done, otherwise we will be forced to request an increase in our numbers." Indeed, the number of calls on the gendarmes to search for escapees from Mettray rose from 56 in 1932 to 70 in 1933, 122 in 1934, and 166 in 1935. Most of the calls were answered by the brigade at Membrolle, whose territory included the colony of Mettray, for which, according to the official, it had spent "one-third of its time searching for escaped *colons*" in 1935. Finally, he noted that while a fifteen-franc reward was "allotted for each pupil returned to the colony," this sum failed to compensate for the costs of the searches.[62] Although there are scattered examples in the historical record of citizens claiming such rewards, Éric Pierre has noted that this was a relatively rare occurrence.[63]

The responsibility for retrieving and returning a captured prisoner from a local jail lay not with the police but with officials of the colony from which he had escaped. The returns sometimes turned violent, particularly when they involved older youths. In March 1909 Éric P., a seventeen-year-old pupil of Mettray, escaped from the hospital in Tours where he was recovering from influenza and was eventually recaptured in Lyon. When the agent from Mettray arrived to take him back to the colony, he "put up a fierce resistance by throwing himself on the agent, striking, kicking, spitting and swearing at him" before he was eventually apprehended by police. He was sent to Val d'Yèvre rather than returned to Mettray.[64]

In another case, Charles G. was captured by police in Tours two days after escaping from Mettray in May 1913. Cornered by police, the young man grabbed from his pocket a large compass whose points had been sharpened in the atelier where he worked and frantically tried to slit his wrists, yelling that he would "not go back to Mettray," before he was physically subdued. The agent from the colony who was dispatched to retrieve the young man the next day had been advised by the director to bring handcuffs because the prisoner was "inclined to resistance . . . and has displayed a deplorable attitude since his arrival." Indeed, as he was led away through the streets of Tours he reportedly "yelled and insulted every person he encountered. . . . He addressed sev-

eral women in the coarsest fashion imaginable, [and] called out for the help
of thugs on the street while raising the handcuffs that bound his wrists in the
air." During the journey back to Mettray by carriage, the youth somehow managed to raise his manacled hands over the agent's back and there was a "veritable battle" until the guard subdued his aggressor and retook control of the
reins. Arriving at a local farm, the agent asked for rope and bound the subject's hands and feet before returning him to Mettray.[65]

While Charles G. was eventually sent to Eysses, the initial request was
blocked by the Ministry of Justice, which indicated to the local prefect that
Eysses was "at present full," and that moving forward, "All directors, NOTA-
BLY THE DIRECTOR OF THE METTRAY COLONY [original emphasis]
should reduce by at least one-quarter the number of demands for reintegra-
tion and take special measures regarding undisciplined subjects until the day
when it will be possible to change establishments." While the prohibition from
the ministry was intended for all directors, Mettray was the only colony sin-
gled out, in large measure due to the institution's inability to forestall escapes.[66]
Ironically, given the complaints of administrators at Mettray, ministerial officials had long suspected that private colonies were dumping their worst inmates on public institutions such as Eysses. A communiqué issued from the
Ministry of the Interior to the préfet du Cher in 1884 noted: "The directors of
the private colonies give in to the temptation to get rid of their most recalcitrant subjects by sending them to a correctional colony, and thus dispensing
with the costs associated with placing them in their own punishment cells for
supervision. These same directors, if they have elite subjects, workers who are
zealous, whose labor is valuable, will sometimes withhold or delay the award
of the provisional release thereby depriving the young subject of a valuable
reward for his good behavior."[67] This is the same complaint that had been leveled against private colonies by the Voisin committee over a decade earlier.

Before the outbreak of the First World War, officials at Mettray had im-
plored authorities to investigate a purported safe house in Tours that had
been brought to their attention after the capture and return of four escapees
in June 1912. In a letter addressed to the prefect, Brun maintained that when
questioned, the boys said they had been given refuge in the home of a man
named Poulain, who in the past had "given many escapees old clothes, a little
money and directions to the train station. . . . I would be very obliged if you
would kindly consider whether it is possible to put a stop to those involved in
these actions, specifically M. Poulain and whatever accomplices he may have."[68]
The prefect twice requested a formal investigation into the matter but the prosecutor refused, writing in a rather terse note that there was insufficient evidence for the claims.[69] Unfortunately, there is nothing more in the extant

correspondence that reveals whether the matter was pursued at a later date, but the prosecutor's cavalier attitude to escapes and the management of affairs at Mettray is noteworthy. As Ramsland points out, the claim about the safe house also demonstrates that at least among a few citizens, there was "some sympathy for the inmates of Mettray."[70]

Not only administrators but also lower-level staff members were disturbed by the presence of older youths in the juvenile colonies. Director Voisin noted in a report that he had been approached by M. Baudet, chief of the disciplinary quarter, who asked what he and his subordinates should do "if they found themselves amid a violent revolt or in the presence of a violent older pupil. I replied that although force is allowed by regulation to restore order, there are always two guards present in the quarter and that the use of the baton should not be necessary . . . yet these good words did not appear to alleviate his concerns or those of the staff who serve in the quarter."[71] In a note forwarded to the local prefect complaining that they felt constrained by regulations, particularly when dealing with older youths, the surveillants of Aniane evinced similar misgivings:

> Our "petits enfants," as they are referred to in the press, come to us with anarchist ideas and with this revolutionary spirit they only want to do as they please. It is impossible to order them to line up or make a count in the ranks. If we "paternally" invite them to line up by taking them gently by the arm, most of them will scowl or act disrespectfully by jostling or pulling away. "You have no right to touch us," they say. Within the space of just a few days, three officers have been slapped by our "petits enfants." You do not think that the Popular Front government would authorize legislation which would encourage a child to strike his father, do you? Given the indiscipline that exists in the school, dining hall, workshops and dormitories, the staff no longer knows what to do. If one is struck and then defends himself, he is in violation of regulations. . . . At eighteen years of age one can enter a regiment as a man and be punished as such. Here, our "petits enfants" remain children until they are twenty. Why not employ the discipline of the regiment in what is supposed to be the pupil's second family? The notions of order and discipline that once guided Aniane would be useful for them.[72]

Twenty-five years earlier, a contingent of guards had forwarded a similar complaint to the local prefect regarding "the attitude of the pupils of the colony toward their surveillants," effectively bypassing Director Jules Rochet, whom they believed had removed all their "authority" in dealing with rebellious youths by adhering to the regulations issued by the Penitentiary Administration in 1869. They wrote, "Revocations have been pronounced against surveillants who have struck pupils in self-defense . . . one of whom received numerous kicks to the head and groin while lying on the ground as these young thugs were shouting 'Kill him!'"[73] The prefect forwarded the letter to Rochet, who dismissed the charges, calling them a "tissue of lies and inaccuracies written by cowards who hide behind their anonymity. I have nothing to answer for. Everything has been done according to the regulations."[74] This was precisely the point that his men had made to the prefect. There is no information in the historical record on the cited incident, however, and there is no indication that the prefect pursued the matter further.

The Penitentiary Administration frequently reminded local officials that the "idea of repression has given way to more humane principles surrounding education" and that deviations from official policy on the treatment of inmates in the juvenile colonies would not be tolerated. One such reminder that made its way to the préfet de l'Hérault in 1898 (the department where Aniane was located) noted that "the children entrusted to the administration . . . must be led not by inflexible leaders, but by guides who operate on the principle of goodwill and who have, as their primary objective, a desire to teach them a useful trade so that they can earn an honest living. It is important that children feel loved. . . . Punishments must never effect either the health or dignity of the pupil." The invocation of love is fascinating because Aniane's regime was both highly restrictive and harshly punitive, not paternal or familial. The prefect was also instructed to remind Aniane's director that there could be no reduction in daily rations and that the use of handcuffs as a disciplinary measure remained strictly prohibited.[75]

Aniane had a well-deserved reputation as a violent institution, and internal records show that attacks on guards and staff were a relatively common feature of daily life. While most of these assaults did not result in serious physical harm, there were occasions when the violence was grave. In perhaps the most notorious assault in the colony's history, a seventeen-year-old pupil, Louis M., murdered forty-year-old Fulcrand Terme, a cobbler who was his workshop supervisor. Witnesses recalled that on 20 September 1911 the young man waited until the surveillant who guarded the atelier had left the building to attend to other duties before striking Terme from behind and then fatally stabbing him with a leather knife. The assailant was quickly subdued by the guard, who hurried back to the shop when he heard shouting from pupils, but Terme died at the scene, leaving behind a wife, two young children, and an invalid father.[76]

Although he had worked at Aniane as a workshop supervisor for over eleven years earning 5.50 francs per day, Terme had accumulated only a

Table 6.   Assault Rate, 1853–1923

INSTITUTION	1853–63	1863–73	1873–83	1883–93	1893–1903	1903–13	1913–23
Mettray	6.04%	7.61%	4.03%	1.91%	2.05%	1.85%	2.43%
Private	3.57%	3.38%	2.76%	1.47%	1.62%	5.21%	2.24%
Public	3.65%	6.39%	5.80%	5.69%	4.10%	4.64%	4.98%

modest pension at the time of his death. His widow brought a civil suit against Aniane seeking damages for negligence, which she won on 13 July 1912, and the court ordered the state to pay her 12,000 francs to be evenly split between herself and her two children. However, because Terme's seventy-five-year-old father, Frédéric, was not included in the settlement, he brought a separate suit in the Montpellier Civil Court seeking 45,000 francs in damages. The position of the state was that it had no legal obligation beyond what had already been paid to the immediate family. While the elder Terme did not win a separate judgment, his suit laid bare how dangerous Aniane could be for workshop supervisors. According to Marius Nougaret, the father's attorney, "The absence of this surveillant from the workshop, and that of others as well, is reflected in the numerous reports of the directorate which have for a long time created a potentially dangerous situation and provided an opportunity for the inmate Louis M. to act upon his excited hostility." Indeed, Terme had been seriously wounded eight years before his death when he was inadvertently stabbed in the stomach with a leather knife while trying to separate two inmates who were fighting—at the time, no surveillants were present. Nougaret argued that the "absence or irregularity of surveillance has been ignored by the administration for years" and that "despite the energetic protests of M. Terme and others, monitoring has never become more active," which constituted an act of "culpable negligence" on the part of local officials.[77]

In contrast to Aniane, Mettray had a relatively low rate of assault throughout the twentieth century. Including attacks on both fellow *colons* and staff, assaults accounted for less than 2 percent of all infractions committed in the decade from 1883 to 1893, whereas the average in public institutions stood at nearly 6 percent. Indeed, the rate at Mettray steadily declined from a rate of well over 7 percent from 1863 to 1873 to slightly below 2 percent from 1903 to 1913, although there was a slight upward trend in the following decade (see Table 6). Thus, inmate violence was significantly more prevalent under Demetz's directorship than under his successors, who oversaw a dramatic drop.[78]

Unlike assaults, escapes from Mettray were common, and there was a general feeling among administrators in Paris, as well as the public, that this was evidence that the colony was in a state of serious disorder and decline. In his inspection report of December 1931, M. Auzemat, inspecteur general des services administratifs, attributed the escapes not to the changing nature of the *colons* but rather to an "insufficient number of supervisors owing to poor recruitment, a staff who do not fulfil their duties with the necessary awareness and punctuality," and a director (Lardet) who "lacks the energy required to lead an institution of this importance." Auzemat also noted that "children are sent to the disciplinary quarter for what are often the most frivolous faults and the penalty is therefore not proportionate to the misdeed committed." Indeed, he discovered that fifty-four of the fifty-seven pupils in the quarter at the time of his visit were being punished for minor infractions, and most were there for indeterminate periods (i.e., "until further notice"). Finally, and unsurprisingly, considering the administration's long intransigence on the issue, Auzemat remarked on the "difficulty in obtaining the exact statement of funds in the colony's bank account. The exact state of the treasury should be given to any inspector who is entitled to request it."[79]

On the heels of the report, Mettray's board of directors officially relieved Lardet of his duties in March 1932 (M. Deluce, an inspector, was appointed interim director as of 1 January). To attract a more qualified pool of applicants and to aid in the retention of capable personnel, the board increased salaries and benefits to a level roughly commensurate with those offered by the state (see Table 7).

Guards saw pay increases in amounts ranging from 2,840 to 3,540 francs per annum, the implementation of a new a wage scale that rewarded continued service at Mettray, and an increase in the annual entry-level salary from 5,480 to 8,500 francs (see Table 8).

Staff were also paid annual allowances for dependents of 400 francs per child, an increase of 220 francs.[80]

A meeting of all staff was convened to announce the reforms on 11 January 1932. Georges Goüin, the son of Eugène, who had been president of the board of directors during the 1887 scandal, proclaimed that the "first thing necessary to ensure a good staff, one that is conscious of its obligations, is that they receive benefits like those offered by the state," a declaration that reportedly met with the unanimous support of those present. He added that there was also an expectation that the increased salaries would instill a greater sense of pride and purpose among the staff, who must avoid "crude talk, drunkenness or the harsh treatment of *colons*" or risk facing serious reprimands, a policy that one might have mistakenly assumed had always been in force. Two

Table 7.   Salaries of Service Personnel as of 1932

SERVICE ADMINISTRATION	CURRENT ANNUAL SALARIES	NEW ANNUAL SALARIES
Director	16,000	20,000
Inspector	12,360	18,000
Chief of Agriculture	12,360	16,000
Clerk	10,360	15,000
Cashier	9,960	13,000
Surveillant Chief	8,760	12,000
Teacher	4,000	8,000

Table 8.   Salaries of Surveillants as of 1932

Surveillant First Class	More than 24 years of service	10,000
Surveillant Second Class	More than 20 years of service	9,700
Surveillant Third Class	More than 16 years of service	9,500
Surveillant Fourth Class	More than 12 years of service	9,300
Surveillant Fifth Class	More than 9 years of service	9,100
Surveillant Sixth Class	More than 6 years of service	8,900
Surveillant Seventh Class	More than 3 years of service	8,700
Surveillant	Less than 3 years of service	8,500

elderly guards, M. Marout and M. Haudebourg, both of whom were seventy-eight years old and whose "state of health did not allow them to fulfil their functions to the satisfaction of their supervisor," were dismissed with pensions. A third guard, M. Leday, was dismissed for "intemperance." Finally, the disciplinary quarter was effectively cleared out; during the month of January the number of *colons* in cellular confinement dropped to a daily average of sixteen and a maximum of twenty-three as the practice of confining inmates for minor infractions was abandoned, albeit temporarily.

While the rhetoric on homosexuality at Mettray had always been quite harsh, officials in the interwar period seemed lackadaisical about policing it. The administration severely punished those whom they suspected of engaging in homosexual acts, but they were seemingly oblivious to what happened in the cottages at night, perhaps secure in their belief that the panoptic presence of the *chef de famille* would curtail such activity. Auzemat's report characterized the surveillance of the dormitories as "poorly organized," with guards making only "one inspection per night and always at the same hour, which permits the *colons* to engage in the most reprehensible acts."[81]

Adhering to the inspector's recommendations, officials increased the number of nightly rounds and staggered the times when guards inspected the dormitories, setting aside a fund to pay those who took on these added responsibilities. Although there was a general expectation that all personnel, including those in the service administration (office staff), would at some point assume nightwatch duties, the extant records do not show whether this happened. In a later examination of Mettray's entire operation, the administrative council concluded: "One of the most serious reproaches made against Mettray is that the common dormitory leads to immorality. The director has completed a study as to how we might transform one or two of the dormitories currently in use. The construction of forty cells in each of the dormitories would be accompanied by the installation of windows, walls and ceilings which would cost approximately 80,000 francs. The council hereby authorizes the expenditure of such funds so that work may begin as soon as possible."[82]

There are three points worth noting here. First, the proposed "solution" to homosexuality was far from ideal because it made the surveillance of the cottages more cumbersome and less cost-efficient. Second, it was an admission that the cottage's architecture of visibility had failed to inhibit and curtail homosexual impulses and relations, particularly at night when officials were most uneasy about the maintenance of moral order. In other words, the totalizing assumption of a panoptic gaze, at least as it pertained to sexual surveillance, was more in the realm of myth than reality. Third, the recourse to a cellular ward represented a last gasp by officials to extend sexual immaturity and "innocence"—even in cases where the youthful body had matured well beyond childhood—by placing *colons* in a state of arrested sexual development.

Most agricultural colonies were explicitly based on Mettray's cottage model, so the dormitory had been a compromised space from the outset in both private and public institutions. Thirty years before the rather belated effort by officials at Mettray to reconfigure the dormitory, the director of the colony at Val d'Yèvre characterized the design of its cottages as "defective and insufficient. As they sleep in hammocks that are only seventy centimeters apart from one another, we have a general level of promiscuity that is deplorable from all points of view." To attenuate the "pernicious effects" of the cottage layout, "it is necessary to exercise a constant surveillance at the expense of our agents who are overworked." As at Mettray, the director requested that the cottages be redesigned to allow for individual cells or rooms and that new buildings be constructed to house inmates. While the préfet du Cher was sympathetic to the "defective situation" in the colony, the award of "extraordinary budget credits" for such a redesign was not possible and Val d'Yèvre remained largely unchanged until its close in 1924.[83]

In a frank report outlining the daily regime and the causes of a prisoner rebellion at Aniane, an unnamed inspector from the Penitentiary Administration argued, "It is in the dormitories that we must look for the obscure causes of the acts of indiscipline and the threat of a revolt that seemingly had no motive." He continued:

> Three hundred and seventy-five inmates are divided into four dormitories in beds aligned in tight rows while monitored by eleven guards who sleep in rooms with doors that are equipped with peepholes. But these guards, tired by their daytime service, are accustomed to their sounds. They sleep well and watch little; we cannot reproach them. . . . After each round is completed, the prisoners are left free. And they make use of this freedom. . . . The types of passions that arise resemble nothing that is human. . . . How could one possibly be morally improved under conditions which exist outside nature and in which there is an apprenticeship of passions among young men who experience morbid paroxysms of love, jealousy, hatred, anger and revenge.[84]

In the eyes of the inspector, the daytime operation at Aniane was generally efficient and effective: "Thanks to the excellent organization of work, the pupil may believe he is simply the resident of a vocational school." However, "when night comes they are thrown together pell-mell and left to fend for themselves while in the most deplorable states of promiscuity." Thus, power and order were maintained through the daily schedule, represented by the regimented segmentation of time; when that authority waned, as it did when the prisoners returned in the evening to the dormitory, they were no longer subjects to be disciplined and controlled. To address the problem, the inspector did not recommend the discontinuation of communal sleeping arrangements but rather a selection process that would separate, on their arrival at colony, "the younger and weaker pupils who are at the mercy of those older and stronger." In addition, he suggested that dormitories be reduced in size to house perhaps only twenty to twenty-five pupils who would be placed under the surveillance of one guard, which to his mind would be more akin to what one sees in college dormitories.[85] While the inspection report acknowledged that crowded forms of confinement exacerbated illegitimate forms of intimacy among inmates, little was done to address the situation at Aniane. The recommended construction of two-story pavilions with two subdivided dormitory spaces on each floor was never pursued by officials.

To address behavioral problems at Mettray, particularly the attempts to escape, Director Voisin instituted measures to reform the regime by improving the quality, quantity, and variety of daily rations; allowing pupils to grow out their hair; allowing eight-day releases to visit families; and increasing the variety of recreational activities available to pupils, such as the staging of theatrical productions and screenings of Hollywood films. Yet, as he noted, "The amelioration of the material conditions has had little effect on the sick urge to escape which seems to grow every day in the minds of our pupils." Indeed, he was astounded that many of the escapees were "youths with excellent records, many of whom were nearly at the point of obtaining their liberation." When interrogated after capture, "they cannot provide any reason or excuse for their escape. They usually shrug their shoulders and say, 'I was bored. It was a lark. I had the blues.'"[86] As Mettray's last director, it was Voisin who wrote the final official report on the *colons*, which was noteworthy for its sense of resignation. "The mentality of the new pupils does not vary. Laziness is the dominant failing; we have the greatest difficulty in obtaining work from them. When it accompanies, as it frequently does, a vicious nature inclined to destroy or brutalize animals, improvement is obtained slowly, if at all. . . . The effect of puberty on their nature and the behavioral traits inherited from their parents last a long time. . . . Beyond age eighteen, if their perversity persists, there is no longer any hope of improvement."[87]

Despite his vague reference to the problems posed by adolescence and heredity, Voisin nonetheless maintained that the proximate cause of the escapes was "the result of the events at Belle-Île and the idiotic and the mendacious press campaign to which we have been subjected and which has certainly affected the rather unbalanced minds of our pupils, as we have heard many declare: 'Since the escapes of the *colons* of Belle-Île have been approved by the newspapers we too have reasons to escape.'"[88] The revolt at Belle-Île, a correctional colony on an island off the coast of Brittany, was the most notorious of the numerous rebellions that rocked state-run institutions throughout the 1920s and 1930s. On 2 August 1934 a guard at the colony beat an inmate for a minor infraction, sparking a riot, and fifty-six youths fled the facility. It took a few days for the boys to be recaptured, even with the aid of locals who were paid a twenty-franc reward for each escapee they apprehended. National and regional newspapers provided breathless coverage of the mass escape, and the incident was critical in arousing public sympathy for the plight of young men held in such institutions. It also inspired the poet and screenwriter Jacques Prévert to pen a poem about the escape, "La chasse à l'enfant" ("The Hunt for the Child"), which was later set to music and popularized by the cabaret singer Marianne Oswald.[89]

In the wake of the events at Belle-Île, the juvenile colonies became a cause célèbre as crusading journalists such as Alexis Danan and Louis Roubaud exposed, in graphic detail, the conditions to which youths were subjected. While most of the press campaign was aimed at state-run institutions, Mettray escaped neither journalistic scrutiny nor the pejorative label *bagnes d'enfants* that was attached to all juvenile colonies. The term *bagne*, which originally referred to the dockyard prisons of the early modern period, was extended to the overseas penal colonies of French Guiana and New Caledonia during the second half of the nineteenth century. The use of the term recalled that those overseas penal colonies had been under sustained attack from journalists such as Albert Londres for their abject cruelty and inhumanity since the 1920s.[90] Not unlike Londres, journalists in newspapers across the political spectrum were now engaged in a similar campaign to expose abuses at Mettray and other juvenile colonies.

Attention was particularly intense due to a new reportorial practice that might be termed, in contemporary parlance, "investigative journalism." Rather than merely reciting daily events, an individual staff reporter undertook a longer-term investigation (*enquête*) of a subject, which typically culminated in a series of articles that were often republished in book form. No longer dependent on the events of the day, this practice, referred to as *grand reportage*, allowed for the "creation" of news.[91] Yet, the themes that dominated the press coverage of Mettray during the 1930s were not unlike those in the scandals of the late nineteenth and early twentieth centuries. The colony had survived those earlier attacks, but obviously things had not improved. There were still concerns about the exploitation of inmate labor for profit; the brutality and incompetence of guards and staff; the institution's clericalism; the lack of state oversight; the rudimentary efforts to educate the *colons*; and the adherence to an anachronistic vision of a rural France that no longer existed. The challenge facing reformers was to catalyze political support for a fundamental change in the entire system of juvenile corrections, a task that had long been hindered by the continual governmental churn that marked the Third Republic and effectively eliminated any real possibility of enacting sweeping legislative reforms.

With front-page photographs and bold headlines such as "The Pastors of Lost Children" and "A Shame: Mettray, Private Establishment of Torture," Danan and Roubaud styled many of their articles as essentially open letters to various high officials in order to command the government's attention. Danan reminded Georges Pernot, the minister of the interior, that it was his duty "to control the use made by Mettray's board of directors of the important subsidies that the national budget allocates to it for the maintenance, reeducation, and rehabilitation of the children entrusted to its care by Public Assistance and the juvenile courts. Where do the profits come from? From the product of the enterprise? Or inhuman deprivations inflicted on the pupils? Accomplish your duty as I accomplish mine."[92] Like the inspector Auzemat, Danan claimed that officials sanctioned *colons* for the slightest faults and "take back, in the form of fines, the meager money the *colons* have earned in workshops and agriculture. The salary is a few centimes a day. The fines are five francs." One young man, imprisoned for twenty-two months, had earned only 27.70 francs by the time of his release from Mettray, according to Danan. The other penalty for minor infractions, putting pupils on a ration of bread and water, was also decried: "The national budget pays for bread, meat, and vegetables. When the prisoner goes hungry under the pretext of discipline, into whose pockets goes the money that is saved?"[93] Roubaud asked Henri Berthélemy if he and all of his predecessors at Mettray had not been mistaken about the institution's effectiveness: "Is your conscience not troubled by the failure of your efforts? Mettray, as you must know, holds the record for escapes (an average of 150 per year, out of 300 pupils) and the record for punishments (4,000 for 300 children in 365 days). The admirable proposition of M. Demetz, 'to improve the earth by the man and the man by the earth,' has been nothing but a deceptive slogan at Mettray. Will you soon be celebrating, in your heart and soul, the centenary of such a mistake?"[94]

Grand reportage effectively expanded the journalistic repertoire—moving beyond the picaresque crime stories that had been the bread and butter of fin-de-siècle journalists—by stimulating a "variety of unconscious fears and impulses which activate the collective imagination and bring into play various forms of projection and identification."[95] Roubaud, who had been a student in the Maison Paternelle some thirty-five years earlier, introduced the reader to the imagined horrors that awaited the *colon* in the dormitory at night, where amid "the unfolded hammocks, one will discover the troubled hour of inner despair, concentrated anger, malice and vice. Mettray holds the record for vice. Whether of good or bad will, the weak must accept the corruption of the strong."[96] In what was an extremely rare interview with Berthélemy, the journalist Jacqueline Albert-Lambert asked how the practice of communal sleeping arrangements at Mettray could possibly be defended: "You certainly must know that the dormitory system when applied to this kind of youth is dangerous, deplorable, so much so that other similar houses are trying to move towards the construction of small, individual cells." Outraged by what he saw as the journalist's impertinence—Berthélemy remarked that if he had known the line of questioning in advance, he would have never agreed to their meeting—he angrily replied: "I know, as you do, that dormitories are regrettable to use for vicious and terrible children, but we have cells in which we enclose the most difficult subjects. For the others, we do not have the necessary credits for the construction of individual cells."[97] Danan wrote of *colons* who, to avoid the "suffering and nameless agonies" inflicted by the guards, "put quicklime in their eyes, swallow crésyl and paint. They inflame their wounds with shards of glass and their mutilated and wounded bodies are marked by abscesses and ulcers in the hope of dying."[98]

In contradistinction to the attitudes of local officials, the newspaper accounts of Mettray in the 1930s made use of what Sarah Fishman has characterized as "the rhetoric of childhood, referring even to older adolescents as children, denying that they were cold-blooded future criminals."[99] Thus a conceptual hurdle was cleared as the adolescent was effectively infantilized and more easily portrayed as a victim of his circumstances in the journalistic treatments of the *bagnes d'enfants*. Albert-Lambert, in lamenting the inadequate provision of rations at Mettray, noted the "hundreds of children who are in the colony from ages ten to eighteen, that is to say, a period when children are growing, during which time they do not have enough to eat."[100] In referring to his own stay at Mettray's Maison Paternelle as an eighteen-year-old, Roubaud maintained that the only crime he had committed was evincing "a crippling indiscipline, an impatience to live while still a boy. . . . My senses were troubled at too early an age."[101] Danan referred to Mettray as a "children's prison" comparable to a bordello of young girls drawn from the white slave trade who could regain their freedom only through the "dividends" generated by their labor.[102]

Because of this suggestion of "dividends" or profits paid out to Mettray's high-level administrators—whether through the embezzlement of the state-allocated per diems or from the exploitation of inmate labor—Danan and *Paris-Soir* were hit with a 300,000-franc libel suit filed by Berthélemy in April 1938, after the colony was closed. Although the head of Mettray's board of directors won the suit—he was awarded a symbolic sum of one franc—*Paris-Soir* was not forced to publish an apology as the plaintiff had demanded. Indeed, the court ruling was a final repudiation of Mettray and a deeply humiliating experience for its former president, who according to Fishman, still had "occasional outbursts of anger about the Mettray affair" years later when he served as Vichy's minister of justice.[103]

Lower-level staff did not have the wherewithal to bring a lawsuit, so Danan's most stunning accusation—that M. Guépin, a retired employee (first a guard, then *surveillant chef*), had murdered two *colons* during his forty years of service—went unchallenged. In advancing this claim Danan relied on the statements of former *colons*, and he had forwarded the names of Guépin's alleged victims to Minister of Justice Marc Rucard. Danan also characterized Khalifa Chaouch, an Algerian guard and chief of the disciplinary quarter, as a "torturer" who "hits you so hard that one faints. Khalifa is an illiterate Arab, with the face and fists of a killer. When he unties his leather belt, your soul is recommended to God." Danan considered the *chefs de famille* to be similarly ill-suited to their positions and generally inclined to violence: "Most are illiterate, which is a little embarrassing when you must teach rudimentary reading to school-age pupils. . . . These ignorant overseers do not remain unoccupied, however, since in the absence of knowledge and science, they have their fists and their whips."[104] According to Evanson, following the publication of Danan's article, Guépin received numerous threats from his neighbors in the Paris banlieue where he had retired, and he died shortly thereafter.[105]

There is little doubt that inmates at Mettray, and the juvenile colonies more generally, suffered abuse at the hands of their overseers. Although the extent of the abuse is difficult to determine given the incompleteness of the historical record, as long as those who "worked in juvenile institutions were hired and trained by the Penal Administration," the institutions were likely to retain their punitive and repressive atmosphere.[106] Albert-Lambert addressed this issue in her interview with Berthélemy: "Your guardians are former prison guards! How can this staff, who has never dealt with anyone other than dangerous criminals in their lives, ever come to think of *petit pensionnaires* as anything more than a ferocious band of animals?"[107] Berthélemy gave no reply. At least some employees of juvenile colonies were dismayed by the widely publicized characterizations of incompetence and brutality. The guards at Aniane noted in a wide-ranging complaint forwarded to the local prefect: "Any campaign has a goal, as there is no interest without a purpose. The odious campaign and lies of some newspapers against the prison administration and supervised education is aimed to discredit our work and our institutions. We demand that measures be taken against journalists who are briefed by former residents of our *maisons*. They are bad subjects who still struggle with the laws that govern society."[108] Yet, as Éric Pierre has pointed out, it cannot be denied that a chronic state of indiscipline—alcoholism, the abandonment of posts, thefts, and the proclivity for violence—had long existed among lower-level staff at Mettray and it could not be easily resolved with a belated pay raise.[109]

Although the Popular Front's minister of justice, Marc Rucard, did not act on Danan's allegations of murder at Mettray, he did dispatch inspectors to investigate conditions in the colony. As Ramsland has noted, the investigators discovered that the crown jewel of the Tourangelle was in a state of abject disrepair: the buildings were in a decrepit state, the roofs leaked, and the equipment was badly worn.[110] The minister of public health, Henri Sellier, withdrew from Mettray all youths affiliated with Assistance publique as a public safety measure in June 1936. Rucard subsequently removed all other minors and informed juvenile court judges to henceforth stop placing minors at Mettray in April 1937.[111] It took more than six months for all 500 *colons* to be evacuated and placed in other institutions or returned to their parents before Mettray was officially closed on 5 November 1937. France's most acclaimed carceral institution, which had been in operation since the first nine *colons* had arrived in January 1840, was no more.[112]

Conclusion

Mettray's birth in 1840 marked the initial diffusion of the modern disciplinary realm, as Foucault has noted. Yet, by the time of its close in 1937, Mettray was not a laboratory of modernity but a shell of its former self, having devolved from the reformist vision of its founder to little more than a custodial care facility. In tracing the colony's nearly century-long existence, the goal of this book has been to confer agency on Mettray's young *colons*, as well as its staff and local administrators, as a counterweight to Foucault, who was never particularly interested in how historical actors impede and complicate presumptions of institutional power. What started out as a progressive and utilitarian project, based on the optimistic belief that juvenile delinquents and wayward youth could be reformed, grew increasingly carceral and punitive amid creeping doubts about whether such changes were, in fact, possible. By the dawn of the twentieth century those doubts had accumulated into a pervasive sense of futility and failure.

Troubled by the dangers of depravity for young offenders held in common jails, Demetz believed that juvenile delinquents had to be separated from their corrupt elders and subjected to a unique rehabilitative regimen as instantiated in the form of the agricultural colony. Encouraged by the success of institutions such as the Rauhe Haus in Prussia, he enlisted the aid of some of France's most prominent figures, who were critical in providing financial assistance and helping to galvanize political support and state recognition of Mettray, and the

agricultural colony more generally, as the principal mechanism for addressing juvenile crime. The Law of 1850 strengthened and regularized the exercise of disciplinary authority as the agricultural colony was inscribed in the
legal structure of the state.

Mettray was a multifaceted institution with aims that extended beyond a
desire to save youthful offenders from the corruption of the communal jail
and help prevent the reproduction of criminality as adults. Early to mid-
nineteenth-century penal reformers and philanthropists had little interest in
examining the relationship between poverty and juvenile crime. Instead, they
viewed delinquency as rooted not in economic misfortune but in the social
environment, particularly the urban environment, which was envisioned as a
physiologically and morally debilitating space. Demetz shared this view and
saw the displacement of the peasantry from the normative geography of an
idealized rural France as a source of disorder, which Mettray, located in the
bucolic Indre-et-Loire, could address by exposing its denizens to a reparative
regime of agrarian life and labor. On his release, the *colon* would choose to
remain in the countryside, becoming a member of a rural society that he
would help to revive and expand, both economically and demographically.

The colony also addressed acute anxieties about the perceived weakness
or ineffectiveness of paternal authority among the poor and working
classes by removing the delinquent from his family. While moral corruption began on the streets of the city, indiscipline emanated from the domestic hearth. Even when the intentions of parents were not malign, their
perceived weakness demanded the intervention of a new site of governance
in the form of the agricultural colony. Mettray would remove such children
from the control of their parents, isolate them from the culture of the
streets, and reshape their physical bodies and moral characters. They would
be refashioned into proper individuals: industrious, disciplined, loyal, deferential, and moral.

Despite rhetoric to the contrary, officials at Mettray did not hesitate to disrupt the natural bonds between parents and their offspring, most particularly
the bond between mother and child. This was especially evident in the colony's visitation policy, which strictly limited contact from the family on grounds
that it might inhibit the child's reformation. Mothers also were subjects of
Mettray, as administrators denied visitations to women who were unwed or
lived in concubinage, effectively severing the maternal link, which could be
reconnected only if they married.

While the agricultural colony was intended to effectuate a moral transformation in the delinquent, the correctional practice raised an ideological conundrum as the state empowered magistrates to commit youths who were

found not guilty of committing a crime, because they had acted *sans discernment*. Thus, innocent children were subjected to what became, in effect, a penal regime. However, Demetz and other proponents of the agricultural colony articulated a vision of the institution that emphasized its "educational" rather than carceral function. This was a rhetorical sleight of hand—Mettray had been created, at least in part, to supplement penal authority—that allowed officials to defend the practice of confining youths who had not been found guilty of a crime alongside those who had, by claiming that the former were provided a "correctional education" whereas the latter were subjected to a regime that was both coercive and punitive.

Agricultural labor was Mettray's ideological cornerstone, conceptualized as spiritually gratifying and physically invigorating. Labor was an effective counterweight to criminality in poor and working-class boys that was rooted, at least in the eyes of bourgeois penal reformers, in idleness and unsupervised time. Work in the French countryside was also envisioned as not only an educational experience but also a purifying one that effectively reshaped the delinquent into a productive citizen. Young men from the cities would find meaning in the planting and harvesting of crops, the feeding and tending of livestock, and the performance of other tasks that supported the daily operation of the colony. While there was most certainly, as Barbara Arneil has noted, an ethical component to agrarian labor based on a "republican emphasis on the redemptive moral and political qualities of a country life,"[1] there was also an economic imperative, as local officials had to harness the labor power of their subjects to maximize the potential of arable land and generate a sufficient level of agricultural production to offset the costs of maintaining the colony. By the late nineteenth century this practice was considered exploitative by critics who charged that Mettray was driven more by a desire for profit than for the redemption of its subjects and that little effort was made to impart useful training or skills beyond those associated with agrarian pursuits.

The idyllic image of the family and its power to save juvenile delinquents and wayward youth was central to Demetz's imagining of Mettray. The use of the word *family* to denote a group of forty *colons* who lived together in a dormitory, led by a "paternal" *chef de famille*, was a critical component of the colony's rehabilitational rhetoric. Yet the term was little more than a principle of spatial organization, and something of an empty signifier. Military drills and competitive sports were intended, at least in part, to establish an identity as a distinct dormitory group, but they were oriented more toward the formation of a masculine identity rather than familial bonds. The regimented and hierarchical aspects of Mettray's regime were designed to instill feelings of citizenship and patriotism, which were considered more important than domesticity to French manhood, This martial masculinity that venerated bourgeois notions of honor and duty reflected Demetz's class presumptions, for he never intended his subjects to rise above their station in life. After leaving Mettray, the former *colon* would be a disciplined and obedient worker and perhaps, as was frequently the case, a loyal soldier. On the heels of the humiliating defeat in the Franco-Prussian War, this took on even greater urgency as France looked to the military to reestablish a masculine standard.

A wide range of scholars, most notably Norbert Elias and Max Weber, have argued that as modern society grew more complex and diversified—with its impersonal cities, bureaucracies, industrial workforce, mass voting, and mass press—the importance of honor in everyday life diminished over time.[2] This is an oversimplification of their positions on the subject (Nye's work on the prevalence of the duel among the French bourgeoisie demonstrates the significance of honor up to the First World War) but honor grew less relevant as the twentieth century progressed. The sociologist Peter Berger has argued that modernity brought with it the demise of honor and the ascendance of the concept of dignity. Whereas honor "implies that identity is essentially, or at least importantly, linked to institutional roles," dignity "implies that identity is essentially independent of institutional roles." The shift to a world of dignity, where the "individual can only discover his true identity by emancipating himself from his socially imposed roles," is a product of modernization, epitomized by technology and bureaucracy. In short, industrialization and the democratization of French society undermined the paternalistic and deferential relations that had once served a hierarchical corporate society. Notions of honor were "rooted in a world of relatively intact, stable institutions," only a few of which survived into the modern era, most notably in military culture.[3] Demetz's successors were obsessed with the concept of honor precisely because they were living through this period of great transformation in which the concept was becoming obsolete, which implied that their own value system, essentially their own characters, were anachronistic. Whereas officials saw doing one's duty as the highest form of virtue, a demonstration of one's honor, some *colons*, many of whom were more than a generation removed from their keepers, considered such notions antiquated betrayals of one's true self. It is likely that some young men of Mettray, particularly its adolescents, were anxious to emancipate themselves from their institutional roles, and that the invocations of honor and duty meant to address their transgressions and induce feelings of shame often fell on deaf ears.

Although the inculcation of masculinity at Mettray was something to which every *colon* was subjected—whether through the colony's martial aspects, its glorification of labor, or its heteronormative vision of sex roles—its definition was not necessarily shared by all. Officials pathologized homosexuality, circumscribing the variety of ways to be a "normal" man at Mettray and inhibiting the possibilities of forging intimacies and affective relationships. Yet, many *colons* were adept at circumnavigating the panoptic gaze of the common dormitory, and inmates governed themselves accordingly. Homosexuality was conceptualized as a clandestine "contagion" that spread in secrecy and silence, and its presence highlighted the limitations of the omniscient eye of surveillance. Finally, while some prisoners were willing participants in a shared homosexual subculture, there is evidence that others were forced into a world they had not chosen that was linked to violence and domination, a practice that represented a particularly dark aspect of masculine identity.

Mettray's history was marked by an enduring tension between participation and resistance, cooption and coercion. Most inmates were acquiescent, completing their agricultural labor dutifully, adhering to the regimented routine without complaint, and ultimately serving their time quietly with an eye toward release. Where compliance and defiance intersected, some *colons* carved out their own spaces of limited autonomy—zones of noncompliant consent, or what Alf Lüdtke has termed *Eigensinn*—within Mettray's carceral landscape. While such nonacquiescent compliance allowed the colony to maintain its veneer of uniformity and order, Mettray was also a site of hostility and resentment, which were manifested in various forms of resistance. Some *colons* slowed down the carceral machinery, both symbolically and literally, by engaging in activities that frustrated the colony's daily operation. Others responded to the various indignities and resentments of institutional life by engaging in demonstrations of bravado via "verbal retorts" aimed at their keepers. Still others committed acts of violence that served no purpose other than as brutal expressions of frustration and rage.

It is tempting to posit that documented acts of prisoner resistance, in tandem with undocumented actions, or what James C. Scott has termed "everyday resistance," ultimately made Mettray unviable. Such an interpretation is appealing because it turns our attention away from domination, forcing us to consider the actions of those seen as powerless. In the interwar period collective and individual acts of resistance became increasingly visible to the public via press accounts and the complaints of civil and municipal officials weary of the economic and bureaucratic pressures on their communities from dealing with crimes committed by escaped *colons*. A successful escape undermined Mettray's legitimacy in the eyes of not only its subjects but also lawmakers and the public, laying bare the limitations of its power.

The fact that Mettray's administration seriously considered establishing a cellular arrangement and doing away with the communal dormitories was an indication that the institution had been affected by the actions of its denizens. Additionally, the belated move in the 1930s toward a more ameliorative regime was a tacit acknowledgement that Mettray had to offer its charges more incentives for compliance than just inspirational portraits, billfolds, enshrinement on the wall of honor, and the opportunity to carry the colony flag at parade day. Yet, Mettray's rigid regimen and elaborate regulations remained largely unchanged, and punishment registers indicate that the colony grew increasingly punitive as *colons* were sanctioned for a myriad of minor offenses, usually by cellular confinement for extended periods of time, often with draconian reductions in daily rations.

The liminality of Mettray's cohort, and the lack of a precise definition of adolescence, was central to the group's perceived threat. Of course, the boundary between childhood and adulthood does not exist as a single point in time; rather, a child's maturation and development into an adult is an extended period of transition. This understanding became increasingly common after the turn of the twentieth century and passage of the Law of 1906 that raised the age of penal majority from sixteen to eighteen.

Faced with youths who inhabited the very upper reaches of childhood, the imprecise line between adult and minor was seen as potentially dangerous in the eyes of staff, particularly guards, who feared violence. Mettray's directors not only shared this basic and pragmatic concern with their lower-level personnel but also evinced a deeply pessimistic vision of the adolescent as a nearly fully formed adult beyond the reach of the colony's importunities for reform. This conceptualization stood in contradistinction to nascent medico-legal understandings of adolescence as a stage of life marked by an inherent malleability and impressionability, which, while potentially dangerous, nonetheless implied that moral reformation was at least possible.[4]

Mettray was not the carefully controlled environment envisioned by Demetz and reimagined by Foucault. Its staff, particularly the guards charged with surveillance, were often incompetent and brutal, and attempts to attract more suitable candidates for such positions were hindered by the jobs' low pay and low status. During the First World War and well into the interwar period, the colony was staffed by makeshift personnel with uneven levels of commitment to modern ideas of punishment and rehabilitation. Moreover, apart from Brun and Voisin, Mettray's directors had no training in the treatment of children and were for the most part drawn from the military, or in the case of De Cayla, from adult corrections. Thus, most of those who oversaw Mettray's operation were relative neophytes in comparison to Demetz, who, though he had no experience managing an institution, had spent years studying corrections from a theoretical perspective and as a former magistrate, possessed a keen understanding of the law as it pertained to minors.

Mettray was not unlike a standard prison in that its keepers were generally preoccupied with escapes, violence, and rebellion rather than noble rehabilitative aims. As the American sociologist and criminologist Gresham Sykes has noted, "Far from being omnipotent rulers who have crushed all signs of rebellion against their regime, the custodians are engaged in a continuous struggle to maintain order—and it is a struggle in which they frequently fail."[5] One could argue that the Mettray directors who followed in Demetz's footsteps were not all that different from the administrators whom Sykes analyzed in his study of the New Jersey State Prison, whose "allegiance to the goal of rehabilitation tended to remain on the verbal level, as an expression of hope for public consumption, rather than a coherent program with an integrated, professional staff."[6]

Like most keepers of "total institutions," Mettray's administrators endeavored to project a positive image of the institution to officials in the Ministry of the Interior and the Penitentiary Administration. This proved difficult, however, as the gap between rhetoric and reality on the ground grew ever wider during the twentieth century. As Goffman observed, while many "total institutions seem to function merely as storage dumps for inmates . . . they usually present themselves to the public as rational organizations designed consciously, through and through," most notably "as effective machines of producing inmates in the direction of some ideal standard. This contradiction, between what the institution does and what its officials must say it does, forms the basic context of the staff's daily activity."[7] Nevertheless, local administrators at Mettray characterized their subjects as irredeemably intractable, and there was little to no pretense of reformation in their communications with officials in Paris, particularly during the interwar period, which raises a question about the role the institution played in the larger carceral network.

Although the problems of inmate resistance disrupted Mettray's regime and generated conflict and confusion among staff and officials, it is too simplistic to attribute the colony's downfall to the actions of the *colons*. Penal reformers and social theorists had long criticized the state for what they saw as an abdication of its role as a caretaker of its youngest and most vulnerable citizens, and they demanded greater state involvement in the form of funding and the creation of more public colonies for juvenile delinquents. Unsurprisingly, once the state began to expand its own efforts in this area, its support for private institutions such as Mettray dried up and the colony's financial situation became precarious. The state per diem—only 2.50 francs in 1929—did not keep pace with increases in the cost of living. In the national budget of 1930 it was raised to six francs for all colonies, which officials at Mettray indicated was still insufficient to meet the basic needs of the colony during a period of strong inflation. At that point, local officials could not spend money on deteriorating buildings and the colony's debt ballooned to over one million francs, which forced the Société paternelle to borrow heavily to continue operation.[8]

One could also point to Demetz's initial formulation of Mettray, which combined an imagining of France's rural past with a prescription for its future, as effectively sealing the colony's fate. On the one hand, as Arneil points out, it was initially due to the "rapid move toward industrialization and urbanization on a massive scale" that domestic colonialists such as Demetz "thought a return to the soil was so critical to reversing the bad habits and corruption of the city streets for the idle and irrational of Europe."[9] But on the other hand, by tying the *colons* to the fertile soil of the Loire, Mettray ultimately drove its young subjects into a rural wage economy that had little need for their labor by the dawn of the twentieth century. Unlike in the overseas *bagnes*, to which the juvenile colonies were frequently compared during the 1920s and 1930s, there was never any promise of land concessions to former *colons*. Thus, there was no mechanism by which Demetz could facilitate their settlement in the French interior, aside from placing them with local farmers as unskilled laborers, most of whom typically returned to the city once they had fulfilled their contract obligations, which typically lasted only a few months.

Demetz sought to create a utopian social space that would allow for the realization of a masculine ideal in young men whom many believed represented a significant threat to social stability. Grounded in a mythic past, the agricultural colony was part of a broader bourgeois program focused on the inculcation of a work-based identity premised on the abstract order of an agrarian-centered life. Mettray was steeped in nostalgia, a simulacrum of the past whose origins lay as much in the imagination as in relation to external forces. Demetz's upbringing was entirely bourgeois—his father, also a lawyer, had served several times as the mayor of Dourdan in the department of Seine-et-Oise. As he himself was neither a cultivator nor a soldier the presence of these worlds at Mettray embodied a longing for a bygone agrarian idyll and a masculine code of honor associated with preindustrial norms and cultural practices.

Throughout the twentieth century state power was extended to better regulate social relations in France. In the July Monarchy there had been a reliance on the rehabilitative prison to counter social disorder, but this link was severed by the creation of a modern welfare state. Social security schemes, economic stabilization programs, unemployment and accident insurance, income redistribution to families and support of abandoned and abused children, public housing and rent subsidies, minimum work requirements, community and neighborhood development plans, medical insurance, life insurance, and counseling programs were all intended to reduce economic instability and assure the social integration of every French citizen, young and old. When the preservation of the collectivity and the promotion of social equality became the fundamental political goals, a new type of criminal justice policy became possible. Thus, the trend toward the secular and centralized state control of welfare, education, the economy, and the prison system that had commenced with the birth of the Third Republic continued unabated throughout the century.

The passage of the law of 12 July 1912 that instantiated juvenile tribunals (Tribunal d'enfance et d'adolescence, or TEA) was the first step in the creation of a distinctly welfare-oriented approach to the problem of juvenile delinquency. Reasoning that casting a minor as a criminal defendant did more harm than good, TEA proceedings were not open to the public because lawmakers hoped to shield youths from public scrutiny that might induce feelings of pride rather than shame or regret for their actions. Concerned about minors' capacity to grasp the nature and ramifications of their criminal acts, republican legislators also removed the standard of *discernement* for children under the age of thirteen, retaining it for youths thirteen to eighteen. Thus the law established a demarcation between childhood and adolescence. Both cohorts were adjudicated in the TEA, where employees of the courts investigated the circumstances surrounding their crimes, their domestic situations, and their psychological development before arriving at individualized resolutions. Finally, the TEA established a probation system (*liberté surveillée*) that monitored youths who were returned to their families or remanded to a private or public patronage.[10]

Vagrancy, which accounted for 30 to 40 percent of all juvenile offenses, was decriminalized in October 1935. As Fishman has noted, families and domestic situations were investigated by TEA officials to determine whether vagrant youths had run away or been abandoned or orphaned and whether they were engaged in prostitution when they were apprehended.. Rather than being placed in a juvenile colony, depending on their individual circumstances these youths were either returned to their homes or sent to a charitable institution, a public preservation school, or Public Assistance. Five years earlier, La

Roquette, the first prison built expressly for juveniles, had become a women's prison, and juveniles who resided there were transferred to Fresnes Supervised Education House, a separate wing of the Fresnes jail established by the neuropsychiatrists Jacques Roubinovitch and George-Paul Boncour to study and "treat" juvenile deviance.[11]

As programs focused on therapeutic treatment rather than "reeducation" gained greater currency during the interwar period, medico-legal experts claimed jurisdiction over the delinquent, largely at the expense of private, philanthropic interests. This epistemological shift was part of a much broader trend in corrections focused on the psychological and medical treatment of deviants—recidivists, alcoholics, drug addicts, and the insane—which began to replace security measures such as transportation and relegation to the overseas penal colonies. Thus, the pessimism of late nineteenth-century medicine concerning the "degenerate" criminal gave way to a guarded optimism, a turn that extended to the juvenile delinquent. As a result, the reliance on segregation and a corrective program of work and moral training that attempted to contain delinquency—while at the same time restricting the role of state institutions—was superseded by a criminal justice strategy that emphasized the integration of delinquent youth into French society.

At the end of the Second World War the leftist government passed the Law of 2 February 1945 (*L'ordonnance du 2e février 1945*), which further transformed the juvenile justice system. The new *juge des enfants* (who replaced the three-judge panel in the 1912 configuration) was presented with a more flexible array of sentencing alternatives, including warnings and the return of offenders back to their families; community service sentences; supervised probation; psychological and social work counseling (for both the youth and his or her family); short-term placements in foster care and nonpunitive alternative home settings; and official placements in carceral institutions for youth, a sanction that became increasingly rare.[12] The primary objective was not to punish but to situate the offense in the broader context of the juvenile's life before arriving at an individualized disposition of the case. The most common disposition by far was an "Education Action in an Open Environment" (*Action éducative en milieu ouvert*), a court order that required that the child and his or her family meet regularly with a social worker who devised an intervention plan to address the youth's specific needs and identified problems (educational, psychological, occupational, medical, or familial) in an attempt to change behaviors and prevent criminal recidivism. Thus, the priority was not to ascertain the precise acts that occurred and characterize them as criminal, but to offer new channels of socialization that forestall the recourse to incarceration.[13] While this approach to juvenile crime has been widely hailed as a humane and effective strategy for dealing with delinquency and a stark repudiation of the past emphasis on incapacitation and punishment, it has come under increasingly harsh criticism in recent years from voices on the right who argue that it is insufficiently punitive.

What are we to make of Mettray's inauspicious denouement? While it is apparent that the institution had long been failing in its basic charge to socialize its subjects—to transform *colons* into what Foucault termed "docile bodies"—administrators and staff were highly resistant to change and firmly convinced that Mettray had become a dumping ground for a state that no longer valued its role in French society. Internal documents reveal an acute anxiety and pessimism about the colony's subjects, in terms of both their propensity to escape and, more fundamentally, their adolescent subjectivity. While the former could be attributed to their basic rejection of authority and discipline, the latter proved far more vexing as officials were confounded by the attitudes and actions of the *colons*. This was a problem exacerbated by the deprivations of the First World War and a staff that had become aged and overburdened. But there was also something more fundamental at play as the inmates of the colony profoundly challenged what was a nineteenth-century imagining of youth, in terms of both what it meant to be young and the perceived capacity of the young for wrongdoing. The sheer volume and diversity of correspondence and other documents from Mettray and other juvenile colonies are testament to the inability of officials to understand the characters and behaviors of their charges.

As a practical matter, officials found themselves out of step with a widely held conceptualization of youth that was more expansive, extending beyond the boundaries of childhood to include adolescence. Thus, the laws and regulations issued by the National Assembly and the Penitentiary Administration that effectively instantiated this reimagining were deeply resented, and sometimes resisted, by those who worked at Mettray. The limitations of the colony's design, in terms of both the dormitory space and the pedagogy based on Demetz's vision of a premodern rural France, was also problematic. As Fishman has aptly noted, "Even aside from the fact that the correctional houses were most often cruel and abusive, most people in the juvenile delinquency establishment considered them fundamentally flawed," and Mettray was certainly no exception.[14]

Finally, whether all the allegations made by journalists such as Danan and Roubaud were entirely accurate is perhaps beside the point, for their stories generated a national dialogue that ultimately condemned the juvenile justice system, forcing officials of the Popular Front government into a period of critical reexamination that ultimately led to Mettray's closure. Henceforth, the state, rather than private philanthropy, would serve as the ultimate arbiter of discipline, punishment, and rehabilitation for the juvenile delinquents and wayward youth of twentieth-century France.

NOTES

Introduction

1. The viscount was a former soldier, local politician, and penal reformer who headed a committee that examined the regime of the Tours prison. His report, *Les condamnés et les prisons ou la réforme morale, criminelle et pénitentiaire* (Paris: Perrotin, 1838), was harshly critical of conditions there. He was subsequently sued for defamation by the prison physician but acquitted on 16 March 1839.

2. *Colonie agricole de Mettray: Assemblée générale des fondateurs tenue à Paris, le 20 mai 1841* (Tours: Imprimerie de H. Fournier et Cie, 1841), 2. Unless otherwise indicated all translations are my own.

3. Henri Gaillac, *Les maisons de correction, 1830–1945* (Paris: Cujas, 1971), appendices B, C.

4. Jeroen Dekker, *The Will to Change the Child: Re-education Homes for Children at Risk in Nineteenth-Century Western Europe* (Frankfurt: Peter Lang, 2001), 67. See also Felix Driver, "Discipline without Frontiers? Representations of the Mettray Reformatory Colony in Britain, 1840–1880," *Journal of Historical Sociology* 3, no. 3 (1990).

5. Chris Leonards, "Priceless Children? Penitentiary Congresses Debating Childhood: A Quest for Social Order in Europe, 1846–1895," in *Social Control in Europe*, vol. 2, ed. Clive Emsley, Eric Johnson, and Pieter Spierenburg (Columbus: Ohio State University Press, 2004), 126n6.

6. Barbara Arneil, *Domestic Colonies: The Turn Inward to Colony* (Oxford: Oxford University Press, 2017), 226.

7. For more on Mettray, see Éric Pierre, "F. A. Demetz et la colonie agricole de Mettray entre réformisme 'romantique' et injonctions administratives," *Paedagogica Historica* 38, no. 2–3 (2002); Dekker, *Will to Change the Child*; Christian Carlier, *La prison aux champs: Les colonies des enfants délinquants du nord de la France au XIXe siècle* (Paris: Éditions de l'Atelier, 1994); Frédéric Chauvaud, "Les jeunes délinquants de Seine-et-Oise et la colonie agricole de Mettray," in *Répression et prison politiques au XIXe siècle*, ed. Alain Faure (Paris: Créaphis, 1990), 253–67; John Ramsland, "The Agricultural Colony at Mettray: A Nineteenth-Century Approach to the Institutionalization of Delinquent Boys," *Critical Studies in Education* 29, no. 1 (1987), 64–80.

8. To mark the occasion of the opening of the archival collection, an edited volume of scholarly works on Mettray was published: Sophie Chassat, Luc Forlivesi, and Georges-François Pottier, eds., *Éduquer et punir: La colonie agricole et pénitentiaire de Mettray* (Rennes: Presses Universitaires de Rennes, 2005).

9. Oliver Davis, "Mettray Revisited in Jean Genet's *Le langage de la muraille*," *French History* 30, no. 4 (2016): 548.

10. Michel Foucault, *Discipline and Punish: The Birth of the Prison*, trans. Alan Sheridan (New York: Random House, 1977).

11. Mary Gibson, "Global Perspectives on the Birth of the Prison," *American Historical Review* 111, no. 4 (2011): 1041.

12. The Panopticon of Jeremy Bentham was based on the notion of total supervision through rational prison architecture (i.e., four cellblocks radiating from a central tower from which officials could visually monitor all the cells simultaneously).

13. Foucault, *Discipline and Punish*, 293–94.

14. Ann Laura Stoler, *Along the Archival Grain: Epistemic Anxieties and Colonial Common Sense* (Princeton, NJ: Princeton University Press, 2009), 131. As Éric Pierre has noted, however, despite repeated efforts by Demetz to establish an agricultural colony in Algeria, he was ultimately unsuccessful. See Pierre, "Mettray-Algérie-Mettray, 1839–1937: Allers et retours sur fond d'éducation correctionnelle," *Les Études Sociales* 152 (2010).

15. Chris Philo, "Foucault's Children," in *Geographies of Children, Youth and Families*, ed. Louise Holt (New York: Routledge, 2011), 31.

16. Frédéric Demetz, *Fondation d'une colonie agricole de jeunes détenus à Mettray* (Paris: B. Duprat, 1839).

17. Foucault, *Discipline and Punish*, 128–29.

18. David Rothman, *Conscience and Convenience: The Asylum and Its Alternatives in Progressive America*, 2nd ed. (New York: Aldine, 2002 [1980]), 11.

19. David Garland, *Punishment and Modern Society: A Study in Social Theory* (Chicago: University of Chicago Press, 1993), 173.

20. Dario Melossi and Massimo Pavarini, *The Prison and the Factory: Origins of the Penitentiary System*, trans. Glynis Cousin (Totowa, NJ: Barnes and Noble, 1981), 192.

21. For more on Foucault's seeming indifference to agency and resistance, see Garland, *Punishment and Modern Society*, especially chap. 7.

22. Robert Adams, *Prison Riots in Britain and the United States* (New York: St. Martin's Press, 1992), 34.

23. Michelle Perrot, "Delinquency and the Penitentiary System in Nineteenth-Century France," in *Deviants and the Abandoned in French Society*, ed. Robert Forster and Orest Ranum (Baltimore: Johns Hopkins University Press, 1978), 215.

24. Patricia O'Brien, *The Promise of Punishment: Prisons in Nineteenth-Century France* (Princeton, NJ: Princeton University Press, 1982), 6–7, 9.

25. "Prison 'reform' is virtually contemporary with the prison itself: it constitutes, as it were, its program." Foucault, *Discipline and Punish*, 234–35.

26. Michel Foucault, *The Foucault Reader: An Introduction to Foucault's Thought*, ed. Paul Rabinow (New York: Pantheon, 1994), 245.

27. Lila Abu-Lughod, "The Romance of Resistance: Tracing Transformations of Power through Bedouin Women," *American Ethnologist* 17, no. 1 (1990): 41.

28. Michel Foucault, "Questions of Method: An Interview with Michel Foucault," *Ideology and Consciousness* 8 (Spring 1981): 4.

29. Alec McHoul and Wendy Grace, *A Foucault Primer: Discourse, Power and the Subject* (New York: New York University Press, 1997), 85.

30. O'Brien, *Promise of Punishment*, 76–77.

31. There is a rich criminological literature on the strategies by which prisoners attempt to assert some degree of autonomy from the universalizing effects of imprisonment. Much less attention has been paid to the distinctive ways children and youth negotiate and resist certain aspects of the carceral environment, particularly from a historical point of view. For a classic articulation see Gresham Sykes, *The Society of Captives: A Study of a Maximum Security Prison* (Princeton, NJ: Princeton University Press, 1958).

32. Erving Goffman, *Asylums: Essays on the Social Situation of Mental Patients and Other Inmates* (New York: Doubleday, 1961), 11.

33. James C. Scott, *Weapons of the Weak: Everyday Forms of Peasant Resistance* (New Haven, CT: Yale University Press, 1985), 29.

34. Ibid., xvi.

35. Alf Lüdtke, ed., *The History of Everyday Life: Historical Experience and Ways of Life*, trans. William Templer (Princeton, NJ: Princeton University Press, 1995), 313–14.

36. On adolescence, see Agnès Thiercé, *Histoire de l'adolescence, 1850–1914* (Paris: Belin, 1999); Katherine Alaimo, "Adolescence, Gender and Class in Education Reform in France: The Development of Enseignement Primaire Supérieure, 1880–1910," *French Historical Studies* 18, no. 4 (1994); Katherine Alaimo, "Shaping Adolescence in the Popular Milieu: Social Policy, Reformers, and French Youth, 1870–1920," *Journal of Family History* 17, no. 4 (1992).

37. On degeneration, see Daniel Pick, *Faces of Degeneration: A European Disorder, c. 1848–1918* (Cambridge: Cambridge University Press, 1993).

38. Rachel G. Fuchs, *Poor and Pregnant in Paris: Strategies for Survival in the Nineteenth Century* (New Brunswick, NJ: Rutgers University Press, 1992), 251.

39. Alfred Fouillée, "Les jeunes criminelles," *Revue des Deux Mondes* (15 January 1897): 425–26.

40. Alain Corbin, "The Triumph of Virility in the Nineteenth Century," in *A History of Virility*, ed. Alain Corbin, Jean-Jacques Courtine, and Georges Vigarello, trans. Keith Cohen (New York: Columbia University Press, 2016), 216.

41. As Davis has noted, the "documents comprising the archive under 114J in Tours were pre-vetted and the accounts are incomplete." Davis, "Mettray Revisited," 564n71.

42. While many prisoner memoirs contain powerful descriptions of daily life, one must be conscious of their limitations. Apart from the obvious problems arising from sources often written decades after the events they depict, the writers are generally not representative of the prison population. For more information on the possibilities and challenges posed by this genre of literature, see Steve Morgan, "Prison Lives: Critical Issues in Reading Prisoner Autobiography," *Howard Journal* 38, no. 3 (1999).

43. In 1827 the French government began publication of a series of criminal statistics that became a model for other European countries. The *Compte général de l'administration de la justice criminelle* was addressed to magistrates, administrators, legislators, and others interested in the question of crime and punishment. The information contained in the *Compte* provided the foundation for nearly all subsequent studies of criminal behavior in the nineteenth and early twentieth centuries, and it was used by administrators, legislators, and philanthropists to support programs of

penal reform. Michelle Perrot, "Délinquance et système pénitentiaire en France au dix-neuvième siècle," *Annales: Economies, Sociétés, Civilisations* 1 (January–February 1975): 70–71.

44. Mary Jo Maynes, "Age as a Category of Analysis: History, Agency, and Narratives of Childhood," *Journal of Childhood and Youth* 1, no. 1 (Winter 2008): 117.

45. Michael Ignatieff, "Total Institutions and Working Classes: A Review Essay," *History Workshop Journal* 15, no. 1 (1983): 168–69.

46. Pieter Spierenburg, "From Amsterdam to Auburn: An Explanation for the Rise of the Prison in Seventeenth-Century Holland and Nineteenth-Century America," *Journal of Social History* 20, no. 3 (Spring 1987): 439.

47. Foremost in this group is Spierenburg's social-historical work on executions in the Netherlands that effectively demonstrates that the public character of punishment did not disappear as abruptly as Foucault asserts, but slowly diminished over centuries. Informed by the work of Norbert Elias, Spierenburg argues that modes of repression reflected long-term changes in "sensibilities." See Spierenburg, *The Spectacle of Suffering: Executions and the Evolution of Repression* (Cambridge: Cambridge University Press, 1984), vii, xix.

48. Melossi and Pavarini, *The Prison and the Factory*, 195.

49. Philippe Ariès, *Centuries of Childhood: A Social History of Family Life*, trans. Robert Baldick (New York: Vintage, 1962). The list of persons critical of Ariès's approach and methodology (particularly his overreliance on iconography) and his general conclusion that "childhood" did not exist prior to the early modern period is too long to reproduce.

50. Under the Napoleonic Code the age of majority was sixteen. In 1906 the age was raised to eighteen.

51. Most prominently, on changing understandings of childhood and French law, see Sylvia Schafer, *Children in Moral Danger and the Problem of Government in Third Republic France* (Princeton, NJ: Princeton University Press, 1997). On childhood in France more generally, see Colin Heywood, *Growing Up in France: From the Ancien Régime to the Third Republic* (Cambridge: Cambridge University Press, 2007); Kristin Stromberg Childers, *Fathers, Families, and the State in France, 1914–1945* (Ithaca, NY: Cornell University Press, 2003); Catherine Rollet, *Les enfants au XIXe siècle* (Paris: Hachette, 2001); Maurice Crubellier, *L'enfance et la jeunesse dans la société française, 1800–1950* (Paris: Colin, 1979).

52. Sarah Fishman, *The Battle for Children: World War II, Youth Crime, and Juvenile Justice in Twentieth-Century France* (Cambridge, MA: Harvard University Press, 2002), 5.

53. Laura Lee Downs, *Childhood in the Promised Land: Working-Class Movements and the Colonies de Vacances in France, 1880–1960* (Durham, NC: Duke University Press, 2002), 15, 16.

54. Arneil, *Domestic Colonies*, 44.

55. Annelien de Dijn, "Rousseau and Republicanism," *Political Theory* 46, no. 1 (2018): 72.

56. Jean-Jacques Rousseau, *Politics and the Arts: Letter to M. d'Alembert on the Theatre*, trans. Allan Bloom (Ithaca, NY: Cornell University Press, 1960), 126.

57. Mona Ozouf, *Festivals and the French Revolution*, trans. Alan Sheridan (Cambridge, MA: Harvard University Press, 1988), 9.

58. Rousseau, *Politics and the Arts*, 82.

59. Arneil, *Domestic Colonies*, 37.

60. Ibid., 40.

61. I approach gender as a historically shifting set of power relations informed by understandings of sexual rather than biological difference. On masculinity in the contemporary prison setting, see Regina Kunzel, *Criminal Intimacy: Prison and the Uneven History of Modern American Sexuality* (Chicago: University of Chicago Press, 2008).

62. On French masculinity, see Christopher Forth, *The Dreyfus Affair and the Crisis of French Manhood* (Baltimore: Johns Hopkins University Press, 2004); Christopher Forth and Elinor Accampo, eds., *Confronting Modernity in Fin-de-Siècle France: Bodies, Minds and Gender* (Basingstoke, UK: Palgrave, 2010). See also George Mosse, *The Image of Man: The Creation of Modern Masculinity* (Oxford: Oxford University Press, 1996); R. W. Connell, *Masculinities* (Cambridge: Polity Press, 1995).

63. Robert Nye, *Masculinity and Male Codes of Honor in Modern France* (New York: Oxford University Press, 1993), 32, 42.

64. Edward Berenson, *The Trial of Madame Caillaux* (Berkeley: University of California Press, 1992), 169–207.

65. Julian Pitt-Rivers, "Honour and Social Status," in *Honour and Shame: The Values of Mediterranean Society*, ed. John G. Peristiany (Chicago: University of Chicago Press, 1966), 21.

66. J. G. Peristiany, ed., *Honour and Shame: The Values of Mediterranean Society* (Chicago: University of Chicago Press, 1966), 11.

67. Jean Genet, "L'enfant criminel," in *Œuvres complètes*, vol. 5 (Paris: Gallimard, 1979), 225.

68. According to O'Brien, "the juvenile offender in the nineteenth century was in most cases male. . . . Four out of every five young prisoners were boys." O'Brien, *Promise of Punishment*, 112.

69. The 1850 legislation establishing agricultural colonies for boys also created special institutions for girls known as "penitentiary houses." According to O'Brien, "girls were not given agricultural training, as most boys were, perhaps because the fear of girls as the dangerous classes in urban areas was less strong. Once confined, girls were taught to be seamstresses, laundresses, and housekeepers. . . . Within two years after the passage of the legislation . . . the penitentiary houses for girls were replaced by convent-like, privately directed establishments. By 1873, with one exception, all houses for young girls were controlled by religious communities." O'Brien, *Promise of Punishment*, 139–40.

70. Ibid., 140–42.

71. On this point I echo Arneil, who argues that domestic colonies were based on the principle of segregation from the outside world and belief in moral improvement through labor, particularly the tilling of the soil. See Arneil, *Domestic Colonies*.

72. Rothman, *Conscience and Convenience*.

Chapter 1

1. As Barrie Ratcliffe has noted, contemporary observers failed to take into account both short- and long-term patterns of circular migration. See Ratcliffe, "The Chevalier Thesis Reexamined," *French Historical Studies* 17, no. 2 (Fall 1991).

2. Ann La Berge, *Mission and Method: The Early Nineteenth-Century French Public Health Movement* (Cambridge: Cambridge University Press, 1992); William Coleman, *Death Is a Social Disease: Public Health and Political Economy in Early Industrial France* (Madison: University of Wisconsin Press, 1982).

3. Louis Chevalier, *Laboring Classes and Dangerous Classes in Paris during the First Half of the Nineteenth Century*, trans. Frank Jellinek (Princeton, NJ: Princeton University Press, 1973).

4. Between 1840 and 1850, when the geographic origins of criminals were first recorded systematically, 58 to 59 percent of felonies were committed by rural denizens, whereas 37 to 38 percent were attributed to residents of urban areas (i.e., cities with populations of 2,000 or more). See Abdul Lodhi and Charles Tilly, "Urbanization, Crime and Collective Violence in Nineteenth-Century France," *American Journal of Sociology* 79, no. 2 (1974).

5. Antoine-Honoré Frégier, *Des classes dangereuses de la population dans les grandes villes et des moyens de le rendre meilleures*, vol. 1 (Paris: J.-B. Baillière, 1840), 7.

6. Louis Mathurin Moreau-Christophe, *Débats du congrès*, cited in O'Brien, *Promise of Punishment*, 65.

7. Ariès, *Centuries of Childhood*, 341.

8. L. Boulangé d'Aytré, *De l'éducation professionnelle pour les enfants pauvres* (Paris: Imprimerie de Baudouin, 1842), 28.

9. Un Détenu (anon.), *L'intérieur des prisons: Réforme pénitentiaire, system cellulaire, emprisonnement en commun* (Paris: Jules Labitte, 1846), 88.

10. Léon Faucher, *De la réforme des prisons* (Paris: Angé, 1838), 110.

11. George Rudé, among others, demonstrated that the "crowds" who manned the barricades of 1830 and 1848 were not comprised of the quintessential *"classes dangereuses"* but were primarily artisans desperate to maintain their way of life amid large-scale economic change. See Rudé, *The Crowd in the French Revolution* (New York: Oxford University Press, 1959).

12. Alphonse Bérenger de la Drôme, *Premier compte rendu des travaux de la Société pour le patronage des jeunes libérés du département de la Seine* (Paris: H. Fournier, 1834), 13.

13. Augustin Cochin, *Notice sur le Mettray* (Tours: Imprimerie Ladevèze, 1851), 17.

14. Kathleen Nilan, "'Crimes Inexplicables': Murderous Children in the Discourse of Monstrosity in Romantic-Era France," in *Becoming Delinquent: British and European Youth, 1650–1950*, ed. Pamela Cox and Heather Shore (Aldershot, UK: Ashgate, 2002), 79.

15. Perrot, "Delinquency and the Penitentiary System," 214.

16. J.-F. Ginouvrier, *Tableau de l'intérieur des prisons de France, ou études sur la situation et les souffrances morales et physiques de toutes les classes de prisonniers ou détenus* (Paris: Baudoin Frères, 1824), 136, 134–35.

17. Benjamin Appert, *Journal des prisons, hospices, écoles primaires et établissements de bienfaisance*, vol. 4 (Paris: Baudoin Frères, 1828), 42.

18. Louis Mathurin Moreau-Christophe, "Les détenus," in *Les français peints par eux-mêmes*, vol. 4, ed. Paul Gavarni et al. (Paris: L. Curmer, 1840), 1–3.

19. *The Times*, 10 October 1855, 12. Demetz was engaged in various civic organizations and activities while a judge, most notably as honorary president of the Société

libre d'instruction d'éducation and vice president of the Société d'encouragement au bien.

20. For instance, see G. M. A. Ferrus, *Des prisonniers, de l'emprisonnement et des prisons* (Paris: J.-B. Baillière, 1850), 44–45.

21. See, for example., F. A. F. La Rochefoucauld-Liancourt, *Examen de la théorie pratique du système pénitentiaire* (Paris: Delaunay, 1840), 372–73.

22. La Rochefoucauld-Liancourt, Benjamin Constant, and François Guizot were just a few of the prominent figures in French society who were members of the Société de la morale chrétienne. For more on this organization and similar, see Catherine Duprat, "Punir et guérir: En 1819, la prison des philanthropes," in *L'impossible prison: Recherches sur le système pénitentiaire au XIXe siècle,* ed. Michelle Perrot (Paris: L'Univers Historique, 1980), 64–122.

23. Gordon Wright, *Between the Guillotine and Liberty: Two Centuries of the Crime Problem in France* (Oxford: Oxford University Press, 1983), 132.

24. O'Brien, *Promise of Punishment,* 20–21.

25. Demetz, *Fondation d'une colonie agricole,* 6–7.

26. A. J.-B. Parent-Duchâtelet, *De la prostitution dans la ville de Paris: Considérée sous le rapport d'hygiène publique de la morale et de l'administration,* vol. 1 (Paris: J.-B. Baillière, 1836), 93–94.

27. Kathleen Nilan, "Incarcerating Children: Prison Reformers, Children's Prisons and Child Prisoners in the July Monarchy" (PhD diss., Yale University, 1996).

28. Frégier, *Des classes dangereuses,* 1:7, 115; 2:500–503.

29. Ibid., 2:115–21.

30. Frédéric Demetz, *Exposé du système d'éducation employé à la colonie agricole et pénitentiaire de Mettray et à la Maison Paternelle* (Paris: Pougin, 1873), 1.

31. Frédéric Demetz, *Assemblée générale des fondateurs* (Tours: Duprat, 1841), 12.

32. Demetz, *Fondation d'une colonie agricole,* 23.

33. While Blouet is perhaps best known today as the architect of the attic story of the Arc de Triomphe, in the 1830s he was one of a group of radical young architects who advocated using architecture to realize social reform. Indeed, he became a recognized authority on prison design and on his return from the United States was named inspecteur general des prisons in 1839. For more on this see Colin Ripley, "Safe as Houses: The Mettray Colony as Seen by Jean Genet," *Space and Culture* 9, no. 4 (2006), 401.

34. See Michel Lepeltier de Saint-Fargeau, "Rapport sur le projet de code pénal, fait à l'Assemblée constituante au nom des comités de constitution et de législation criminelle," in *Œuvre* (Brussels: Imprimerie Lacrosse, 1826), 89–150.

35. Whereas the Quaker-inspired Walnut Street prison in Philadelphia was the first to strictly isolate prisoners in individual cells both day and night, the Auburn prison in New York state was based on a regimen where prisoners were placed in individual cells only at night and worked together with other inmates during the day, "with absolute silence rigorously enforced using the whip." Wright, *Between the Guillotine and Liberty,* 64.

36. Gustave de Beaumont and Alexis de Tocqueville, *On the Penitentiary System in the United States and Its Application in France,* trans. Francis Lieber (Carbondale: Southern Illinois University Press, 1964), 81.

37. Ibid., 22.

38. Tocqueville to Ernest du Chabrol, 19 November 1831, cited in George Wilson Pierson, *Tocqueville and Beaumont in America* (Oxford: Oxford University Press, 1938), 473.

39. There were nine official visits to the United States to study modern prison technology including Demetz and Blouet's tour.

40. Davis, "Mettray Revisited," 556. As Davis points out, these elements of prison life remained subjects of prisoner protests, carried forward by Foucault and the Groupe d'information sur les prisons in the 1970s.

41. Frédéric Demetz and Abel Blouet, *Rapports à M. le comte de Montalivet, ministre secrétaire d'état au Département de l'intérieur, sur les pénitenciers des États-Unis* (Paris: Imprimerie Royale, 1837), 6.

42. Ibid., 3–4.

43. Ibid., 19–22.

44. Ibid., 26.

45. Ibid, 42.

46. Ibid., 27.

47. Frédéric Demetz, *Résumé sur le système pénitentiaire* (Paris: Claye et Taillefer, 1844), 3.

48. Demetz and Blouet, *Rapports*, 45.

49. Ibid., 43.

50. Ibid., 18.

51. Melossi and Pavarini, *The Prison and the Factory*, 129.

52. Davis, "Mettray Revisited," 554.

53. *Le Siècle*, 20 June 1839.

54. Marie-Sylvie Dupont-Bouchat and Éric Pierre, *Enfance et justice au XIXe siècle* (Paris: Presses Universitaires de France, 2001), 65.

55. Chris Leonards, "Priceless Children? Penitentiary Congresses Debating Childhood: A Quest for Social Order in Europe, 1846–1895," in *Social Control in Europe,* vol. 2, ed. Clive Emsley, Eric Johnson, and Pieter Spierenburg (Columbus: Ohio State University Press, 2004), 131n24.

56. Beaumont and Tocqueville, *On the Penitentiary System*, 104, 167.

57. Albert Schrauwers, "The 'Benevolent' Colonies of Johannes van den Bosch: Continuities in the Administration of Poverty in the Netherlands and Indonesia," *Comparative Studies in Society and History* 43, no. 2 (2001): 302.

58. Arneil, *Domestic Colonies*, 44.

59. L.-F. Huerne de Pommeuse, *Des colonies agricoles et de leurs avantages pour assurer le secours à l'honnête indigence* (Paris: Imprimerie Huzard, 1832); Louis-François Benoiston de Chateauneuf, *De la colonisation des condamnes, et de l'avantage qu'il y aurait pour la France à adopter cette mesure* (Paris: Hachette, 2016 [1827]).

60. Jean-Paul Alban de Villeneuve-Bargemont, *Economie politique chrétienne ou recherches sur la nature et les causes du paupérisme en France et en Europe et sur les moyens de la soulager et prévenir*, 2nd ed., vol. 2 (Brussels: Mélines, 1837), 537, cited in Frances Gouda, *Poverty and Political Culture: The Rhetoric of Social Welfare in the Netherlands and France, 1815–54* (Lanham, MD: Rowman and Littlefield, 1994), 241.

61. N.A., "Reformatory Education," *American Journal of Education* 1 no. 1 (1855): 615.

62. W.-H. Suringar, *Une visite à Mettray en 1848* (Leeuwarden, Netherlands: Imprimerie de G. T. N., 1845), 15.

63. Frédéric Demetz, "Report on Agricultural Colonies," *Irish Quarterly Review* (1855): 1.

64. Demetz cited in Edward Carpenter, *Socialism and Agriculture* (London: A. C. Fifield, 1910), 53–54. While his efforts to establish an institution like the Rauhe Haus had failed, Pestalozzi's role in the development of modern pedagogy, particularly his emphasis on active or hands-on learning, cannot be overstated. In this regard his ideas were shaped by Rousseauian notions of child development detailed in *Emile* (1762).

65. Frédéric Demetz, *Colonie agricole et pénitentiaire de Mettray* (Paris: Lemercier, 1847), 15.

66. On this point, see Dupont-Bouchat and Pierre, *Enfance et justice*, 70.

67. Demetz, *Fondation d'une colonie agricole*, 8.

68. Ibid.

69. Over the last quarter of the nineteenth century the term *pupille* gradually replaced *colon* in administrative nomenclature as the agricultural imperative that had guided the colony during its early years diminished in importance.

70. *Rapport annuel*, 1841.

71. Isidore Sarramea, *Considérations sur la maison central d'éducation correctionnelle de Bordeaux et sur les divers systèmes pénitentiaires appliques en France au jeunes détenus* (Bordeaux: T. Lafargue, 1842), 13.

72. Arneil, *Domestic Colonies*, 43.

73. Ceri Crossley, "Using and Transforming the French Countryside: The 'Colonies Agricoles,' 1820–1850," *French Studies* 65, no. 1 (1991): 52.

74. Cochin, *Notice sur Mettray*, 2–3.

75. Francesca Ashurst and Couze Venn, *Inequality, Poverty, Education: A Political Economy of School Exclusion* (Aldershot, UK: Palgrave, 2014), 123.

76. Michel Foucault, *Madness and Civilization: A History of Insanity in the Age of Reason*, trans. Richard Howard (London: Tavistock, 1967), 59–60.

77. Foucault, *Discipline and Punish*, 34–35.

78. Charles Lucas, "Économie politique: De l'extinction de la mendicité de l'agriculture," *Le Cultivateur* 15 (1839): 359.

79. Faucher, *De la réforme des prisons*, 150. It was never entirely clear to which region they were referring, though there were occasional mentions of lands in the southwest of France. For more, see Louis-Auguste Marquet-Vasselot, *La ville du refuge: Rêve philanthropique* (Paris: Ladvocat, 1832).

80. Louis-René Villermé, *Tableau d'état moral physique des ouvrières*, vol. 2 (Paris: Imprimerie Renouard, 1840), 360–62.

81. *Statuts constitutifs de la Société paternelle* (Tours: J. Claye, 1898), Article 31.

82. Jacques Bourquin and Éric Pierre, "Une visite à Mettray par l'image: L'album de gravures de 1844," *Sociétés et Représentations* 18, no. 2 (2004): 208.

83. Wright, *Between the Guillotine and Liberty*, 90.

84. Frédéric Demetz, "Exposé du système d'éducation employé à la colonie agricole et pénitentiaire de Mettray et à la Maison Paternelle," in *Congres de l'Alliance universelle de l'ordre et de la civilisation* (Paris: A. Pougin, 1872), 3.

85. A. Corne, "Rapport et projet de loi sur le patronage des jeunes détenus, présents au nom de la commission de l'assistance publique," in *Compte-rendu de l'Assemblée législative*, vol. 4, séance du 14 Décembre 1849 (Paris: Imprimerie Nationale, 1850), 67.

86. Ibid.

87. Wright, *Between the Guillotine and Liberty*, 90n29.

88. The Falloux Law granted legal status to independent secondary schools in France and was sponsored by the minister of education, Frédéric-Alfred-Pierre de Falloux. Under the guise of freedom of education, it restored much of the church's traditional influence.

89. *Statistique des prisons et établissements pénitentiaires* (Paris: Imprimerie Nationale, 1853), xx–xxi.

90. Pierre, "F.-A. Demetz et la colonie agricole de Mettray," 456.

91. A. Corne, *France: Compte rendu des séances de l'Assemblée* (Paris: Imprimerie Nationale, 1850), 66–67.

92. Jean-Jacques Yvorel, "Le discernement: Construction et usage d'une catégorie juridique en droit pénale des mineures," *Recherches Familiales* 9 (2012): 153–62.

93. Berlier de Vauplane, *Le cinquantenaire de Mettray* (Paris: Soye et Fils, 1890), 5.

94. The cost for each cottage was 8,300 francs, or as calculated by Demetz, 193 francs per inmate. *Rapport annuel*, 1841.

95. Demetz, *Fondation d'une colonie agricole*, 8.

96. Dupont-Bouchat and Pierre, *Enfance et justice*, 188.

97. Henry Barnard, *Reformatory Education: Papers on Preventive, Correctional and Reformatory Institutions and Agencies* (Hartford, CT: Brownell, 1857), 21.

98. François Cantagrel, "Examen critique de la colonie de Mettray," *La Phalange* vol. 9, no. 1 (1843): 1320.

99. Davis, "Mettray Revisited," 557. See also Bourquin and Pierre, "Une visite à Mettray;" Driver, "Discipline without Frontiers."

100. Barillet-Deschamps is most widely known for designing the gardens of the Bois de Boulogne, the Bois de Vincennes, the Parc des Buttes-Chaumont and for reconfiguring the Jardin du Luxembourg during the Second Empire. See Luisa Limido, *L'art des jardins sous le second empire: Jean-Pierre Barillet-Deschamps* (Paris: Champs Vallon, 2002), 73.

101. *Bulletin Société Générale des Prisons* 8, no. 2–3 (1884): 295.

102. Ibid.

103. Charles Fourier, *The Utopian Vision of Charles Fourier: Selected Texts on Work, Love, and Passionate Attraction*, ed. and trans. Jonathan Beecher and Richard Bienvenu (Boston: Beacon Press, 1971).

104. Ripley, "Safe as Houses," 403.

105. Pamela Pilbeam, *French Socialists before Marx: Workers, Women and the Social Question in France* (Montreal: McGill–Queen's University Press, 2000), 63.

106. Pierre, "F.-A. Demetz et la colonie agricole de Mettray," 456.

107. Considérant kept all of Mettray's annual reports in his personal library. Pilbeam, *French Socialists before Marx*, 64.

108. François Cantagrel, *Mettray et Ostwald: Étude sur ces deux colonies agricoles* (Paris: Librairie de l'École Sociétaire, 1842), 11.

109. *Annual Report of the Executive Committee of the Prison Association of New York* (Albany: Prison Association of New York, 1869), 255.

110. Arnould Bonneville de Marsangy, *Mettray: Colonie pénitentiaire, maison paternelle* (Paris: Henri Plon, 1866), 19–22. See also Ripley, "Safe as Houses."

111. *Notice sur la colonie agricole de Mettray 1852*, 2.

112. Pierre, "F. A. Demetz et la colonie agricole de Mettray," 460.

113. Ibid., 460, 458.

114. Dupont-Bouchat and Pierre, *Enfance et justice*, 183.

115. Terry Nichols Clark, *Prophets and Patrons: The French University System and the Emergence of the Social Sciences* (Cambridge, MA: Harvard University Press, 1973), 104–15, 122–42.

116. Cited in Arnould Bonneville de Marsangy, *L'amélioration de la loi criminelle*, vol. 1 (Paris: Cotillon, 1855), 1.

117. Howard C. Payne, *The Police State of Louis-Napoleon Bonaparte* (Seattle: University of Washington Press, 1966), 4–131.

118. Marcel Le Clère, *Histoire de la police* (Paris: Presses Universitaires de France, 1964), 85–87.

Chapter 2

1. Edmund White, *Genet: A Biography* (New York: Knopf, 1993), 64. One must be careful in utilizing Genet as a historical reference because Mettray was the site for his erotic fantasies and many of his claims regarding his own exploits at the colony were fictitious.Nevertheless, many of Genet's descriptions of aspects of the daily regime are substantiated in biographies and autobiographies of other former inmates, as well as by internal documentation.

2. Demetz, *Exposé du système d'éducation*, 8.

3. Michael J. Hughes, *Forging Napoleon's Grande Armée: Motivation, Military Culture, and Masculinity in the French Army, 1800–1808* (New York: New York University Press, 2012).

4. Ibid., 57.

5. Michael J. Hughes, "Making Frenchmen into Warriors: Martial Masculinity in Napoleonic France," in *French Masculinities: History, Politics and Culture*, ed. Christopher Forth and Bertrand Taithe (Aldershot, UK: Palgrave, 2007), 51–55.

6. Charles Sauvestre, *Une visite à Mettray* (Paris: Librairie Hachette, 1864), 8. The work was initially published as a series of columns in the Paris journal *L'Opinion Nationale* and later published as a book that was sold for the benefit of the colony.

7. Hill, "Mettray," 271–72.

8. Paul Huot, *Trois jours à Mettray: Rapports lus au Congrès scientifique de Tours et à la Société des sciences morales de Seine-et-Oise* (Paris: Claye and Taillefer, 1848), 25.

9. Demetz, *Exposé du système d'éducation*, 9.

10. Hill, "Mettray," 271.

11. Ibid.

12. Foucault, *Discipline and Punish*, 188.

13. Hill, "Mettray," 261–62.

14. Huot, *Trois jours*, 51.

15. Ibid.

16. Ibid., 55.

17. Jules Lamarque, *Des colonies pénitentiaires et du patronage des jeunes libérés* (Paris: Veuve Berger-Levrault et Fils, 1863), 170.

18. Almire Lepelletier de la Sarthe, *Colonie de Mettray: Solution pratique du problème des jeunes détenus* (Paris: Librairie de Guillaumin, 1856), 37. As with many early publications on Mettray, the profits from this particular work were earmarked for the colony.

19. Édouard Ducpétiaux, *Colonies agricoles, écoles rurales et écoles de réforme* (Brussels: Imprimerie de T. Lesigne, 1851), 68.

20. A. Giraud, *Colonie de Mettray: Devoirs du colon* (Tours: Imprimerie de Pornin, 1843), 32–33.

21. *Rapport annuel*, 1843.

22. Demetz cited in Henry Barnard, *Reformatory Education Papers on Preventive, Correctional, and Reformatory Institutions and Agencies in Different Countries* (Hartford, CT.: Brownell, 1857), 181.

23. James C. Scott, *Domination and the Arts of Resistance: Hidden Transcripts* (New Haven, CT: Yale University Press, 1990), 26.

24. Foucault, *Discipline and Punish*, 175–76.

25. Frédéric Demetz, *Rapport sur les colonies agricoles* (Tours: Ladevèze, 1855), 119.

26. Jean Genet, *Miracle of the Rose*, trans. Bernard Frechtman (New York: Grove Press, 1988 [1946]), 114.

27. Jean-Guy Le Dano, *La mouscaille* (Paris: Flammarion, 1973), 23–24.

28. Directeur to Préfet d'Hérault, 10 March 1893 (Archives départementales de Hérault [hereafter cited as ADH] 1 Y 353).

29. Ibid.

30. "Reformatory Schools," *The Quarterly Review* vol. XCVIII (January-April 1856), 25.

31. Lamarque, *Des colonies pénitentiaires*, 180.

32. Giraud, *Colonie de Mettray*, 3.

33. Genet, *Miracle of the Rose*, 200.

34. Raoul Léger, *La colonie agricole pénitentiaire de Mettray: Souvenirs d'un colon 1922–1927*, edited by Jacques Bourquin and Éric Pierre (Paris: L'Harmattan, 1998), 46.

35. Genet, *Miracle of the Rose*, 200. On this point, see also Le Dano, *La mouscaille*, 17.

36. Inspection générale de 1889 (Archives départementales du Cher [hereafter cited as ADC] 1 Y 157).

37. Inspection générale de 1892 (ADC 1 Y 157).

38. Lamarque, *Des colonies pénitentiaires*, 184.

39. Giraud, *Colonie de Mettray*, 9.

40. Ibid., 8.

41. Jean-Jacques Rousseau, *Emile* (New York: Dover, 2013 [1762]), 340.

42. Foucault, *Discipline and Punish*, 168.

43. *Mettray: Statuts constitutifs de la Société Paternelle de Mettray* (Tours: Impremerie Tourangelle 1920), Article 11.

44. For more on industrial time and proletarianization, see E. P. Thompson, *The Making of the English Working Class* (London: Vintage, 1980), 393–400.

45. Inspection générale des prisons du département du Cher, 1891 (ADC 1 Y 157).

46. Foucault, *Discipline and Punish*, 135.

47. Giraud, *Colonie de Mettray*, 7.

48. Lamarque, *Des colonies pénitentiaires*, 60.

49. Foucault, *Discipline and Punish*, 169.

50. Connell, *Masculinities*, 45.

51. *Bulletin Société Générale des Prisons* Vol. 4. (April 1880): 425.

52. Ivan Jablonka, "Childhood or the 'Journey toward Virility,'" in *A History of Virility*, ed. Alain Corbin, Jean-Jacques Courtine, and Georges Vigarello, trans. Keith Cohen (New York: Columbia University Press, 2016), 235–36.

53. Stoler, *Along the Archival Grain*, 110.

54. *Mettray: Statuts constitutifs*, Article 18.

55. Mosse, *Image of Man*, 44–45.

56. *Rapport annuel*, 1842, 12.

57. M. de la Baume, *Des colonies pénitentiaires agricoles: Mettray et Les Matelles* (Montpellier: Gras, 1859), 9.

58. Christopher Forth, *Masculinity in the Modern West: Gender, Civilization and the Body* (Aldershot, UK: Palgrave, 2008), 136.

59. Rapport d'ensemble sur les différents services de l'établissement d'Aniane de l'année 1936 (ADH 1 Y 328).

60. Inspection générale des prisons du département du Cher, 1891 (ADC 1 Y 157).

61. Rapport d'ensemble sur les différents services de l'établissement d'Aniane.

62. *Rapport annuel*, 1846.

63. Ibid.

64. Demetz cited in Patrick Joseph Murray, *Reformatory Schools in France and England* (London: W. F. G. Cash, 1854), 32.

65. William H. McNeill, *Keeping in Time: Dance and Drill in Human History* (Cambridge: Cambridge University Press, 1995), 131, 124.

66. Forth, *Masculinity in the Modern West*, 123.

67. *Bulletin Société Générale des Prisons* Vol. 8 (May 1884): 291.

68. Jean-Jacques Rousseau, *Discourse on the Sciences and Arts*, ed. Roger D. Masters, trans. Roger D. Masters and Judith R. Masters (New York: St. Martin's Press, 1964), 55.

69. Mosse, *Image of Man*, 23.

70. P.-F. Martin-Dupont, *Mes impressions, 1803–1876* (Paris: Sandoz et Fischbacher, 1878), 217–18.

71. See *Bulletin Société Générale des Prisons* 12 (May 1888): 628. *Canne de combat* (stick fighting) was quite popular as a martial art and as a means of self-defense in nineteenth-century France because the cane was an indispensable fashion accessory that could also serve as a weapon. Some fencing and boxing teachers naturally began to include the practice in their instruction. For more, see M. Larribeau, *Nouvelle théorie du jeu de la canne* (Paris: Verdeau, 1856); Fernand Legrange, *L'art de la boxe française et de la canne: Nouveau traité, théorique, pratique* (Paris: L'Académie de la Boxe, 1899).

72. Lamarque, *Des colonies pénitentiaires*, 180.

73. *Rapport annuel*, 1843.

74. Ducpétiaux, *Colonies agricoles*, 59.

75. Sauvestre, *Une visite à Mettray*, 42.

76. Cantagrel, *Mettray et Ostwald*, 20.

77. *Statuts constitutifs de la Société paternelle*, Article 21.

78. *Rapport annuel*, 1841.

79. Ibid.

80. Gaillac describes the *cellules obscures* as "low, unlit, poorly ventilated, and entirely painted in black." *Les maisons de correction*, 81. Davis notes that some of the cells were painted with *goudron* (tar), a common practice in French military prisons. Davis, "Mettray Revisited," 557n52.

81. *Rapport annuel*, 1841.

82. Le Dano, *La mouscaille*, 29.

83. Huot, *Trois jours*, 29.

84. Ibid.

85. Sauvestre, *Une visite à Mettray*, 30.

86. For example, see Charles Lucas, *Du système pénitentiaire en Europe et aux États-Unis*, vol. 2 (Paris: Bossange et Bechet, 1828), xxvi.

87. L. to Ministère de l'Intérieur, 6 August 1851 (Archives départementales d'Indre-et-Loire [hereafter cited as ADIL] 1 Y 176).

88. Directeur to Préfet d'Indre-et-Loire, 8 October 1851 (ADIL 1 Y 176). Paul Niquet's cabaret (located in Les Halles) was an infamous haunt of the Parisian demimonde that gained world renown through the literary works of Eugène Sue and Gérard de Nerval.

89. Ministère de l'Intérieur to Préfet d'Indre-et-Loire, n.d. (ADIL 1 Y 176).

90. Directeur to Préfet d'Indre-et-Loire, 30 August 1851 (ADIL 1 Y 176).

91. *Rapport annuel*, 1849.

92. Hill, "Mettray," 299.

93. Ducpétiaux, *Colonies agricoles*, 58.

94. Hill, "Mettray," 299.

95. *Rapport annuel*, 1845.

96. Ministère de l'Intérieur et des Cultes, 21 December 1901 (ADC 1 Y 157).

97. Goffman, *Asylums*, 14.

98. *Rapport annuel*, 1841. The clothing provided to each inmate on entry consisted of three shirts, three pairs of pants, two pairs gaiters, one straw hat, one pair of shoes, one pair of wooden shoes (sabots), two blacking brushes, one hairbrush, one comb, one black scarf, one woolen shirt, one woolen waistcoat for winter, and one pair of wool pants, all of which together had a value of 10.20 francs.

99. Préfet du Cher à Ministère de l'Intérieur, Direction de l'Administration pénitentiaire, 28 February 1887 (ADC 1 Y 157).

100. Ministère de l'Intérieur to Préfet du Cher, 6 April 1887 (ADC 1 Y 157).

101. *Mettray: Statuts constitutifs*, Articles 29–30. Visitors were also forbidden from giving letters, money, or any other items to their family member during their visit, and they were not allowed to speak or have contact with any other *colons*.

102. *Rapport annuel*, 1850.

103. There is no evidence that this extended to fathers who lived in concubinage with someone other than the inmate's mother.

104. Fuchs, *Poor and Pregnant*, 21.

105. Cluze directed Mettray from January 1887 until his death on 12 February 1905.

106. Préfet d'Indre-et-Loire to Commissaire Général, 30 June 1899 (ADIL 1 Y 176).

107. Commissaire Général to Préfet d'Indre-et-Loire, 2 July 1899 (ADIL 1 Y 176).

108. Directeur to Préfet d'Indre-et-Loire, 20 July 1899 (ADIL 1 Y 176).

109. Mme. F. to Préfet d'Indre-et-Loire, 9 March 1905 (ADIL 1 Y 176).

110. Mme. F. to Préfet d'Indre-et-Loire, 23 March 1905 (ADIL 1 Y 176).

111. Préfet d'Indre-et-Loire to Directeur, 20 March 1905 (ADIL 1 Y 176).

112. Directeur to Préfet d'Indre-et-Loire, 21 July 1906 (ADIL 1 Y 176).

113. Directeur to Préfet d'Indre-et-Loire, 25 July 1906 (ADIL 1 Y 176).

114. Gavignon to Préfet d'Indre-et-Loire, 9 May 1907 (ADIL 1 Y 176).

115. Directeur to Préfet d'Indre-et-Loire, 14 May 1907 (ADIL 1 Y 176).

116. Mme. B. to Préfet d'Indre-et-Loire, 25 May 1897 (ADIL 1 Y 176).

117. Directeur to Préfet d'Indre-et-Loire, 27 May 1897 (ADIL 1 Y 176).

118. Directeur to Préfet d'Indre-et-Loire, 24 September 1920 (ADIL 1 Y 176).

119. Directeur to Préfet d'Indre-et-Loire, 21 December 1920 (ADIL 1 Y 176).

120. Directeur de l'Administration pénitentiaire to Préfet d'Indre-et-Loire, 14 May 1921 (ADIL 1 Y 176).

121. Maire de Saint-Cyr-sur-Loire to Préfet d'Indre-et-Loire, 25 May 1921 (ADIL 1 Y 176).

122. V. to Préfet d'Indre-et-Loire, 10 April 1923 (ADIL 1 Y 175).

123. Directeur to Préfet d'Indre-et-Loire, 28 April 1923 (ADIL 1 Y 175).

124. Ibid.

125. Préfet d'Indre-et-Loire to V., 1 May 1923 (ADIL 1 Y 175).

126. Sykes, *Society of Captives*.

127. Alf Lüdtke, "Polymorphous Synchrony: German Industrial Workers and the Politics of Everyday Life," in *The End of Labour History?*, ed. Marcel van der Linden (Cambridge: Cambridge University Press, 1993), 56.

128. Brun was the colony's director from 1911 to 1921. Unlike his predecessors, he was not drawn from the military but from the public sector, as he had directed a few state-operated agricultural colonies before accepting the post at Mettray.

129. Report on the C. incident, 9 June 1912 (ADIL 1 Y 176).

130. Directeur to Préfet d'Indre-et-Loire, 10 June 1912 (ADIL 1 Y 176).

131. Directeur to Préfet d'Indre-et-Loire, 27 April 1909 (ADIL 1 Y 220).

132. Préfet de la Vendée to Directeur, 22 April 1909 (ADIL 1 Y220).

133. Ministère de l'Intérieur. Direction de l'Administration pénitentiaire, jeunes détenus. Notice sur le nommé G. ND. (ADIL 1 Y 220).

134. Préfet d'Indre-et-Loire to Préfet de la Vendée, 4 May 1909 (ADIL 1 Y 220).

135. *Rapport annuel*, 1872.

136. Dupont-Bouchat and Pierre, *Enfance et justice*, 189.

137. Foucault, *Discipline and Punish*, 194.

Chapter 3

1. Michel Foucault, *The History of Sexuality: Volume One, An Introduction* (New York: Vintage, 1990 [1984]), 104.

2. Vernon Rosario, *The Erotic Imagination: French Histories of Perversity* (Oxford: Oxford University Press, 1997), 42.

3. Foucault, *History of Sexuality*, 27.

4. Robert A. Nye, "Sex Difference and Male Homosexuality in French Medical Discourse, 1830–1930," *Bulletin of the History of Medicine* 63, no. 1 (1989): 32.

5. Auguste Ambroise Tardieu, *Étude médico-légale sur les attentats aux mœurs* (Paris: J. Millon, 1878), 198. The word *homosexual*, an invention of German origin, did not appear in French until the 1890s and was not widely used until after the Second World War. The word *pederast* was improperly used to identify homosexuals until that time. See Claude Courouve, *Vocabulaire de l'homosexualité masculine* (Paris: Payot, 1985).

6. Perrot, "Delinquency and the Penitentiary System," 225.

7. Patricia O'Brien, "The Prison on the Continent: Europe, 1865–1965," in *Oxford History of the Prison: The Practice of Punishment in Western Society*, ed. Norval Morris and David Rothman (Oxford: Oxford University Press, 1997), 206. On subcultures in the nineteenth-century French prison, see O'Brien, *Promise of Punishment*, 5, 11, 77–89. For a classic articulation of prison subculture in the American prison system, see Sykes, *Society of Captives*.

8. Le Dano, *La mouscaille*, 24.

9. Caffler was interviewed for a series of investigative articles on Mettray that appeared in *Détective*. See Louis Roubaud, *Détective*, 21 April 1937.

10. Henri Danjou, *Enfants du malheur!* (Paris: Albin-Michel, 1932), 101.

11. Hugo characterized argot as "nothing more than the ugly, restless, sly, treacherous, venomous, cruel, crooked, vile, deadly language of misery. . . . We can hardly recognize it. Is it truly the French tongue? We distinguish questions and answers, we perceive, without understanding, a hideous murmur, sounding almost like human tones, but nearer a howling than speech. This is argot." Hugo, *Les misérables* St. Denis, book VII. Hugo, *Les misérables* trans. Charles E. Wilbour (New York: Carleton, 1862), 91.

12. Genet, *Miracle of the Rose*, 64. The expression "to doe" translates to *se bicher* (to clear out [escape]) and *biche* (a doe). See 98n1.

13. Le Dano, *La mouscaille*, 43.

14. Léger, *La colonie agricole pénitentiaire de Mettray*, 56.

15. Genet, *Miracle of the Rose*, 114–15.

16. Directeur to Préfet d'Indre-et-Loire, 17 December 1910 (ADIL 1 Y 194). To preserve the anonymity of prisoners I have used pseudonyms.

17. Télégramme Directeur de la colonie d'Aniane to Préfet d'Hérault, 23 March 1909 (ADH 1 Y 348).

18. Directeur de la colonie d'Aniane to Préfet d'Hérault, 24 March 1909 (ADH 1 Y 348).

19. Peter L. Berger, Brigitte Berger, and Hansfried Kellner, *The Homeless Mind: Modernization and Consciousness* (New York: Random House, 1973), 86.

20. Huot, *Trois jours*, 28.

21. Directeur to Préfet d'Indre-et-Loire, 21 July 1911 (ADIL 1 Y 204).

22. Préfet d'Indre-et-Loire to Ministre de la Justice, 19 August 1911 (ADIL 1 Y 204).

23. Préfet de l'Hérault to Ministère de l'Intérieure pénitentiaire, 14 February 1911 (ADH 1 Y 331).

24. Le Président du Conseil, Ministère de l'Intérieure pénitentiaire to Préfet de l'Hérault, 22 February 1900 (ADH 1 Y 331).

25. This is not to dismiss the possibility that coercion was involved in this case; it is possible that there was fear involved in the relationship and it was therefore not voluntary. The extant documentation does not allow for a definitive determination.

26. Victoria Thompson has examined the sexual and affective bonds among adult prisoners with a shared sense of commitment and solidarity in the relationship. See Thompson, "Creating Boundaries: Homosexuality and the Changing Social Order in France, 1830–1870," in *Homosexuality in Modern France*, ed. Jeffrey Merrick and Bryant T. Ragan (Oxford: Oxford University Press, 1996), 102–27.

27. Mary Bosworth and Eamonn Carrabine, "Reassessing Resistance: Race, Gender and Sexuality in Prison," *Punishment and Society* 3, no. 4 (2001): 501.

28. Thomas Laqueur, *Solitary Sex: A Cultural History of Masturbation*, 2nd ed. (New York: Zone Books, 2003), 249.

29. Robert A. Nye, *Crime, Madness and Politics in Modern France: The Medical Concept of National Decline* (Princeton, NJ: Princeton University Press, 1984), 143.

30. Claude François Lallemand, *Des pertes séminales involontaires* (Paris: Bechet Jeune, 1839).

31. On this point, see Ellen Bayuk Rosenman, "Body Doubles: The Spermatorrhea Panic," *Journal of the History of Sexuality* 12, no. 3 (2003).

32. Foucault, *History of Sexuality*, 6.

33. André Mailhol, *La colonie industrielle et agricole d'Aniane* (Montpellier: Imprimerie de Causse, Graille et Castelnau, 1927), 50–51.

34. *Rapport annuel*, 1874. Blanchard directed Mettray from November 1873 to December 1884.

35. Henri Joly, *À la recherche de l'éducation correctionnelle à travers l'Europe* (Paris: V. Lecoffre, 1902), 180–81. See also O'Brien, *Promise of Punishment*, 132n70.

36. Rapport, Directeur de la colonie pénitentiaire d'Aniane, 11 January 1899 (1 Y347).

37. Caffler quoted in Roubaud, *Détective*, 22 April 1937, 12–14.

38. See White, *Genet*, 69n58.

39. Le Dano, *La mouscaille*, 29.

40. Inspection générale des prisons du département du Cher, 1891 (ADC 1 Y 157).

41. Ripley, "Safe as Houses," 411.

42. Goffman, *Asylums*, 40.

43. Genet, *Miracle of the Rose*, 146, 151.

44. White, *Genet*, 76n86.

45. O'Brien, *Promise of Punishment*, 80, 87.

46. Étienne Martin, "Le tatouage chez les enfants," *Archives d'Anthropologie Criminelle* 25 (1910): 81.

47. Gemma Angel, "Roses and Daggers: Expressions of Emotional Pain and Devotion in Nineteenth-Century Tattoos," in *Probing the Skin: Culture Representations of Our Contact Zones*, ed. Caroline Rosenthal and Dirk Vanderbeke (Cambridge: Cambridge Scholars Press, 2015), 226, 226n19.

48. Alexandre Lacassagne, *Les tatouages, étude anthropologique et médico-légale* (Paris: J.-B. Baillière et Fils, 1881), 99.

49. Lombroso argued that tattoos were a "specific and entirely new anatomic-legal characteristic" "born criminal." Cesare Lombroso, "The Savage Origin of Tattooing" cited in Simon A. Cole, *Suspect Identities: A History of Fingerprinting and Criminal Identification* (Cambridge, MA: Harvard University Press, 2001), 58.

50. For more information on the similarities and differences between the Italian and French "schools" of criminology, see Laurent Mucchielli, "Hérédité et milieu social: Le faux antagonisme franco-italien," in *Histoire de la criminologie française*, ed. Laurent Mucchielli (Paris: L'Harmattan, 1995), 189–214.

51. Martine Kaluszynski, "The International Congresses of Criminal Anthropology and the Shaping of the French and International Criminological Movement, 1886–1914," in *The Criminal and His Scientists: Essays on the History of Criminology*, ed. Peter Becker and Richard F. Wetzell (Cambridge: Cambridge University Press, 2006), 303.

52. Louis Vervaeck, "Le tatouage en Belgique," cited in Jane Caplan, "'National Tattooing': Traditions of Tattooing in Nineteenth-Century Europe," in *Written on the Body: The Tattoo in European and American History*, ed. Jane Caplan (Princeton, NJ: Princeton University Press, 2000), 165n23.

53. Martin, "Le tatouage chez les enfants," 83.

54. Ibid., 75.

55. For more on tattooing in the French overseas penal colonies, see Stephen A. Toth, *Beyond Papillon: A History of the French Overseas Penal Colonies, 1854–1952* (Lincoln: University of Nebraska Press, 2006), 55–56.

56. Martin, "Le tatouage chez les enfants," 82.

57. Alan Kerdavid, *Bagne de gosses* (Paris: La Pensée Universelle, 1978), 7.

58. Directeur to Préfet d'Indre-et-Loire, 6 November 1911 (ADIL 1 Y 194).

59. Danjou, *Enfants du malheur!*, 28.

60. Directeur de Maison d'education surveillée d'Eysses to M. Ministre de la Justice, 22 November 1937 (Archives départementales de Lot-et-Garonne [hereafter cited as ADLEG] 1 Y 114).

61. Ibid.

62. Le Dano, *La mouscaille*, 17.

63. Kerdavid, *Bagne des gosses*, 85.

64. Inspection rapport 22-2-1935 (ADIL 114 J 271).

65. For instance, see reports from 1916 to 1919, Commission permanence de Tours. Procès-verbaux (ADIL 114 J 182).

66. White, *Genet*, 69.

67. Conseil d'administration assemble des fondateurs, comité des finances et commission permanente, 23 June 1932 (ADIL 114 J 177).

68. Directeur to Préfet d'Indre-et-Loire, 17 June 1916 (ADIL 114 J 252).

69. Tamara Myers and Joan Sangster, "Retorts, Runaways and Riots: Patterns of Resistance in Canadian Reform Schools for Girls, 1930–1960," *Journal of Social History* 34, no. 3 (2001): 673.

70. Rapport individuel, 3 July 1924 (ADIL 1 Y 176).

71. According to Scott, gossip "consists typically of stories that are designed to ruin the reputation of some identifiable person or persons. . . . Above all, gossip is about social rules that have been violated." Scott, *Domination and the Arts of Resistance*, 143.

72. Rapport individuel, 3 June 1919 (ADIL 1 Y 176).

73. Sauvestre, *Une visite à Mettray*, 64.

74. Bertrand Taithe, "Neighborhood Boys and Men: The Changing Space of Masculine Identity in France, 1848–71," in *French Masculinities: History, Politics and Culture* (Basingstoke, UK: Palgrave Macmillan, 2007), 68.

75. Richard Klein, *Cigarettes Are Sublime* (Durham, NC: Duke University Press, 1993), 8.

76. Genet, *Miracle of the Rose*, 18, 151–52.

77. Erving Goffman, "On the Characteristics of Total Institutions: The Inmate World," in *The Prison: Studies in Institutional Organization and Change*, ed. Donald R. Cressey (New York: Holt, 1961), 53–54.

78. There is a vast literature on underground economies in the prison. For classic articulations, see Donald Clemmer, *The Prison Community* (New York: Rinehart, 1940); Sykes, *Society of Captives*.

79. Letter of Jean-Pierre B., 21 June 1912 (ADIL 1 Y 204). Regarded as one of the most infamous anarchists of his day, Jacques Liabeuf was known for wearing a bulletproof waistcoat, a suit with brass sleeves, and wristbands with sharp points that could inflict grave violence on anyone whom he might encounter. He was arrested and guillotined in July 1910 for murdering a policeman.

80. 236 *colons* to Directeur, 2 April 1912 (ADC 1 Y 158).

81. Directeur to Ministère de la Justice, 3 April 1912 (ADC 1 Y 158).

82. Perhaps most common, however, was the socialist standard of the nineteenth century, "l'Internationale," particularly during the First World War and the interwar period.

83. Directeur to Préfet du Cher, 26 January 1899 (ADC 1 Y 157).

84. Report of Brigadier Rodolphe, Commandant de la brigade à cheval de Bourges, 26 January 1899 (ADC 1 Y 157).

85. Directeur to Préfet d'Indre-et-Loire, 1 October 1897 (ADIL 1 Y 203).

86. *Mettray: Statuts constitutifs*, Article 16.

87. Directeur Cluze to Préfet d'Indre-et-Loire, 26 June 1895 (ADIL 1 Y 203).

88. Punishment record of Jean K., n.d. (ADIL 1 Y 203).

89. In a provocative article based on a cross-referencing of death tolls and admissions to the local hospital in Tours, Idelette Ardouin-Weiss and Georges-François Pottier discovered that officials at Mettray underreported prisoner deaths by not including *colons* who had died in hospital, thereby giving the appearance that the colony was more salubrious than it was. See "Les décès des enfants de la colonie agricole et pénitentiaire de Mettray," *Histoire de la Touraine* 21, no. 1 (2008).

90. Jacques M., "Actes insensés," 9 May 1920 (ADIL 1 Y 204).

91. "Actes insensés commis par divers pupilles pour se nuire à eux-mêmes" (ADIL 1 Y204).

92. Pierre B., "Actes insensés," 14 November 1925 (ADIL 1 Y 204). See also *Compte-rendu de la situation morale et financière*, 1925 (ADIL 114 J 252). Lardet was director of Mettray from January 1922 to March 1932.

93. Leroy L., "Actes insensés," 6 January 1926 (ADIL 1 Y 204).

94. White, *Genet*, 67–68.

95. "Actes insensés,"

96. Ibid.

97. Observations of Inspecteur General Granier, 25 August 1890 (ADIL 114 J 271).

98. Harry Alis [Jules-Hippolyte Percher], *Mettray, la colonie agricole. Étude parue dans le* Journal des Débats (Tours: Imprimerie de Mame, 1890), 8. In 1895 Percher was killed in a duel outside Le Moulin Rouge by an angry reader of an article he had published in *Journal des Débats* related to French territorial acquisitions in Africa.

99. *Compte-rendu de la situation morale et financière*, 1925 (ADIL 114 J 252).

100. "Actes insensés commis par divers pupilles pour se nuire à eux-mêmes," (ADIL 1 Y 204).

101. Thomas Ugelvik, *Power and Resistance in Prison: Doing Time, Doing Freedom* (Aldershot, UK: Palgrave, 2014), 11.

102. Michael Hardt, "Prison Time," *Yale French Studies* 91 (1997): 65.

103. Le Dano, *La mouscaille*, 58, 61.

Chapter 4

1. David Garland and Peter Young, eds., *The Power to Punish: Contemporary Penality and Social Analysis* (Aldershot, UK: Gower, 1979).

2. Foucault, *Discipline and Punish*, 10.

3. Christian Carlier, *Histoire du personnel des prisons françaises du XVIIIe siècle à nos jours* (Paris: Éditions de l'Atelier, 1997), 10.

4. Matthew Davenport Hill, *Suggestions for the Repression of Crime: Charges Delivered to Grand Juries of Birmingham* (London: John W. Parker, 1857), 121.

5. "Visit to Mettray," *Chambers' Journal of Popular Literature, Sciences and Arts* 98 (17 November 1855), 309.

6. Cochin, *Notice sur Mettray*, 13–14.

7. Enoch Cobb Wines, "The Agricultural and Penitentiary Colony of Mettray," in *Report on the International Penitentiary Congress of London, 3–13 July 1872* (Washington, DC: Government Printing Office, 1873), 265.

8. Frédéric Demetz, *Notice sur l'école préparatoire de Mettray* (Paris: Claye Taillefer, 1846), 7.

9. The *certificat d'études* represented the successful completion of primary schooling in France, usually by age twelve.

10. Robert Hall, *Mettray: A Lecture Read before the Leeds Philosophical and Literary Society* (London: Cash, 1854), 27.

11. Mary Carpenter, *Reformatory Schools for the Children of the Perishing and Dangerous Classes and for Juvenile Delinquents* (London: Routledge, 2006 [1851]), 328.

12. John Ramsland, "Mettray: A Corrective Institution for Delinquent Youth in France, 1840–1937," *Journal of Educational Administration and History* 22, no. 1 (1990): 40.

13. Wines, "Agricultural and Penitentiary Colony," 265.

14. Foucault, *Discipline and Punish*, 295.

15. Driver, "Discipline without Frontiers?"

16. Foucault, *Discipline and Punish*, 294.

17. Jean-Jacques Yvorel, "Les premières campagnes contre les bagnes d'enfants," in *L'indignation: Histoire d'une émotion (XIXe–XXe siècles)*, ed. Anne-Claire Ambroise-Rendu and Christian Delaporte (Paris: Nouveau Monde, 2008), 105–28; Frédéric Chauvaud, "Le scandale de Mettray (1909): Le trait enténébré et la campagne de

presse," in *Éduquer et punir: La colonie agricole et pénitentiaire de Mettray*, ed. Sophie Chassat, Luc Forlivesi, and Georges-François Pottier (Rennes: Presses Universitaires de Rennes, 2005), 175–93; Pascale Quincy-Lefebvre, "Emotion et opinion dans la justice des mineurs en France durant l'entre-deux-guerres," *Revue d'Histoire de l'Enfance "Irrégulière"* 17 (2015). See also Pascale Quincy-Lefebvre, *Combats pour l'enfance. Itinéraire d'un faiseur d'opinion: Alexis Danan, 1890–1979* (Paris: Beauchesne, 2014).

18. Louis Roubaud, "Bagnes d'enfants," *Détective*, 15 November 1934. Roubaud later admitted to readers that as a youth he had been confined—via the power of paternal correction—to Mettray's Maison Paternelle (see chapter 5 for more in this regard). *Le Petit Parisien*, 5 April 1937.

19. Jean Castagnez, *Extrait du journal officiel, Chambre des députes*, 5 February 1935 (ADIL 114 J 582).

20. Genet, *Miracle of the Rose*, 180.

21. Félix Voisin, "Rapport sur le projet de loi relative à l'éducation des jeunes détenus," in *Enquête parlementaire sur le régime des établissements pénitentiaires*, vol. 8 (Paris: Imprimerie Nationale, 1875), 30.

22. Ibid., 47.

23. Ibid.

24. Chauvaud, "Les jeunes délinquants de Seine-et-Oise," 258.

25. *Annales de l'Assemblée nationale, 1871–75* (Versailles: Cerf, 1875), 56.

26. Voisin, "Rapport sur le projet de loi," 128.

27. Ibid., 127–30.

28. Ibid., 42.

29. Louis Herbette, cited in Gaillac, *Les maisons de correction*, 156.

30. Voisin, "Rapport sur le projet de loi," 28–30.

31. On industrial labor law pertaining to children, see Hugh Cunningham, *Children in Nineteenth-Century France: Work, Health and Education among the Classes Populaires* (Cambridge: Cambridge University Press, 1988), 312–15. On the Tallon Law, see Schafer, *Children in Moral Danger*, 53–57. For more on the Roussel Law, see Rachel G. Fuchs, *Abandoned Children: Foundlings and Child Welfare in Nineteenth-Century France* (Albany: State University of New York Press, 1984), 164–65.

32. The law of 1881 made primary education free and the law of 1882 made school compulsory for boys and girls aged six to thirteen. Through several laws passed between 1882 and 1889 education was secularized. For more on this, see Linda Clark, *Schooling the Daughters of Marianne* (Albany: State University of New York Press, 1985).

33. Local councils typically covered salaries for teachers rather than building or operating costs.

34. The Catholic share of primary school students rose from 29 percent in 1850 to 44 percent in 1876. See Raymond Grew and Patrick J. Harrigan, "The Catholic Contribution to Universal Schooling in France, 1850–1906," *Journal of Modern History* 57, no. 2 (1985): 219.

35. Lacroix served as mayor of the eleventh arrondissement in 1866, *conseiller municipal* from 1874 to 1881, and *député de la Seine* from 1883 to 1889.

36. For more on moral abandonment, see Schafer, *Children in Moral Danger*.

37. Sigismond Lacroix, "Une visite à Mettray," *Le Radical*. 22 December 1882.

38. Ibid.

39. Ibid.

40. After establishing *La Lanterne* in 1868, Rochefort was arrested and then exiled to the island of New Caledonia for his political activities during the Paris Commune (along with 3,858 other Communards) after a new deportation law was enacted on 23 March 1872. He returned to France following the general amnesty of the Communards in 1880 and later established the socialist newspaper *L'Intransigeant*. For more on this, see Toth, *Beyond Papillon*.

41. Henri Rochefort, "Les enfants moralement abandonnés," pt. 3, *La Lanterne*, 1 January 1883.

42. Henri Rochefort, "Les enfants moralement abandonnés," pt. 2, *La Lanterne*, 31 December 1882.

43. Pierre-Paul Chapon, "L'historique de la profession d'éducateur technique spécialisé," in *Educateurs techniques spécialisés*, ed. Manuel Sanz and Paul Sanchou (Paris: ERES, 2007), 17.

44. "Exposé de l'état actuel du système pénitentiaire en France," in *Actes du Congrès pénitentiaire international de Bruxelles, août 1900*, vol. 4 (Brussels: Bureau de la Commission pénitentiaire international, 1901), 415.

45. Thomas Grimm, "La colonie de Mettray," *Le Petit Journal*, 8 September 1887.

46. Article 7 read: "No person belonging to an unauthorized religious community can govern a public or private educational establishment of whatever order or to give instruction therein."

47. John W. Bush, "Education and Social Status: The Jesuit College in the Early Third Republic," *French Historical Studies* 9, no. 1 (1975): 125.

48. John W. Padberg, *Colleges in Controversy: The Jesuit Schools in France, from Revival to Suppression, 1815–1880* (Cambridge, MA: Harvard University Press, 1969), 267.

49. J. Messire, "La colonie de Mettray," *L'Univers*, 30 January 1887.

50. Ramsland, "Mettray: A Corrective Institution," 41.

51. *L'Univers*, 3 March 1887.

52. *Enquête parlementaire sur le régime des établissements pénitentiaires*, vol. 45 (Paris: Imprimerie et Librairie du journal officiel, 1876), 172. For more on Casabianda, see Paul-Roger Gontard, "Le centre de détention de Casabianda: Emblématique prison de paradoxes" (master's thesis, Université Paul Cézanne Aix-Marseille III, 2008).

53. *Rapports et délibérations, Conseil général d'Indre-et-Loire* (Tours: Conseil général, 1886), 141.

54. Goüin was one of nine deputies in the National Assembly closely affiliated with Adolphe Thiers during the early years of the Third Republic. He later founded and served as president of the Banque de Paris et des Pays-Bas. For more on Goüin, see Robert C. Locke, *French Legitimists and the Politics of Moral Order in the Early Third Republic* (Princeton, NJ: Princeton University Press, 1974), 130.

55. De Cayla to Eugène Goüin, 14 July 1886 (ADIL 1 Y 141).

56. Ibid.

57. On this point, see Arneil, *Domestic Colonies*, 45.

58. A. Comte de Tourdonnet, *Des colonies agricoles d'éducation*, vol. 3: *Régime financier* (Paris: P. Brunet, 1867), 195.

59. M. Gillon, représentant de la Meuse, cited in Ducpétiaux, *Colonies agricoles*, 55.

60. Frédéric Demetz, *Notice sur la colonie agricole de Mettray 1863* (Tours: Imprimerie Ladevèze, 1864), 6.

61. Marsangy, *Mettray: Colonie pénitentiaire*, 45–46.

62. Huot, *Trois jours*, 57.

63. De Cayla to Goüin 14 July 1886.

64. De Cayla to Eugène Goüin, 26 January 1887 (ADIL 1 Y 141).

65. De Cayla to Goüin, 14 July 1886.

66. Colonie de Mettray, Personnel, 26 October 1886 (ADIL 1 Y 141).

67. De Cayla to Goüin, 14 July 1886.

68. De Cayla to Eugène Goüin, 5 December 1886 (ADIL 1 Y 141).

69. *L'Univers* (3 March 1887).

70. De Cayla to Goüin, 5 December 1886.

71. De Cayla to Goüin, 26 January 1887 (ADIL 1 Y 141).

72. Ibid. For more on the Maison Paternelle, see chapter 5.

73. Ibid. The will is not part of the historical record.

74. Ibid.

75. Ibid.

76. Ibid.

77. According to Davis, "as the documents comprising the archive were pre-vetted . . . there is no realistic prospect of historians being able to get to the bottom of the matter [re financial improprieties] with those documents alone." See Davis, "Mettray Revisited," 564.

78. White, *Genet*, 71.

79. Davis, "Mettray Revisited," 549.

80. Wilson was the son of a wealthy English entrepreneur by the same name. His father had made his fortune by developing a gas lighting system in Paris and then investing in railways, property, and metallurgy at Le Creusot in Burgundy. His son was implicated in a scandal selling honors and government contracts from his office in the Elysée palace in 1887. For more on this, see Daniel Palmer, "Daniel Wilson and the Decorations Scandal of 1887," *Modern and Contemporary France* 1, no. 2 (1993).

81. *L'Union Libérale de Tours*, 28 January 1887.

82. An unnamed member of the Société paternelle noted in an 1856 meeting that news of the colony's lack of profitability should be closely guarded so as not to attract attention from critics. See *Procès-verbaux des séances du conseil de la Société paternelle*, 16 July 1856 (ADIL 114 J 175).

83. *Le Petit Journal*, 11 September 1887.

84. On this point, see Yvorel, "Les premières campagnes," 112.

85. Mettray's surveillance council was established only belatedly, on 17 June 1874. It officially constituted a representative of the Penitentiary Administration, a delegate appointed by the prefect of Indre-et-Loire, two delegates from the Conseil général, a member of the civil court elected by his colleagues, and a clergyman appointed by the archbishop of Tours.

86. Rapport du Préfet et procès-verbaux des séances et délibérations du conseil général, 19 April 1887 (Tours: Imprimerie E. Mazerau, 1887), 46–47.

87. Heywood, *Growing Up in France*, 163.

88. Directeur de la colonie industrielle d'Aniane to M. Préfet de l'Hérault, 24 October 1923 (ADH 1 Y 348).

89. Directeur de la maison d'education surveillée d'Aniane to Ministère de la Justice Administration pénitentiaire (Service du personnel), 28 October 1934 (ADH 1 Y 348).

90. Directeur de la Maison d'education surveillée d'Aniane to M. Ministère de la Justice Administration pénitentiaire (Service du personnel), 4 February 1930 (ADH 1 Y 348).

91. René Goblet, Ministre de l'Intérieur to Préfet d'Indre-et-Loire, 9 March 1887 (ADIL 1 Y 141).

92. Guillon estimates that approximately two-thirds of the population was drawn from the Service des enfants moralement abandonnés de la Seine. Jean-Marie Guillon, "Enfance assistée, enfance exploitée? La colonie agricole de Porquerolles," in *Enfants au travail: Attitudes des élites en Europe occidentale et méditerranéenne aux XIXe et XXe siècles*, ed. Roland Caty (Aix-en-Provence: Presses Universitaires de Provence, 2002), 137–52.

93. The couple's marital status did not escape the scrutiny of conservative newspapers, which frequently noted that they lived in concubinage. Lapeyre wrote under two pseudonyms: Pierre Ninous (the name of her first husband) and after the trial involving child abuse at Porquerolles in 1887, Paul d'Aigremont. For more on this, see Yves Olivier-Martin, *Histoire du roman populaire en France: De 1840 à 1980* (Paris: Albin Michel, 1980).

94. Schafer, *Children in Moral Danger*, 175.

95. Guillon, "Enfance assistée, enfance exploitée?"

96. Edmond Le Roy, "L'affaire de Porquerolles," *Le Gaulois*, 28 July 1886.

97. Guillon, "Enfance assistée, enfance exploitée?"

98. *Journal d'Indre-et-Loire*, 26 March 1887. See also *Soleil*, 26 March 1887.

99. J. Messire, "Un scandale à Mettray," *L'Univers*, 28 March 1887.

100. J. Messire, "Un scandale à Mettray," *L'Univers*, 29 March 1887.

101. Rapport du Préfet et procès-verbaux des séances et délibérations du conseil general, 47.

102. "Le scandale de Mettray," *La Petite France*, 23 March 1887.

103. *L'Union Libérale de Tours*, 27 March 1887.

104. Jean Frollo, "Les corrections corporelles," *Le Petit Parisien*, 2 April 1887, 2–3.

105. Strauss was later elected to the senate and then named minister of hygiene after the First World War. "Les scandales de Mettray," *L'Union Libérale: Journal de Tours et de département d'Indre-et-Loire*, 2 April 1887.

106. "À Mettray: Un scandale a la colonie pénitentiaire," *La Lanterne*, 25 March 1887.

107. Alexandre Millerand, "Yzeure et Mettray," *La Justice*, 28 March 1887.

108. *La Petite France*, 1 April 1887.

109. Léon Millot, "À Mettray," *La Justice*, 5 April 1887.

110. *La Petite France*, 31 March 1887.

111. *La Petite France*, 28 March 1887.

112. *Annuaire statistique de la France* (Paris: Bureau de la statistique générale, 1884), 245; *Annuaire statistique de la France* (Paris: Bureau de la statistique générale, 1885), 245.

113. René Goblet, Ministre de l'Intérieur to Préfet d'Indre-et-Loire, 30 March 1887 (ADIL 1 Y 141).

114. Ibid.

115. Ibid.

116. J. Messire, "Un scandale à Mettray," *L'Univers*, 29 March 1887.

117. *Le Messager d'Indre-et-Loire*, (27 March 1887.

118. Ramsland, "Mettray: A Corrective Institution," 41.

119. "Question de M. Vaillant sur les événements de Mettray," *Bulletin Municipal Officiel de la Ville de Paris* 6, no. 85 (Paris: Imprimerie Nationale, 1887): 732–35.

120. *Annuaire statistique de la France* (Paris: Bureau de la statistique générale, 1887), 204; *Annuaire statistique de la France* (Paris: Bureau de la statistique générale, 1888), 195.

121. *L'Univers*, 4 April 1887.

122. *Annales de la Chambre des députés: Débats parlementaires*, 31 March 1887 (Paris: Imprimerie Nationale, 1887), 899.

123. Ibid.

124. *Rapport du préfet et procès-verbaux des séances et délibérations du Conseil général*, 19 April 1887 (Tours: Imprimerie E. Mazerau, 1887), 30, 37, 39.

125. Ibid., 38–39.

126. Ibid., 42, 51.

127. *Procès-verbaux des séances et délibérations du Conseil général*, 28 August 1887 (Tours: Imprimerie E. Arrault, 1887), 160–61.

128. Ibid., 167–69.

129. Ibid., 177.

130. His remarks were transcribed and published in the *Bulletin Société Générale des Prisons* 13 (1889): 375–76.

131. Republican newspapers made allusions to a riot and/or colony-wide disturbance, which were rebutted in conservative journals. There is no evidence of such an event in the archival record, but that does not preclude the possibility of unrest at the time. For examples of the claims and rebuttals, see *La Petite France*, 23 March 1887, and *Journal d'Indre-et-Loire*, 25 March 1887.

132. Cluze to Préfet d'Indre-et-Loire, 1 July 1887 (ADIL 1 Y 108).

Chapter 5

1. The use of ether as an intoxicant was relatively rare in France compared to other countries such as Ireland. Ether was typically ingested orally, usually mixed with alcohol such as cognac. See John Frederick Logan, "The Age of Intoxication," *Yale French Studies* 50, no. 1 (1974).

2. Each cell was furnished with a bed, desk, chair, bookshelf, and armoire for clothing.

3. The Maison Paternelle, more than Mettray as a whole, fits Goffman's notion of a "total institution," "symbolized by the barrier to social intercourse with the outside and to departure that is often built right into the physical plant such as locked doors, high walls, barbed wire, cliffs, water, forests, or moors." Goffman, *Asylums*, 4.

4. "Those who, without order of the proper authorities and except in those cases in which the law prescribes the seizure, arrest, detention or restraint of any persons,

shall be punished with a term of hard labor." *Code Napoléon*, Article 341, 7th ed. (Paris, 1852).

5. Chauvaud, "Le scandale de Mettray"; John Ramsland, "La Maison Paternelle: 'A College of Repression' for Wayward Bourgeois Adolescents in Nineteenth- and Early Twentieth-Century France," *History of Education* 18, no. 1 (1989): 52. See also Gaillac, *Les maisons de correction*, 85.

6. Although the Napoleonic Code allowed fathers to send their children for paternal correction to adult prisons, few minors served time in these establishments. Most boys were sent to public *colonies pénitentiaires* and most girls were sent to *écoles de préservation*. See O'Brien, *Promise of Punishment*, 31, 119.

7. For more on the *lettres de cachet*, see Brian Strayer, Lettres de cachet *and Social Control in the Ancien Régime, 1659–1789* (Bern: Peter Lang, 1991).

8. Schafer, *Children in Moral Danger*.

9. Bernard Schnapper estimates that most of these cases emanated from Paris and that nearly half of those submitted to paternal correction were girls. See Schnapper, "La correction paternelle et le mouvement des idées au XIXe siècle 1789–1935," in *Voies nouvelles en histoire du droit, la justice, la famille et la répression pénale, XVI–XXe* (Paris: Presses Universitaires de France, 1991), 536. O'Brien estimates that three-fourths of the paternal correction cases in 1881 involved girls, though this figure declined by the turn of the century. O'Brien, *Promise of Punishment*, 119.

10. Childers, *Fathers, Families and the State in France*, 19.

11. Frédéric Demetz, *Lettre de M. Demetz aux membres du Conseil général de département de la Seine sur le régime de la colonie de Mettray* (Tours: Imprimerie Nationale, 1860), 9.

12. *Instruction religieuse et morale* (ADIL 1 Y 139).

13. Enoch Wines, *Report to the International Penitentiary Congress of London* (Washington, DC: Government Printing Office, 1872), 734.

14. H. Latham, "The Maison Paternelle at Mettray," *Macmillan's Magazine* 21 (April 1870): 46.

15. Parents provided pants, shirts, undergarments, and towels. *Maison paternelle de Saint-Antoine* (Tours: Imprimerie Tourangelle, 1901), 60–61 (ADIL 114 J 217).

16. Georges Delegorgue, *La correction paternelle et l'école de reforme* (Paris: Larose, 1900), 86–87.

17. Demetz, "Exposé du système d'éducation," 23.

18. Marsangy, *Mettray: Colonie pénitentiaire*, 42.

19. Ibid.

20. Latham, "Maison Paternelle," 48.

21. Wines, *Report to the International Penitentiary Congress*, 735.

22. Demetz, "Exposé du système d'éducation," 22–23.

23. J.-M. Guardia, *La maison paternelle* (Tours: Ladevèze, 1872), 7–8.

24. Henri Joly, "Rapport à la société des prisons," *Revue Pénitentiaire: Bulletin de la Société Générale des Prisons* (1894): 25.

25. Louis Proal, "Education et suicide d'enfants," *Archives d'Anthropologie Criminelle* 20, no. 3 (1905): 387–88.

26. Maurice Bruyère, "Rapport à la société des prisons," *Revue Pénitentiaire: Bulletin de la Société Générale des Prisons* (1897): 1322.

27. Delegorgue, *La correction paternelle*, 24.

28. Ibid., 24–25.

29. Bruyère, "Rapport à la société des prisons," 1322.

30. Joly, "Rapport à la société des prisons," 12.

31. Gabriel Tarde, "La jeunesse criminelle," *Archives d'Anthropologie Criminelle et des Sciences Pénales* 12 (1897): 458.

32. Tarde, "La jeunesse criminelle," 460.

33. Proal, "Education et suicide," 373–74.

34. Delegorgue, *La correction paternelle*, 23.

35. Judith Surkis, *Sexing the Citizen: Morality and Masculinity in France, 1870–1920* (Ithaca, NY: Cornell University Press, 2006), 73–90.

36. Theodore Zeldin, *France, 1848–1945: Ambition and Love* (Oxford: Oxford University Press, 1979), 315.

37. Alphonse Dumas, *De la maison paternelle de Mettray* (Nîmes: Imprimerie de Clavel-Balivet, 1867), 10.

38. Guardia, *La maison paternelle*, 6.

39. Matilda Betham-Edwards, *Home Life in France* (London: Methuen, 1907), 44.

40. Marsangy, *Mettray: Colonie pénitentiaire*, 37–38.

41. Dumas, *De la maison paternelle*, 3–4, 14.

42. Sauvestre, *Une visite à Mettray*, 69.

43. Latham, "Maison Paternelle," 47.

44. Demetz, "Exposé du système d'éducation," 21.

45. Marsangy, *Mettray: Colonie pénitentiaire*, 41.

46. Ibid.

47. Betham-Edwards, *Home Life in France*, 230.

48. Wines, *Report to the International Penitentiary Congress*, 735.

49. Demetz, "Exposé du système d'éducation," 20–21.

50. Wines, *Report to the International Penitentiary Congress*, 735.

51. Gustave de Beaumont and Alexis de Tocqueville, *On the Penitentiary System in the United States and Its Application in France* (Philadelphia: Carey, Lea and Blanchard, 1833), 22.

52. Marsangy, *Mettray: Colonie pénitentiaire*, 41.

53. *Le Temps*, 29 September 1891.

54. *Maison paternelle de Saint-Antoine*, 58.

55. Latham, "Maison Paternelle," 44–45.

56. Betham-Edwards, *Home Life in France*, 232.

57. *Le Temps*, 29 September 1891.

58. Surkis, *Sexing the Citizen*, 84–85.

59. Guardia, *La maison paternelle*, 6.

60. Demetz, "Exposé du système d'éducation," 23.

61. *Code Napoléon*, Article 382.

62. *L'Union Libérale d'Indre-et-Loire*, 23 January 1909 (ADIL 1 Y 195).

63. Letter from Lorenzo to parents, 17 January 1909 (ADIL 114 J 277).

64. Ibid.

65. Enquête du 19 janvier 1909, Student Number 613 (ADIL 114 J 277).

66. Enquête du 19 janvier 1909, Student Number 628 (ADIL 114 J 277).

67. Enquête du 19 janvier 1909, Student Number 625 (ADIL 114 J 277).

68. Enquête du 19 janvier 1909, Student Number 592 (ADIL 114 J 277).

69. Enquête du 19 janvier 1909, Student Number 614 (ADIL 114 J 277).

70. Enquête du 19 janvier 1909, Student Number 551 (ADIL 114 J 277).

71. Enquête du 19 janvier 1909, Observations (ADIL 114 J 277).

72. *Le Journal*, 28 January 1909; *La Touraine Républicaine*, 31 January 1909.

73. *La Dépêche*, 28 January 1909.

74. *La Dépêche*, 29 January 1909 (ADIL 1 Y 187).

75. *Colonie de Mettray: Discours à la chambre des députes* 8 November 1909 (ADIL 1 Y 140).

76. Enquête du 23 janvier 1909, Observations (ADIL 114 J 277).

77. Enquête du 23 janvier 1909, Student Number 628.

78. Enquête du 23 janvier 1909, Student Number 651 (ADIL 114 J 277).

79. Interrogatoire du M. Chanloup, 27 January 1909 (ADIL 114 J 277).

80. Ibid.

81. Interrogatoire du M. Devos, 27 January 1909.

82. Interrogatoire du M. Juigner, 27 January 1909.

83. Interrogatoire du M. Touchent, 27 January 1909.

84. Interrogatoire du M. Guepin, 27 January 1909.

85. Interrogatoire du M. Juigner.

86. Latham, "Maison Paternelle," 48.

87. Interrogatoire du Juigner.

88. *L'Union Libérale d'Indre-et-Loire*, 23 January 1909.

89. A. Poittevin and E. Garçon, "Consultation sur la nature juridique de l'internement des enfants confiés à la Maison Paternelle" (ADIL 1 Y 140).

90. *La Dépêche*, 10 February 1910.

91. H. Du Buit, "Consultation sur la nature juridique de l'internement des enfants confiés à la Maison Paternelle" (ADIL 1 Y 140).

92. Du Buit, "Consultation sur la nature juridique."

93. *Journal d'Indre-et-Loire*, 29 January 1909 (ADIL 1 Y 187).

94. *La Dépêche*, 24 January 1909.

95. *L'Assiette au Beurre*, 13 February 1909. For more on the press campaign against the Maison Paternelle, particularly by *L'Assiette au Beurre*, see Chauvaud, "Le scandale de Mettray."

96. *Le Journal*, 24 January 1909.

97. Letter to Lorenzo from anonymous, 10 January 1909 (ADIL 114 J 277).

98. H. Berthélemy, "Consultation sur la nature juridique de l'internement des enfants confiés à la Maison Paternelle" (ADIL 1 Y 140).

99. Poittevin and Garçon, "Consultation sur la nature juridique."

100. Ibid.

101. Berthélemy, "Consultation sur la nature juridique."

102. Du Buit, "Consultation sur la nature juridique."

103. H. Devin, "Consultation sur la nature juridique de l'internement des enfants confiés à la Maison Paternelle" (ADIL 1 Y 140).

104. *Journal d'Indre-et-Loire*, 29 January 1909.

105. *L'Intransigeant*, 23 January 1909 (ADIL 114 J 582).

106. Delegorgue, *La correction paternelle*, 76–77.

107. *La Touraine*, 20 February 1910.

108. *La Touraine*, 30 January 1910.

109. *Le Journal*, 24 January 1909.

110. *La Dépêche*, 24 January 1909.

111. *Le Matin*, 22 January 1909.

112. Jacques Donzelot, *The Policing of Families*, trans. Robert Hurley (New York: Pantheon, 1979), 56–70.

113. Schafer, *Children in Moral Danger*, 100.

114. *La Libre Parole*, 17 February 1910.

115. *Le Petit Parisien*, 18 February 1909.

Chapter 6

1. Préfet d'Indre-et-Loire to Président du Conseil, Ministre de l'Intérieur et des Cultes, 3 July 1903 (ADIL 1 Y 194).

2. Ibid. Cluze's opinion on the collective work stoppage was summarized in the prefect's letter.

3. *Compte-rendu triennal présenté à l'Assemblée générale des membres fondateurs de la Société paternelle* (Tours: Imprimerie Tourangelle, 1901), 17.

4. Directeur Brun to Préfet d'Indre-et-Loire, 17 June 1916 (ADIL 114 J 252).

5. *Compte-rendu de la situation morale et financière*, 1922 (Tours: Imprimerie Tourangelle, 1923), 12. A fourth category of inmate was added with the passage of a law in June 1904 which allowed state authorities to send "incorrigible" minors—those housed in orphanages, hospices or who lived with families that received aid from Assistance publique—to correctional institutions such as Mettray.

6. *Compte-rendu de la situation morale et financière, la colonie de Mettray*, 1926 (ADIL 114 J 252). See also 1923, 1925, 1930.

7. *Bulletin des Assemblée générale des fondateurs* (Tours: Imprimerie Rouille-Ladeveze, 1883), 2.

8. Gaillac, *Les maisons de correction*, appendices B and C.

9. O'Brien, *Promise of Punishment*, 139.

10. *Compte rendu triennale*, 1889–1891 (ADIL 1 Y 131).

11. Robert Picot, *De la défiance manifestée par les pouvoirs publics à l'égard des colonies pénitentiaire, privées: Comité de défense des enfants traduits en justice de Paris* (Paris: Imprimerie Kugelmann, 1907), 17–19.

12. Picot, *De la défiance manifestée*, 7.

13. On the Apaches, see Dominique Kalifa, *L'encre et le sang: Récits de crimes et société à la Belle Époque* (Paris: Fayard, 1995); Michelle Perrot, "Dans le Paris de la Belle Époque, les 'Apaches': Premières bandes de jeunes," *La lettre de l'enfance et de l'adolescence* 67, no. 1 (2007).

14. Directeur Brun to Préfet d'Indre-et-Loire, 17 June 1916 (ADIL 114 J 252).

15. Ramsland, "Mettray: A Corrective Institution," 42.

16. Directeur Brun to Préfet d'Indre-et-Loire au sujet du projet de mutinerie (copy attachment 1), 6 November 1911 (ADIL 1 Y 194).

17. Directeur Brun to Préfet d'Indre-et-Loire au sujet du projet de mutinerie (copy attachment 2), 6 November 1911 (ADIL 1 Y 194).

18. Directeur Brun to Préfet d'Indre-et-Loire au sujet du projet de mutinerie (copy attachment 3), 6 November 1911 (ADIL 1 Y 194).

19. Directeur Brun to Préfet d'Indre-et-Loire, 5 January 1912 (ADIL 1 Y 194).

20. Directeur Brun to Préfet d'Indre-et-Loire au sujet du projet de mutinerie, 6 November 1911 (ADIL 1 Y 194).

21. Alyson Brown, *Inter-war Penal Policy and Crime in England: The Dartmoor Convict Prison Riot* (Houndmills, UK: Palgrave Macmillan, 2013), 136.

22. Directeur Brun to Préfet d'Indre-et-Loire au sujet du projet de mutinerie, 6 November 1911 (ADIL 1 Y 194).

23. The basic ration consisted of 750 grams of bread per day plus a meal containing beef or pork three times a week, along with vegetables and soup. The former *colon* Caffler described a tripe soup served at noon three times per week that was a mixture of beans, peas, rice, and potatoes, all in a mush, with an occasional piece of tough meat sometimes added. He estimated that each inmate consumed the equivalent of three baguettes a day. See White, *Genet*, 7.

24. Directeur to Préfet du Cher, 29 August 1910 (ADC 1 Y 163).

25. Yvorel, "Les premières campagnes," 125. For more on the child as the victim of the family, see also Jean-Claude Vimont, "De coupables aux victimes, l'archéologie de l'identité du mineur délinquant au 19e siècle," in *Jeunes, déviances et identités, 18e–20e siècles* (Mont-Saint-Aignan: Publications des Universités de Rouen et du Havre, 2005), 35–47; Jean-Marie Renouard, *De l'enfant coupable à l'enfant inadapté: Le traitement social et politique de la déviance* (Paris: Centurion, 1990).

26. Georges Bonjean, "Discussion sur les écoles industrielles et la législation relative à l'éducation correctionnel," *Bulletin Société Générale des Prisons* vol. 3, no. 4 (1879): 363–64.

27. Alfred Fouillée, *La France au point de vue moral* (Paris: Alcan, 1900), 153–57.

28. Auguste Motet, "Discussion sur les écoles industrielles," *Bulletin Société Générale des Prisons* vol. 3, no. 4 (1879): 318–19.

29. Ernest Passez, "Du vagabondage et de la prostitution des mineurs de seize ans et des reformes à apporter au mode actuel de répression," *Bulletin Société Générale des Prisons* vol. 3, no. 3 (1879): 978–79.

30. Gaillac, *Les maisons de correction*, 156–58.

31. Schafer, *Children in Moral Danger*, 194.

32. For instance, see Henri Taudière, "Quelques réformes législatives en matière de puissance paternelle," *La Reforme Sociale* 5 (1898).

33. Kari Evanson, "Writing Scandal: Popular Media and the *Bagnes d'enfants*, 1920–1945" (PhD diss., New York University, 2012), 30.

34. Schafer, *Children in Moral Danger*, 194.

35. *Bulletin des Assemblée générale des fondateurs* (Tours: Imprimerie Rouille-Ladeveze, 1883), 2.

36. For more, see Alaimo, "Shaping Adolescence."

37. Proal, "Education et suicide," 374, 381.

38. Paul Garnier, "La criminalité juvénile: Étiologie du meurtre," *Annales d'Hygiène Publique et de Médecine Légale* vol. 46, no. 3 (1901): 405–6.

39. Alfred Binet, *Les idées modernes sur les enfants* (Paris: Flammarion, 1909), 329.

40. M. Grosmolard, "La criminalité juvénile," *Archives d'Anthropologie Criminelle* 18 (1903): 166.

41. Rouveyrolis, "Les observations anthropométriques," *Revue Pénitentiaire* (1913): 232–39.

42. J. Maxwell, *Le crime et la société* (Paris: Flammarion, 1909), 332–33.

43. Rouveyrolis, "Les observations anthropométriques," 236.

44. Conseil d'administration assemblée des fondateurs, Comité des finances et commission permanente, séances, 18 September 1918 (ADIL 114 J 177).

45. Éric Pierre, "Mettray dans les années 1920s," in *La colonie agricole pénitentiaire de Mettray: Souvenirs d'un colon, 1922–1927*, ed. Jacques Bourquin and Éric Pierre (Paris: Harmattan, 1997), 146.

46. Conseil d'administration assemblée des fondateurs, Comité des finances et commission permanente, 12 November 1917 (ADIL 114 J 177).

47. Directeur Brun to Préfet d'Indre-et-Loire, 17 June 1916 (ADIL 114 J 252).

48. *Compte rendu de la situation morale et financière*, 1923 (Tours: Imprimerie Tourangelle, 1924), 13.

49. *Compte rendu de la situation morale et financière*, 1925 (Tours: Imprimerie Tourangelle, 1926) 14.

50. Pierre, "Mettray dans les années 1920s."

51. Directeur Brun to Préfet d'Indre-et-Loire, 17 June 1916 (ADIL 114 J 252).

52. Ibid.

53. Rapport de Directeur Brun, 1914–1919 (ADIL 114 J 278).

54. Ibid.

55. Maire de Boulay to Préfet d'Indre-et-Loire, 9 September 1931 (ADIL 1 Y 200).

56. Extrait des délibérations du Conseil général d'Indre-et-Loire, 30 October 1931 (ADIL 1 Y 200).

57. Extrait du registre des délibérations du Conseil municipale de la commune de Saint-Symphorien, 27 November 1927 (ADIL 1 Y 200).

58. Extrait du registre des délibérations du Conseil municipale de la commune de Chanceaux-sur-Choisille, 26 June 1930 (ADIL 1 Y 200).

59. Directeur Lardet to Préfet d'Indre-et-Loire, 5 June 1930 (ADIL 1 Y 200).

60. Directeur Lardet to Préfet d'Indre-et-Loire, 16 November 1927 (ADIL 1 Y 200).

61. Directeur Lardet to Préfet d'Indre-et-Loire, 25 September 1930 (ADIL 1 Y 200).

62. Commandant Tricottet, la Compagnie de gendarmerie d'Indre-et-Loire to Préfet d'Indre-et-Loire, 15 January 1936 (ADIL 1 Y 200).

63. Pierre, "Mettray dans les années 1920s," 137.

64. Directeur de Val d'Yèvre to Préfet du Cher, 27 September 1910 (ADC 1 Y 266).

65. Directeur Brun to Prefect d'Indre-et-Loire, 19 May 1913 (ADIL 1 Y 204).

66. Ministre de la Justice to Prefect d'Indre-et-Loire, 24 May 1913 (ADIL 1 Y 204).

67. Ministère de l'Intérieur Direction a l'Administration pénitentiaire to Préfet du Cher, 12 April 1884 (ADC 1 Y 163).

68. Directeur to Préfet d'Indre-et-Loire, 24 June 1912 (ADIL 1 Y 175).

69. Procureur de la république to Préfet d'Indre-et-Loire, 20 December 1912 (ADIL 1 Y 175).

70. Ramsland, "Agricultural Colony at Mettray," 76.

71. Demandes et réponses, 22 February 1935 (ADIL 114 J 271).

72. Exposé des principales revendications au sujet du maintien de l'ordre, la discipline et la sécurité du personnel, 4 April 1937 (ADH 1 Y 347).

73. J. D.'H [pseud.] to M. le Préfet de l'Hérault, 28 August 1912 (ADH 1 Y 347).

74. Directeur Rochet to Préfet de l'Hérault, 30 August 1912 (ADH 1 Y 347).

75. Le Président du Conseil, Ministère de l'Intérieur et des Cultes to Préfet de l'Hérault, 3 December 1898, (ADH 1 Y 347).

76. Le Garde des Sceaux, Ministre de la Justice to Préfet de l'Hérault, 15 January 1913 (ADH 1 Y 347).

77. Marius Nougaret, avocat, mémoire dans l'intérêt de M. Frederic Terme, cultivateur, demeurant et domicile à Aniane to Préfet de l'Hérault, n.d. (ADH 1 Y 347).

78. *Annuaire statistique de la France, 1861–1923* (Paris: Bureau de la statistique générale, 1924).

79. Rapport de M. Auzemat, Inspecteur Générale des Services Administratifs, cited in Séance du Conseil d'administration, 23 June 1932 (ADIL 114 J 177).

80. Séance du Conseil d'administration, 23 June 1932 (ADIL 114 J 177).

81. Conseil d'administration assemblé des fondateurs, comité des finances et commission permanente, 23 June 1932 (ADIL 114 J 177).

82. Ibid.

83. Inspection générale des prisons du département du Cher, 1901 (ADC 1 Y 157).

84. Rapport, 11 January 1899 (ADH 1 Y 347).

85. Ibid.

86. Directeur Voisin to Préfet d'Indre-et-Loire, 31 January 1936 (ADIL 1 Y 200).

87. *Compte rendu de la situation morale et financière, la colonie de Mettray*, 1935 (ADIL 114 J 252).

88. Ibid.

89. Fishman, *Battle for Children*, 35.

90. For more, see Toth, *Beyond Papillon*, 121–46.

91. Robert W. Desmond, *Windows on the World: The Information Process in a Changing Society, 1900–1920* (Iowa City: University of Iowa Press, 1980), 187.

92. Alexis Danan, "Une honte: Mettray établissement privé . . . et de tortures," *Paris-Soir*, 23 November 1934.

93. Ibid.

94. Louis Roubaud, "Les pasteurs de l'enfant perdu," *Le Petit Parisien*, 22 April 1937.

95. David H. Walker, *Outrage and Insight: Modern French Writers and the Fait Divers* (New York: Berg, 1995), 6.

96. Roubaud, "Les pasteurs de l'enfant perdu."

97. Jacqueline Albert-Lambert, "Que se passe-t-il à Mettray," *l'Intransigeant*, 28 May 1930.

98. Danan, "Une honte."

99. Fishman, *Battle for Children*, 36.

100. Albert-Lambert, "Que se passe-t-il à Mettray."

101. Roubaud, "Les pasteurs de l'enfant perdu."

102. Danan, "Une honte."

103. Gaillac, *Les maisons de Correction*, 290.

104. Danan, "Une honte."

105. Evanson, "Writing Scandal," 144.

106. Fishman, *Battle for Children*, 37.

107. Albert-Lambert, "Que se passe-t-il à Mettray."

108. Exposé des principales, 4 April 1937 (ADH 1 Y 347).

109. Pierre, "Mettray dans les années 1920s," 144.

110. Ramsland, "Agricultural Colony at Mettray," 76.

111. Fishman, *Battle for Children*, 43.

112. Eysses closed its doors on 15 August 1940. Aniane remained in operation until 1953. Val d'Yèvre had been closed in 1924.

Conclusion

1. Arneil, *Domestic Colonies*, 226.

2. For example, see Norbert Elias, *The Civilizing Process* (Oxford: Blackwell, 1994); Max Weber, *Economy and Society*, trans. Guenther Roth and Claus Wittich (Berkeley: University of California Press, 1978).

3. Berger, Berger, and Kellner, *Homeless Mind*, 90, 86.

4. Alaimo, "Shaping Adolescence."

5. Sykes, *Society of Captives*, xii.

6. Ibid., 34.

7. Goffman, *Asylums*, 74.

8. Pierre, "Mettray dans les années 1920s," 140.

9. Arneil, *Domestic Colonies*, 226.

10. Evanson, "Writing Scandal," 31–33.

11. Fishman, *Battle for Children*, 38.

12. Catherine Blatier has noted that among first-time youth offenders, 5 percent were acquitted or discharged, 35 percent received an official warning, 13 percent were left in the care of the family or a guardian, 25 percent received formal or informal probation, 8 percent were required to pay compensation, 6 percent were only fined, 5 percent were placed in care, and 3.4 percent received a sentence of institutional confinement. Second-time offenders were treated much more harshly, however: 55 percent were placed in institutions. See Blatier, "Juvenile Justice in France: The Evolution of Sentencing for Children and Minor Delinquents," *British Journal of Criminology* vol. 39, no. 2 (1999): 240–52.

13. Fishman, *Battle for Children*, 200–13.

14. Ibid., 36.

BIBLIOGRAPHY

Archival Sources

Archives départementales du Cher (ADC) 1 Y 157, 1 Y 158
Archives départementales de Hérault (ADH) 1 Y 353, 1 Y 138, 1 Y 348, 1 Y 347
Archives départementales d'Indre-et-Loire (ADIL) 1 Y 99, 1 Y 100–102, 1 Y 103–38, 1
      Y 139, 1 Y 140, 1 Y 141, 1 Y 142, 1 Y 148, 1 Y 151, 1 Y 152, 1 Y 153–55, 1 Y
      156–58, 1 Y 159–65, 1 Y 174, 1 Y 175, 1 Y 176, 1 Y 177, 1 Y 185–87, 1 Y 194,
      1 Y 195, 1 Y 196–200, 1 Y 201, 1 Y 202–204, 1 Y 220, 1 Y 223, 1 Y 224, 1 Y
      331; 114 J 177, 114 J 182, 114 J 217, 114 J 252, 114 J 271, 114 J 277, 114 J 582,
      114 J 642
Archives départementales de Lot-et-Garonne (ADLEG) 1 Y 107, 1 Y 114

Newspapers and Journals

Archives d'Anthropologie Criminelle et des Sciences Pénales
Bulletin de la Société Générale des Prisons (August 1877–January 1892)
Détective
Journal d'Indre-et-Loire
La Dépêche
La Justice
La Libre Parole
La Lanterne
La Petite France
La Touraine
La Touraine Républicaine
Le Gaulois
Le Journal
Le Matin
Le Petit Journal
Le Petit Parisien
Le Radical
Le Siècle
Le Temps
L'Intransigeant
L'Union Libérale d'Indre-et-Loire
L'Univers

Nation
Paris-Soir
Revue Pénitentiaire: Bulletin de la Société Générale des Prisons (February 1892–1907)
Soleil
Statistique des Prisons et Établissements Pénitentiaires
Tours-Journal

Primary Sources

Alis, Harry [Jules-Hippolyte Percher]. *Mettray, la colonie agricole. Étude parue dans le Journal des Débats* (Tours: Imprimerie de Mame, 1890).

Annales de l'Assemblée nationale, 1871–75 (Versailles: Cerf, 1875).

Annales de la Chambre des députés: Débats parlementaires (Paris: Imprimerie Nationale, 1887).

Appert, Benjamin. *Journal des prisons, hospices, écoles primaires et établissements de bienfaisance*, vol. 4 (Paris: Baudouin Frères, 1828).

Barnard, Henry. *Reformatory Education: Papers on Preventive, Correctional and Reformatory Institutions and Agencies in Different Countries* (Hartford, CT: Brownell, 1857).

Baume, M. de la. *Des colonies pénitentiaires agricoles: Mettray et Les Matelles* (Montpellier: Gras, 1859).

Beaumont, Gustave de, and Alexis de Tocqueville. *On the Penitentiary System in the United States and Its Application in France*, translated by Francis Lieber (Carbondale: Southern Illinois University Press, 1964).

Benoiston de Chateauneuf, Louis-François. *De la colonisation des condamnes, et de l'avantage qu'il y aurait pour la France à adopter cette mesure* (Paris: Hachette, 2016 [1827]).

Bérenger de la Drôme, Alphonse. *Premier compte rendu des travaux de la Société pour le patronage des jeunes libérés du département de la Seine* (Paris: H. Fournier, 1834).

Betham-Edwards, Matilda. *Home Life in France* (London: Methuen, 1907).

Boulangé d'Aytré, L. *De l'éducation professionnelle pour les enfants pauvres* (Paris: Imprimerie de Baudouin, 1842).

Brétignières de Courteilles, Louis-Hermann. *Les condamnés et les prisons ou la réforme morale, criminelle et pénitentiaire* (Paris: Perrotin, 1838).

Bruyère, Maurice. "Rapport à la société des prisons." *Revue Pénitentiaire: Bulletin de la Société Générale des Prisons* (1897): 1320–40.

Cantagrel, François. "Examen critique de la colonie de Mettray." *La Phalange* 9, no. 1 (1843): 1320–30.

Cantagrel, François. *Mettray et Ostwald: Étude sur ces deux colonies agricoles* (Paris: Librairie de l'École Sociétaire, 1842).

Carpenter, Edward. *Socialism and Agriculture* (London: A. C. Fifield, 1910).

Cochin, Augustin. *Notice sur le Mettray* (Tours: Imprimerie Ladevèze, 1851).

Colonie agricole de Mettray. Assemblée générale des fondateurs tenue à Paris (Tours: Imprimerie de H. Fournier et Cie, 1841).

Corne, A. "Rapport et projet de loi sur le patronage des jeunes détenus, présents au nom de la Commission de l'assistance publique." In *Compte rendu de l'Assemblée législative*, vol. 4, séance du 14 Décembre 1849 (Paris: Imprimerie Nationale, 1850).

Danjou, Henri. *Enfants du malheur! Les bagnes d'enfants* (Paris: Albin-Michel, 1932).

Delegorgue, Georges. *La correction paternelle et l'école de réforme* (Paris: Larose, 1900).

Demetz, Frédéric. *Colonie agricole et pénitentiaire de Mettray* (Paris: Lemercier, 1847).

Demetz, Frédéric. *Exposé du système d'éducation employé à la colonie agricole et pénitentiaire de Mettray et à la Maison Paternelle* (Paris: Pougin, 1873).

Demetz, Frédéric. "Exposé du système d'éducation employé à la colonie agricole et pénitentiaire de Mettray et à la Maison Paternelle." In *Congres de l'Alliance universelle de l'ordre et de la civilisation* (Paris: A. Pougin, 1872), 1–24.

Demetz, Frédéric. *Fondation d'une colonie agricole de jeunes détenus à Mettray* (Paris: B. Duprat, 1839).

Demetz, Frédéric. *Lettre de M. Demetz aux membres du Conseil général de département de la Seine sur le régime de la colonie de Mettray* (Tours: Imprimerie Nationale, 1860).

Demetz, Frédéric. *Notice sur la colonie agricole de Mettray 1863* (Tours: Imprimerie Ladevèze, 1864).

Demetz, Frédéric. *Notice sur l'école préparatoire de Mettray* (Paris: Claye Taillefer, 1846).

Demetz, Frédéric. *Rapport sur les colonies agricoles* (Tours: Ladevèze, 1855).

Demetz, Frédéric. "Report on Agricultural Colonies." *Irish Quarterly Review* (1855): 1–12.

Demetz, Frédéric. *Résumé sur le système pénitentiaire* (Paris: Claye et Taillefer, 1844).

Demetz, Frédéric, and Abel Blouet. *Rapports à M. le comte de Montalivet, ministre secrétaire d'état au Département de l'intérieur, sur les pénitenciers des États-Unis* (Paris: Imprimerie Royale, 1837).

Détenu, Un (anon.). *L'intérieur des prisons: Reforme pénitentiaire, system cellulaire, emprisonnement en commun* (Paris: Jules Labitte, 1846).

Ducpétiaux, Édouard. *Colonies agricoles, écoles rurales et écoles de réforme* (Brussels: Imprimerie de T. Lesigne, 1851).

Dumas, Alphonse. *De la maison paternelle de Mettray* (Nîmes: Imprimerie de Clavel-Balivet, 1867).

Faucher, Léon. *De la réforme des prisons* (Paris: Angé, 1838).

Ferrus, G. M. A. *Des prisonniers, de l'emprisonnement et des prisons* (Paris: J.-B. Baillière, 1850).

Fouillée, Alfred. "Les jeunes criminelles." *Revue des Deux Mondes* (15 January 1897): 425–26.

Frégier, Antoine-Honoré. *Des classes dangereuses de la population dans les grandes villes et des moyens de le rendre meilleures*, vol. 1 (Paris: J.-B. Baillière, 1840).

Garnier, Paul. "La criminalité juvénile: Étiologie du meurtre." *Annales d'Hygiène Publique et de Médicine Légale* 46, no. 3 (1901): 403–11.

Genet, Jean. *Miracle of the Rose*, translated by Bernard Frechtman (New York: Grove Press, 1988 [1946]).

Genet, Jean. "L'enfant criminel." In *Œuvres complètes*, vol. 5 (Paris: Gallimard, 1979): 379–93.

Ginouvrier, J.-F. *Tableau de l'intérieur des prisons de France, ou études sur la situation et les souffrances morales et physiques de toutes les classes de prisonniers ou détenus* (Paris: Baudouin Frères, 1824).

Giraud, A. *Colonie de Mettray: Devoirs du colon* (Tours: Imprimerie de Pornin, 1843).

Guardia, J.-M. *La maison paternelle* (Tours: Ladevèze, 1872).

Hall, Robert. *Mettray: A Lecture Read before the Leeds Philosophical and Literary Society* (London: Cash, 1854).

Hill, Matthew Davenport. *Suggestions for the Repression of Crime: Charges Delivered to Grand Juries of Birmingham* (London: John W. Parker, 1857).

Hugo, Victor. *Les misérables* trans. Charles E. Wilbour (New York: Carleton, 1862).

Huot, Paul. *Trois jours à Mettray: Rapports lus au Congrès scientifique de Tours et à la Société des sciences morales de Seine-et-Oise* (Paris: Claye and Taillefer, 1848).

Joly, Henri. *À la recherche de l'éducation correctionnelle à travers l'Europe* (Paris: V. Lecoffre, 1902).

Joly, Henri. "Rapport à la société des prisons." *Revue Pénitentiaire: Bulletin de la Société Générale des Prisons* (1894): 20–32.

Lacassagne, Alexandre. *Les tatouages, étude anthropologique et médico-légale* (Paris: J.-B. Baillière, 1881).

Lamarque, Jules. *Des colonies pénitentiaires et du patronage des jeunes libérés* (Paris: Veuve Berger-Levrault et Fils, 1863).

La Rochefoucauld-Liancourt, F. A. F. *Examen de la théorie pratique du système pénitentiaire* (Paris: Delaunay, 1840).

Lallemand, Claude François. *Des pertes séminales involontaires* (Paris: Bechet Jeune, 1839).

Larribeau, M. *Nouvelle théorie du jeu de la canne* (Paris: Verdeau, 1856).

Latham, H. "The Maison Paternelle at Mettray." *Macmillan's Magazine* 21 (April 1870): 44–50.

Léger, Raoul. *La colonie agricole pénitentiaire de Mettray: Souvenirs d'un colon 1922–1927*, edited by Jacques Bourquin and Éric Pierre (Paris: L'Harmattan, 1998).

Legrange, Fernand. *L'art de la boxe française et de la canne: Nouveau traité, théorique, pratique* (Paris: L'Académie de la Boxe, 1899).

Lepelletier de la Sarthe, Almire. *Colonie de Mettray: Solution pratique du problème des jeunes détenus* (Paris: Librairie de Guillaumin, 1856).

Lepeltier de Saint-Fargeau, Michel. "Rapport sur le projet de code pénal, fait à l'Assemblée constituante au nom des comités de constitution et de législation criminelle." In *Œuvre*, 89–150 (Brussels: Imprimerie Lacrosse, 1826).

Lucas, Charles. "Économie politique: De l'extinction de la mendicité de l'agriculture." *Le Cultivateur* 15 (1839): 358–85.

Lucas, Charles. *Du système pénitentiaire en Europe et aux États-Unis*, vol. 2 (Paris: Bossange et Bechet, 1828).

Mailhol, André. *La colonie industrielle et agricole d'Aniane* (Montpellier: Imprimerie de Causse, Graille et Castelnau, 1927).

Marquet-Vasselot, Louis-Auguste. *La ville du refuge: Rêve philanthropique* (Paris: Ladvocat, 1832).

Marsangy, Arnould Bonneville de. *L'amélioration de la loi criminelle* (Paris: Cotillon, 1855).

Marsangy, Arnould Bonneville de. *Mettray: Colonie pénitentiaire, maison paternelle* (Paris: Henri Plon, 1866).

Martin, Étienne. "Le tatouage chez les enfants." *Archives d'Anthropologie Criminelle et des Sciences Pénales* 25 (1910): 75–90.

Martin-Dupont, P.-F. *Mes impressions, 1803–1876* (Paris: Sandoz et Fischbacher, 1878).

Mettray: Statuts constitutifs de la Société Paternelle de Mettray (Tours: Impremerie Tourangelle 1920).

Moreau-Christophe, Louis-Mathurin. "Les détenus." In *Les français peints par eux-mêmes*, vol. 4, edited by Paul Gavarni et al. (Paris: L. Curmer, 1840): 1–98.

Murray, Patrick Joseph. *Reformatory Schools in France and England* (London: W. F. G. Cash, 1854).

Parent-Duchâtelet, A. J.-B. *De la prostitution dans la ville de Paris: Considérée sous le rapport d'hygiène publique de la morale et de l'administration*, vol. 1 (Paris: J.-B. Baillière, 1836).

Picot, Robert. *De la défiance manifestée par les pouvoirs publics à l'égard des colonies pénitentiaire, privées: Comité de défense des enfants traduits en justice de Paris* (Paris: Imprimerie Kugelmann, 1907).

Pommeuse, L.-F. Huerne de. *Des colonies agricoles et de leurs avantages pour assurer le secours à l'honnête indigence* (Paris: Imprimerie Huzard, 1832).

Proal, Louis. "Education et suicide d'enfants." Archives d'Anthropologie Criminelle et des Sciences Pénales vol. 20, no. 3 (1905): 369–404.

Rapports et délibérations, Conseil général d'Indre-et-Loire (Tours: Conseil général, 1886).

Rapport du préfet et procès-verbaux des séances et délibérations du Conseil général, 19 April 1887 (Tours: Imprimerie E. Mazerau, 1887).

"Reformatory Schools," *The Quarterly Review* vol. XCVIII (January-April 1856): 17–36.

Rousseau, Jean-Jacques. *Politics and the Arts: Letter to M. d'Alembert on the Theatre*, translated by Allan Bloom (Ithaca, NY: Cornell University Press, 1960).

Rousseau, Jean-Jacques. *Emile* (New York: Dover, 2013 [1762]).

Rousseau, Jean-Jacques. *Discourse on the Sciences and Arts*, edited by Roger D. Masters, translated by Roger D. Masters and Judith R. Masters (New York: St. Martin's Press, 1964).

Sarramea, Isidore. *Considérations sur la maison central d'éducation correctionnelle de Bordeaux et sur les divers systèmes pénitentiaires appliques en France au jeunes détenus* (Bordeaux: T. Lafargue, 1842).

Sauvestre, Charles. *Une visite à Mettray* (Paris: Librairie Hachette, 1864).

Statistique des prisons et établissements pénitentiaires (Paris: Imprimerie Nationale, 1840–1914).

Statuts constitutifs de la Société paternelle (Tours: J. Claye, 1898).

Suringar, W.-H. *Une visite à Mettray en 1848* (Leeuwarden, Netherlands: Imprimerie de G. T. N., 1845).

Tarde, Gabriel. "La jeunesse criminelle." *Archives d'Anthropologie Criminelle et des Sciences Pénales* 12 (1897): 452–72.

Tardieu, Auguste Ambroise. *Étude médico-légale sur les attentats aux mœurs* (Paris: J. Millon, 1878).

Tocqueville, Alexis de, and Gustave de Beaumont. *Democracy in America*, translated by Gerald Bevan (New York: Penguin, 2003 [1837]).Vauplane, Berlier de. *Le cinquantenaire de Mettray* (Paris: Soye et Fils, 1890).

Villermé, Louis René. *Tableau d'état moral physique des ouvrières*, vol. 2 (Paris: Imprimerie Renouard, 1840).

Voisin, Félix. "Rapport sur le projet de loi relative à l'éducation des jeunes détenus." In *Enquête parlementaire sur le régime des établissements pénitentiaires*, vol. 8 (Paris: Imprimerie Nationale, 1875).

Wines, Enoch Cobb. "The Agricultural and Penitentiary Colony of Mettray." In *Report on the International Penitentiary Congress of London, 3–13 July 1872* (Washington, DC: Government Printing Office, 1873): 260–69.

Wines, Enoch. *Report to the International Penitentiary Congress of London* (Washington, DC: Government Printing Office, 1872).

Secondary Sources

Abu-Lughod, Lila. "The Romance of Resistance: Tracing Transformations of Power through Bedouin Women." *American Ethnologist* 17, no. 1 (1990): 41–55.

Adams, Robert. *Prison Riots in Britain and the United States* (New York: St. Martin's Press, 1992).

Alaimo, Katherine. "Adolescence, Gender and Class in Education Reform in France: The Development of Enseignement primaire supérieure, 1880–1910." *French Historical Studies* 18, no. 4 (1994): 1025–55.

Alaimo, Katherine. "Shaping Adolescence in the Popular Milieu: Social Policy, Reformers, and French Youth, 1870–1920." *Journal of Family History* 17, no. 4 (1992): 419–38.

Angel, Gemma. "Roses and Daggers: Expressions of Emotional Pain and Devotion in Nineteenth-Century Tattoos." In *Probing the Skin: Culture Representations of Our Contact Zones*, edited by Caroline Rosenthal and Dirk Vanderbeke, 211–38 (Cambridge: Cambridge Scholars Press, 2015).

Ardouin-Weiss, Idelette, and Georges-François Pottier. "Les décès des enfants de la colonie agricole et pénitentiaire de Mettray." *Histoire de la Touraine* 21, no. 1 (2008): 47–66.

Ariès, Philippe. *Centuries of Childhood: A Social History of Family Life*, translated by Robert Baldick (New York: Vintage, 1962).

Arneil, Barbara. *Domestic Colonies: The Turn Inward to Colony* (Oxford: Oxford University Press, 2017).

Ashurst, Francesca, and Couze Venn. *Inequality, Poverty, Education: A Political Economy of School Exclusion* (Aldershot, UK: Palgrave, 2014).

Berenson, Edward. *The Trial of Madame Caillaux* (Berkeley: University of California Press, 1992).

Berger, Peter L., Brigitte Berger, and Hansfried Kellner. *The Homeless Mind: Modernization and Consciousness* (New York: Random House, 1973).

Blatier, Catherine. "Juvenile Justice in France: The Evolution of Sentencing for Children and Minor Delinquents." *British Journal of Criminology* 39 (1999): 240–52.

Bosworth, Mary, and Eamonn Carrabine. "Reassessing Resistance: Race, Gender and Sexuality in Prison." *Punishment and Society* 3, no. 4 (2001): 501–15.

Bourquin, Jacques, and Éric Pierre. "Une visite à Mettray par l'image: L'album de gravures de 1844." *Sociétés et Représentations* 18, no. 2 (2004): 207–16.

Brown, Alyson. *Inter-war Penal Policy and Crime in England: The Dartmoor Convict Prison Riot* (Houndmills, UK: Palgrave Macmillan, 2013).

Bush, John W. "Education and Social Status: The Jesuit College in the Early Third Republic." *French Historical Studies* 9, no. 1 (1975): 125–40.

Caplan, Jane, ed. *Written on the Body: The Tattoo in European and American History* (Princeton, NJ: Princeton University Press, 2000).

Carlier, Christian. *Histoire du personnel des prisons françaises du XVIIIe siècle à nos jours* (Paris: Éditions de l'Atelier, 1997).

Carlier, Christian. *La prison aux champs: Les colonies des enfants délinquants du nord de la France au XIXe siècle* (Paris: Éditions de l'Atelier, 1994).

Chapon, Pierre-Paul. "L'historique de la profession d'éducateur technique spécialisé." In *Educateurs techniques spécialisés*, edited by Manuel Sanz and Paul Sanchou, 11–20 (Paris: ERES, 2007).

Carpenter, Mary. *Reformatory Schools for the Children of the Perishing and Dangerous Classes and for Juvenile Delinquents* (London: Routledge, 2006 [1851]).

Chassat, Sophie, Luc Forlivesi, and Georges-François Pottier, eds. *Éduquer et punir: La colonie agricole et pénitentiaire de Mettray* (Rennes: Presses Universitaires de Rennes, 2005).

Chauvaud, Frédéric. "Le scandale de Mettray (1909): Le trait enténébré et la campagne de presse." In *Éduquer et punir: La colonie agricole et pénitentiaire de Mettray*, edited by Sophie Chassat, Luc Forlivesi, and Georges-François Pottier, 175–93 (Rennes: Presses Universitaires de Rennes, 2005).

Chauvaud, Frédéric. "Les jeunes délinquants de Seine-et-Oise et la colonie agricole de Mettray." In *Répression et prison politiques au XIXe siècle*, edited by Alain Faure, 253–67 (Paris: Créaphis, 1990).

Chevalier, Louis. *Laboring Classes and Dangerous Classes in Paris during the First Half of the Nineteenth Century*, translated by Frank Jellinek (Princeton, NJ: Princeton University Press, 1973).

Childers, Kristin Stromberg. *Fathers, Families, and the State in France, 1914–1945* (Ithaca, NY: Cornell University Press, 2003).

Clark, Linda. *Schooling the Daughters of Marianne* (Albany: State University of New York Press, 1985).

Clark, Terry Nichols. *Prophets and Patrons: The French University System and the Emergence of the Social Sciences* (Cambridge, MA: Harvard University Press, 1973).

Clemmer, Donald. *The Prison Community* (New York: Rinehart, 1940).

Coleman, William. *Death Is a Social Disease: Public Health and Political Economy in Early Industrial France* (Madison: University of Wisconsin Press, 1982).

Connell, R. W. *Masculinities* (Cambridge: Polity Press, 1995).

Corbin, Alain. "The Triumph of Virility in the Nineteenth Century." In *A History of Virility*, edited by Alain Corbin, Jean-Jacques Courtine, and Georges Vigarello, translated by Keith Cohen, 215–20 (New York: Columbia University Press, 2016).

Courouve, Claude. *Vocabulaire de l'homosexualité masculine* (Paris: Payot, 1985).

Crossley, Ceri. "Using and Transforming the French Countryside: The 'Colonies Agricoles,' 1820–1850." *French Studies* 65, no. 1 (1991): 36–54.

Crubellier, Maurice. *L'enfance et la jeunesse dans la société française, 1800–1950* (Paris: Colin, 1979).

Cunningham, Hugh. *Children in Nineteenth-Century France: Work, Health and Education among the Classes Populaires* (Cambridge: Cambridge University Press, 1988).

Davis, Oliver. "Mettray Revisited in Jean Genet's *Le langage de la muraille*." *French History* 30, no. 4 (2016): 546–66.

Dekker, Jeroen. *The Will to Change the Child: Re-education Homes for Children at Risk in Nineteenth-Century Western Europe* (Frankfurt: Peter Lang, 2001).

Desmond, Robert W. *Windows on the World: The Information Process in a Changing Society, 1900–1920* (Iowa City: University of Iowa Press, 1980).

Dijn, Annelien de. "Rousseau and Republicanism." *Political Theory* 46, no. 1 (2018): 59–80.

Donzelot, Jacques. *The Policing of Families*, translated by Robert Hurley (New York: Pantheon, 1979).

Downs, Laura Lee. *Childhood in the Promised Land: Working-Class Movements and the Colonies de Vacances in France, 1880–1960* (Durham, NC: Duke University Press, 2002).

Driver, Felix. "Discipline without Frontiers? Representations of the Mettray Reformatory Colony in Britain, 1840–1880." *Journal of Historical Sociology* 3, no. 3 (1990): 272–93.

Dupont-Bouchat, Marie-Sylvie, and Éric Pierre. *Enfance et justice au XIXe siècle* (Paris: Presses Universitaires de France, 2001).

Duprat, Catherine. "Punir et guérir: En 1819, la prison des philanthropes." In *L'impossible prison: Recherches sur le système pénitentiaire au XIXe siècle*, edited by Michelle Perrot, 64–122 (Paris: L'Univers Historique, 1980).

Elias, Norbert. *The Civilizing Process* (Oxford: Blackwell, 1994).

Evanson, Kari. "Writing Scandal: Popular Media and the *Bagnes d'enfants*, 1920–1945." PhD diss., New York University, 2012.

Fishman, Sarah. *The Battle for Children: World War II, Youth Crime, and Juvenile Justice in Twentieth-Century France* (Cambridge, MA: Harvard University Press, 2002).

Forth, Christopher. *The Dreyfus Affair and the Crisis of French Manhood* (Baltimore: Johns Hopkins University Press, 2004).

Forth, Christopher. *Masculinity in the Modern West: Gender, Civilization and the Body* (Aldershot, UK: Palgrave, 2008).

Forth, Christopher, and Elinor Accampo, eds. *Confronting Modernity in Fin-de-Siècle France: Bodies, Minds, and Gender* (Basingstoke, UK: Palgrave, 2010).

Foucault, Michel. *Discipline and Punish: The Birth of the Prison*, translated by Alan Sheridan (New York: Random House, 1977).

Foucault, Michel. *The Foucault Reader: An Introduction to Foucault's Thought*, edited by Paul Rabinow (New York: Pantheon, 1994).

Foucault, Michel. *The History of Sexuality: Volume One, an Introduction* (New York: Vintage, 1990 [1984]).

Foucault, Michel. *Madness and Civilization: A History of Insanity in the Age of Reason*, translated by Richard Howard (London: Tavistock, 1967).

Foucault, Michel. "Questions of Method: An Interview with Michel Foucault." *Ideology and Consciousness* 8 (Spring 1981): 3–14.

Fourier, Charles. *The Utopian Vision of Charles Fourier: Selected Texts on Work, Love, and Passionate Attraction*, edited and translated by Jonathan Beecher and Richard Bienvenu (Boston: Beacon Press, 1971).

Fuchs, Rachel G. *Abandoned Children: Foundlings and Child Welfare in Nineteenth-Century France* (Albany: State University of New York Press, 1984).

Fuchs, Rachel G. *Poor and Pregnant in Paris: Strategies for Survival in the Nineteenth Century* (New Brunswick, NJ: Rutgers University Press, 1992).

Gaillac, Henri. *Les maisons de correction, 1830–1945* (Paris: Cujas, 1971).

Garland, David. *Punishment and Modern Society: A Study in Social Theory* (Chicago: University of Chicago Press, 1993).

Garland, David, and Peter Young, eds. *The Power to Punish: Contemporary Penality and Social Analysis* (Aldershot, UK: Gower, 1979).

Gibson, Mary. "Global Perspectives on the Birth of the Prison." *American Historical Review* 111, no. 4 (2011): 1040–63.

Goffman, Erving. *Asylums: Essays on the Social Situation of Mental Patients and Other Inmates* (New York: Doubleday, 1961).

Goffman, Erving. "On the Characteristics of Total Institutions: The Inmate World." In *The Prison: Studies in Institutional Organization and Change*, edited by Donald R. Cressey, 15–67 (New York: Holt, 1961).

Gontard, Paul-Roger. "Le centre de détention de Casabianda: Emblématique prison de paradoxes." Master's thesis, Université Paul Cézanne Aix-Marseille III, 2008.

Gouda, Frances. *Poverty and Political Culture: The Rhetoric of Social Welfare in the Netherlands and France, 1815–54* (Lanham, MD: Rowman and Littlefield, 1994).

Grew, Raymond, and Patrick J. Harrigan. "The Catholic Contribution to Universal Schooling in France, 1850–1906." *Journal of Modern History* 57, no. 2 (1985): 211–47.

Guillon, Jean-Marie. "Enfance assistée, enfance exploitée? La colonie agricole de Porquerolles." In *Enfants au travail: Attitudes des élites en Europe occidentale et méditerranéenne aux XIXe et XXe siècles*, edited by Roland Caty, 137–52 (Aix-en-Provence: Presses Universitaires de Provence, 2002).

Hardt, Michael. "Prison Time." *Yale French Studies* 91 (1997): 64–79.

Heywood, Colin. *Growing Up in France: From the Ancien Régime to the Third Republic* (Cambridge: Cambridge University Press, 2007).

Hughes, Michael J. *Forging Napoleon's Grande Armée: Motivation, Military Culture, and Masculinity in the French Army, 1800–1808* (New York: New York University Press, 2012).

Hughes, Michael J. "Making Frenchmen into Warriors: Martial Masculinity in Napoleonic France." In *French Masculinities: History, Politics and Culture*, edited by Christopher Forth and Bertrand Taithe, 51–66 (Aldershot, UK: Palgrave, 2007).

Ignatieff, Michael. "Total Institutions and Working Classes: A Review Essay." *History Workshop Journal* 15, no. 1 (1983): 167–73.

Jablonka, Ivan. "Childhood or the 'Journey toward Virility.'" In *A History of Virility*, edited by Alain Corbin, Jean-Jacques Courtine, and Georges Vigarello, translated by Keith Cohen, 220–44 (New York: Columbia University Press, 2016).

Kalifa, Dominique. *L'encre et le sang: Récits de crimes et société à la Belle Époque* (Paris: Fayard, 1995).

Kaluszynski, Martine. "The International Congresses of Criminal Anthropology and the Shaping of the French and International Criminological Movement, 1886–1914." In *The Criminal and His Scientists: Essays on the History of Criminology*, edited by Peter Becker and Richard F. Wetzell, 301–16 (Cambridge: Cambridge University Press, 2006).

Kerdavid, Alan. *Bagne de gosses* (Paris: La Pensée Universelle, 1978).

Klein, Richard. *Cigarettes Are Sublime* (Durham, NC: Duke University Press, 1993).

Kunzel, Regina. *Criminal Intimacy: Prison and the Uneven History of Modern American Sexuality* (Chicago: University of Chicago Press, 2008).

La Berge, Ann. *Mission and Method: The Early Nineteenth-Century French Public Health Movement* (Cambridge: Cambridge University Press, 1992).

Laqueur, Thomas. *Solitary Sex: A Cultural History of Masturbation*, 2nd ed. (New York: Zone Books, 2003).

Le Clère, Marcel. *Histoire de la police* (Paris: Presses Universitaires de France, 1964).

Le Dano, Jean-Guy. *La mouscaille* (Paris: Flammarion, 1973).

Leonards, Chris. "Priceless Children? Penitentiary Congresses Debating Childhood: A Quest for Social Order in Europe, 1846–1895." In *Social Control in Europe*, vol. 2, edited by Clive Emsley, Eric Johnson, and Pieter Spierenburg, 125–48 (Columbus: Ohio State University Press, 2004).

Limido, Luisa. *L'art des jardins sous le second empire: Jean-Pierre Barillet-Deschamps* (Paris: Champs Vallon, 2002).

Locke, Robert C. *French Legitimists and the Politics of Moral Order in the Early Third Republic* (Princeton, NJ: Princeton University Press, 1974).

Lodhi, Abdul, and Charles Tilly, "Urbanization, Crime and Collective Violence in Nineteenth-Century France." *American Journal of Sociology* 79, no. 2 (1974): 279–318.

Logan, John Frederick. "The Age of Intoxication." *Yale French Studies* 50, no. 1 (1974): 81–94.

Lüdtke, Alf. *The History of Everyday Life: Historical Experience and Ways of Life*, translated by William Templer (Princeton, NJ: Princeton University Press, 1995).

Lüdtke, Alf. "Polymorphous Synchrony: German Industrial Workers and the Politics of Everyday Life." In *The End of Labour History?*, edited by Marcel van der Linden, 39–84 (Cambridge: Cambridge University Press, 1993).

Maynes, Mary Jo. "Age as a Category of Analysis: History, Agency, and Narratives of Childhood." *Journal of Childhood and Youth* 1, no. 1 (Winter 2008): 37–63.

McHoul, Alec, and Wendy Grace. *A Foucault Primer: Discourse, Power and the Subject* (New York: New York University Press, 1997).

McNeill, William H. *Keeping in Time: Dance and Drill in Human History* (Cambridge: Cambridge University Press, 1995).

Melossi, Dario, and Massimo Pavarini, *The Prison and the Factory: Origins of the Penitentiary System*, translated by Glynis Cousin (Totowa, NJ: Barnes and Noble, 1981).

Morgan, Steve. "Prison Lives: Critical Issues in Reading Prisoner Autobiography." *Howard Journal* 38, no. 3 (1999): 328–40.

Mosse, George. *The Image of Man: The Creation of Modern Masculinity* (Oxford: Oxford University Press, 1996).

Mucchielli, Laurent. "Hérédité et milieu social: Le faux antagonisme franco-italien." In *Histoire de la criminologie française*, edited by Laurent Mucchielli, 189–214 (Paris: L'Harmattan, 1995).

Myers, Tamara, and Joan Sangster. "Retorts, Runaways and Riots: Patterns of Resistance in Canadian Reform Schools for Girls, 1930–1960." *Journal of Social History* 34, no. 3 (2001): 669–97.

Nilan, Kathleen. "'Crimes Inexplicables': Murderous Children in the Discourse of Monstrosity in Romantic-Era France." In *Becoming Delinquent: British and European Youth, 1650–1950*, edited by Pamela Cox and Heather Shore, 77–88 (Aldershot, UK: Ashgate, 2002).

Nilan, Kathleen. "Incarcerating Children: Prison Reformers, Children's Prisons and Child Prisoners in the July Monarchy." PhD diss., Yale University, 1996.

Nye, Robert A. *Crime, Madness and Politics in Modern France: The Medical Concept of National Decline* (Princeton, NJ: Princeton University Press, 1984).

Nye, Robert A. *Masculinity and Male Codes of Honor in Modern France* (New York: Oxford University Press, 1993).

Nye, Robert A. "Sex Difference and Male Homosexuality in French Medical Discourse, 1830–1930." *Bulletin of the History of Medicine* 63, no. 1 (1989): 32–51.

O'Brien, Patricia. "The Prison on the Continent: Europe, 1865–1965." In *Oxford History of the Prison: The Practice of Punishment in Western Society*, edited by Norval Morris and David Rothman, 178–206 (Oxford: Oxford University Press, 1997).

O'Brien, Patricia. *The Promise of Punishment: Prisons in Nineteenth-Century France* (Princeton, NJ: Princeton University Press, 1982).

Olivier-Martin, Yves. *Histoire du roman populaire en France: De 1840 à 1980* (Paris: Albin Michel, 1980).

Ozouf, Mona. *Festivals and the French Revolution*, translated by Alan Sheridan (Cambridge: Cambridge University Press, 1988).

Padberg, John W. *Colleges in Controversy: The Jesuit Schools in France, from Revival to Suppression, 1815–1880* (Cambridge, MA: Harvard University Press, 1969).

Palmer, Daniel. "Daniel Wilson and the Decorations Scandal of 1887." *Modern and Contemporary France* 1, no. 2 (1993): 139–50.

Payne, Howard C. *The Police State of Louis-Napoleon Bonaparte* (Seattle: University of Washington Press, 1966).

Peristiany, J. G., ed. *Honour and Shame: The Values of Mediterranean Society* (Chicago: University of Chicago Press, 1966).

Perrot, Michelle. "Dans le Paris de la Belle Époque, les 'Apaches': Premières bandes de jeunes." *La Lettre de l'Enfance et de l'Adolescence* 67, no. 1 (2007).

Perrot, Michelle. "Délinquance et système pénitentiaire en France au dix-neuvième siècle." *Annales: Economies, Sociétés, Civilisations* 1 (January–February 1975): 67–91.

Perrot, Michelle. "Delinquency and the Penitentiary System in Nineteenth-Century France." In *Deviants and the Abandoned in French Society*, edited by Robert Forster and Orest Ranum, 213–45 (Baltimore: Johns Hopkins University Press, 1978).

Perrot, Michelle. "Les enfants de la Petite Roquette." *L'Histoire* 100 (May 1987): 30–38.

Philo, Chris. "Foucault's Children." In *Geographies of Children, Youth and Families*, edited by Louise Holt, 27–54 (New York: Routledge, 2011).

Pick, Daniel. *Faces of Degeneration: A European Disorder, c. 1848–1918* (Cambridge: Cambridge University Press, 1993).

Pierre, Éric. "F. A. Demetz et la colonie agricole de Mettray entre réformisme 'romantique' et injonctions administratives." *Paedagogica Historica* 38, no. 2–3 (2002): 451–66.

Pierre, Éric. "Mettray-Algérie-Mettray, 1839–1937: Allers et retours sur fond d'éducation correctionnelle." *Les Études Sociales* 152 (2010): 13–24.

Pierre, Éric. "Mettray dans les années 1920s." In *La colonie agricole pénitentiaire de Mettray: Souvenirs d'un colon, 1922–1927*, edited by Jacques Bourquin and Éric Pierre, 127–52 (Paris: Harmattan, 1997).

Pierson, George Wilson. *Tocqueville and Beaumont in America* (Oxford: Oxford University Press, 1938).

Pilbeam, Pamela. *French Socialists before Marx: Workers, Women and the Social Question in France* (Montreal: McGill–Queen's University Press, 2000).

Pitt-Rivers, Julian. "Honour and Social Status." In *Honour and Shame: The Values of Mediterranean Society*, ed. J. G. Peristiany (Chicago: University of Chicago Press, 1966): 19–77.

Pottier, G.-F. *Répertoire numérique de la sous-série 114 J: Association la paternelle, colonie agricole et pénitentiaire de Mettray, village des jeunes, 1839–1997* (Tours: Archives Départementales, 2004).

Quincy-Lefebvre, Pascale. *Combats pour l'enfance. Itinéraire d'un faiseur d'opinion: Alexis Danan, 1890–1979* (Paris: Beauchesne, 2014).

Quincy-Lefebvre, Pascale. "Emotion et opinion dans la justice des mineurs en France durant l'entre-deux-guerres." *Revue d'Histoire de l'Enfance "Irrégulière"* 17 (2015): 149–67.

Quincy-Lefebvre, Pascale. *Familles, institutions et déviances: Une histoire de l'enfance difficile* (Paris: Economica, 1997).

Ramsland, John. "The Agricultural Colony at Mettray: A Nineteenth-Century Approach to the Institutionalization of Delinquent Boys." *Critical Studies in Education* 29, no. 1 (1987): 64–80.

Ramsland, John. "La Maison Paternelle: 'A College of Repression' for Wayward Bourgeois Adolescents in Nineteenth- and Early Twentieth-Century France." *History of Education* 18, no. 1 (1989): 47–55.

Ramsland, John. "Mettray: A Corrective Institution for Delinquent Youth in France, 1840–1937," *Journal of Educational Administration and History* 22, no. 1 (1990): 30–46.

Ratcliffe, Barrie. "The Chevalier Thesis Reexamined." *French Historical Studies* 17, no. 2 (Fall 1991): 542–74.

Renouard, Jean-Marie. *De l'enfant coupable à l'enfant inadapté: Le traitement social et politique de la déviance* (Paris: Centurion, 1990).

Ripley, Colin. "Safe as Houses: The Mettray Colony as Seen by Jean Genet." *Space and Culture* 9, no. 4 (2006): 400–17.

Rollet, Catherine. *Les enfants au XIXe siècle* (Paris: Hachette, 2001).

Rosario, Vernon. *The Erotic Imagination: French Histories of Perversity* (Oxford: Oxford University Press, 1997).

Rosenman, Ellen Bayuk. "Body Doubles: The Spermatorrhea Panic." *Journal of the History of Sexuality* 12, no. 3 (2003): 365–99.

Rothman, David. *Conscience and Convenience: The Asylum and Its Alternatives in Progressive America*, 2nd ed. (New York: Aldine, 2002 [1980]).

Rudé, George. *The Crowd in the French Revolution* (New York: Oxford University Press, 1959).

Schafer, Sylvia. *Children in Moral Danger and the Problem of Government in Third Republic France* (Princeton, NJ: Princeton University Press, 1997).

Schnapper, Bernard. "La correction paternelle et le mouvement des idées au XIXe siècle, 1789–1935." In *Voies nouvelles en histoire du droit, la justice, la famille et la répression pénale, XVI–XXe*, 523–53 (Paris: Presses Universitaires de France, 1991).

Schrauwers, Albert. "The 'Benevolent' Colonies of Johannes van den Bosch: Continuities in the Administration of Poverty in the Netherlands and Indonesia." *Comparative Studies in Society and History* 43, no. 2 (2001): 298–328.

Scott, James C. *Domination and Art of Resistance: Hidden Transcripts* (New Haven, CT: Yale University Press, 1990).

Scott, James C. *Weapons of the Weak: Everyday Forms of Peasant Resistance* (New Haven, CT: Yale University Press, 1985).

Smith-Allen, James. *In the Public Eye: A History of Reading in Modern France, 1800–1940* (Princeton, NJ: Princeton University Press, 1991).

Spierenburg, Pieter. "From Amsterdam to Auburn: An Explanation for the Rise of the Prison in Seventeenth-Century Holland and Nineteenth-Century America." *Journal of Social History* 20, no. 3 (Spring 1987): 439–61.

Spierenburg, Pieter. *The Spectacle of Suffering: Executions and the Evolution of Repression* (Cambridge: Cambridge University Press, 1984).

Stoler, Ann Laura. *Along the Archival Grain: Epistemic Anxieties and Colonial Common Sense* (Princeton, NJ: Princeton University Press, 2009).

Strayer, Brian. *Lettres de cachet and Social Control in the Ancien Régime, 1659–1789* (Bern: Peter Lang, 1991).

Surkis, Judith. *Sexing the Citizen: Morality and Masculinity in France, 1870–1920* (Ithaca, NY: Cornell University Press, 2006).

Sykes, Gresham. *The Society of Captives: A Study of a Maximum Security Prison* (Princeton, NJ: Princeton University Press, 1958).

Taithe, Bertrand. "Neighborhood Boys and Men: The Changing Space of Masculine Identity in France, 1848–71." In *French Masculinities: History, Politics and Culture*, 67–84 (Basingstoke, UK: Palgrave Macmillan, 2007).

Thiercé, Agnès. *Histoire de l'adolescence, 1850–1914* (Paris: Belin, 1999).

Thompson, E. P. *The Making of the English Working Class* (London: Vintage, 1980).

Thompson, Victoria. "Creating Boundaries: Homosexuality and the Changing Social Order in France, 1830–1870." In *Homosexuality in Modern France*, edited by Jeffrey Merrick and Bryant T. Ragan, 102–27 (Oxford: Oxford University Press, 1996).

Tilly, Louise, and Miriam Cohen. "Does the Family Have a History?" *Social Science History* 6 (1982): 131–79.

Toth, Stephen A. *Beyond Papillon: A History of the French Overseas Penal Colonies, 1854–1952* (Lincoln: University of Nebraska Press, 2006).

Ugelvik, Thomas. *Power and Resistance in Prison: Doing Time, Doing Freedom* (Aldershot, UK: Palgrave, 2014).

Vimont, Jean-Claude. "De coupables aux victimes, l'archéologie de l'identité du mineur délinquant au 19e siècle." In *Jeunes, déviances et identités, 18e–20e siècles,* 35–47 (Mont-Saint-Aignan: Publications des Universités de Rouen et du Havre, 2005).

Walker, David H. *Outrage and Insight: Modern French Writers and the Fait Divers* (New York: Berg, 1995).

Weber, Max. *Economy and Society*, translated by Guenther Roth and Claus Wittich (Berkeley: University of California Press, 1978).

White, Edmund. *Genet: A Biography* (New York: Knopf, 1993).

Wright, Gordon. *Between the Guillotine and Liberty: Two Centuries of the Crime Problem in France* (Oxford: Oxford University Press, 1983).

Yvorel, Jean-Jacques. "Le discernement: Construction et usage d'une catégorie juridique en droit pénale des mineures." *Recherches Familiales* 9 (2012): 153–62.

Yvorel, Jean-Jacques. "Les premières campagnes contre les bagnes d'enfants." In *L'indignation: Histoire d'une émotion (XIXe-XXe siècles)*, edited by Anne-Claire Ambroise-Rendu and Christian Delaporte, 105–28 (Paris: Nouveau Monde, 2008).

Zeldin, Theodore. *France, 1848–1945: Ambition and Love* (Oxford: Oxford University Press, 1979).

INDEX